BLUE PERIOD

TSUBASA YAMAGUCHI

3

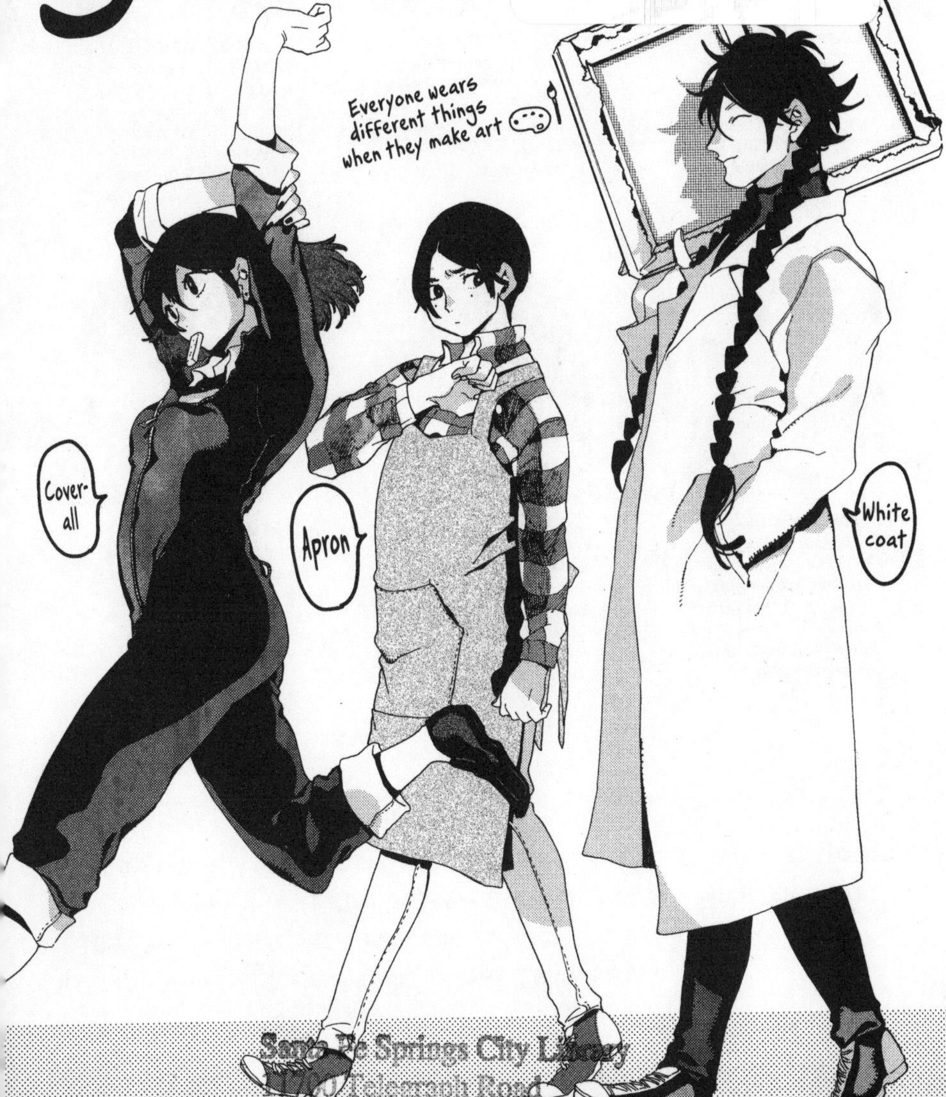
Everyone wears different things when they make art
White coat
Apron
Cover-all

CHARACTERS

Yotasuke Takahashi
A third-year high school
student who attends
the same prep school as
Yatora. His talent, skill, and
unsociable character inspire
Yatora to be a better artist.

Ryuji Ayukawa
Goes by the name Yuka. A
boy who dresses in women's
clothing. A member of the Art
Club who's in the same class
as Yatora. He invited Yatora
to the Art Club.

Yatora Yaguchi
A third-year in high school.
After seeing Mori-senpai's
painting, he discovered the
joy of making art and was
hooked. He sets his sights on
Tokyo University of the Arts,
the most competitive of all
Japanese art colleges.

Saeki-sensei
The advisor for the Art Club.
She uses her skills, insight,
and resourcefulness to give
solid guidance to motivated
students. She also lets less
motivated students enjoy
themselves in their own way.

Ooba-sensei
An instructor at the art prep
school that Yatora attends.
Her height matches the
volume of her voice.

Haruka Hashida
A student who's in the same
year and school as Yotasuke.
He attends the same prep
school as Yatora.

TABLE OF CONTENTS

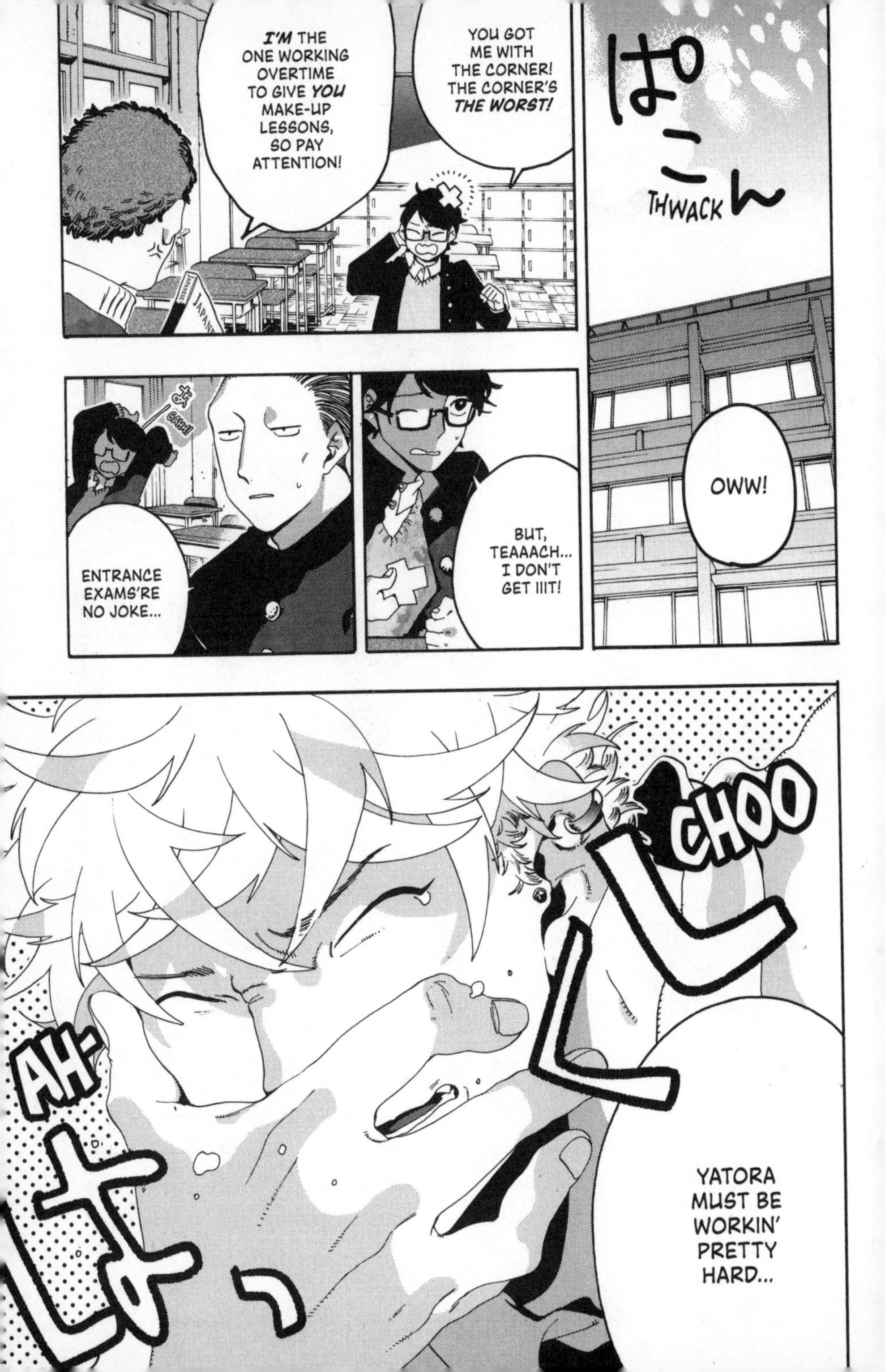
ぱこん
THWACK
OWW!
YOU GOT ME WITH THE CORNER! THE CORNER'S *THE WORST!*
I'M THE ONE WORKING OVERTIME TO GIVE *YOU* MAKE-UP LESSONS, SO PAY ATTENTION!
BUT, TEAAACH... I DON'T GET IIIT!
GAHH!
ENTRANCE EXAMS'RE NO JOKE...
AH-
CHOO
YATORA MUST BE WORKIN' PRETTY HARD...

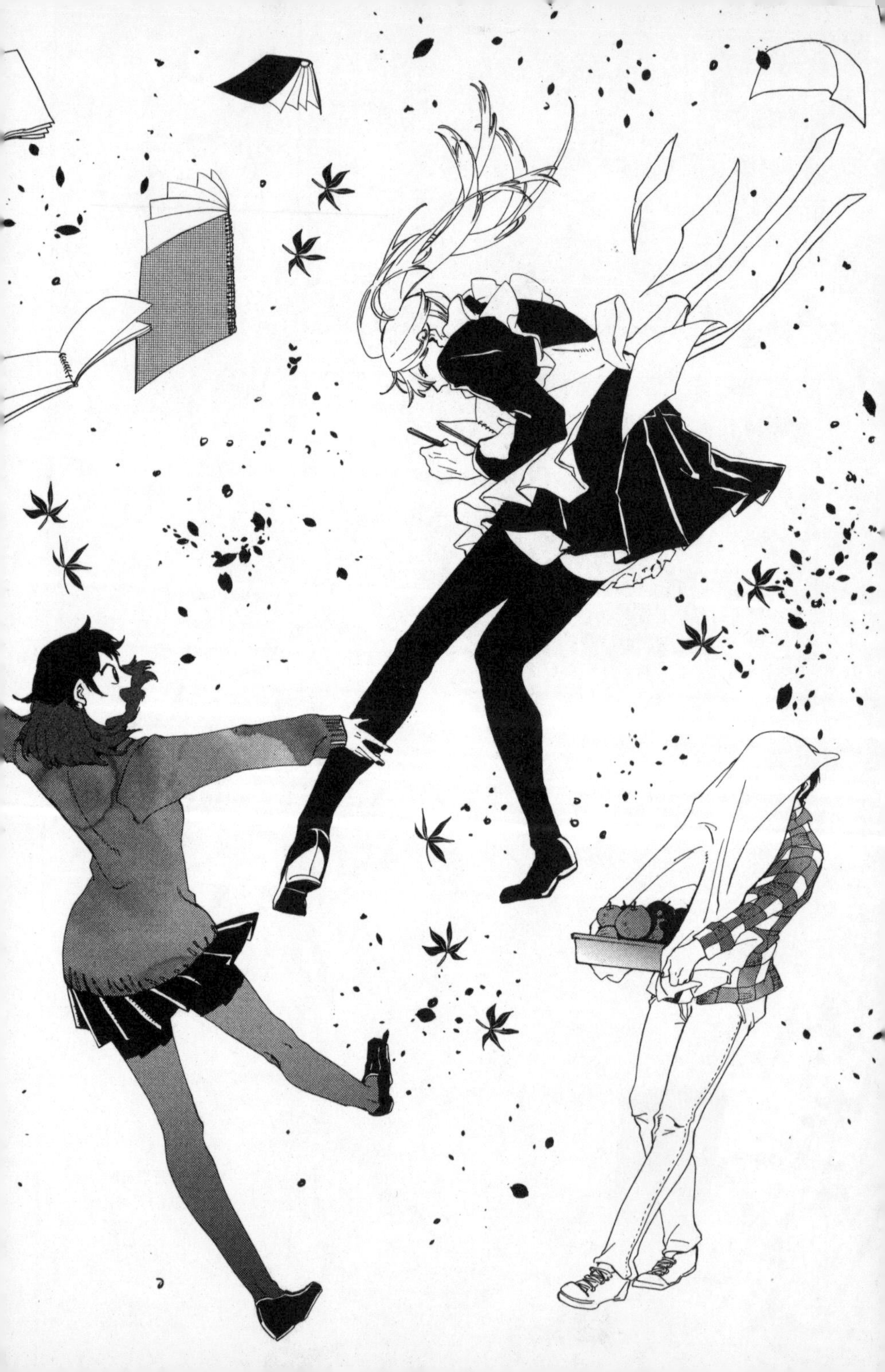

STROKE 9

I KNOW WHAT TO DO, I JUST DON'T KNOW IF I CAN DO IT

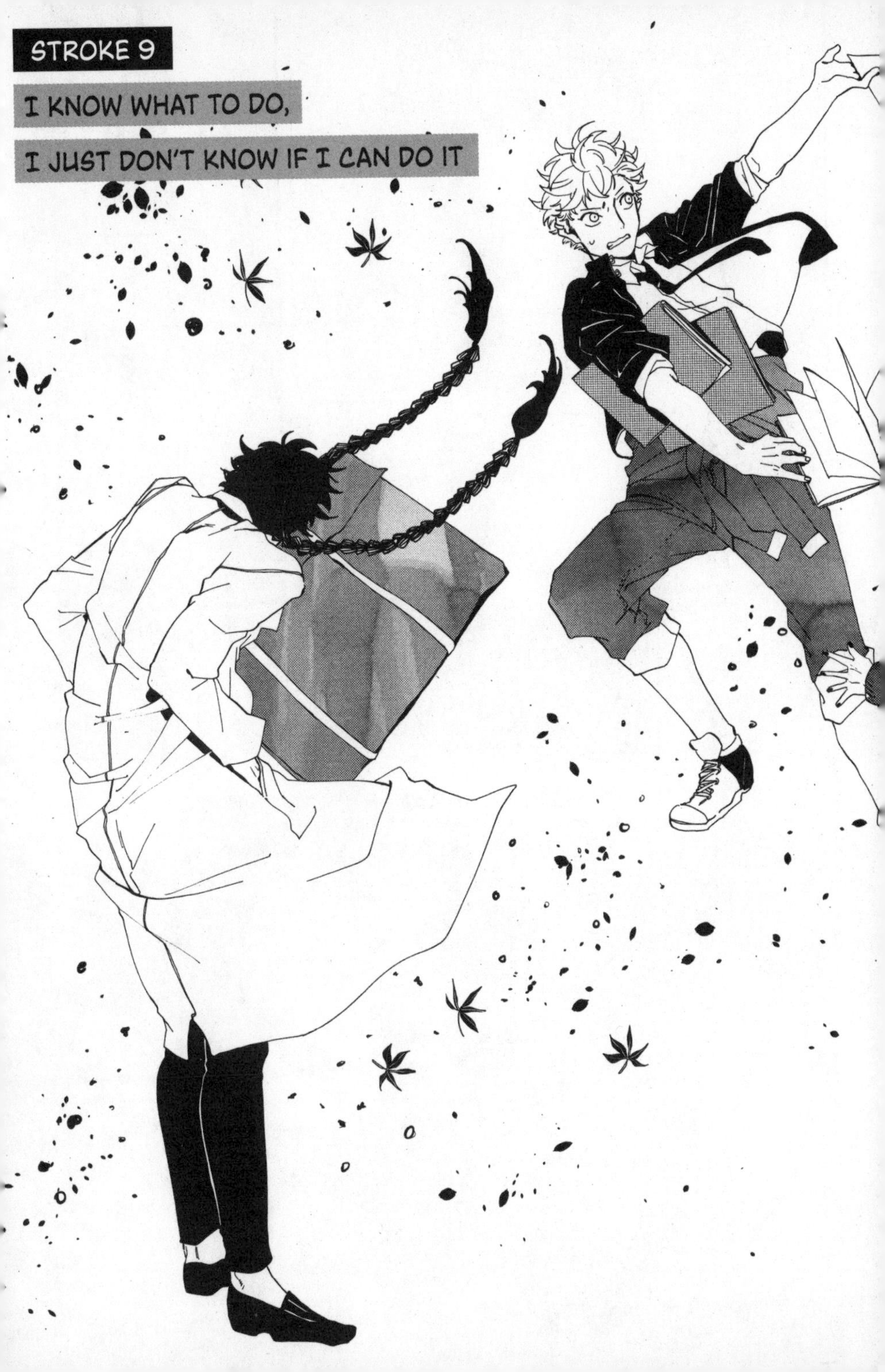

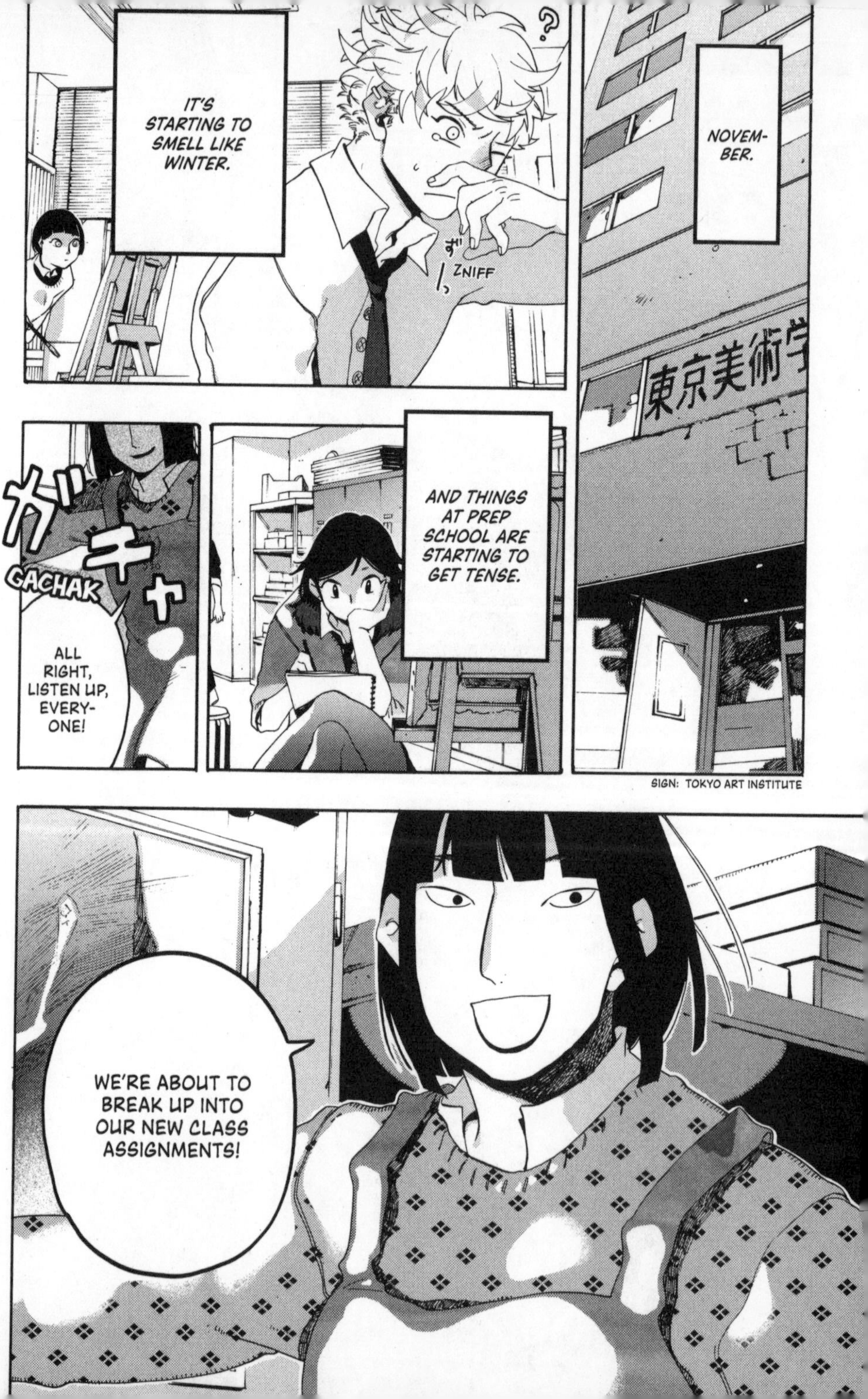
NOVEM-
BER.
東京美術学
SIGN: TOKYO ART INSTITUTE
?
IT'S STARTING TO SMELL LIKE WINTER.
ず
ZNIFF
AND THINGS AT PREP SCHOOL ARE STARTING TO GET TENSE.
ガチャ
GACHAK
ALL RIGHT, LISTEN UP, EVERY-ONE!
WE'RE ABOUT TO BREAK UP INTO OUR NEW CLASS ASSIGNMENTS!

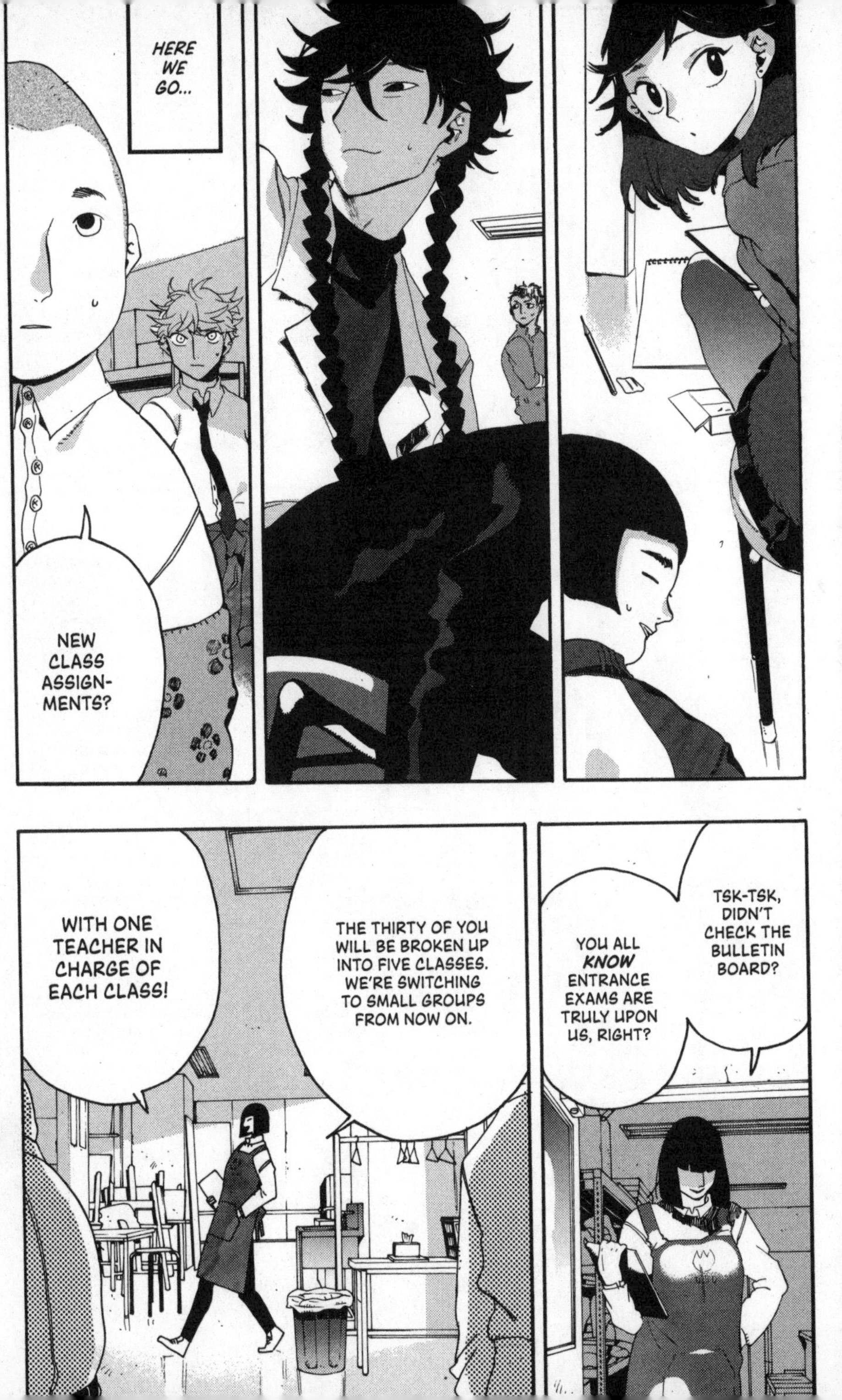
HERE WE GO...
NEW CLASS ASSIGN-MENTS?
TSK-TSK, DIDN'T CHECK THE BULLETIN BOARD?
YOU ALL KNOW ENTRANCE EXAMS ARE TRULY UPON US, RIGHT?
THE THIRTY OF YOU WILL BE BROKEN UP INTO FIVE CLASSES. WE'RE SWITCHING TO SMALL GROUPS FROM NOW ON.
WITH ONE TEACHER IN CHARGE OF EACH CLASS!

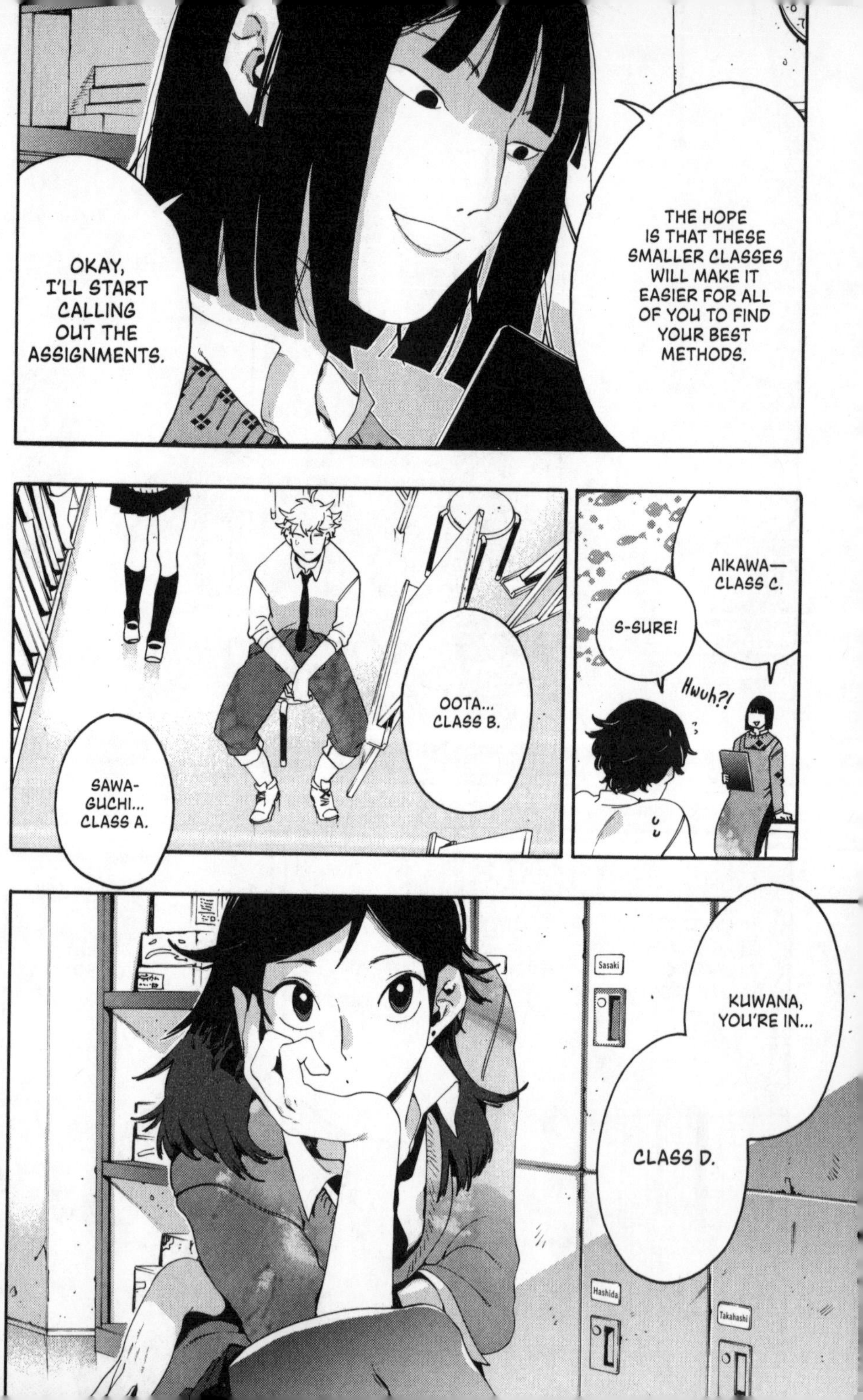
THE HOPE IS THAT THESE SMALLER CLASSES WILL MAKE IT EASIER FOR ALL OF YOU TO FIND YOUR BEST METHODS.
OKAY, I'LL START CALLING OUT THE ASSIGNMENTS.
AIKAWA— CLASS C.
S-SURE!
Hwuh?!
OOTA... CLASS B.
SAWA-GUCHI... CLASS A.
KUWANA, YOU'RE IN...
Sasaki
CLASS D.
Hashida
Takahashi

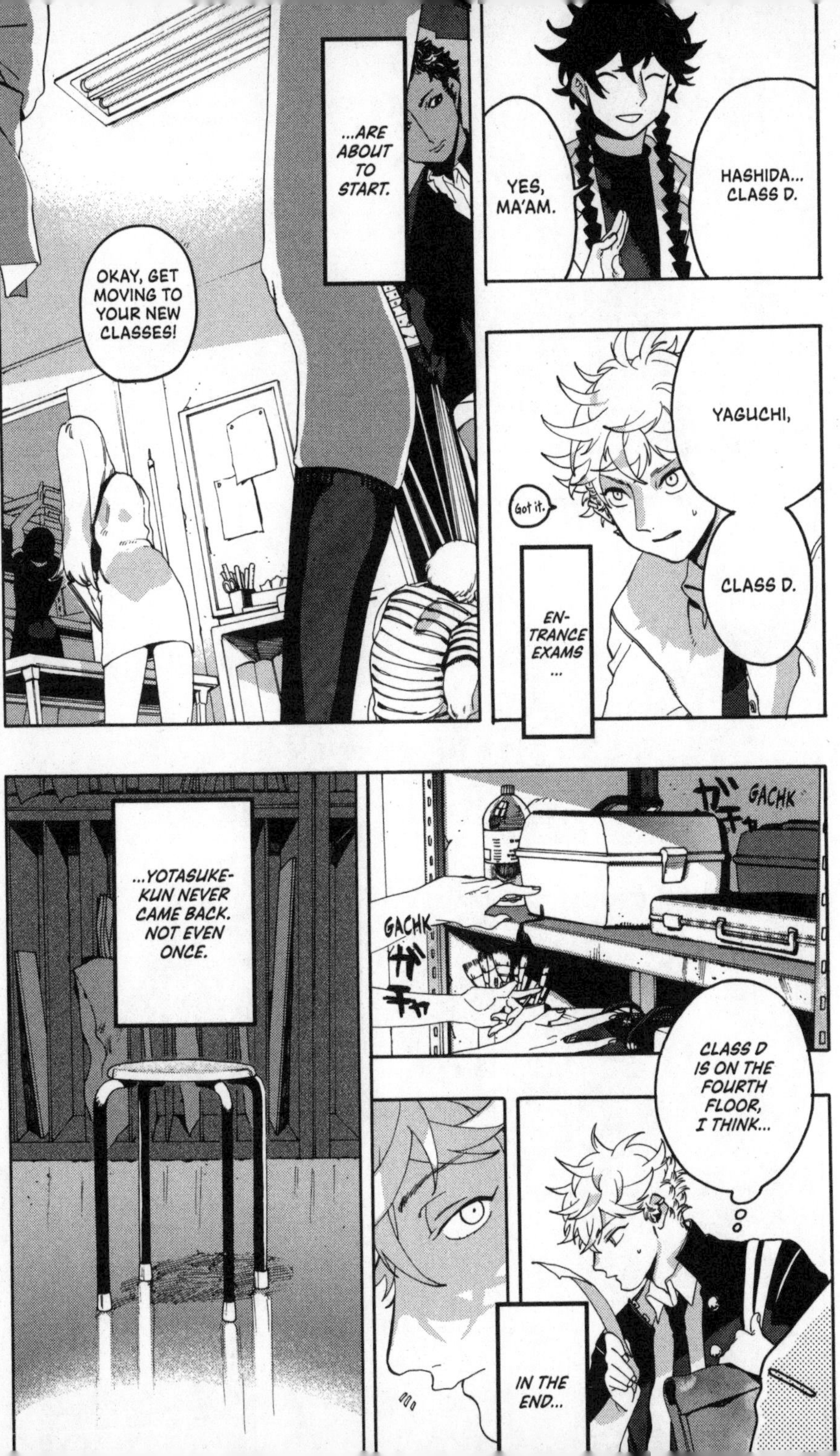
HASHIDA... CLASS D.
YES, MA'AM.
YAGUCHI,
CLASS D.
Got it.
EN-TRANCE EXAMS ...
...ARE ABOUT TO START.
OKAY, GET MOVING TO YOUR NEW CLASSES!
ガチャ
GACHK
GACHK
ガチャ
CLASS D IS ON THE FOURTH FLOOR, I THINK...
IN THE END...
...YOTASUKE-KUN NEVER CAME BACK. NOT EVEN ONCE.

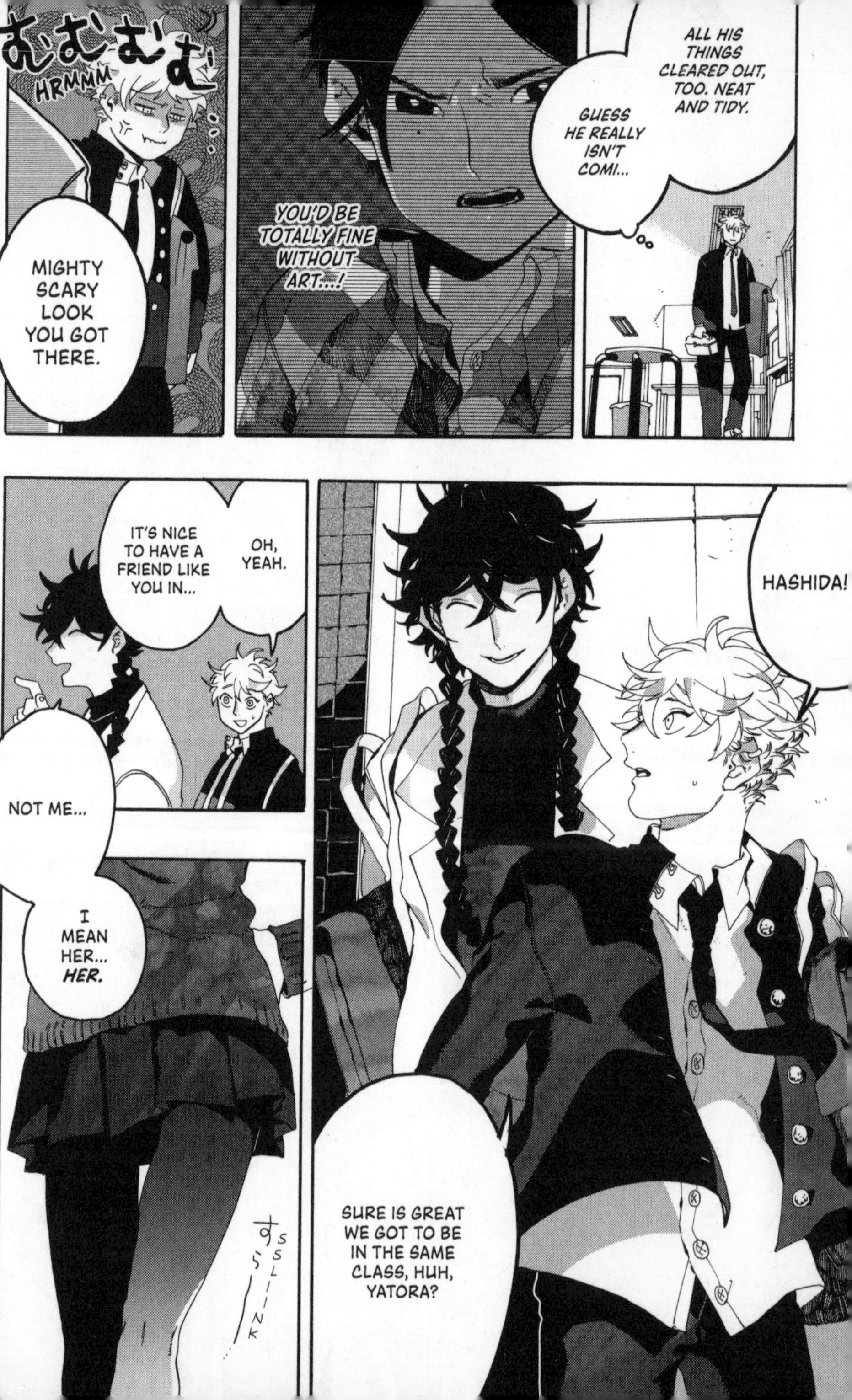
ALL HIS THINGS CLEARED OUT, TOO. NEAT AND TIDY.
GUESS HE REALLY ISN'T COMI...
YOU'D BE TOTALLY FINE WITHOUT ART...!
むむむむ
HRMMM
MIGHTY SCARY LOOK YOU GOT THERE.
HASHIDA!
SURE IS GREAT WE GOT TO BE IN THE SAME CLASS, HUH, YATORA?
OH, YEAH.
IT'S NICE TO HAVE A FRIEND LIKE YOU IN...
NOT ME...
I MEAN HER... *HER.*
すぅ
SSLIINK

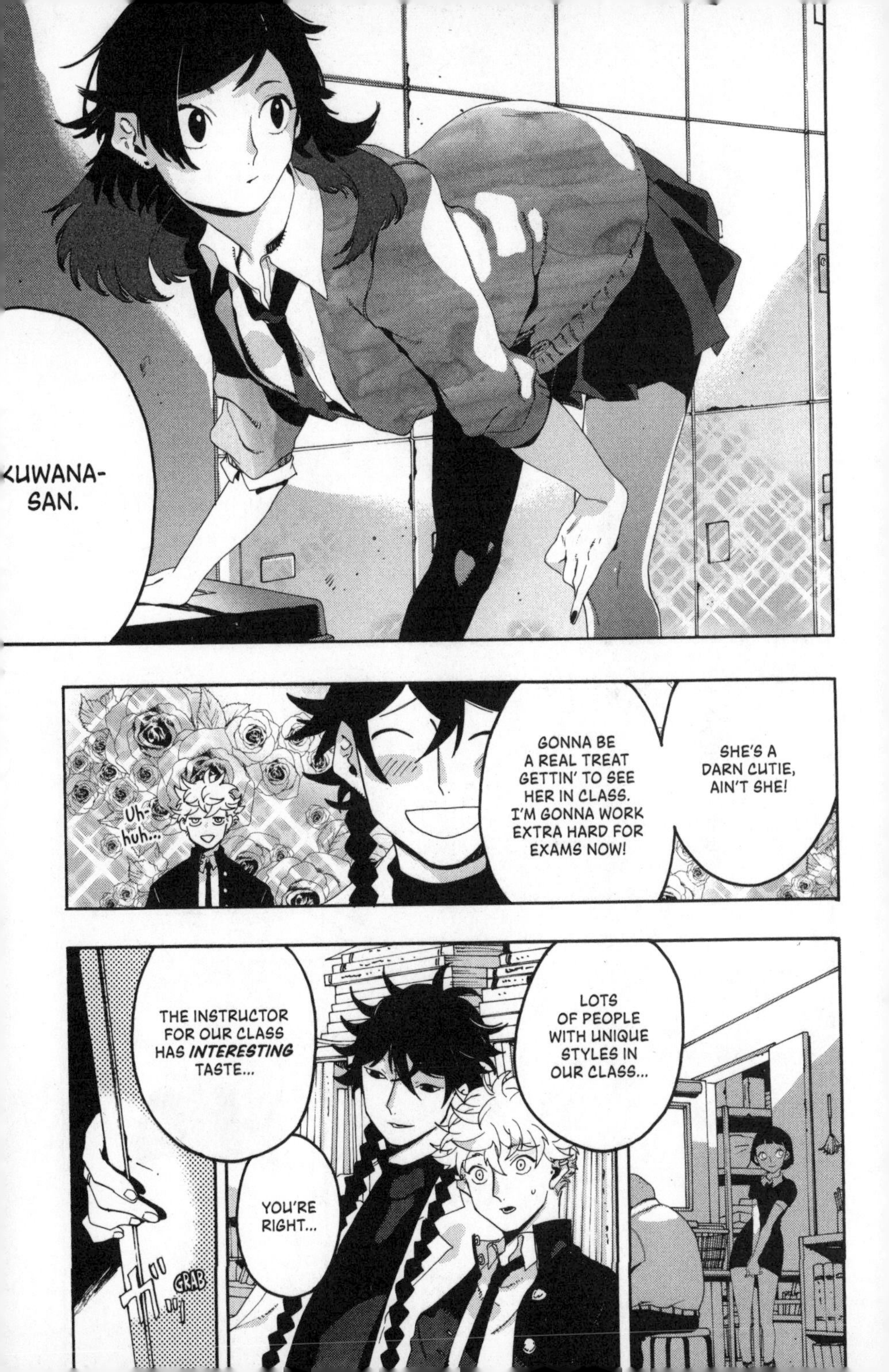
KUWANA-SAN.
SHE'S A DARN CUTIE, AIN'T SHE!
GONNA BE A REAL TREAT GETTIN' TO SEE HER IN CLASS. I'M GONNA WORK EXTRA HARD FOR EXAMS NOW!
Uh-huh...
LOTS OF PEOPLE WITH UNIQUE STYLES IN OUR CLASS...
THE INSTRUCTOR FOR OUR CLASS HAS *INTERESTING* TASTE...
YOU'RE RIGHT...
GRAB

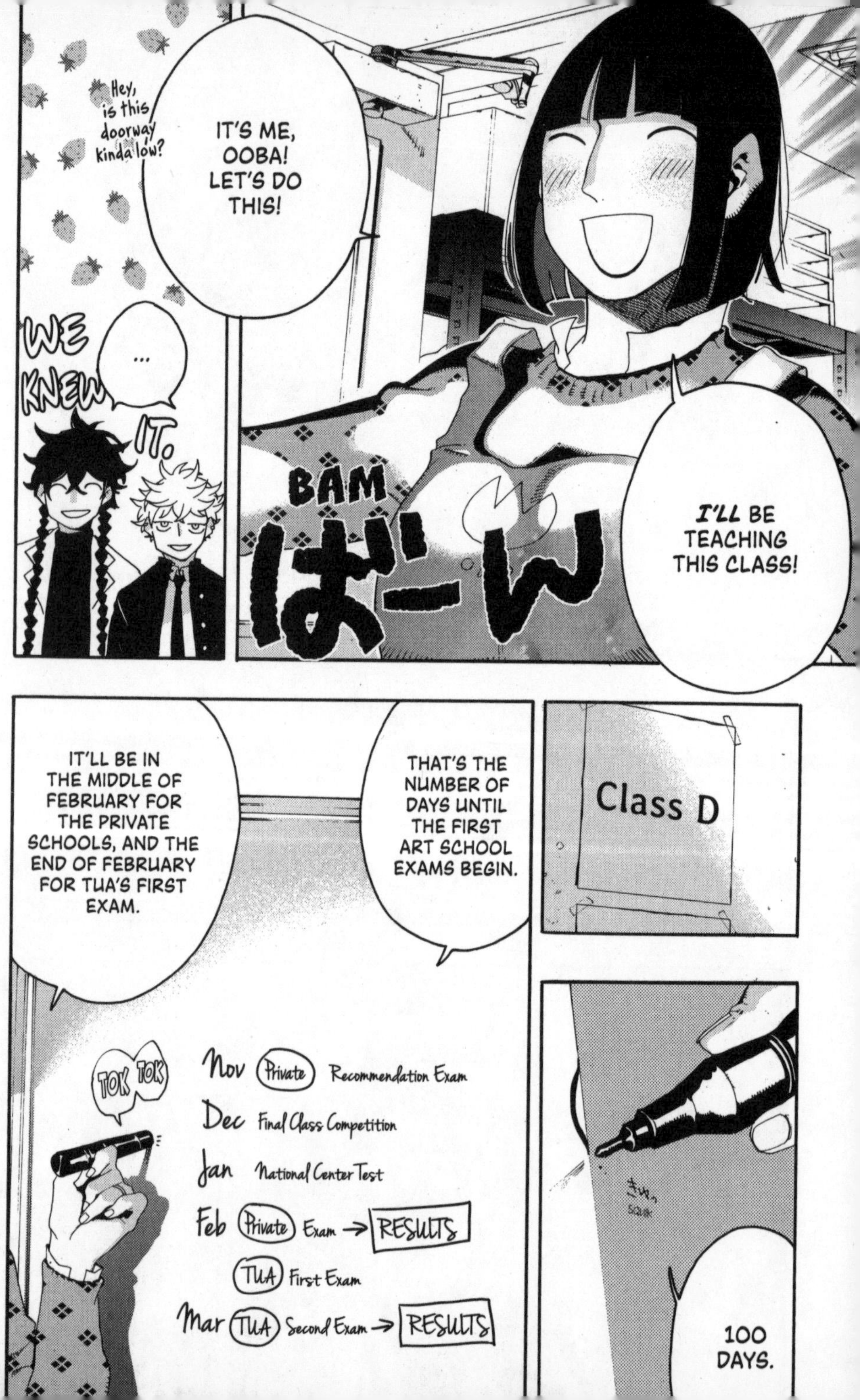
IT'S ME, OOBA! LET'S DO THIS!
I'LL BE TEACHING THIS CLASS!
BAM
ばーん
Hey, is this doorway kinda low?
...
WE KNEW IT.
Class D
SQUIK
100 DAYS.
THAT'S THE NUMBER OF DAYS UNTIL THE FIRST ART SCHOOL EXAMS BEGIN.
IT'LL BE IN THE MIDDLE OF FEBRUARY FOR THE PRIVATE SCHOOLS, AND THE END OF FEBRUARY FOR TUA'S FIRST EXAM.
TOK TOK
Nov (Private) Recommendation Exam
Dec Final Class Competition
Jan National Center Test
Feb (Private) Exam → RESULTS
(TUA) First Exam
Mar (TUA) Second Exam → RESULTS

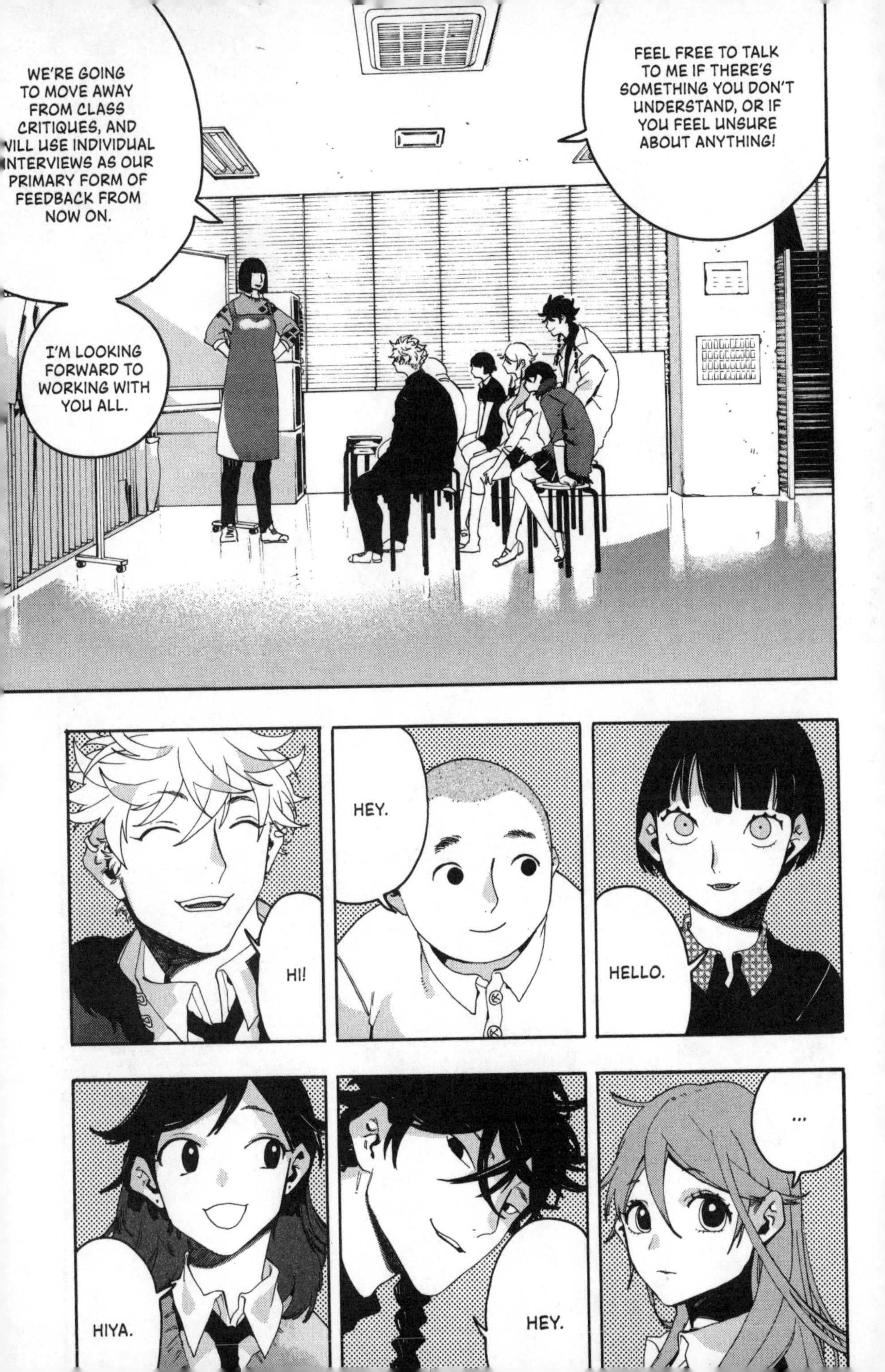
FEEL FREE TO TALK TO ME IF THERE'S SOMETHING YOU DON'T UNDERSTAND, OR IF YOU FEEL UNSURE ABOUT ANYTHING!
WE'RE GOING TO MOVE AWAY FROM CLASS CRITIQUES, AND VILL USE INDIVIDUAL NTERVIEWS AS OUR PRIMARY FORM OF FEEDBACK FROM NOW ON.
I'M LOOKING FORWARD TO WORKING WITH YOU ALL.
HELLO.
HEY.
HI!
...
HEY.
HIYA.

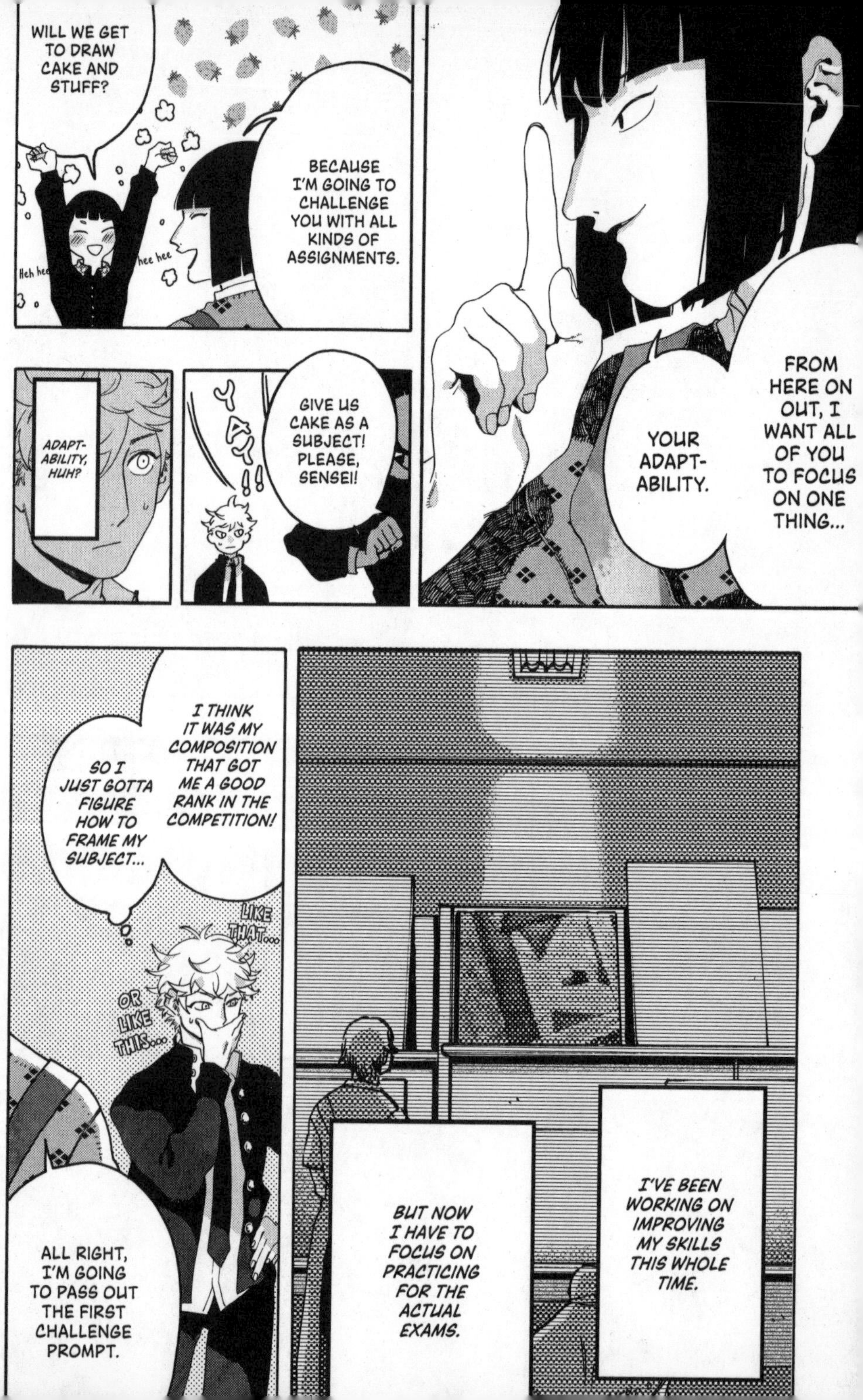
FROM HERE ON OUT, I WANT ALL OF YOU TO FOCUS ON ONE THING...
YOUR ADAPT-ABILITY.
BECAUSE I'M GOING TO CHALLENGE YOU WITH ALL KINDS OF ASSIGNMENTS.
WILL WE GET TO DRAW CAKE AND STUFF?
hee hee
Heh hee
GIVE US CAKE AS A SUBJECT! PLEASE, SENSEI!
YAY!!
ADAPT-ABILITY, HUH?
I'VE BEEN WORKING ON IMPROVING MY SKILLS THIS WHOLE TIME.
BUT NOW I HAVE TO FOCUS ON PRACTICING FOR THE ACTUAL EXAMS.
I THINK IT WAS MY COMPOSITION THAT GOT ME A GOOD RANK IN THE COMPETITION!
SO I JUST GOTTA FIGURE HOW TO FRAME MY SUBJECT...
LIKE THAT...
OR LIKE THIS...
ALL RIGHT, I'M GOING TO PASS OUT THE FIRST CHALLENGE PROMPT.

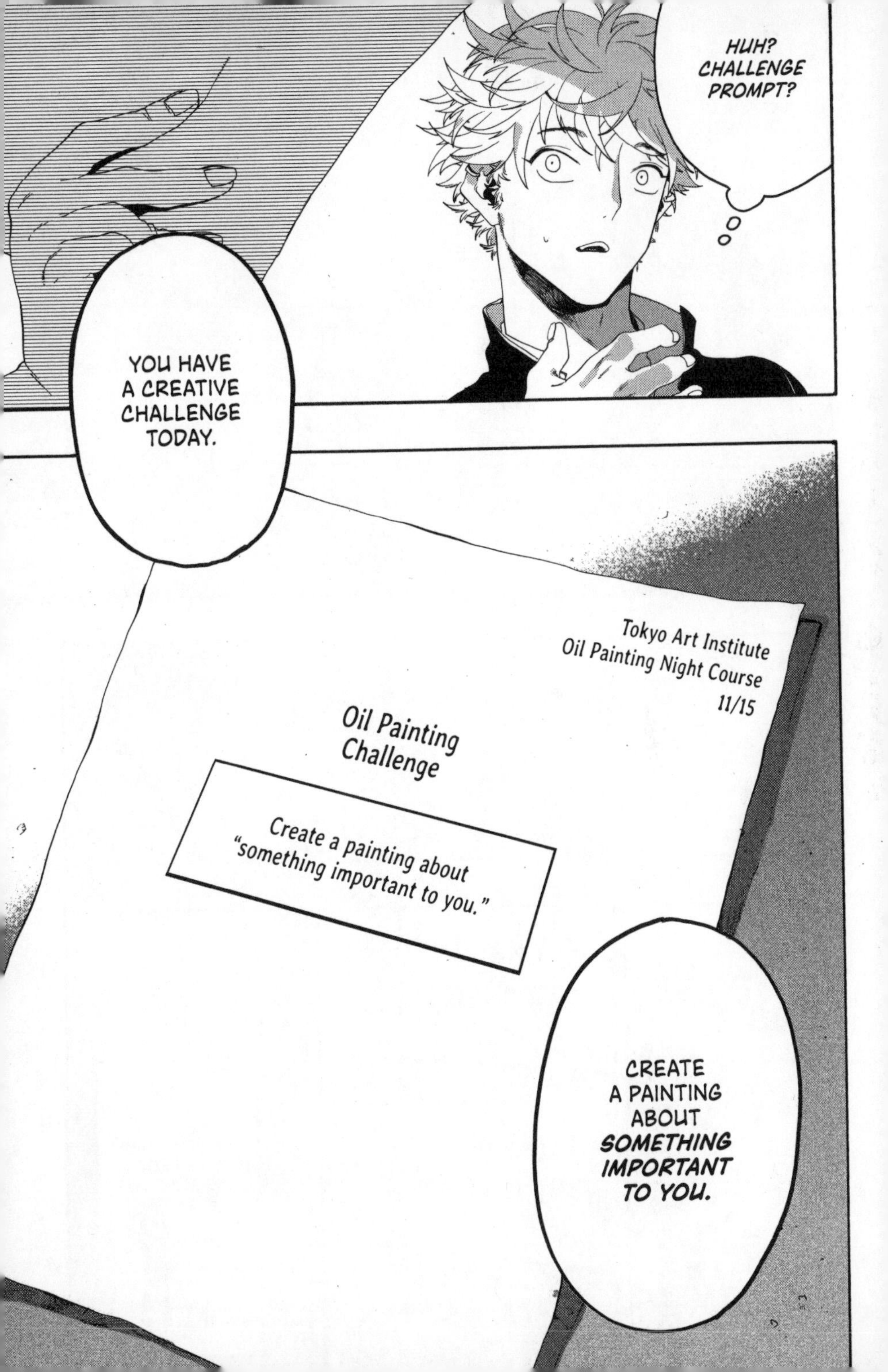
HUH? CHALLENGE PROMPT?
YOU HAVE A CREATIVE CHALLENGE TODAY.
Tokyo Art Institute
Oil Painting Night Course
11/15
Oil Painting Challenge
Create a painting about "something important to you."
CREATE A PAINTING ABOUT SOMETHING IMPORTANT TO YOU.

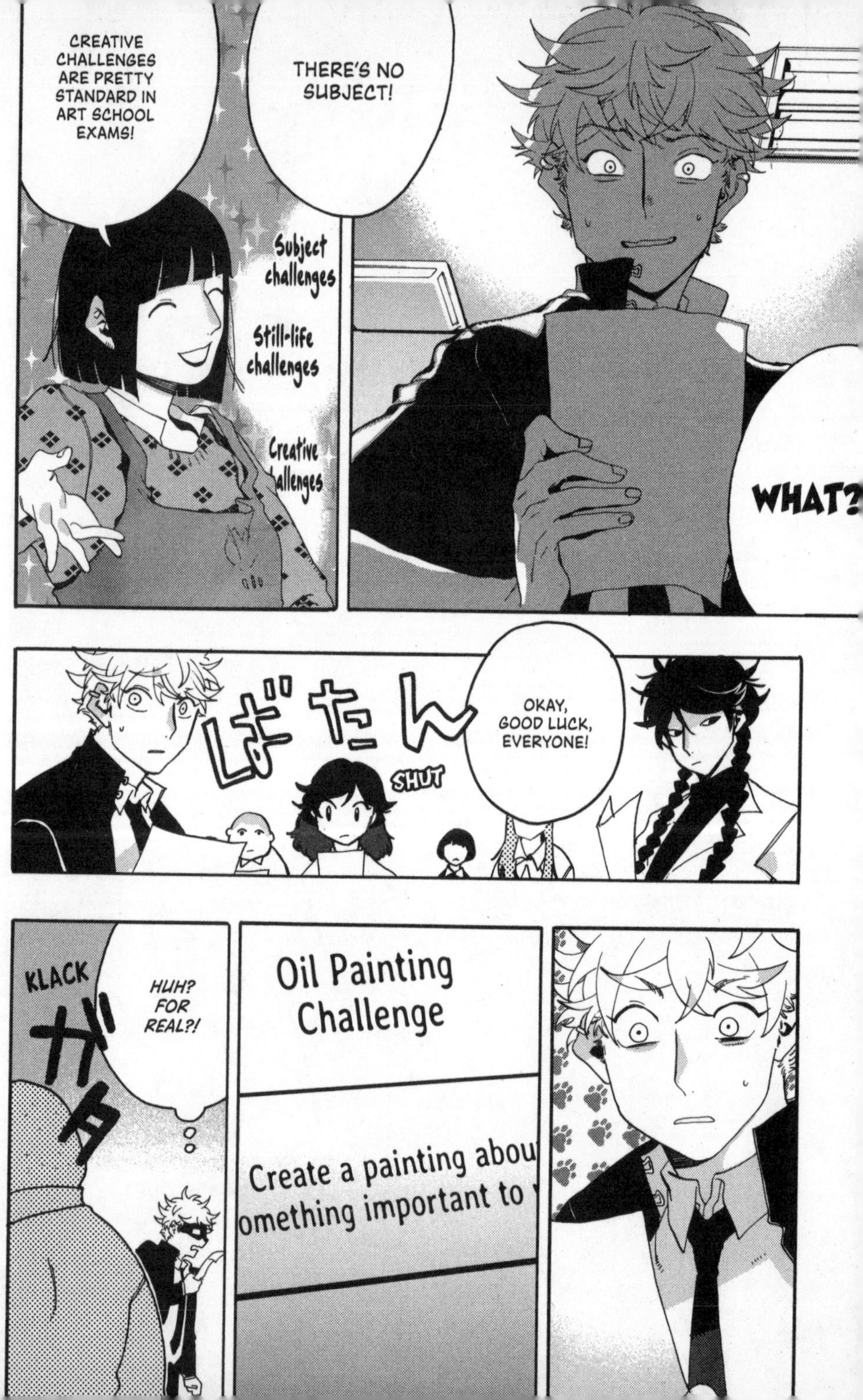
WHAT?
THERE'S NO SUBJECT!
CREATIVE CHALLENGES ARE PRETTY STANDARD IN ART SCHOOL EXAMS!
Subject challenges
Still-life challenges
Creative challenges
OKAY, GOOD LUCK, EVERYONE!
ばたん
SHUT
Oil Painting Challenge
Create a painting abou
omething important to
HUH? FOR REAL?!
KLACK
ガタ

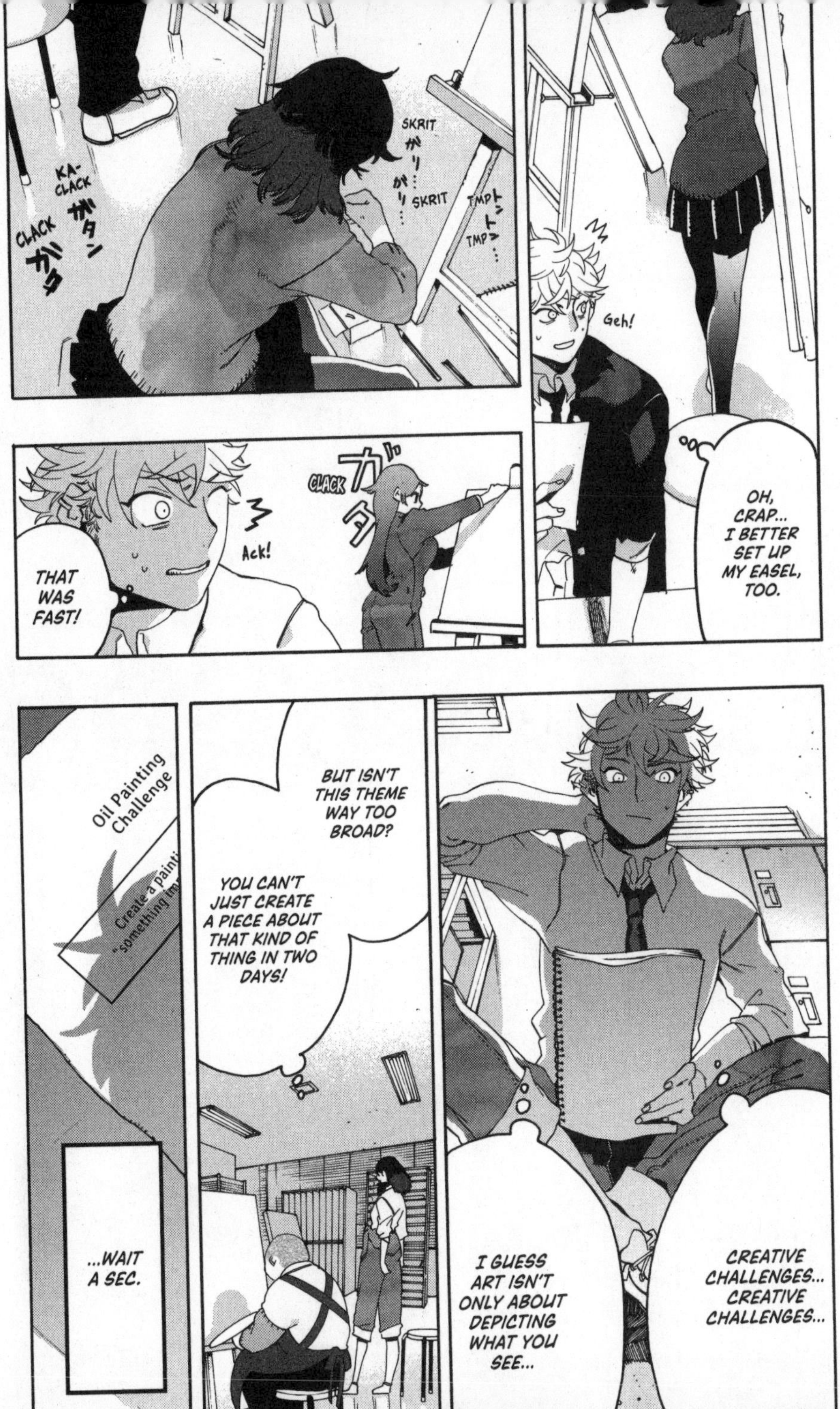
Geh!
OH, CRAP... I BETTER SET UP MY EASEL, TOO.
SKRIT
ガリ…
ガリ…
SKRIT
TMP
TMP
KA-CLACK
ガタン
CLACK
ガタ
CLACK
ガタ
Ack!
THAT WAS FAST!
CREATIVE CHALLENGES... CREATIVE CHALLENGES...
I GUESS ART ISN'T ONLY ABOUT DEPICTING WHAT YOU SEE...
BUT ISN'T THIS THEME WAY TOO BROAD?
YOU CAN'T JUST CREATE A PIECE ABOUT THAT KIND OF THING IN TWO DAYS!
Oil Painting Challenge
...WAIT A SEC.

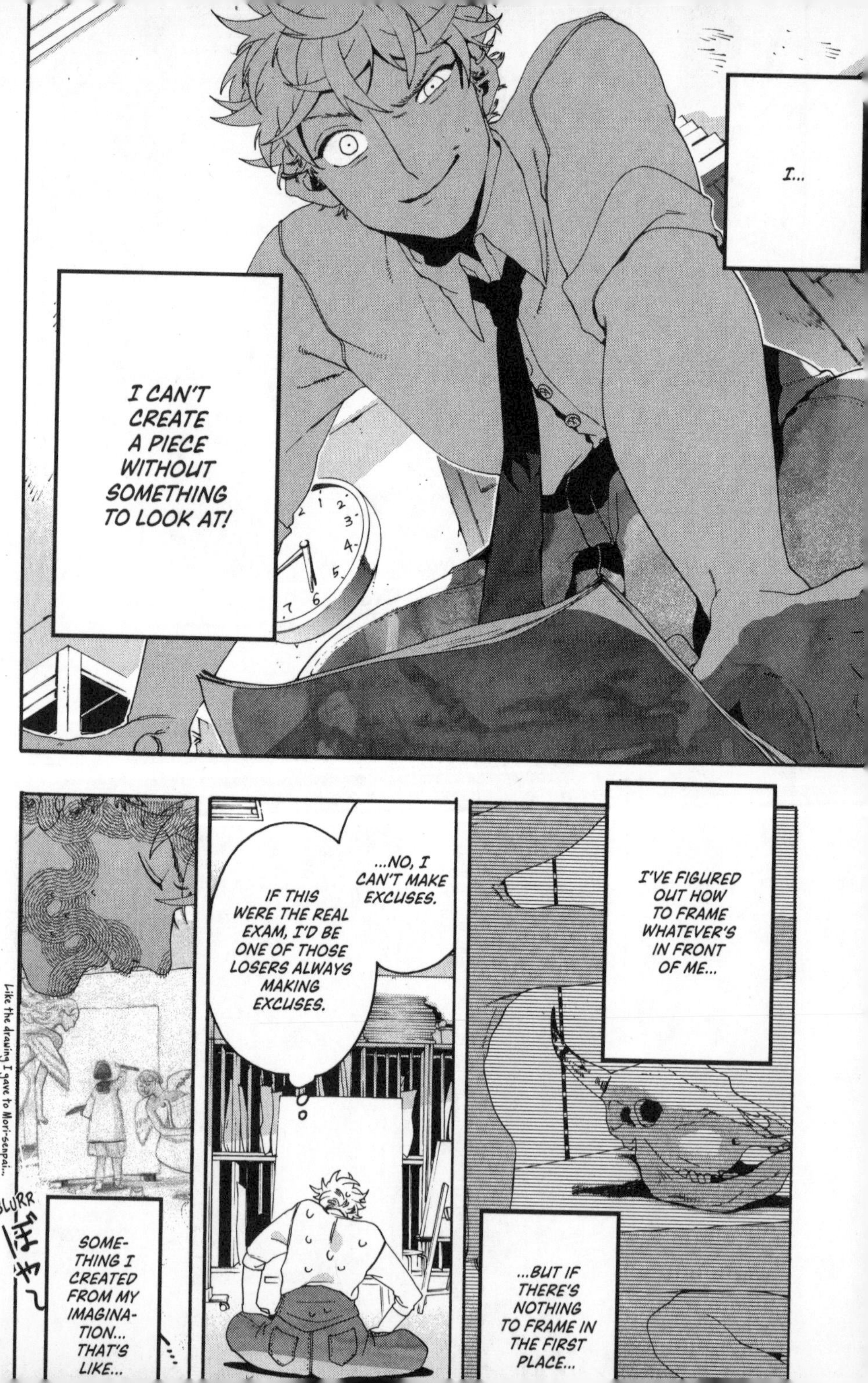
I...
I CAN'T CREATE A PIECE WITHOUT SOMETHING TO LOOK AT!
I'VE FIGURED OUT HOW TO FRAME WHATEVER'S IN FRONT OF ME...
...BUT IF THERE'S NOTHING TO FRAME IN THE FIRST PLACE...
IF THIS WERE THE REAL EXAM, I'D BE ONE OF THOSE LOSERS ALWAYS MAKING EXCUSES.
...NO, I CAN'T MAKE EXCUSES.
BLURR
SOME-THING I CREATED FROM MY IMAGINA-TION... THAT'S LIKE...
Like the drawing I gave to Mori-senpai...

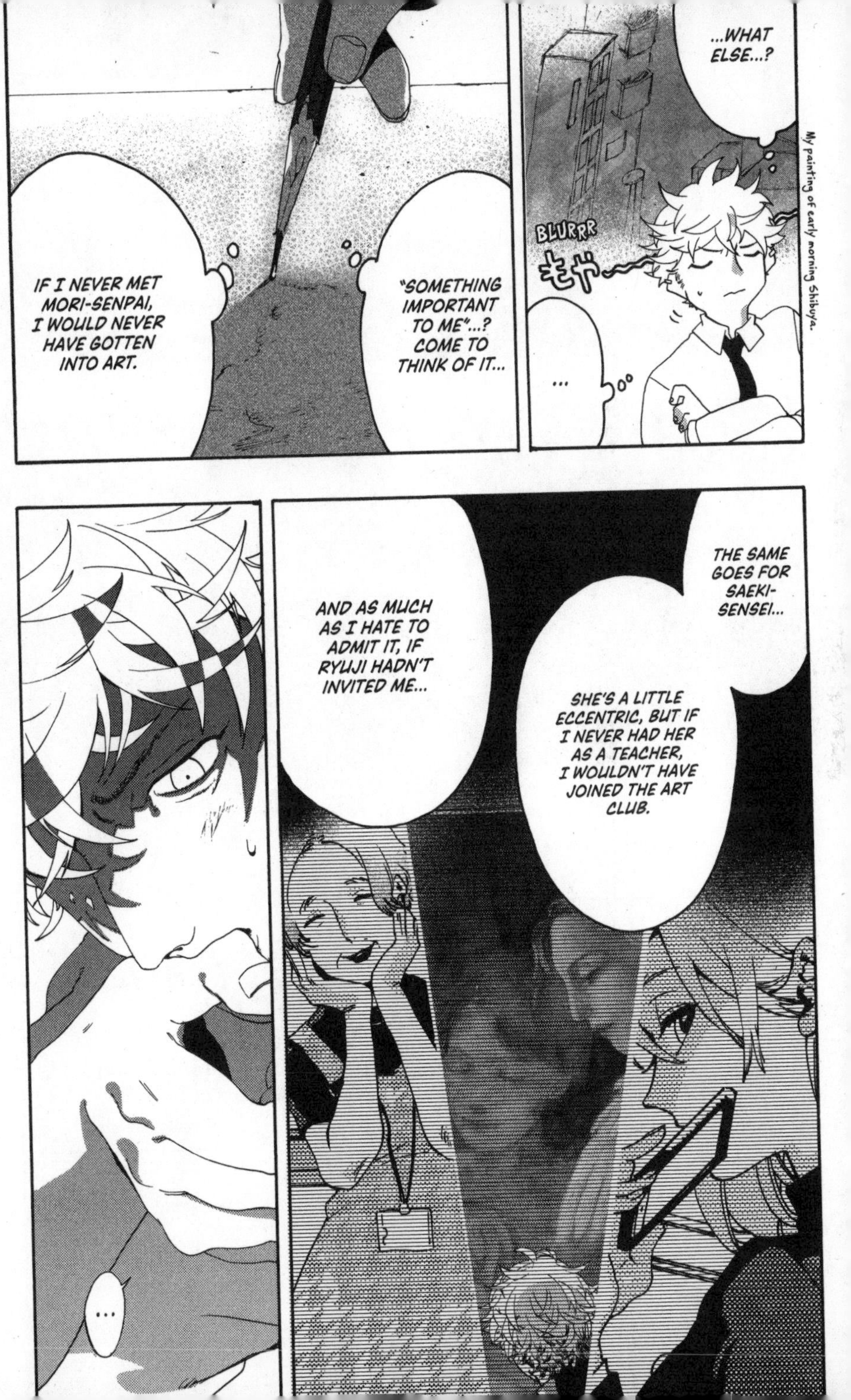
...WHAT ELSE...?
My painting of early morning Shibuya.
BLURRR
もや
...
"SOMETHING IMPORTANT TO ME"...? COME TO THINK OF IT...
IF I NEVER MET MORI-SENPAI, I WOULD NEVER HAVE GOTTEN INTO ART.
THE SAME GOES FOR SAEKI-SENSEI...
SHE'S A LITTLE ECCENTRIC, BUT IF I NEVER HAD HER AS A TEACHER, I WOULDN'T HAVE JOINED THE ART CLUB.
AND AS MUCH AS I HATE TO ADMIT IT, IF RYUJI HADN'T INVITED ME...
...

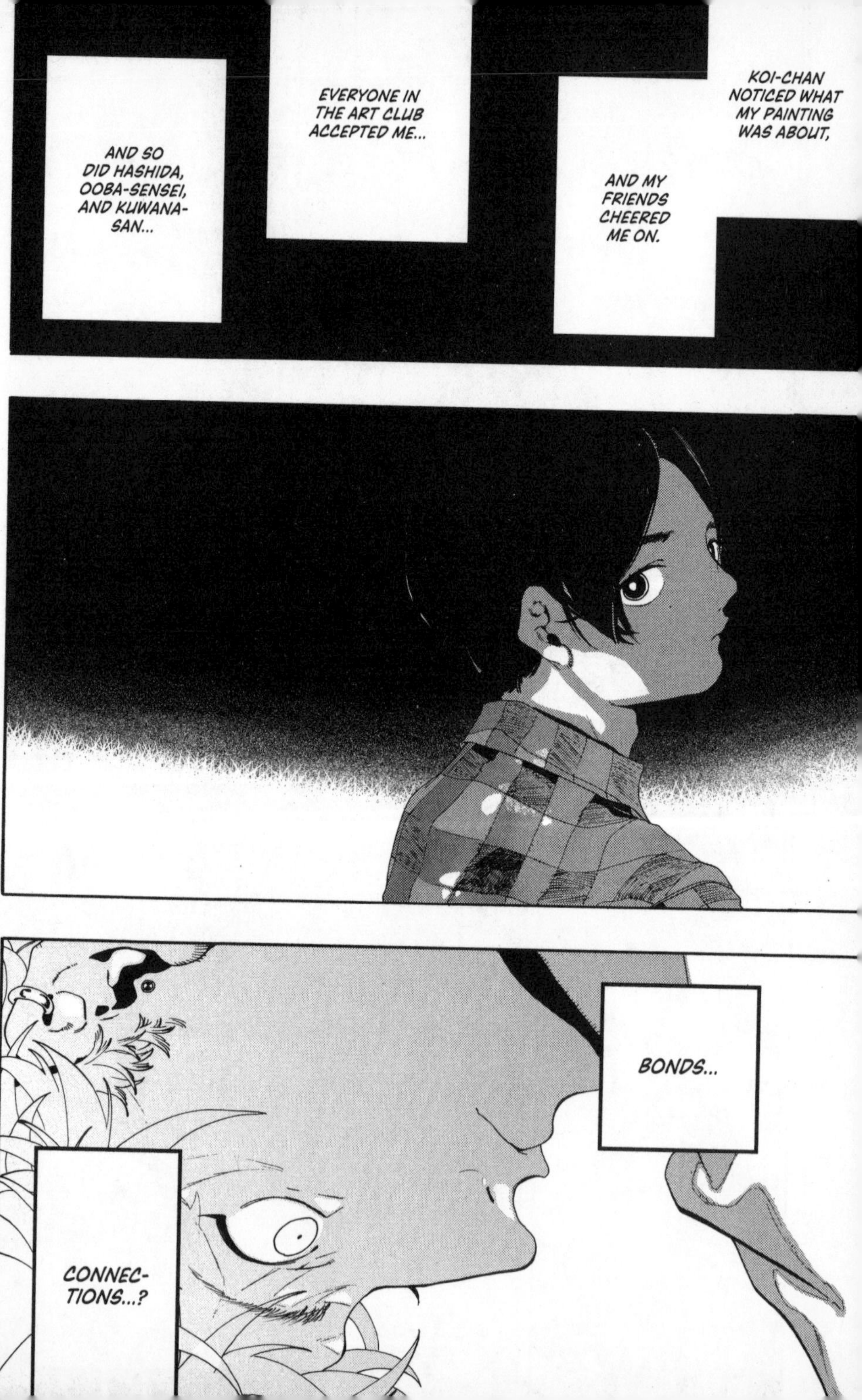
KOI-CHAN NOTICED WHAT MY PAINTING WAS ABOUT,
AND MY FRIENDS CHEERED ME ON.
EVERYONE IN THE ART CLUB ACCEPTED ME...
AND SO DID HASHIDA, OOBA-SENSEI, AND KUWANA-SAN...
BONDS...
CONNEC-TIONS...?

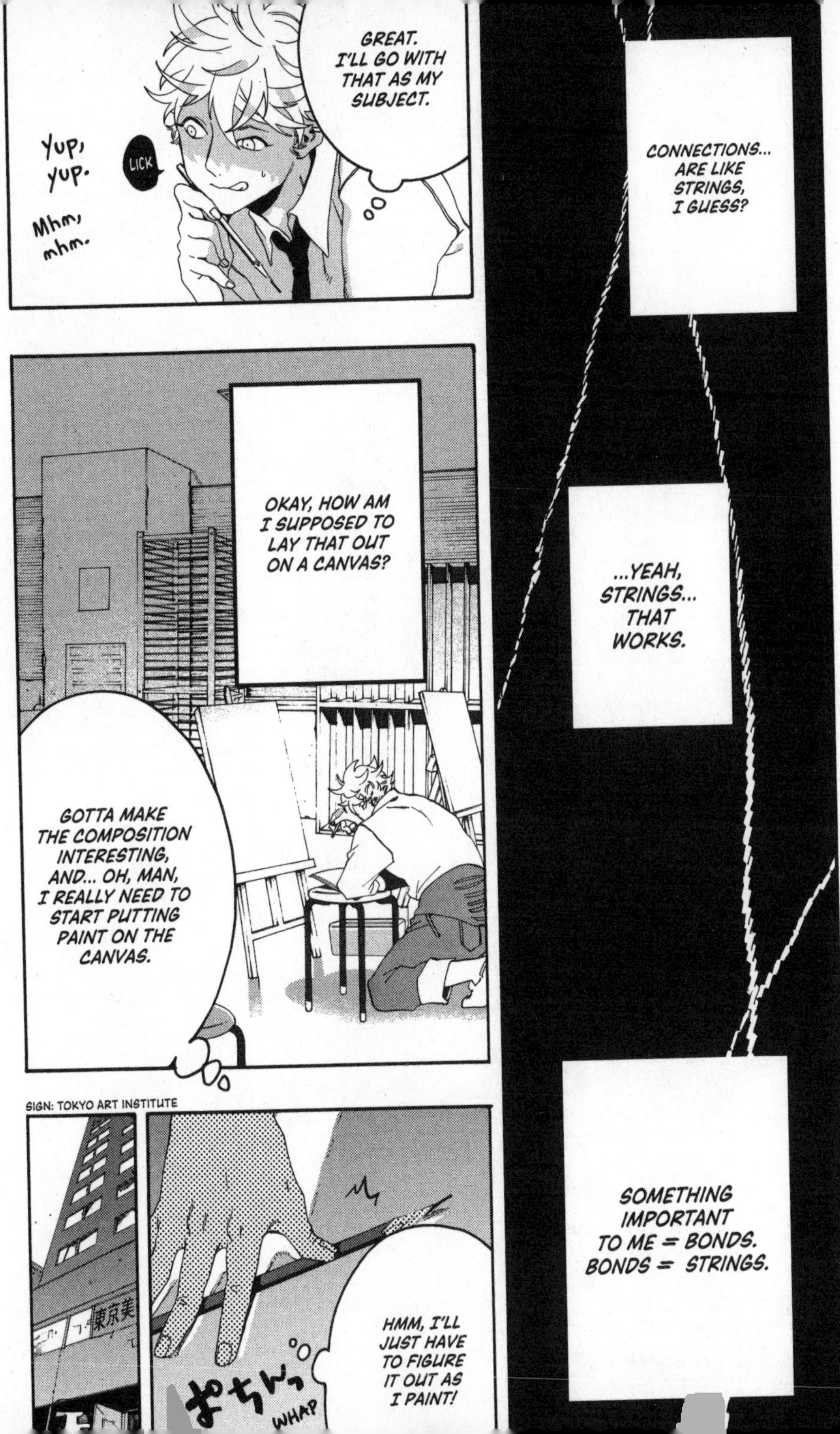
CONNECTIONS... ARE LIKE STRINGS, I GUESS?
...YEAH, STRINGS... THAT WORKS.
SOMETHING IMPORTANT TO ME = BONDS. BONDS = STRINGS.
GREAT. I'LL GO WITH THAT AS MY SUBJECT.
LICK
Yup, yup.
Mhm, mhm.
OKAY, HOW AM I SUPPOSED TO LAY THAT OUT ON A CANVAS?
GOTTA MAKE THE COMPOSITION INTERESTING, AND... OH, MAN, I REALLY NEED TO START PUTTING PAINT ON THE CANVAS.
HMM, I'LL JUST HAVE TO FIGURE IT OUT AS I PAINT!
WHAP
東京美
SIGN: TOKYO ART INSTITUTE

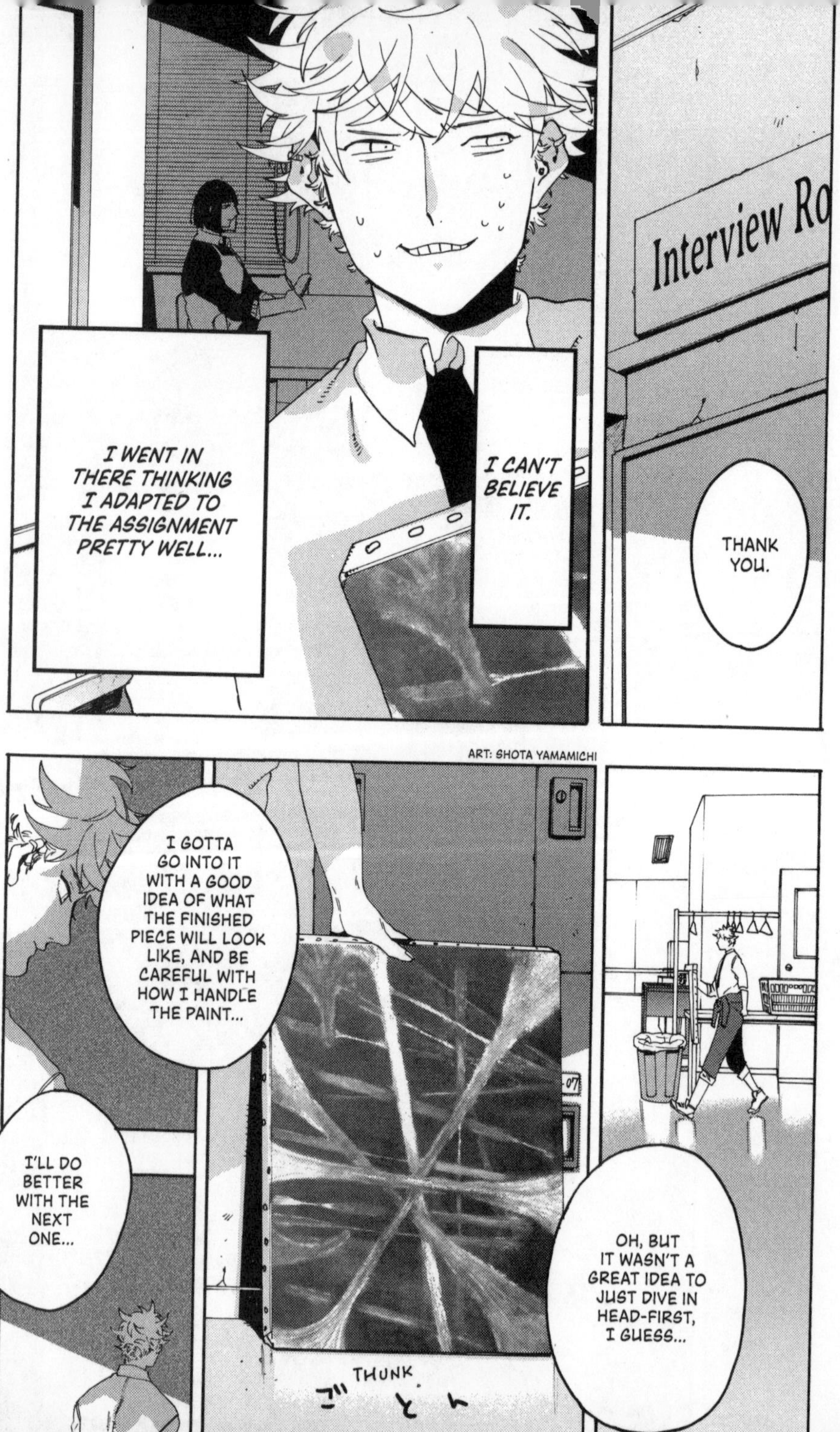
Interview Ro
THANK YOU.
I CAN'T BELIEVE IT.
I WENT IN THERE THINKING I ADAPTED TO THE ASSIGNMENT PRETTY WELL...
ART: SHOTA YAMAMICHI
OH, BUT IT WASN'T A GREAT IDEA TO JUST DIVE IN HEAD-FIRST, I GUESS...
I GOTTA GO INTO IT WITH A GOOD IDEA OF WHAT THE FINISHED PIECE WILL LOOK LIKE, AND BE CAREFUL WITH HOW I HANDLE THE PAINT...
I'LL DO BETTER WITH THE NEXT ONE...
THUNK
ごとん

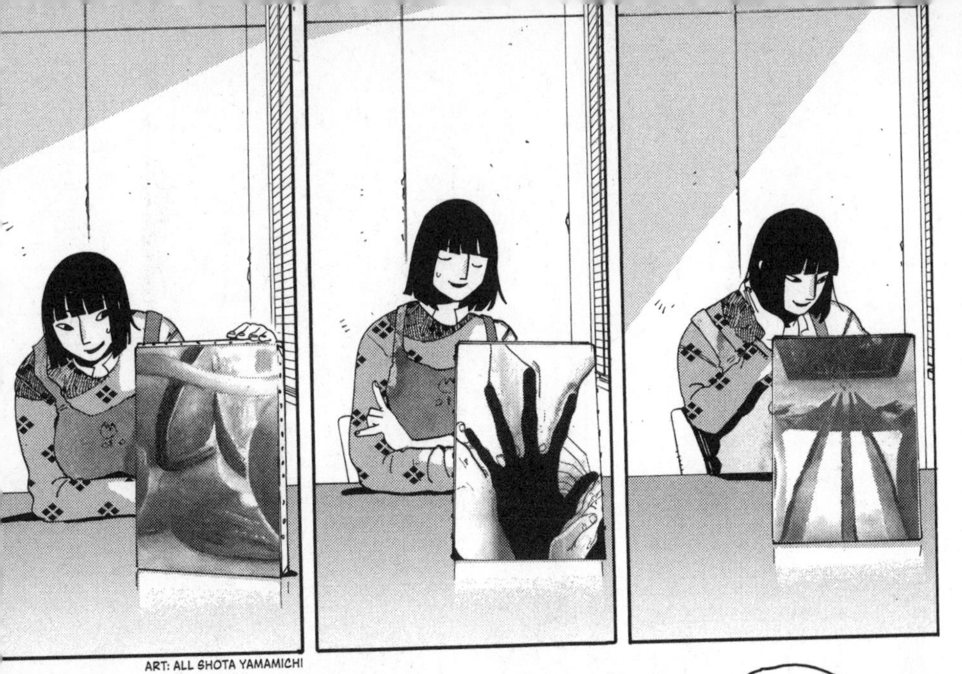

ART: ALL SHOTA YAMAMICHI

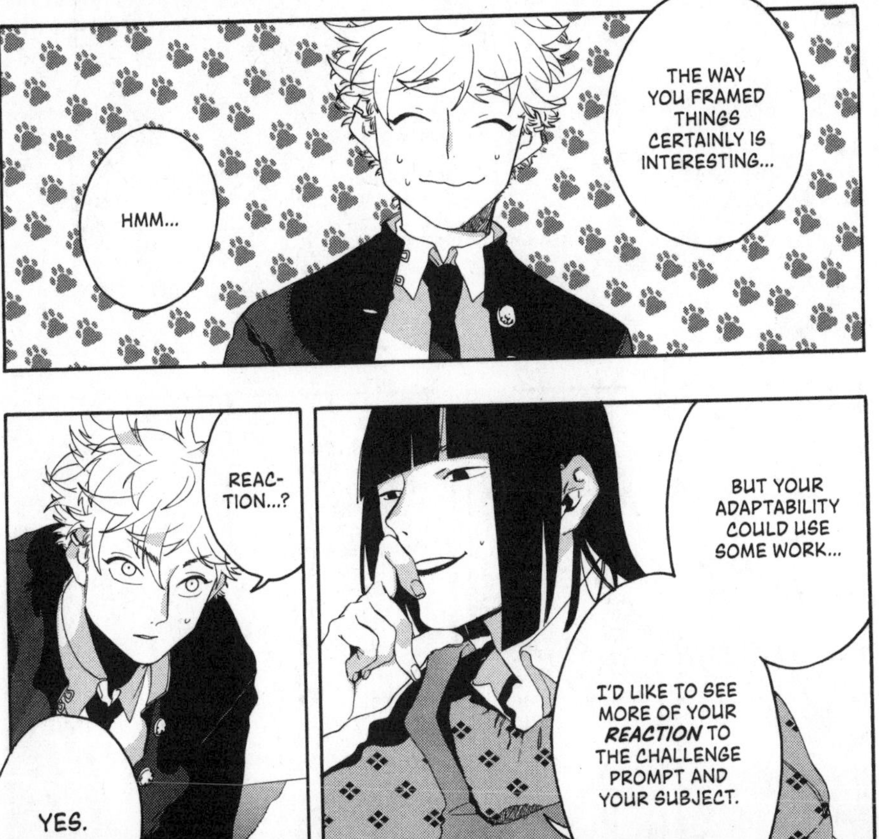
THE WAY YOU FRAMED THINGS CERTAINLY IS INTERESTING...
HMM...
BUT YOUR ADAPTABILITY COULD USE SOME WORK...
I'D LIKE TO SEE MORE OF YOUR *REACTION* TO THE CHALLENGE PROMPT AND YOUR SUBJECT.
REAC-TION...?
YES.

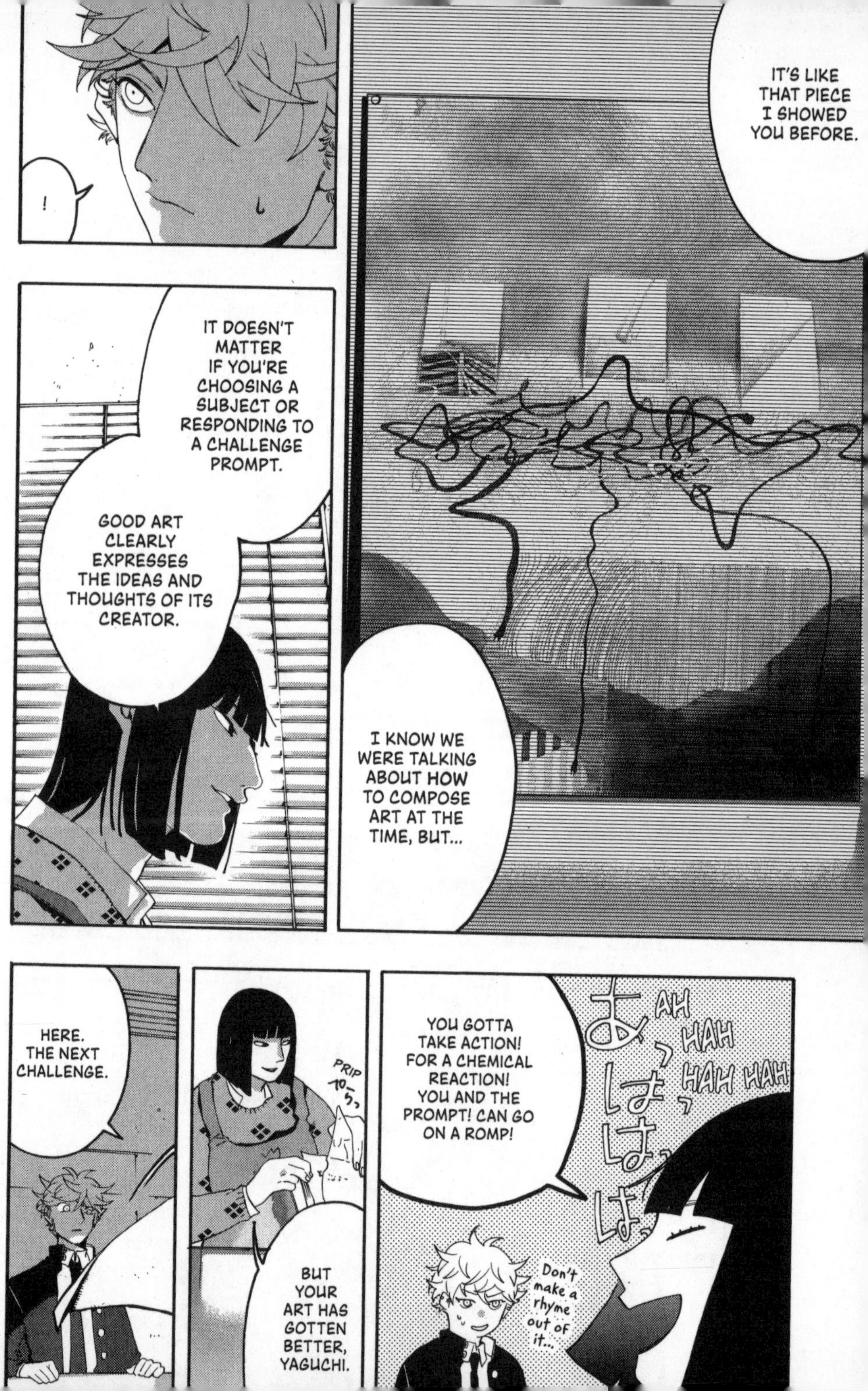
IT'S LIKE THAT PIECE I SHOWED YOU BEFORE.
I KNOW WE WERE TALKING ABOUT HOW TO COMPOSE ART AT THE TIME, BUT...
!
IT DOESN'T MATTER IF YOU'RE CHOOSING A SUBJECT OR RESPONDING TO A CHALLENGE PROMPT.
GOOD ART CLEARLY EXPRESSES THE IDEAS AND THOUGHTS OF ITS CREATOR.
AH HAH HAH HAH HAH
YOU GOTTA TAKE ACTION! FOR A CHEMICAL REACTION! YOU AND THE PROMPT! CAN GO ON A ROMP!
Don't make a rhyme out of it...
PRIP
BUT YOUR ART HAS GOTTEN BETTER, YAGUCHI.
HERE. THE NEXT CHALLENGE.
...

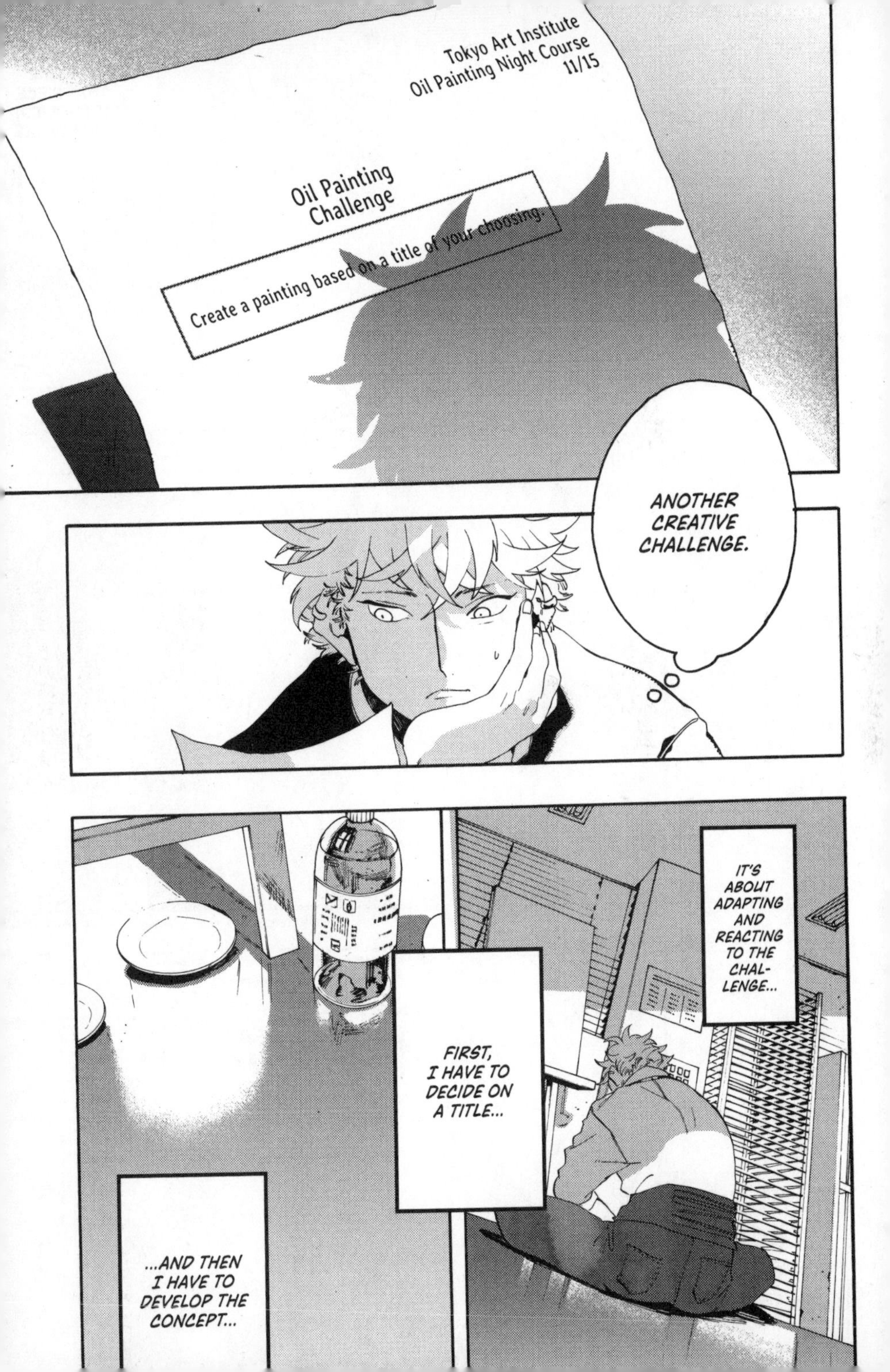
Tokyo Art Institute
Oil Painting Night Course
11/15
Oil Painting Challenge
Create a painting based on a title of your choosing.
ANOTHER CREATIVE CHALLENGE.
IT'S ABOUT ADAPTING AND REACTING TO THE CHAL-LENGE...
FIRST, I HAVE TO DECIDE ON A TITLE...
...AND THEN I HAVE TO DEVELOP THE CONCEPT...

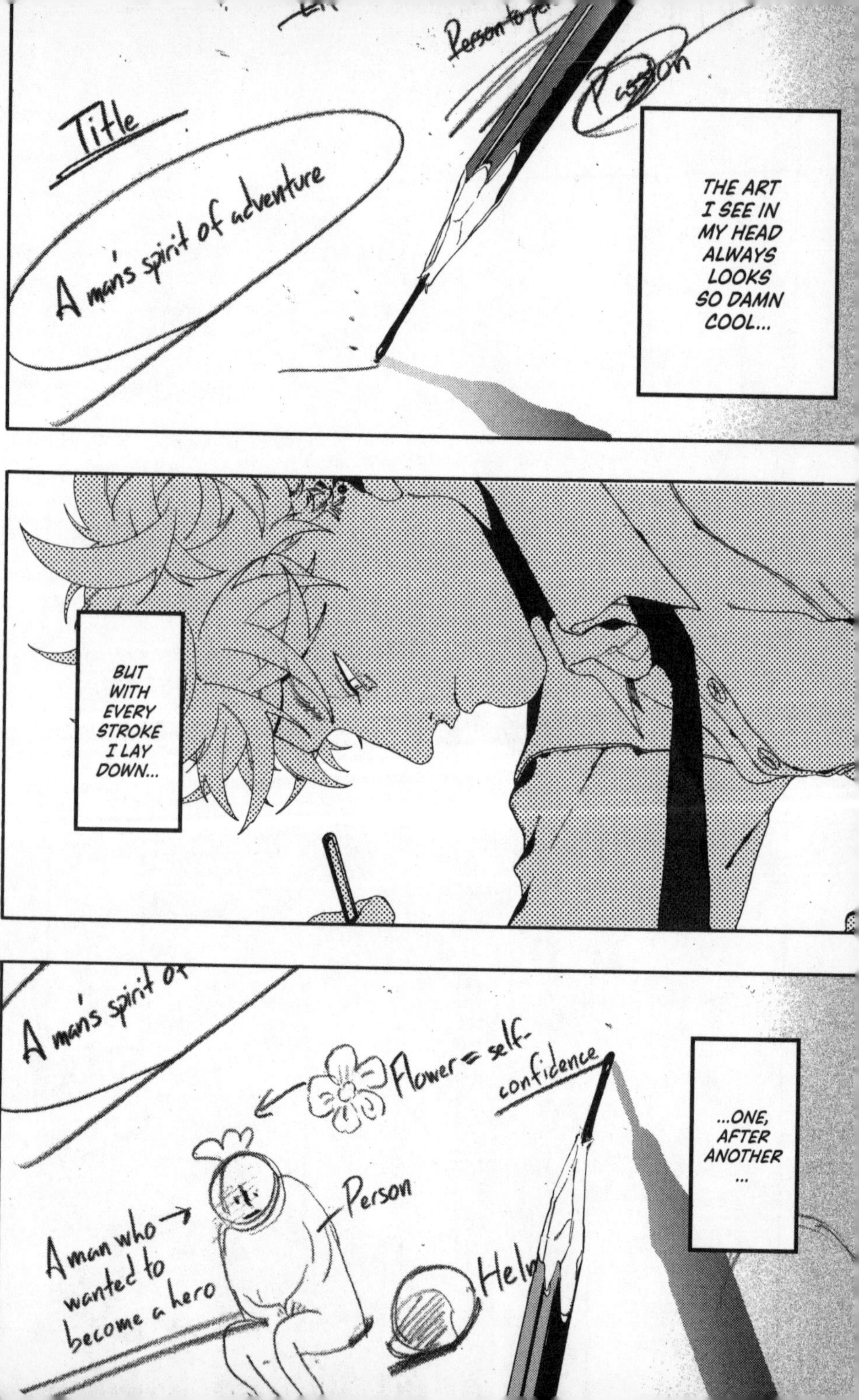
THE ART I SEE IN MY HEAD ALWAYS LOOKS SO DAMN COOL...
Passion
Title
A man's spirit of adventure
BUT WITH EVERY STROKE I LAY DOWN...
...ONE, AFTER ANOTHER...
Flower = self-confidence
A man's spirit of
Person
A man who wanted to become a hero

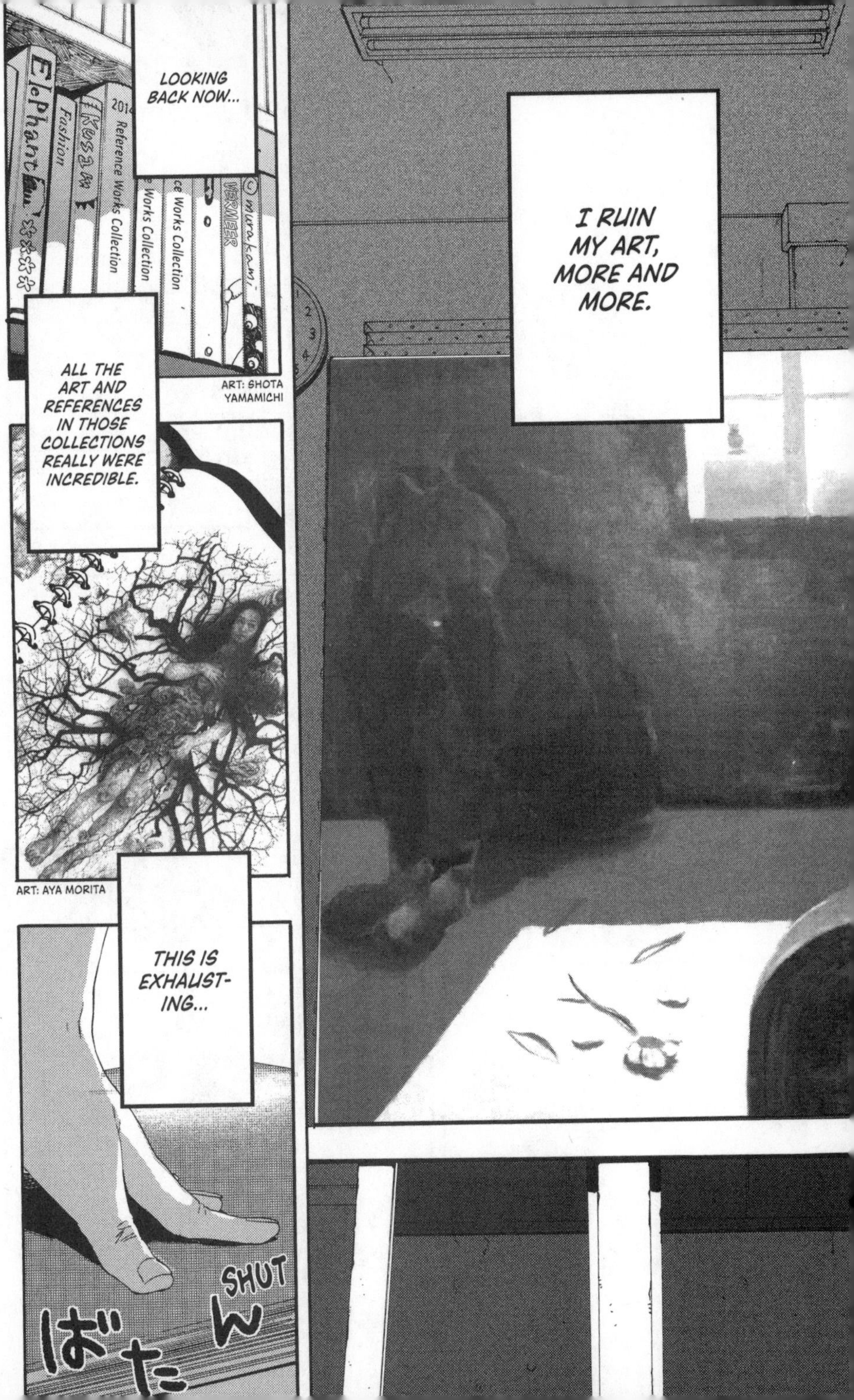
I RUIN MY ART, MORE AND MORE.
LOOKING BACK NOW...
ElePhant
Fashion
2014 Reference Works Collection
Works Collection
Works Collection
murakami
VERMEER
ART: SHOTA YAMAMICHI
ALL THE ART AND REFERENCES IN THOSE COLLECTIONS REALLY WERE INCREDIBLE.
ART: AYA MORITA
THIS IS EXHAUSTING...
ばたん
SHUT

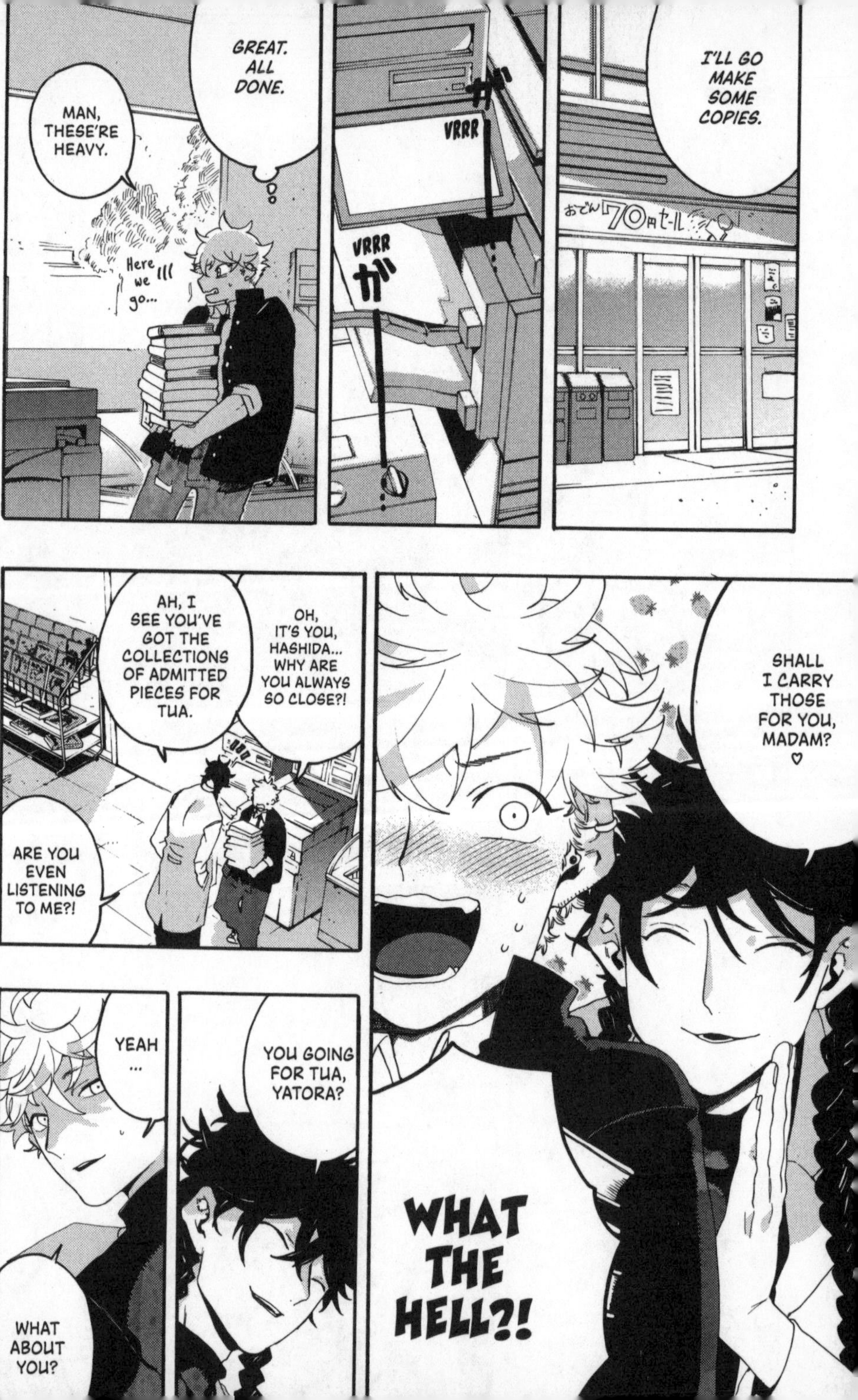
I'LL GO MAKE SOME COPIES.
おでん70円セール
ガ
VRRR
VRRR
ガ
GREAT. ALL DONE.
MAN, THESE'RE HEAVY.
Here we go...
SHALL I CARRY THOSE FOR YOU, MADAM? ♡
WHAT THE HELL?!
OH, IT'S YOU, HASHIDA... WHY ARE YOU ALWAYS SO CLOSE?!
AH, I SEE YOU'VE GOT THE COLLECTIONS OF ADMITTED PIECES FOR TUA.
ARE YOU EVEN LISTENING TO ME?!
YOU GOING FOR TUA, YATORA?
YEAH ...
WHAT ABOUT YOU?

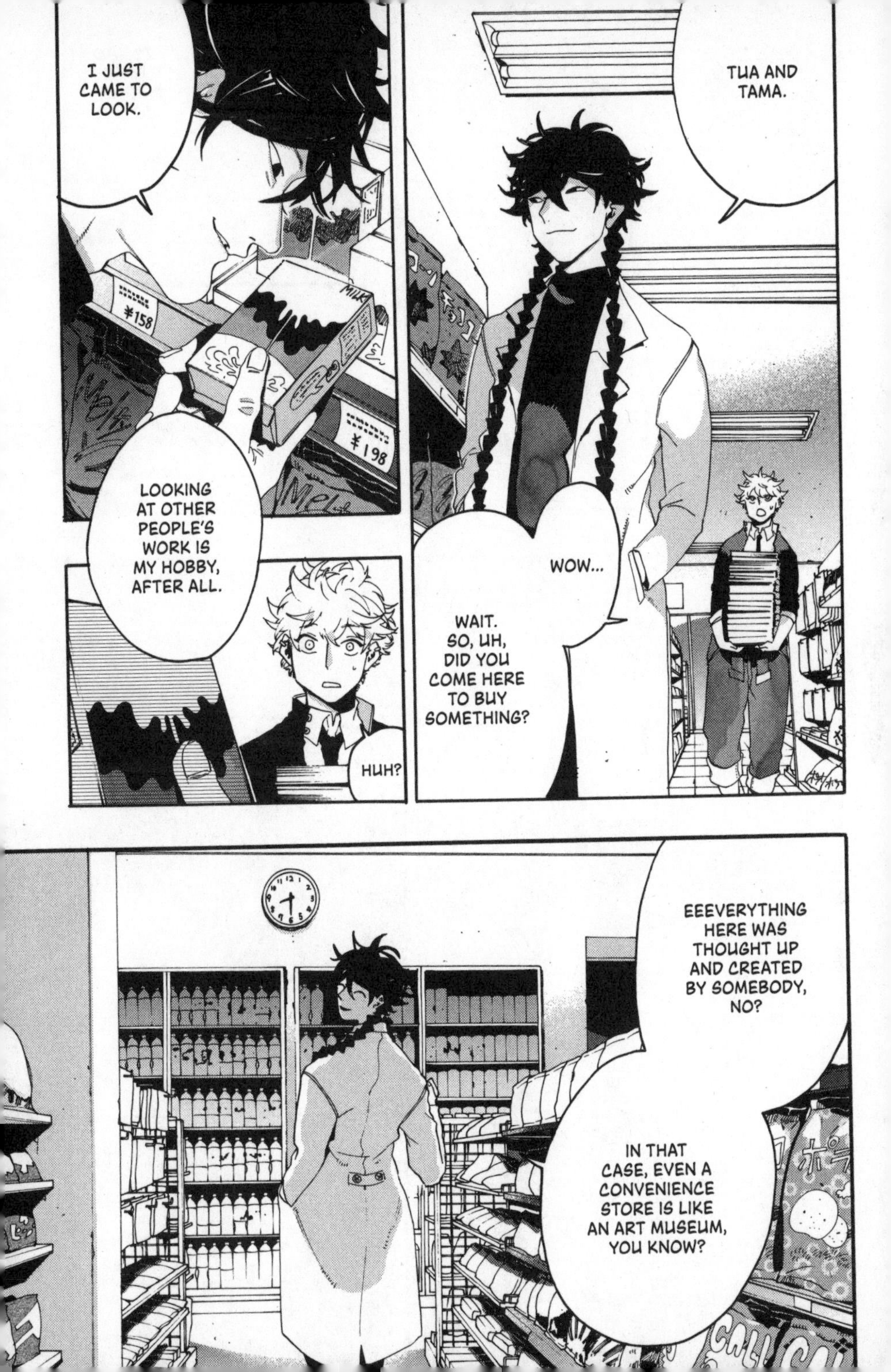
TUA AND TAMA.
WOW...
WAIT. SO, UH, DID YOU COME HERE TO BUY SOMETHING?
I JUST CAME TO LOOK.
LOOKING AT OTHER PEOPLE'S WORK IS MY HOBBY, AFTER ALL.
HUH?
EEEVERYTHING HERE WAS THOUGHT UP AND CREATED BY SOMEBODY, NO?
IN THAT CASE, EVEN A CONVENIENCE STORE IS LIKE AN ART MUSEUM, YOU KNOW?

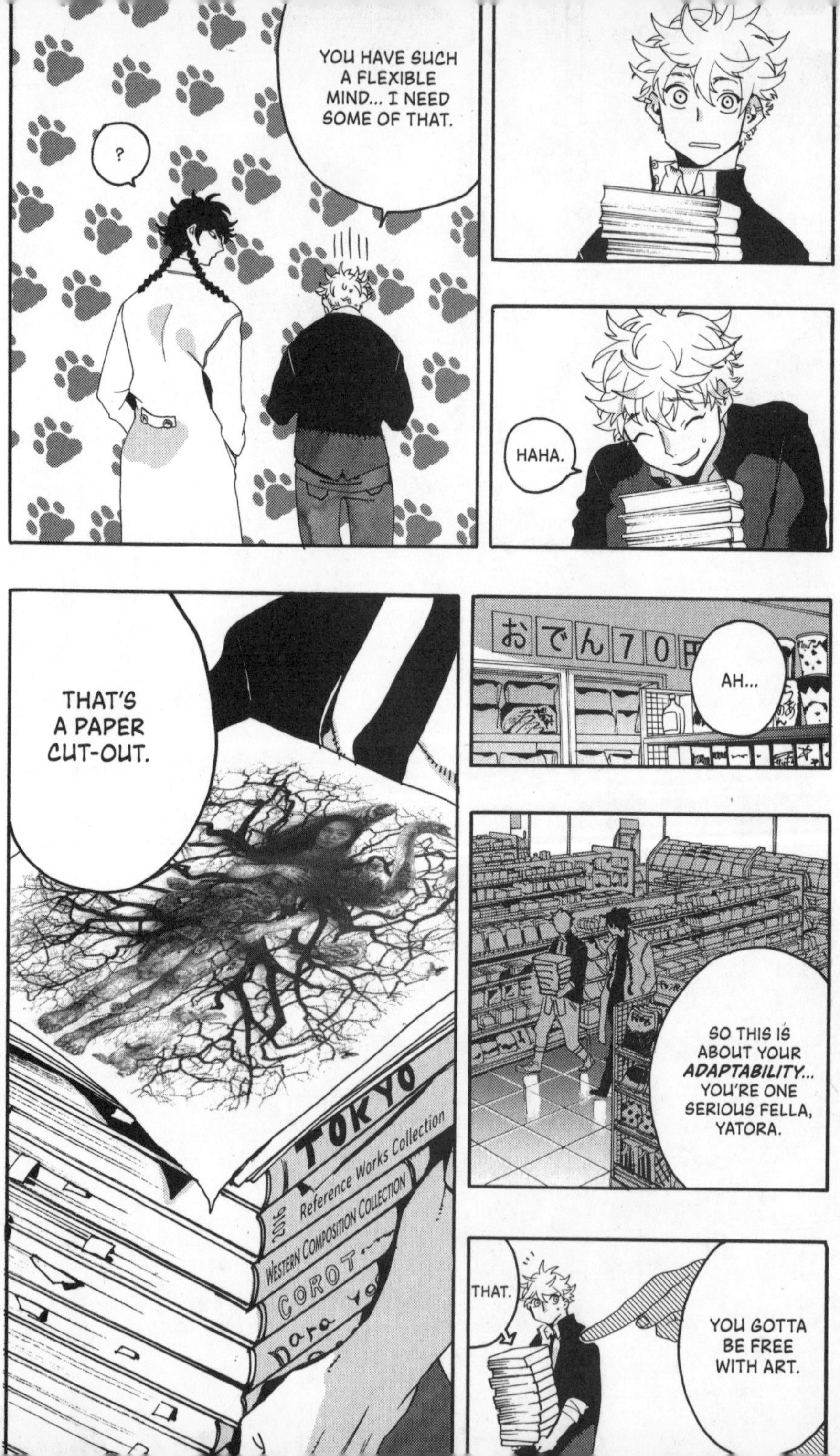
HAHA.
YOU HAVE SUCH A FLEXIBLE MIND... I NEED SOME OF THAT.
?
おでん70
AH...
SO THIS IS ABOUT YOUR *ADAPTABILITY*... YOU'RE ONE SERIOUS FELLA, YATORA.
YOU GOTTA BE FREE WITH ART.
THAT.
THAT'S A PAPER CUT-OUT.
TOKYO
Reference Works Collection
WESTERN COMPOSITION COLLECTION
COROT

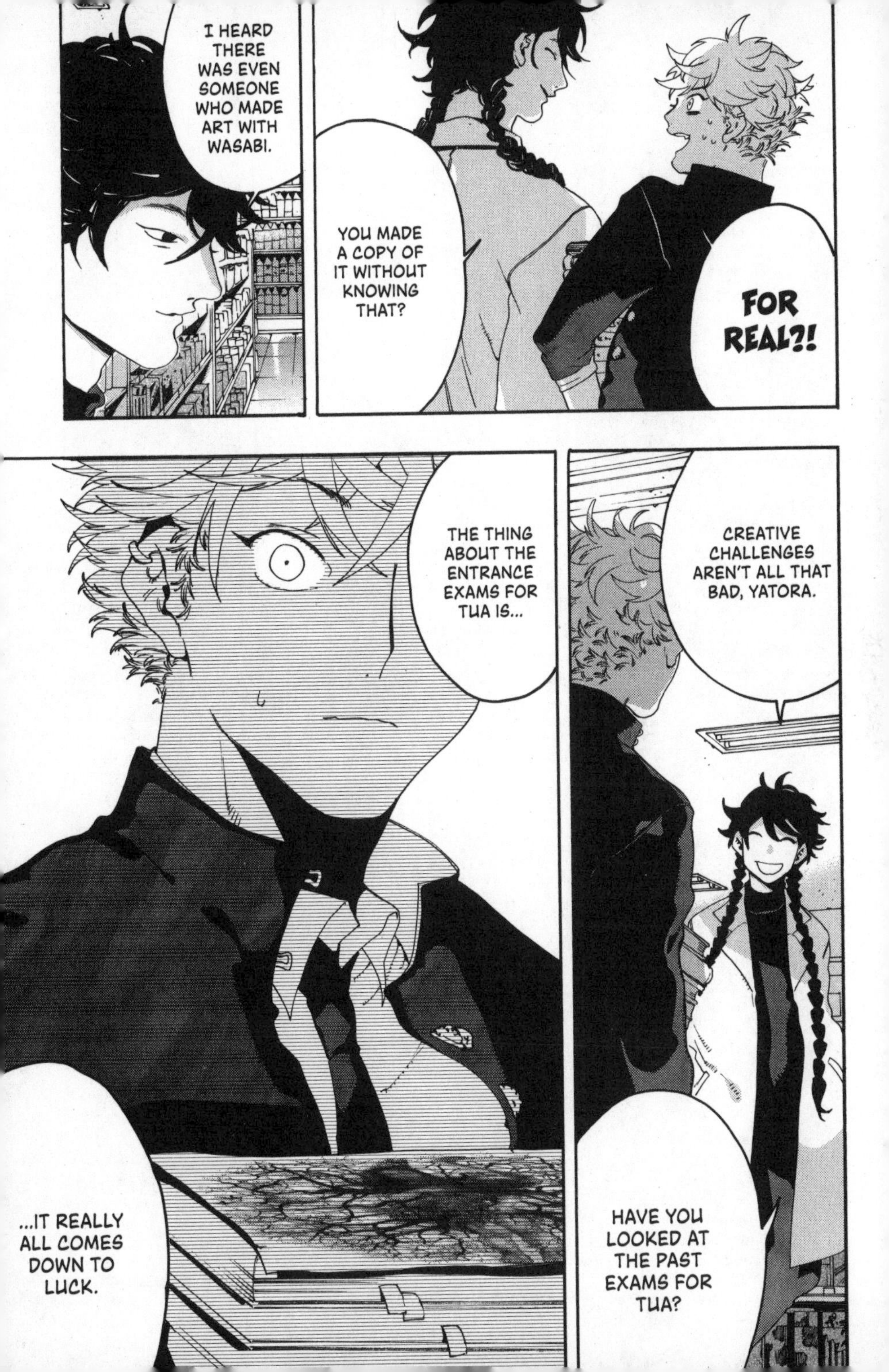
YOU MADE A COPY OF IT WITHOUT KNOWING THAT?
FOR REAL?!
I HEARD THERE WAS EVEN SOMEONE WHO MADE ART WITH WASABI.
CREATIVE CHALLENGES AREN'T ALL THAT BAD, YATORA.
HAVE YOU LOOKED AT THE PAST EXAMS FOR TUA?
THE THING ABOUT THE ENTRANCE EXAMS FOR TUA IS...
...IT REALLY ALL COMES DOWN TO LUCK.

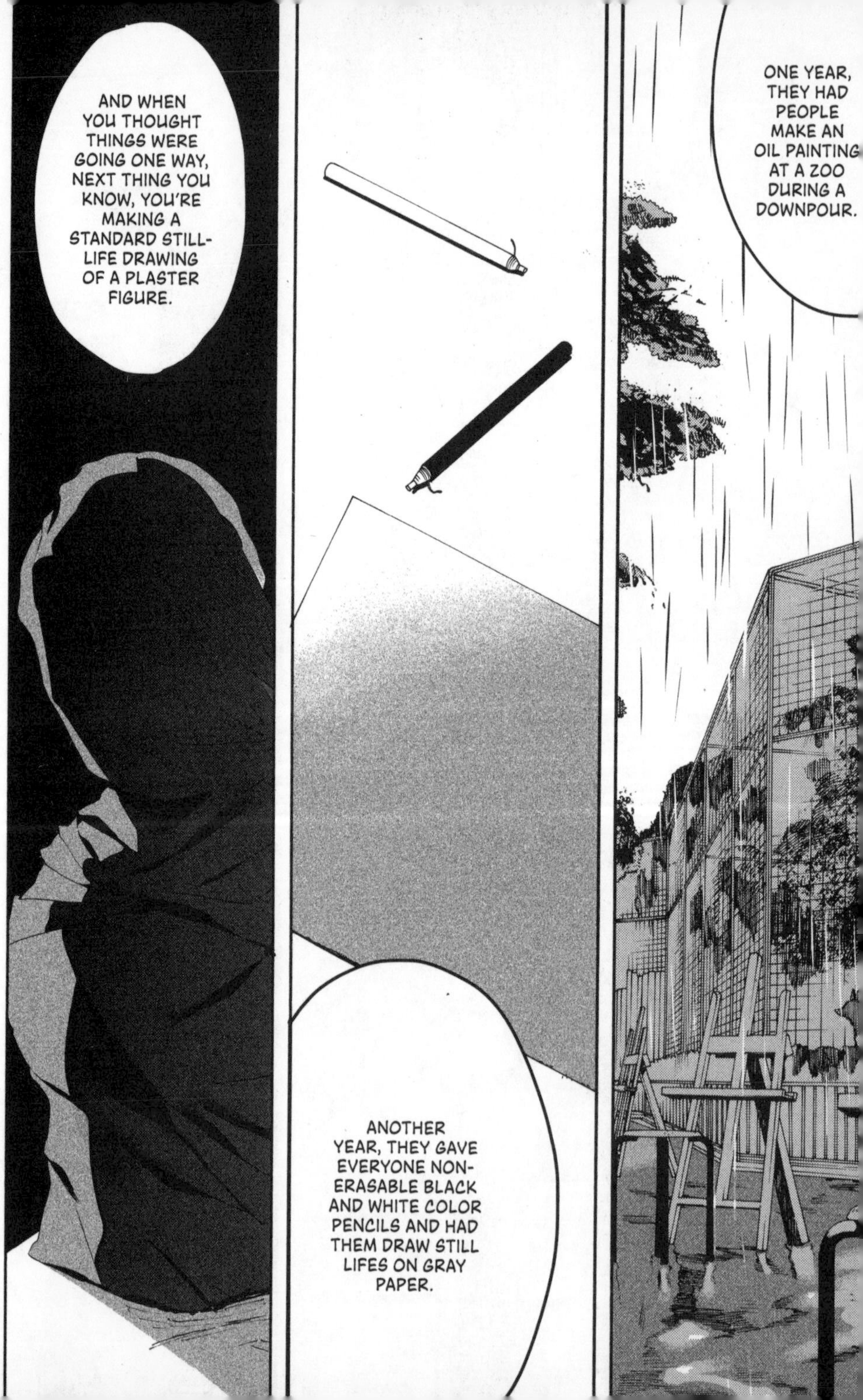
ONE YEAR, THEY HAD PEOPLE MAKE AN OIL PAINTING AT A ZOO DURING A DOWNPOUR.
ANOTHER YEAR, THEY GAVE EVERYONE NON-ERASABLE BLACK AND WHITE COLOR PENCILS AND HAD THEM DRAW STILL LIFES ON GRAY PAPER.
AND WHEN YOU THOUGHT THINGS WERE GOING ONE WAY, NEXT THING YOU KNOW, YOU'RE MAKING A STANDARD STILL-LIFE DRAWING OF A PLASTER FIGURE.

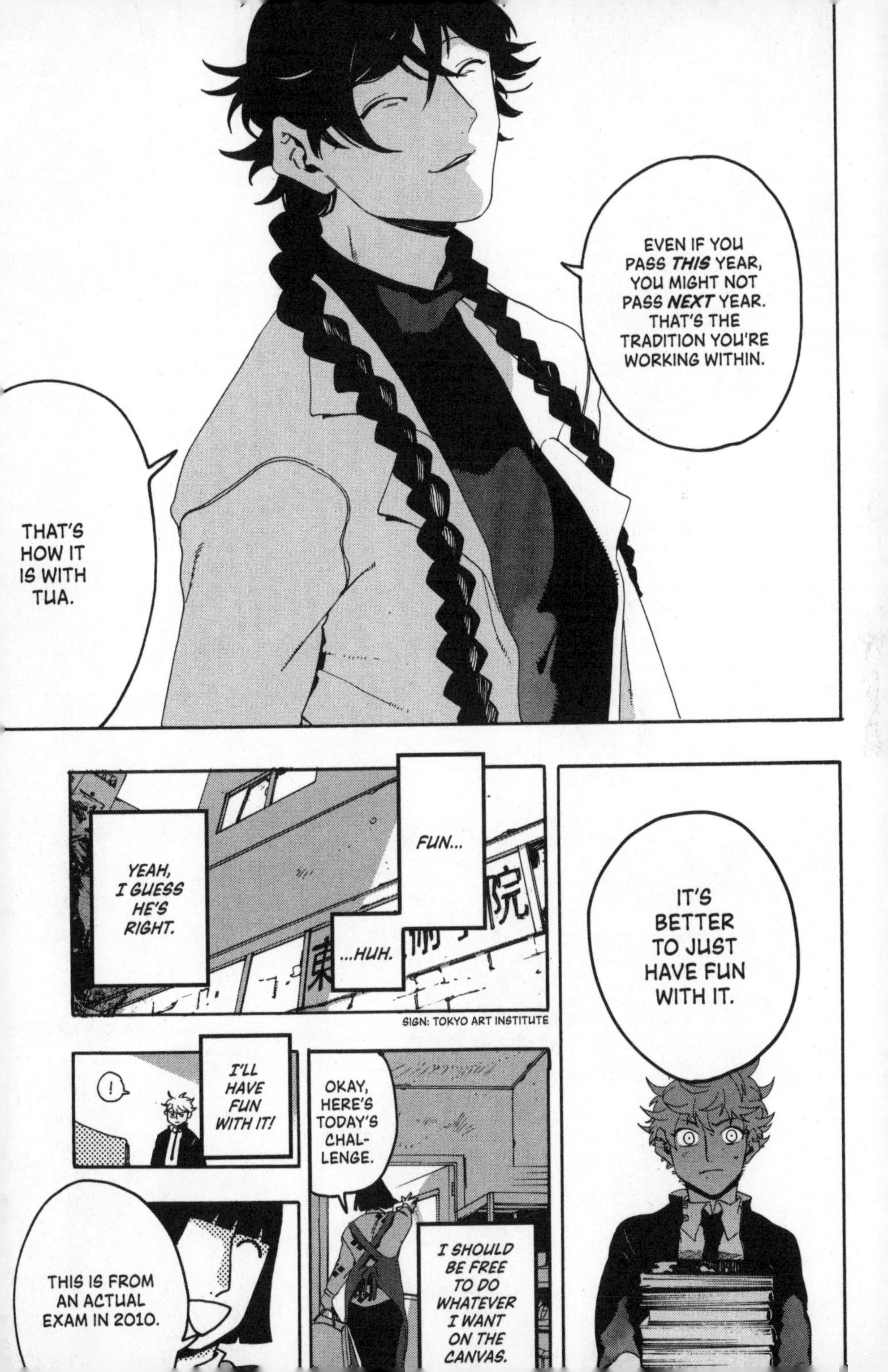
EVEN IF YOU PASS THIS YEAR, YOU MIGHT NOT PASS NEXT YEAR. THAT'S THE TRADITION YOU'RE WORKING WITHIN.
THAT'S HOW IT IS WITH TUA.
IT'S BETTER TO JUST HAVE FUN WITH IT.
FUN...
...HUH.
YEAH, I GUESS HE'S RIGHT.
SIGN: TOKYO ART INSTITUTE
OKAY, HERE'S TODAY'S CHAL-LENGE.
I SHOULD BE FREE TO DO WHATEVER I WANT ON THE CANVAS.
I'LL HAVE FUN WITH IT!
!
THIS IS FROM AN ACTUAL EXAM IN 2010.

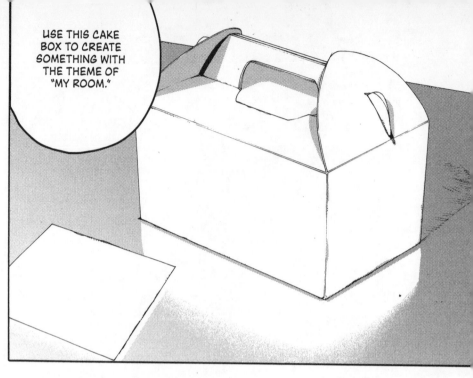

USE THIS CAKE BOX TO CREATE SOMETHING WITH THE THEME OF "MY ROOM."

...

WOW, SHOULD BE FUN.

...

terview Ro

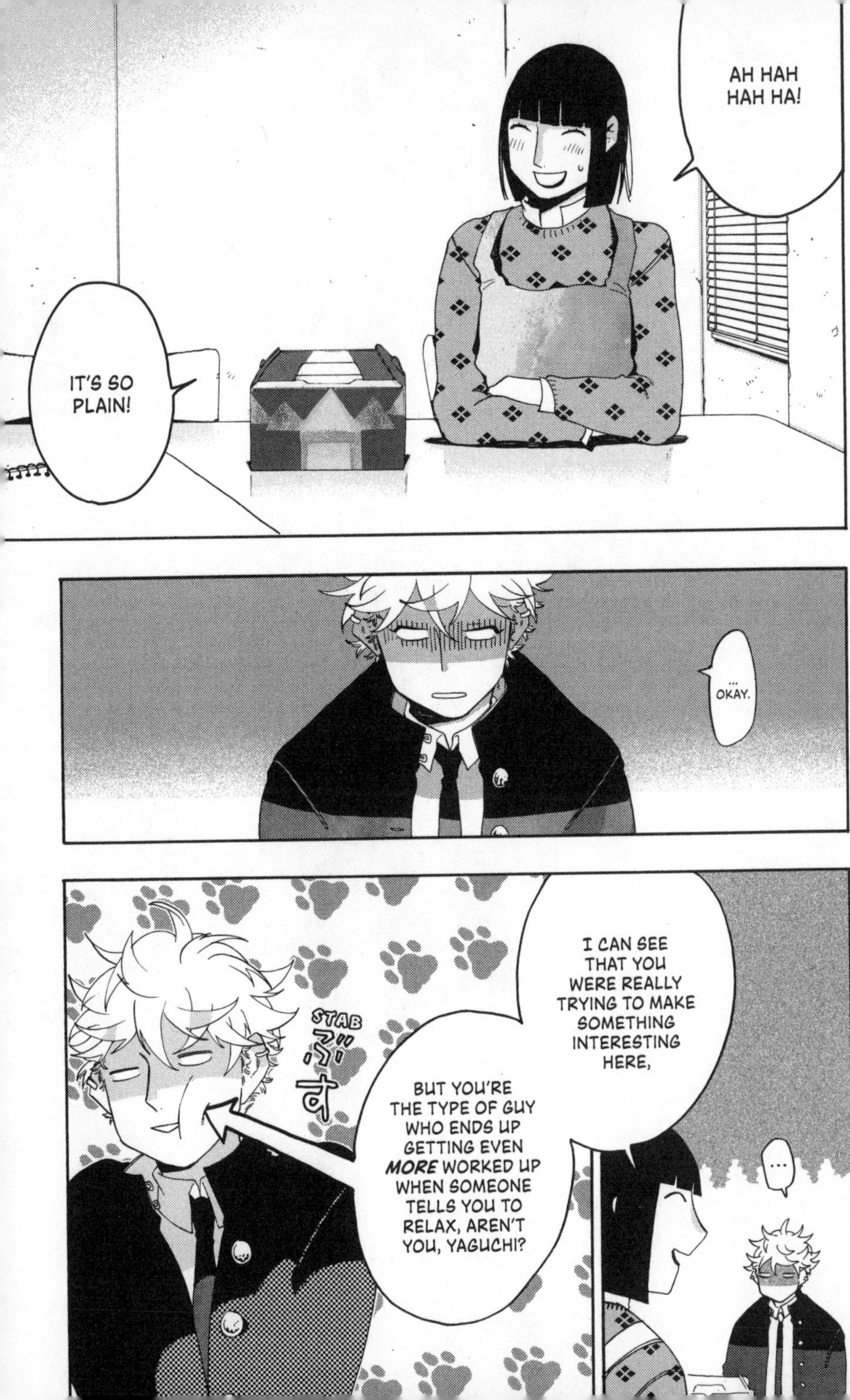
AH HAH HAH HA!
IT'S SO PLAIN!
...OKAY.
I CAN SEE THAT YOU WERE REALLY TRYING TO MAKE SOMETHING INTERESTING HERE,
BUT YOU'RE THE TYPE OF GUY WHO ENDS UP GETTING EVEN *MORE* WORKED UP WHEN SOMEONE TELLS YOU TO RELAX, AREN'T YOU, YAGUCHI?
STAB ぶす
...

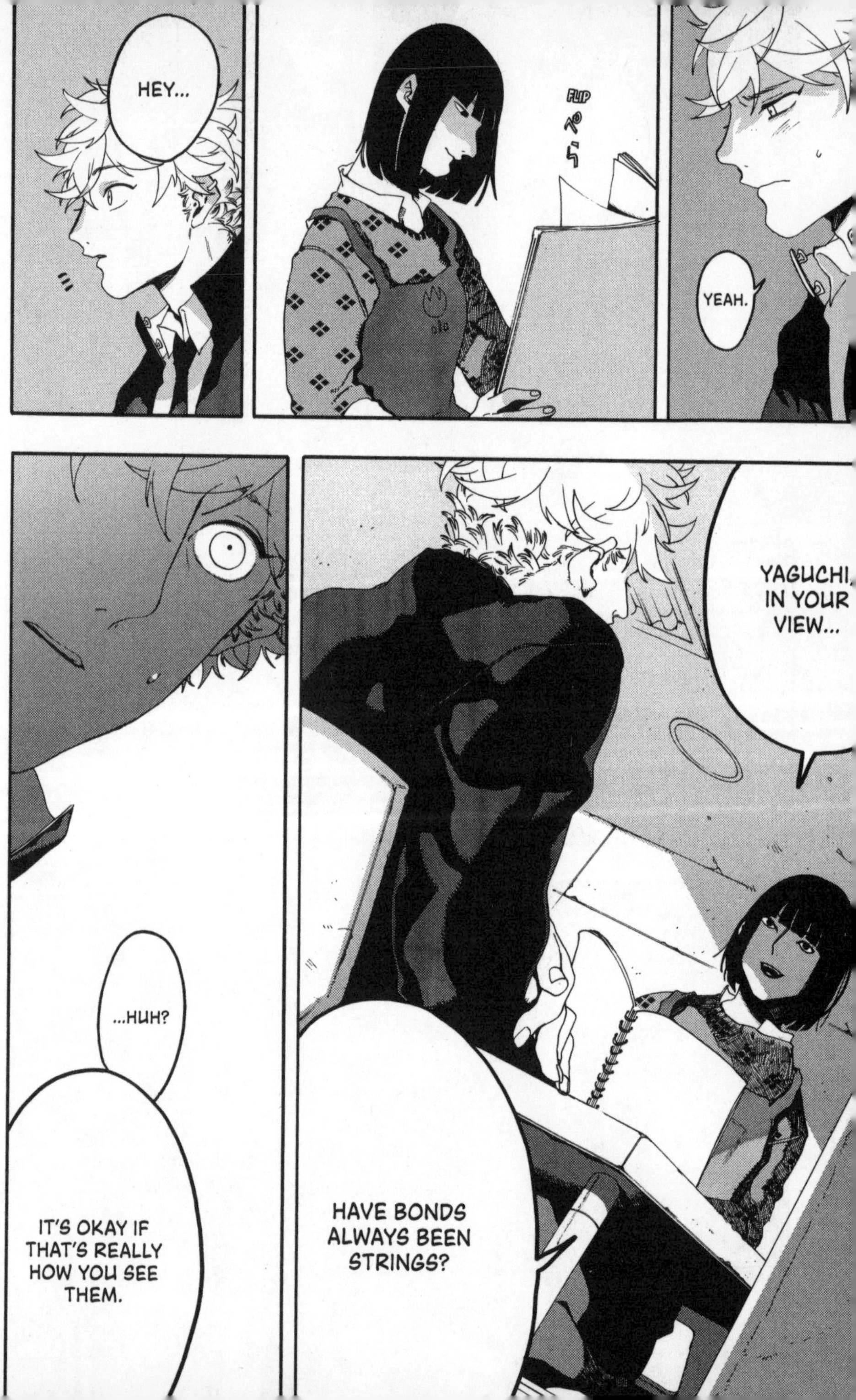
YEAH.
FLIP
HEY...
YAGUCHI, IN YOUR VIEW...
HAVE BONDS ALWAYS BEEN STRINGS?
...HUH?
IT'S OKAY IF THAT'S REALLY HOW YOU SEE THEM.

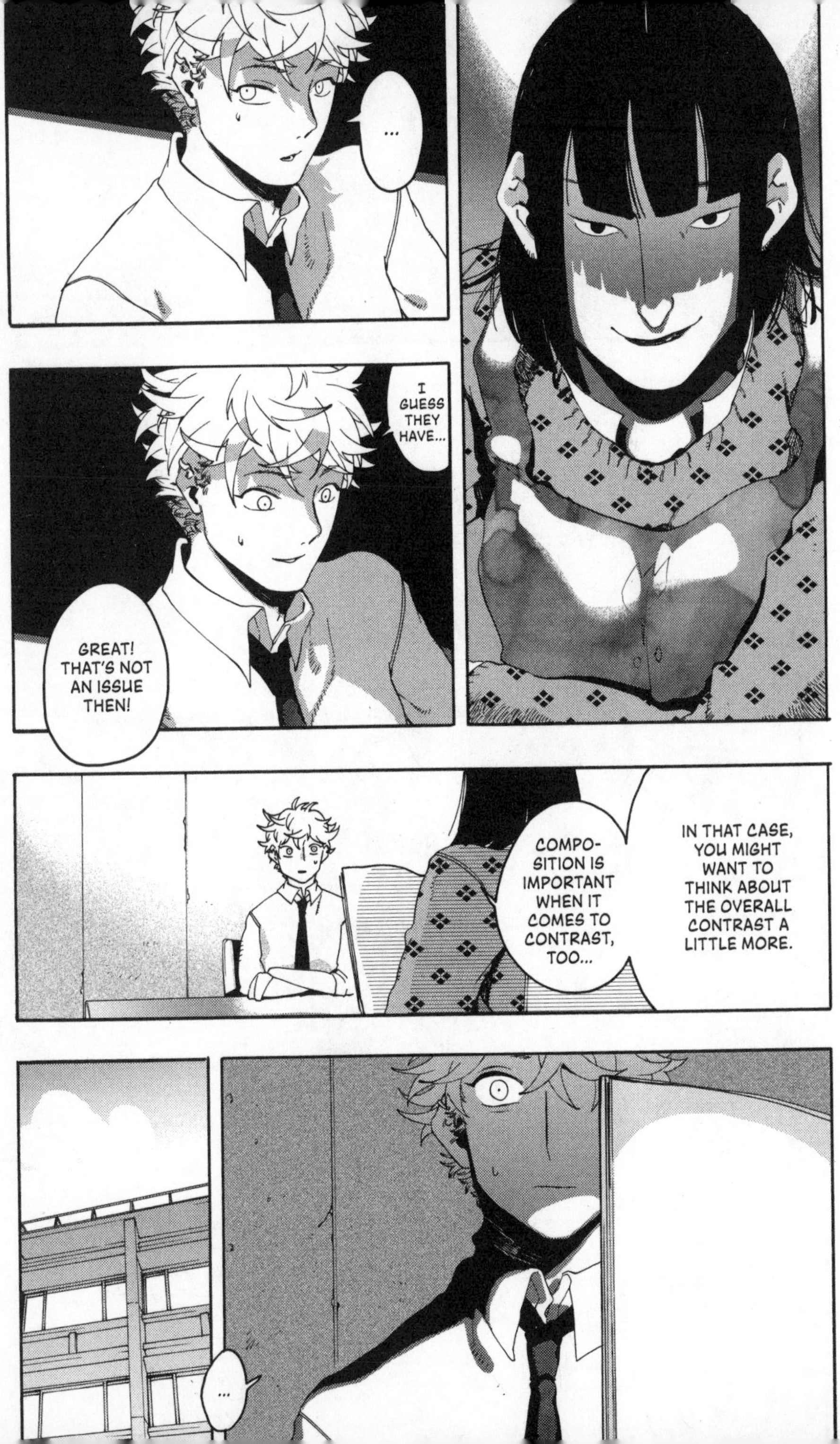
...
I GUESS THEY HAVE...
GREAT! THAT'S NOT AN ISSUE THEN!
IN THAT CASE, YOU MIGHT WANT TO THINK ABOUT THE OVERALL CONTRAST A LITTLE MORE.
COMPOSITION IS IMPORTANT WHEN IT COMES TO CONTRAST, TOO...
...

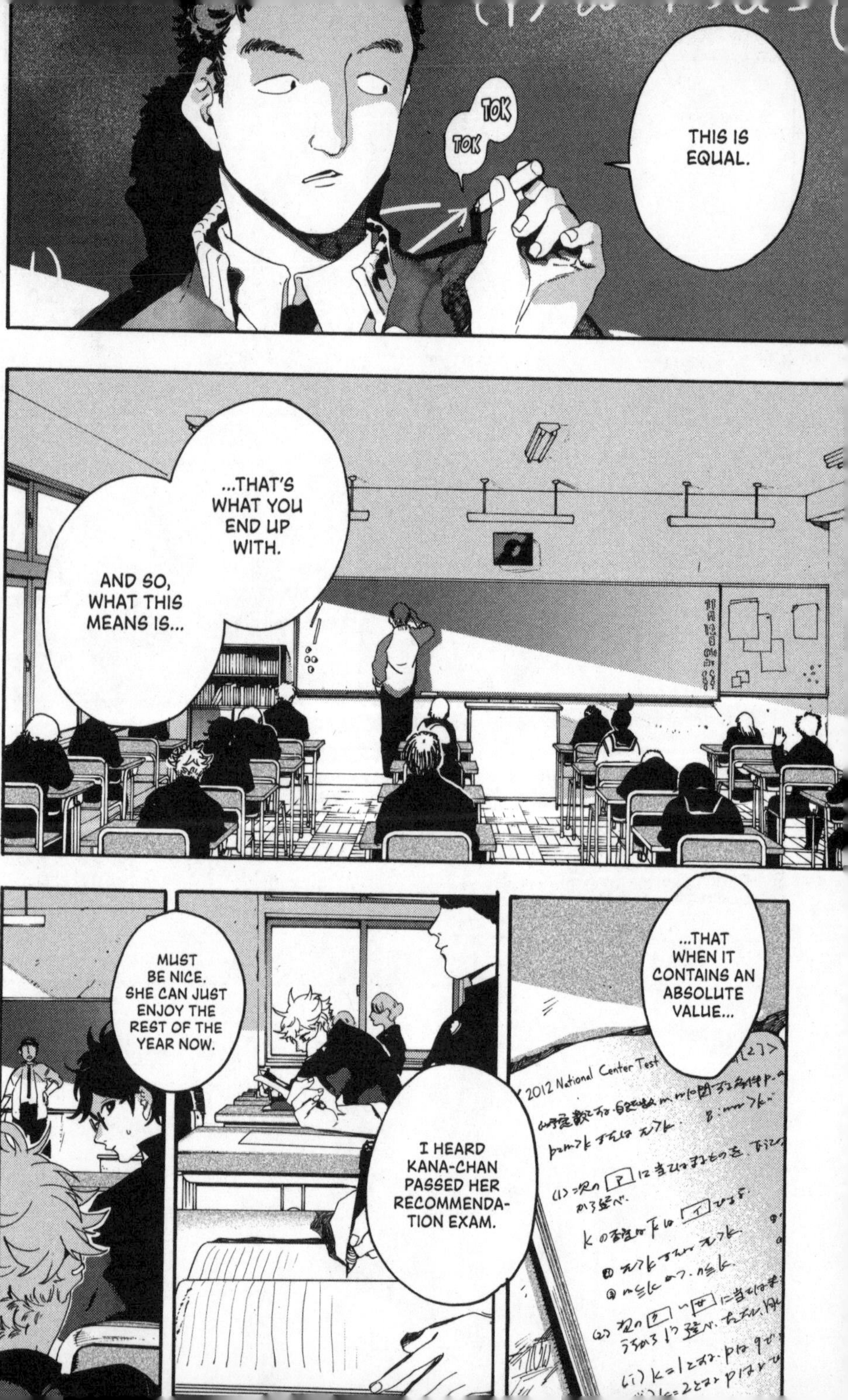
THIS IS EQUAL.
TOK
TOK
...THAT'S WHAT YOU END UP WITH.
AND SO, WHAT THIS MEANS IS...
...THAT WHEN IT CONTAINS AN ABSOLUTE VALUE...
2012 National Center Test
I HEARD KANA-CHAN PASSED HER RECOMMENDATION EXAM.
MUST BE NICE. SHE CAN JUST ENJOY THE REST OF THE YEAR NOW.

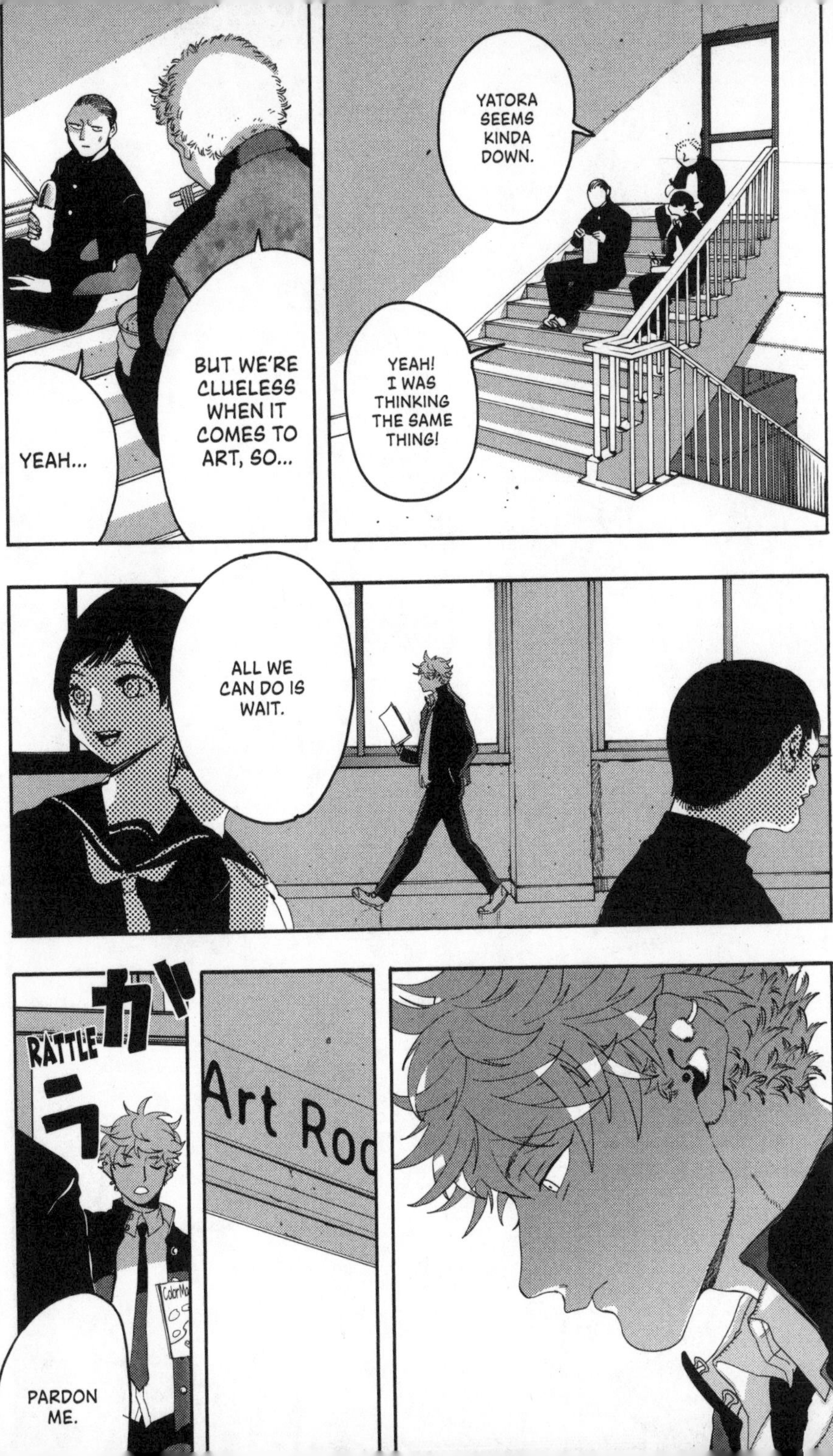
YATORA SEEMS KINDA DOWN.
YEAH! I WAS THINKING THE SAME THING!
BUT WE'RE CLUELESS WHEN IT COMES TO ART, SO...
YEAH...
ALL WE CAN DO IS WAIT.
Art Roo
RATTLE
PARDON ME.

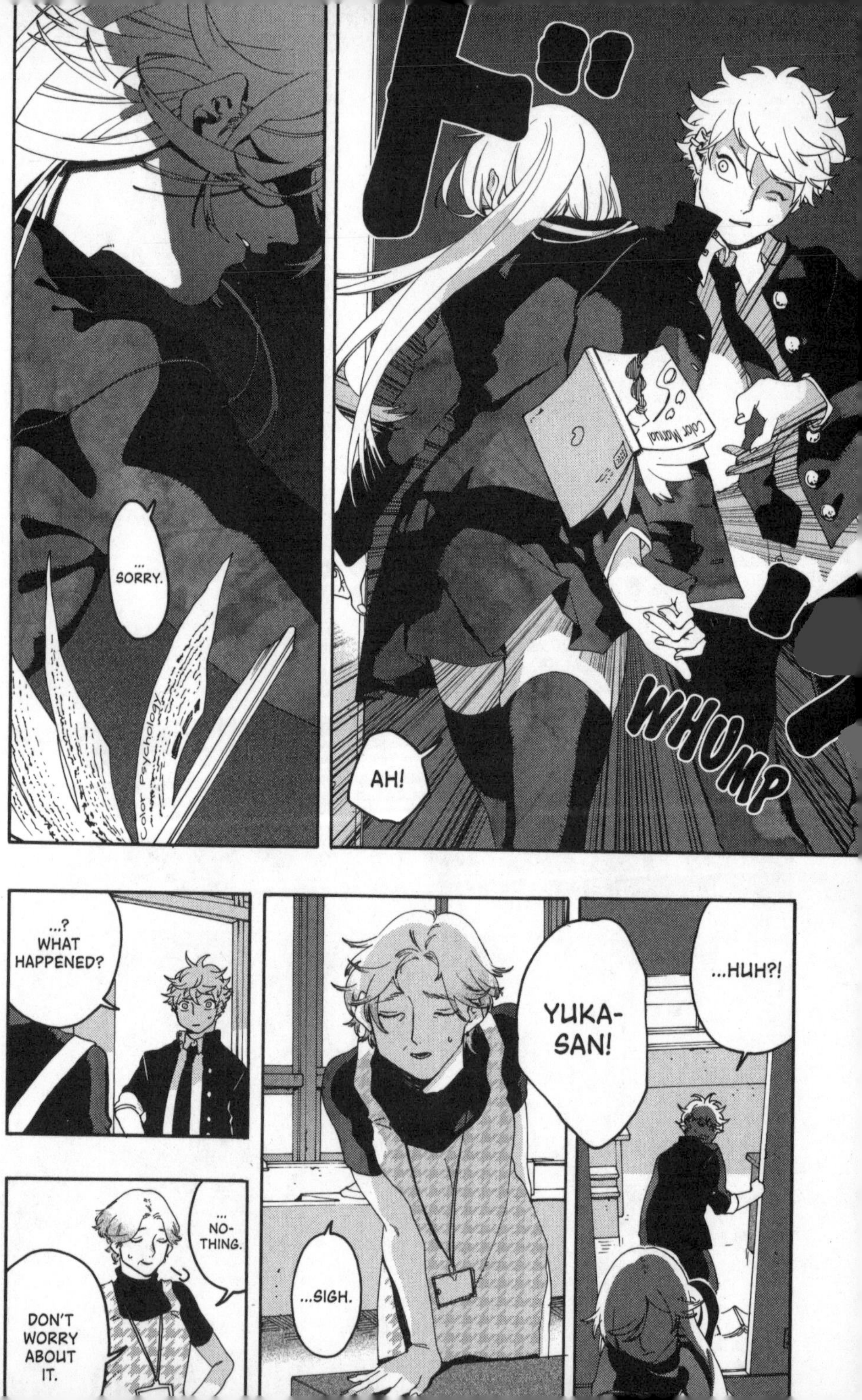
Color Manual
WHUMP
AH!
... SORRY.
Color Psychology
...HUH?!
YUKA-SAN!
...SIGH.
...? WHAT HAPPENED?
... NO-THING.
DON'T WORRY ABOUT IT.

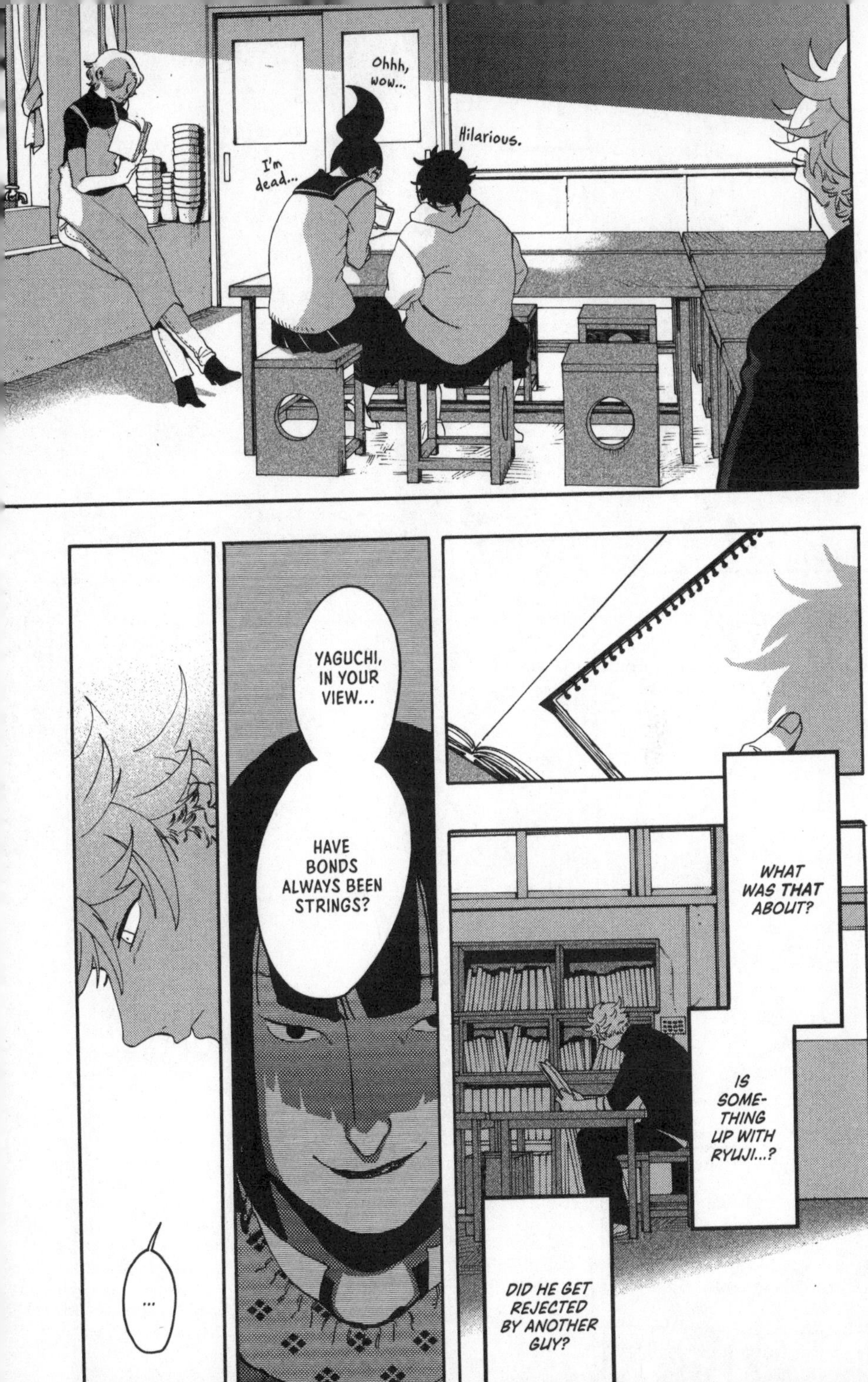
Hilarious.
Ohhh, wow...
I'm dead...
WHAT WAS THAT ABOUT?
IS SOMETHING UP WITH RYUJI...?
DID HE GET REJECTED BY ANOTHER GUY?
YAGUCHI, IN YOUR VIEW...
HAVE BONDS ALWAYS BEEN STRINGS?
...

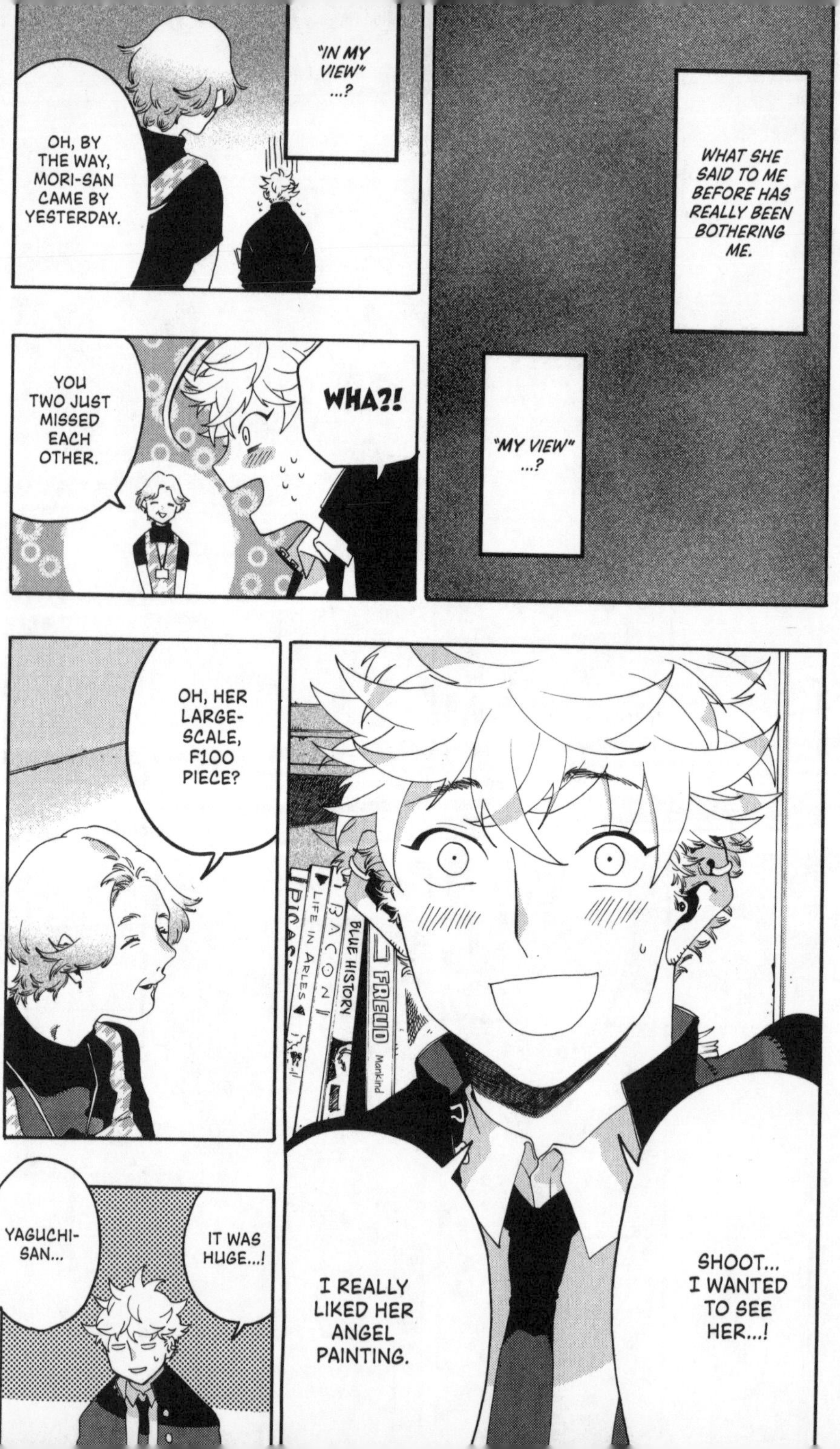
WHAT SHE SAID TO ME BEFORE HAS REALLY BEEN BOTHERING ME.
"MY VIEW" ...?
"IN MY VIEW" ...?
OH, BY THE WAY, MORI-SAN CAME BY YESTERDAY.
WHA?!
YOU TWO JUST MISSED EACH OTHER.
SHOOT... I WANTED TO SEE HER...!
I REALLY LIKED HER ANGEL PAINTING.
FREUD
Mankind
BLUE HISTORY
BACON
LIFE IN ARLES
OH, HER LARGE-SCALE, F100 PIECE?
IT WAS HUGE...!
YAGUCHI-SAN...

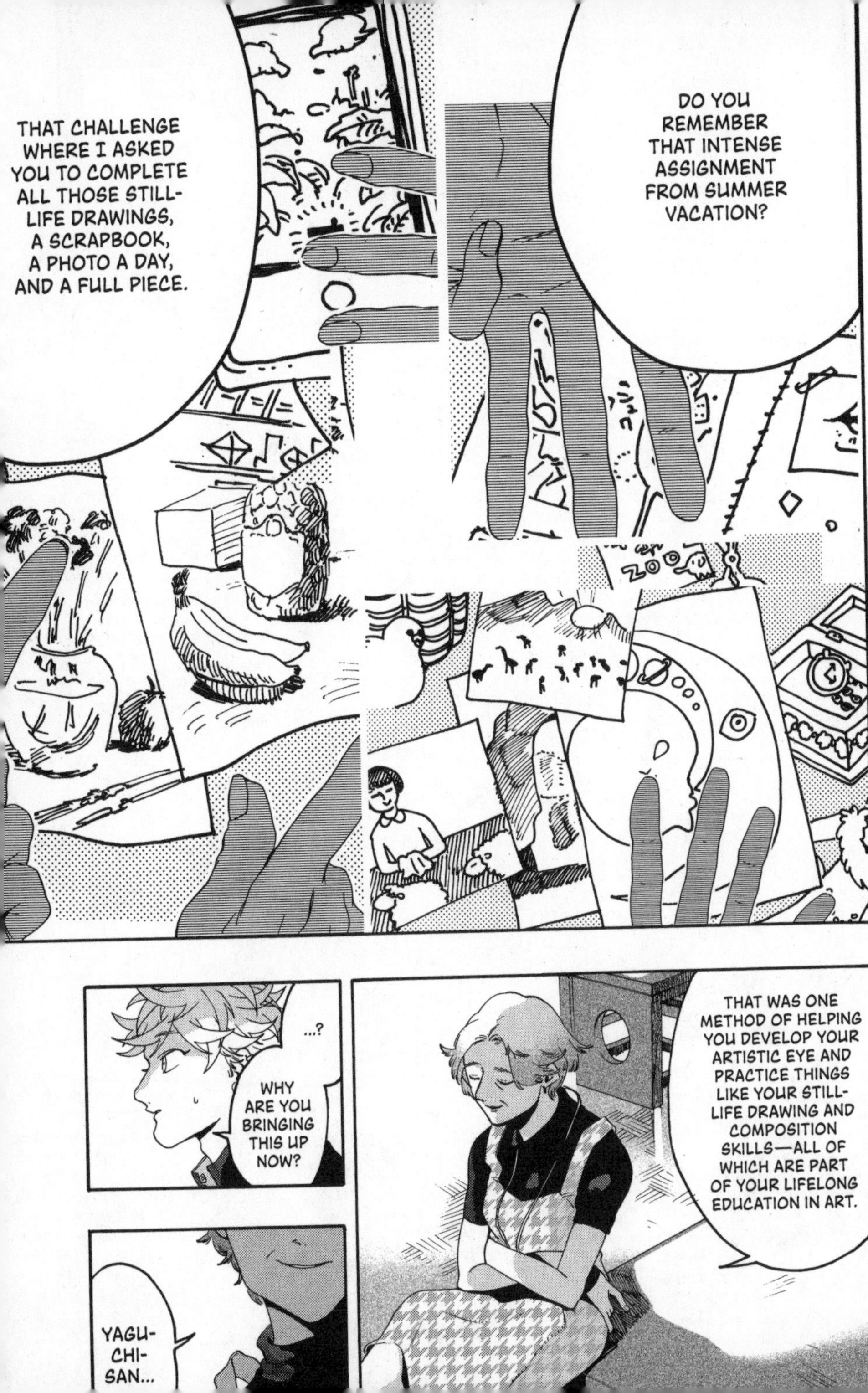
DO YOU REMEMBER THAT INTENSE ASSIGNMENT FROM SUMMER VACATION?
THAT CHALLENGE WHERE I ASKED YOU TO COMPLETE ALL THOSE STILL-LIFE DRAWINGS, A SCRAPBOOK, A PHOTO A DAY, AND A FULL PIECE.
ZOO
THAT WAS ONE METHOD OF HELPING YOU DEVELOP YOUR ARTISTIC EYE AND PRACTICE THINGS LIKE YOUR STILL-LIFE DRAWING AND COMPOSITION SKILLS—ALL OF WHICH ARE PART OF YOUR LIFELONG EDUCATION IN ART.
...?
WHY ARE YOU BRINGING THIS UP NOW?
YAGUCHI-SAN...

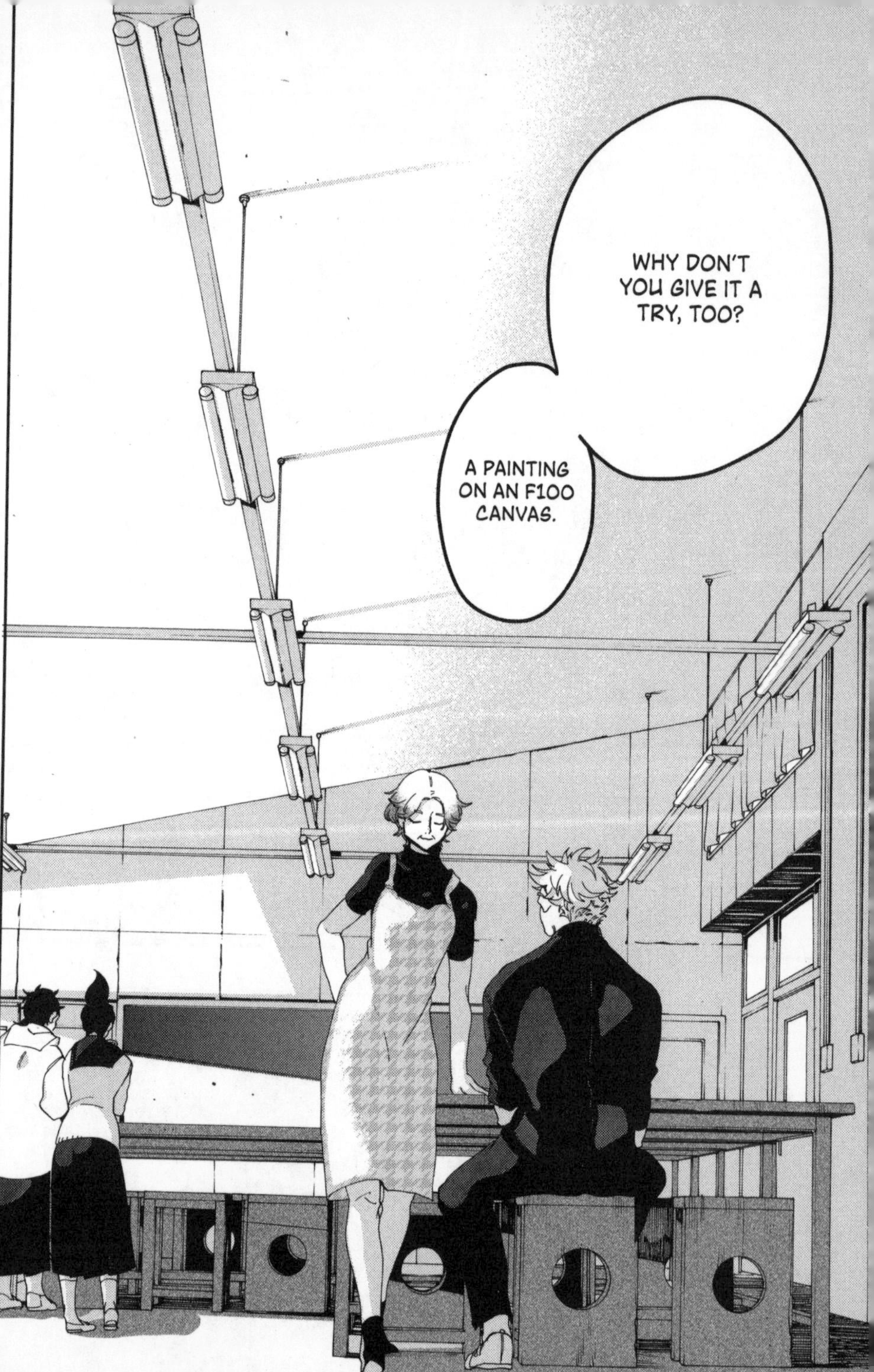
WHY DON'T YOU GIVE IT A TRY, TOO?
A PAINTING ON AN F100 CANVAS.

STROKE 9 END

Relatable Content ①

CH-CHK
CH-CHK
CH-CHK
WITH SOFT B-PENCILS, THE LEAD BREAKS OFF EASILY.
CRMBL..
Ugh...
CRMBL
BUT WITH HARD H PENCILS, THE LEAD BREAKS JUST AS YOU FINISH SHARPENING IT.
SNAP
Arghh!
I was pretty much done...

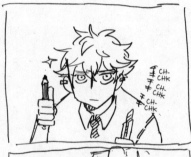

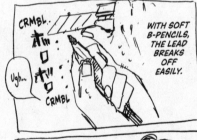

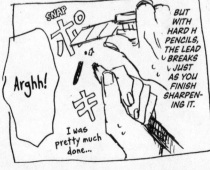

BLUE PERIOD

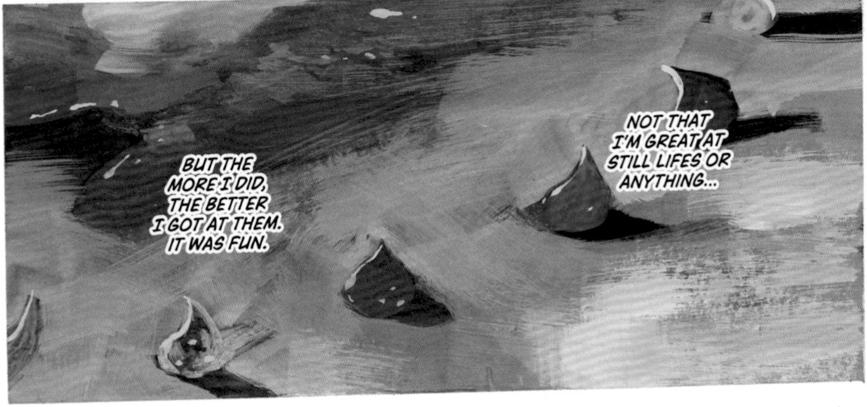
NOT THAT I'M GREAT AT STILL LIFES OR ANYTHING...
BUT THE MORE I DID, THE BETTER I GOT AT THEM. IT WAS FUN.

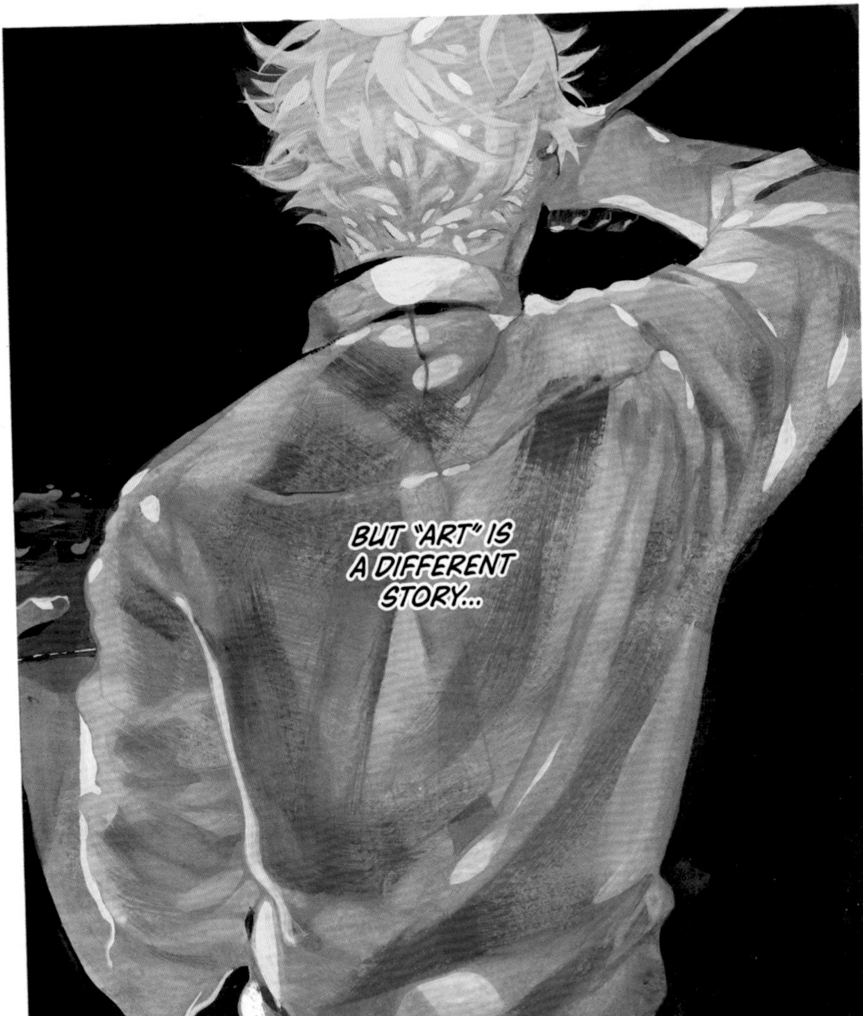
BUT "ART" IS A DIFFERENT STORY...

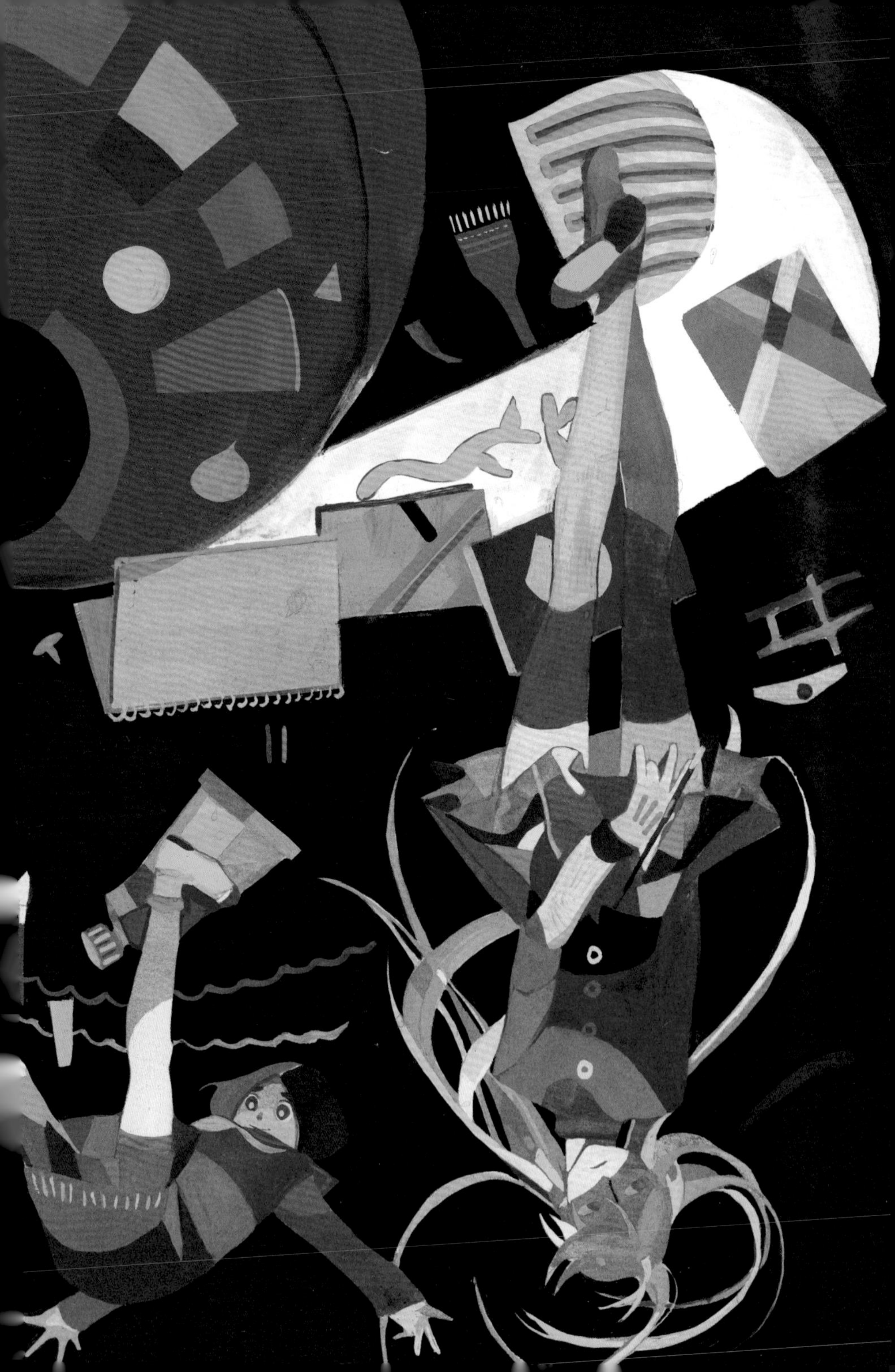

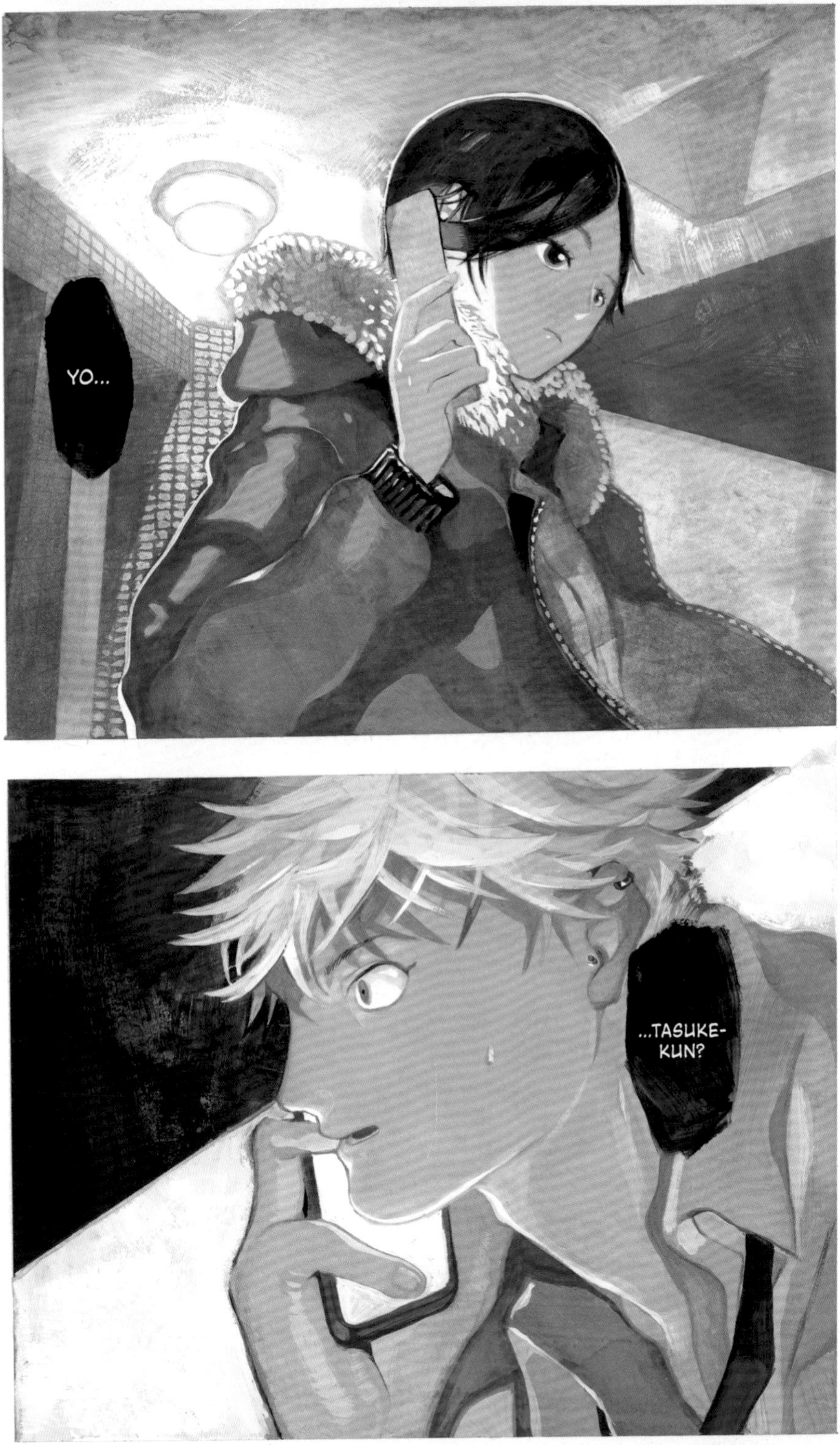
YO...
...TASUKE-KUN?

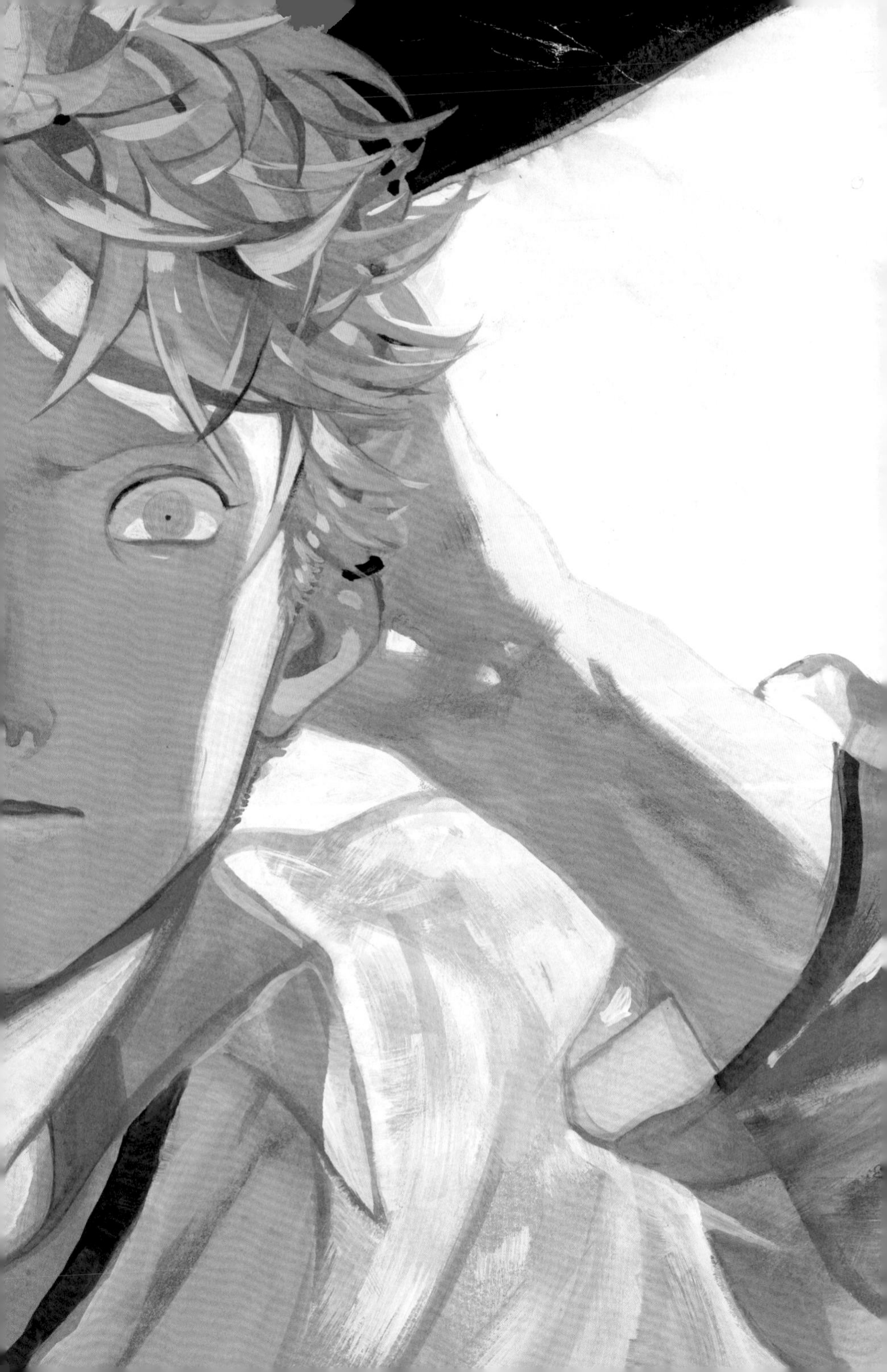

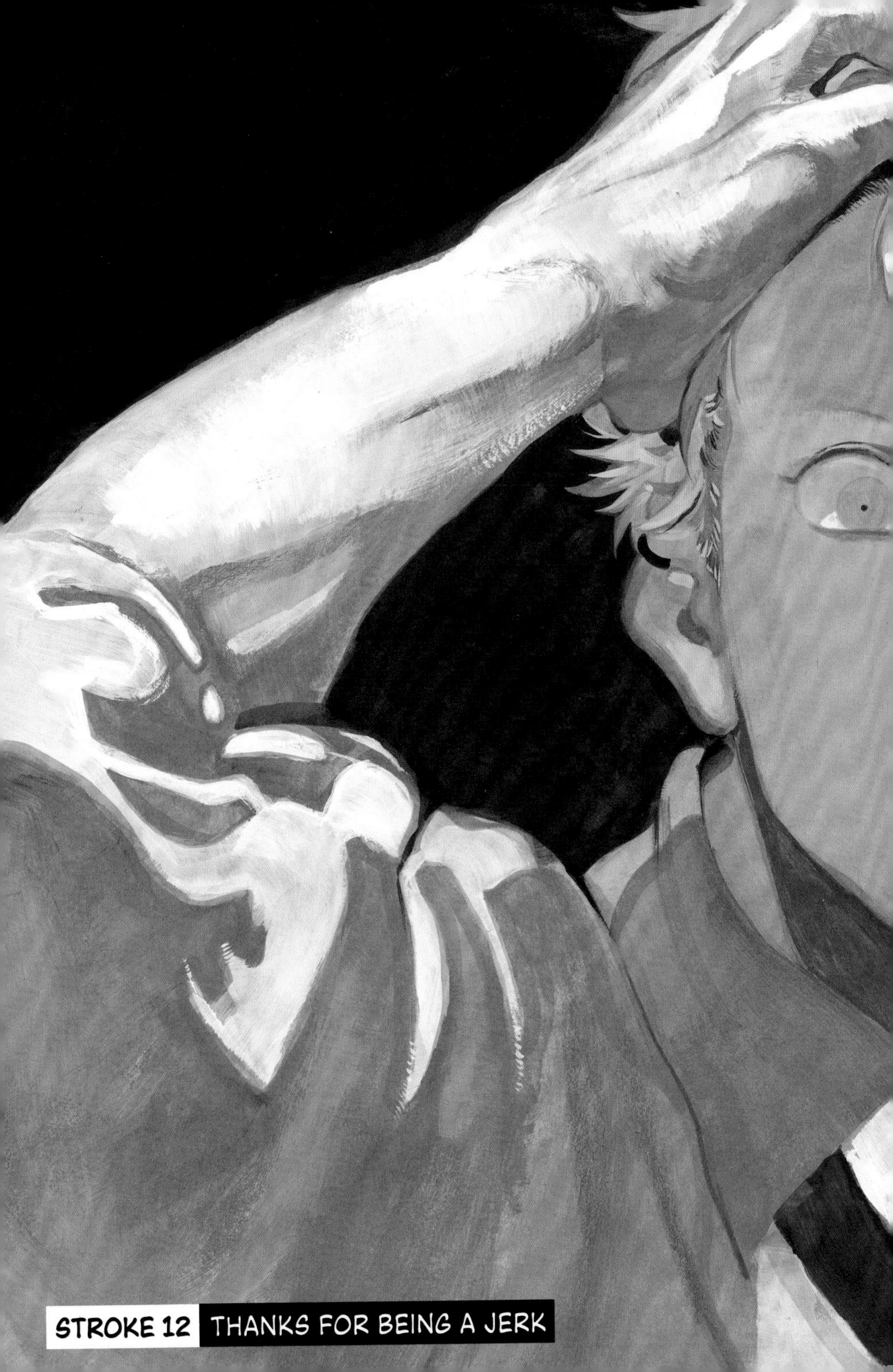

STROKE 12 THANKS FOR BEING A JERK

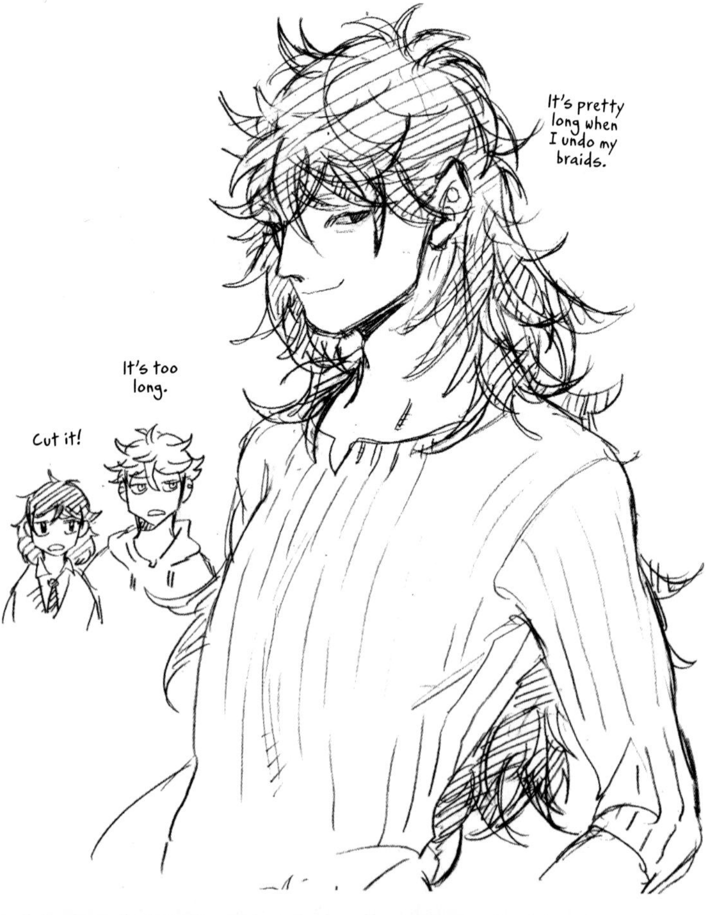
It's pretty long when I undo my braids.
It's too long.
Cut it!

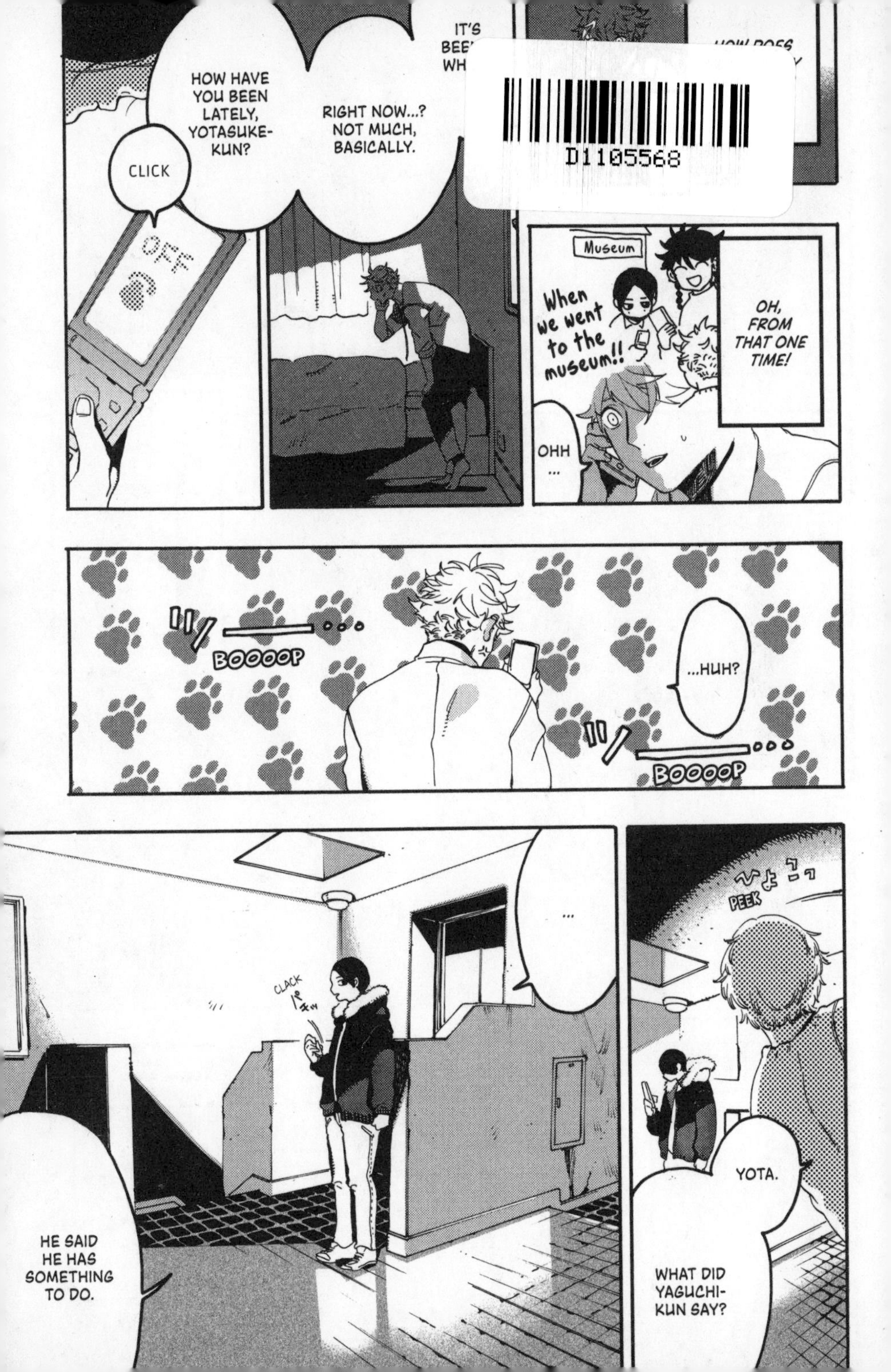
HOW HAVE YOU BEEN LATELY, YOTASUKE-KUN?
RIGHT NOW...? NOT MUCH, BASICALLY.
Museum
OH, FROM THAT ONE TIME!
When we went to the museum!!
OHH ...
CLICK
OFF
...HUH?
BOOOOP
BOOOOP
PEEK
YOTA.
WHAT DID YAGUCHI-KUN SAY?
...
CLACK
HE SAID HE HAS SOMETHING TO DO.

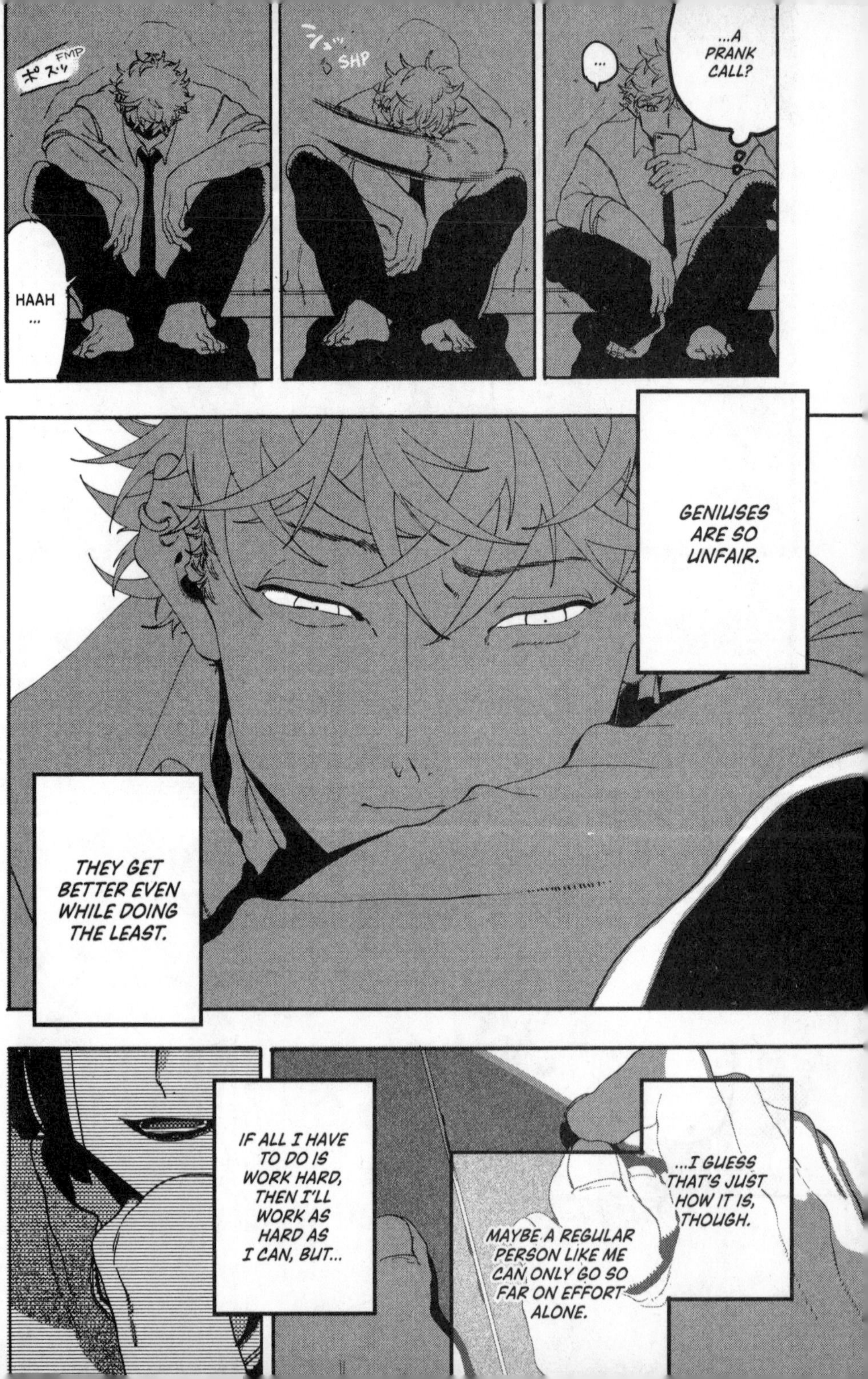
...A PRANK CALL?
...
シュッ
SHP
ポスッ
FMP
HAAH ...
GENIUSES ARE SO UNFAIR.
THEY GET BETTER EVEN WHILE DOING THE LEAST.
...I GUESS THAT'S JUST HOW IT IS, THOUGH.
MAYBE A REGULAR PERSON LIKE ME CAN ONLY GO SO FAR ON EFFORT ALONE.
IF ALL I HAVE TO DO IS WORK HARD, THEN I'LL WORK AS HARD AS I CAN, BUT...

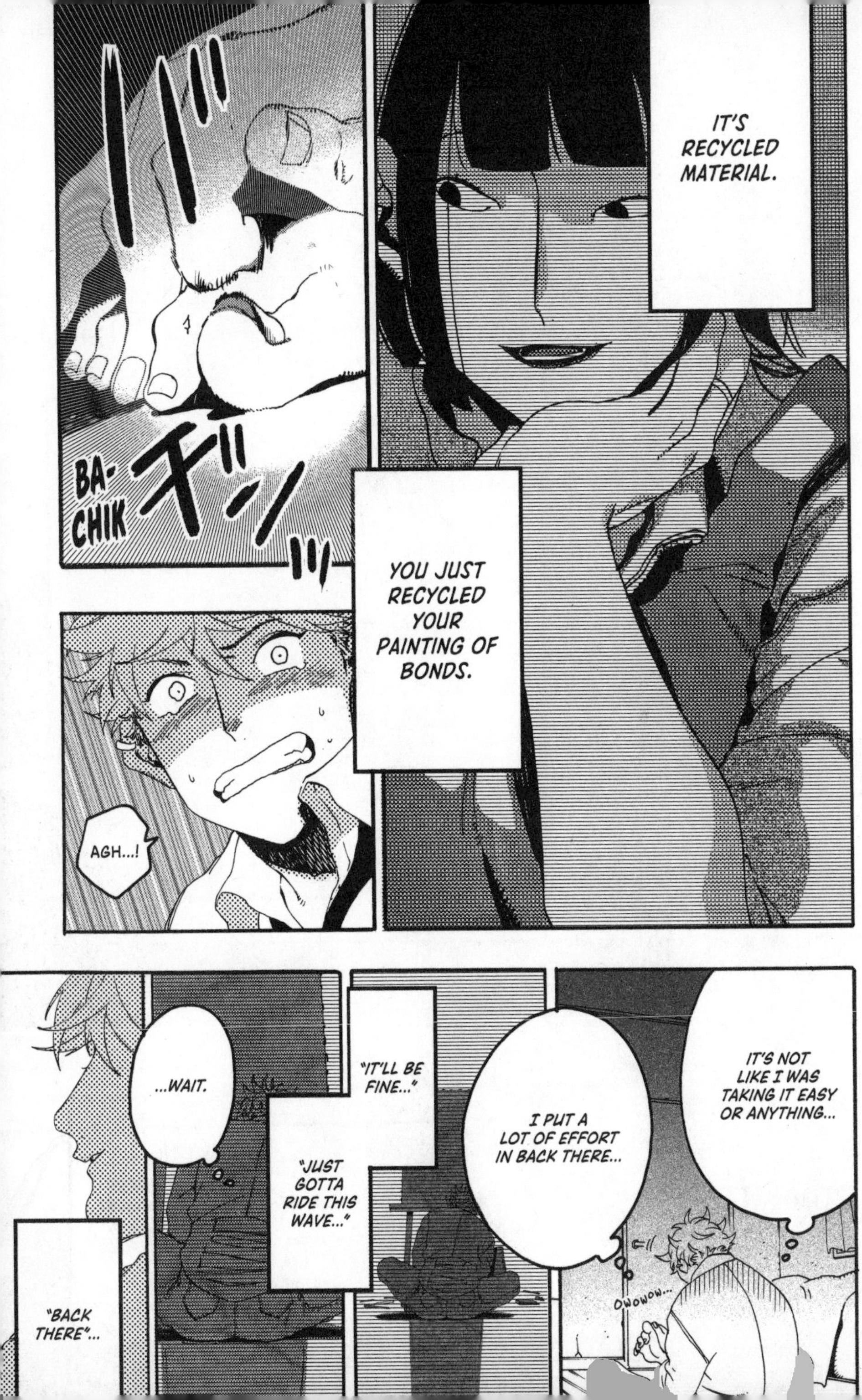
IT'S RECYCLED MATERIAL.
YOU JUST RECYCLED YOUR PAINTING OF BONDS.
BA-CHIK
AGH...!
IT'S NOT LIKE I WAS TAKING IT EASY OR ANYTHING...
I PUT A LOT OF EFFORT IN BACK THERE...
OWOWOW...
"IT'LL BE FINE..."
"JUST GOTTA RIDE THIS WAVE..."
...WAIT.
"BACK THERE"...

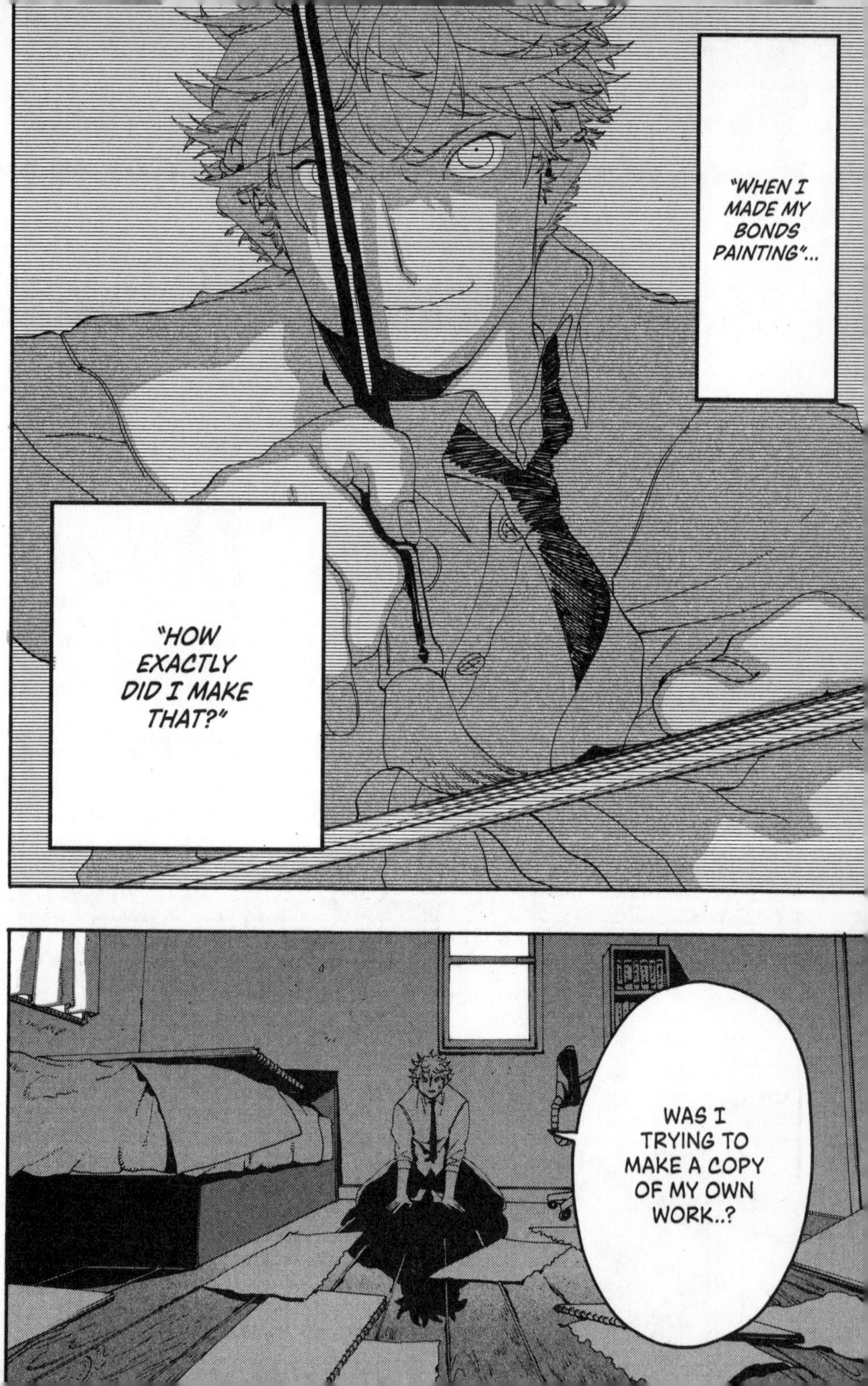
"WHEN I MADE MY BONDS PAINTING"...
"HOW EXACTLY DID I MAKE THAT?"
WAS I TRYING TO MAKE A COPY OF MY OWN WORK..?

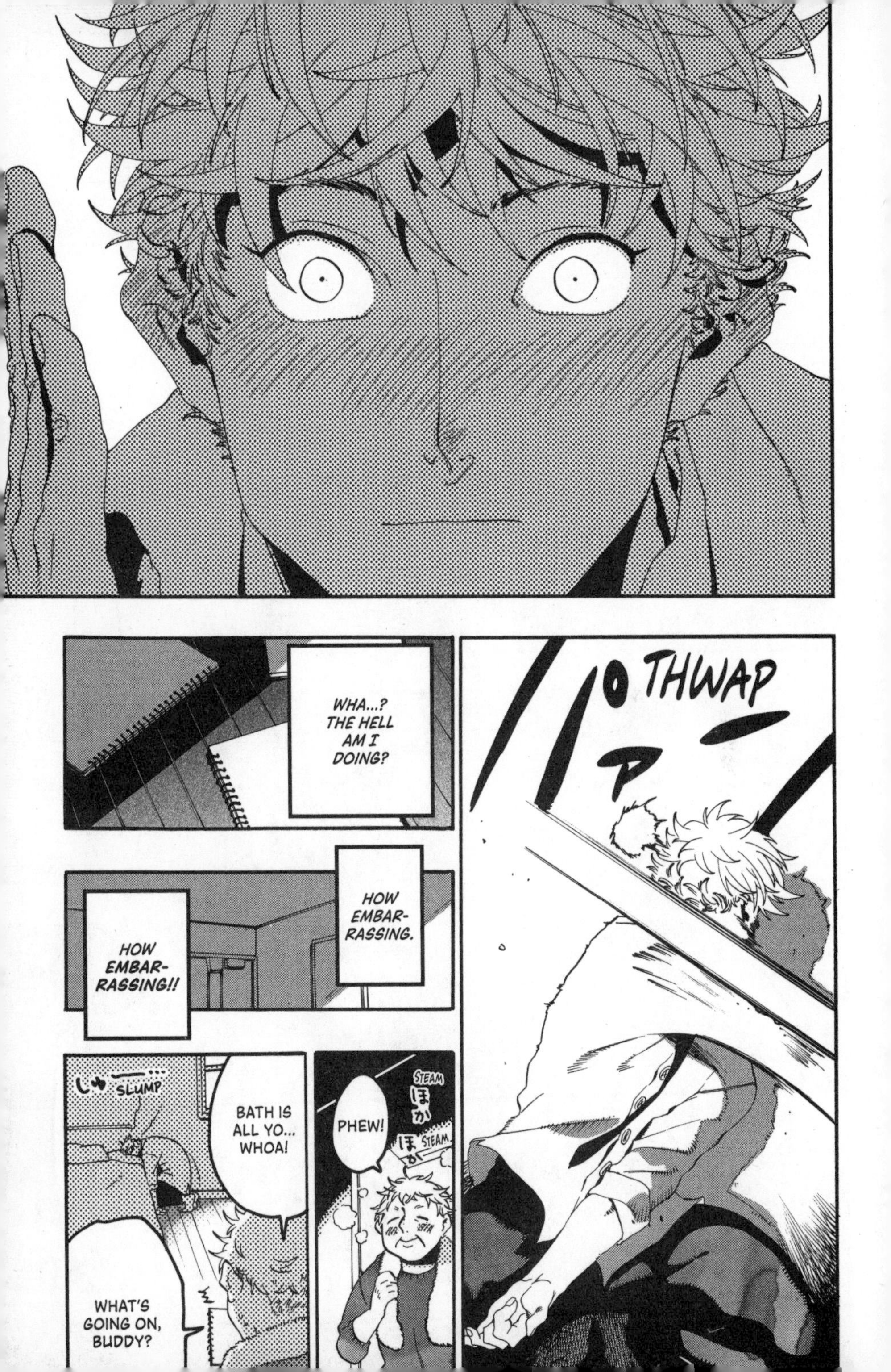
THWAP
WHA...? THE HELL AM I DOING?
HOW EMBARRASSING.
HOW EMBARRASSING!!
PHEW!
ほか STEAM
ほか STEAM
BATH IS ALL YO... WHOA!
SLUMP
WHAT'S GOING ON, BUDDY?

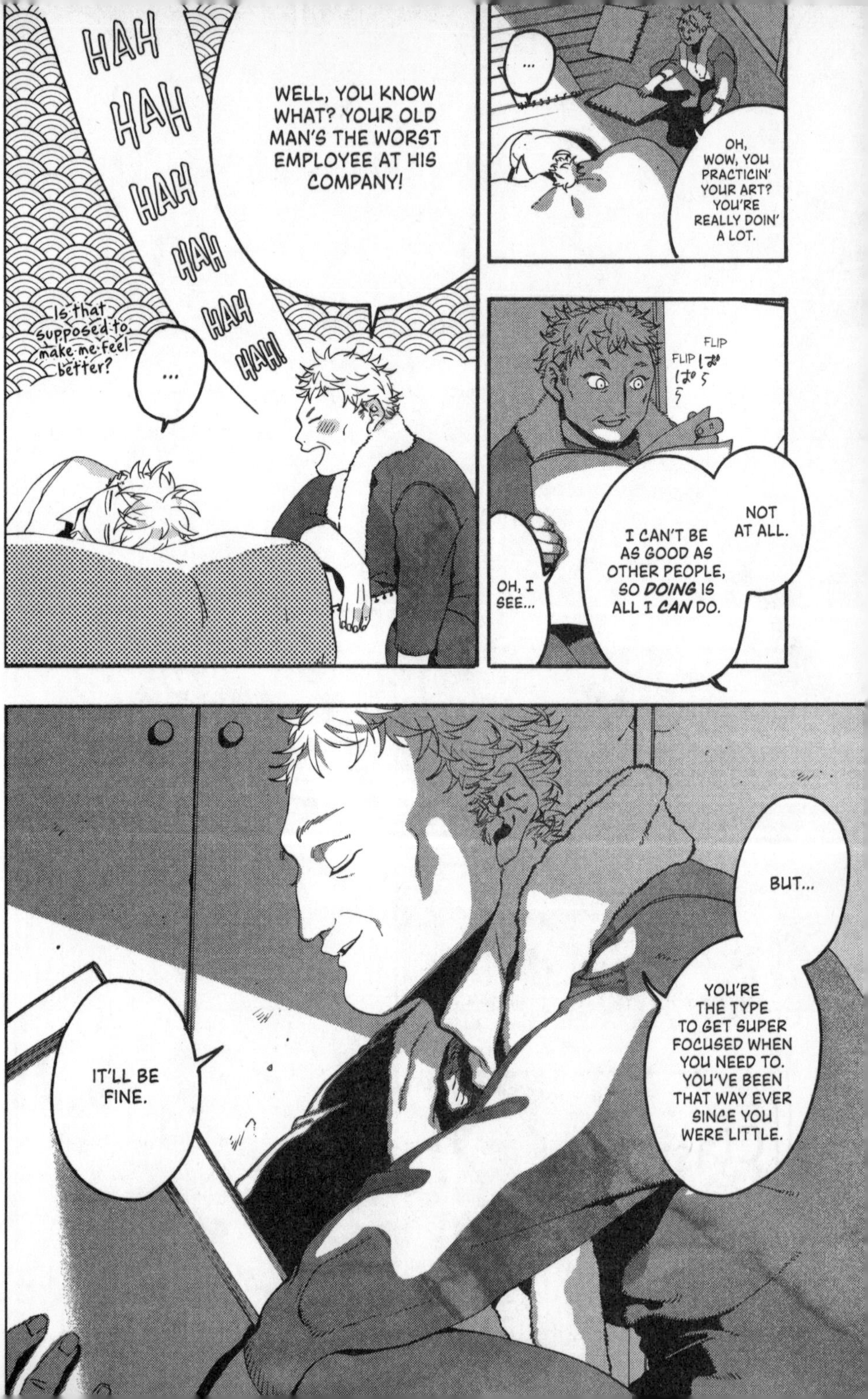
...
OH, WOW, YOU PRACTICIN' YOUR ART? YOU'RE REALLY DOIN' A LOT.
FLIP FLIP
ぱら ぱら
NOT AT ALL.
I CAN'T BE AS GOOD AS OTHER PEOPLE, SO *DOING* IS ALL I *CAN* DO.
OH, I SEE...
WELL, YOU KNOW WHAT? YOUR OLD MAN'S THE WORST EMPLOYEE AT HIS COMPANY!
HAH HAH HAH HAH HAH HAH!
...
Is that supposed to make me feel better?
BUT...
YOU'RE THE TYPE TO GET SUPER FOCUSED WHEN YOU NEED TO. YOU'VE BEEN THAT WAY EVER SINCE YOU WERE LITTLE.
IT'LL BE FINE.

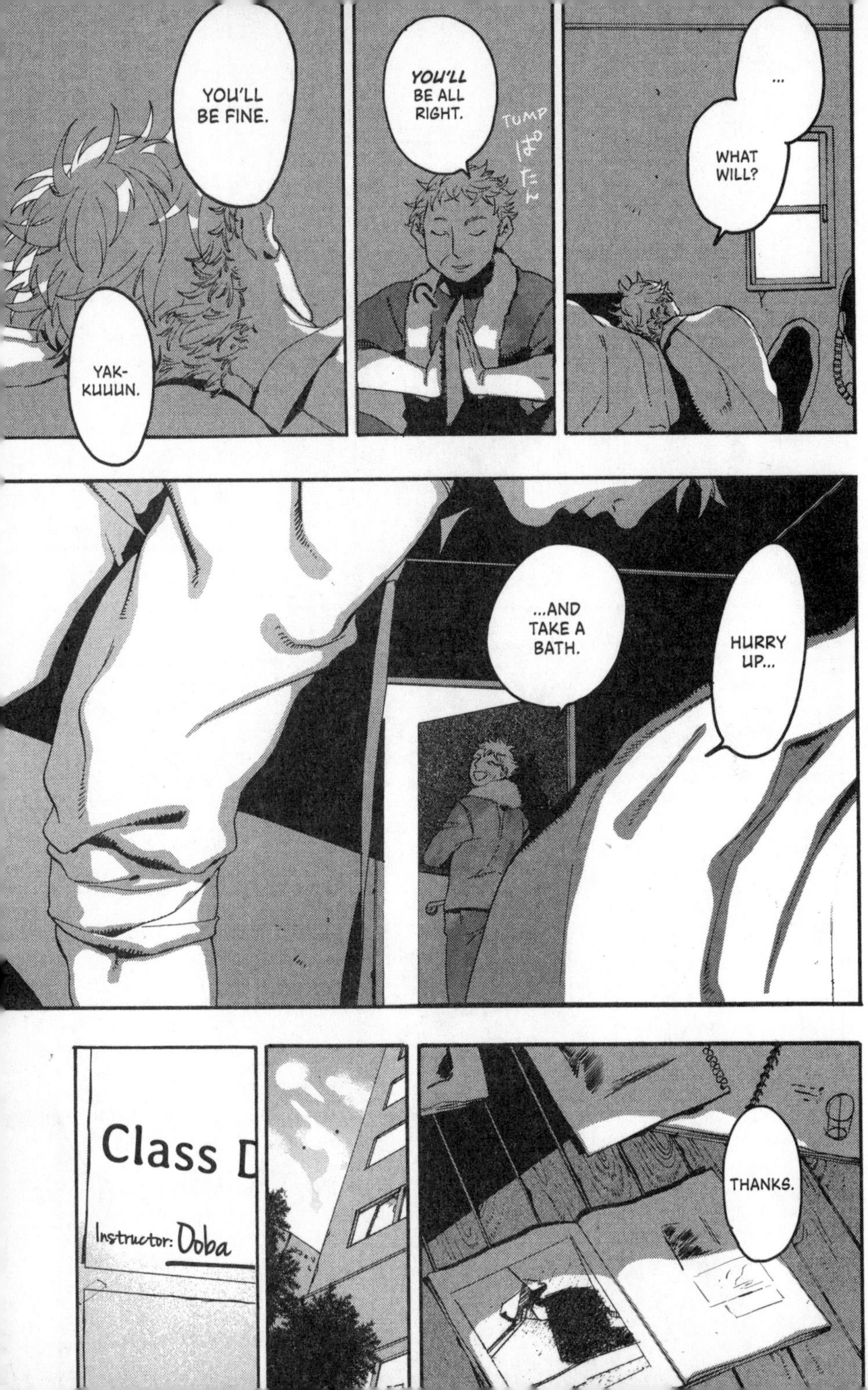
...
WHAT WILL?
YOU'LL BE ALL RIGHT.
TUMP
ぽたん
YOU'LL BE FINE.
YAK-KUUUN.
HURRY UP...
...AND TAKE A BATH.
THANKS.
Class D
Instructor: Doba

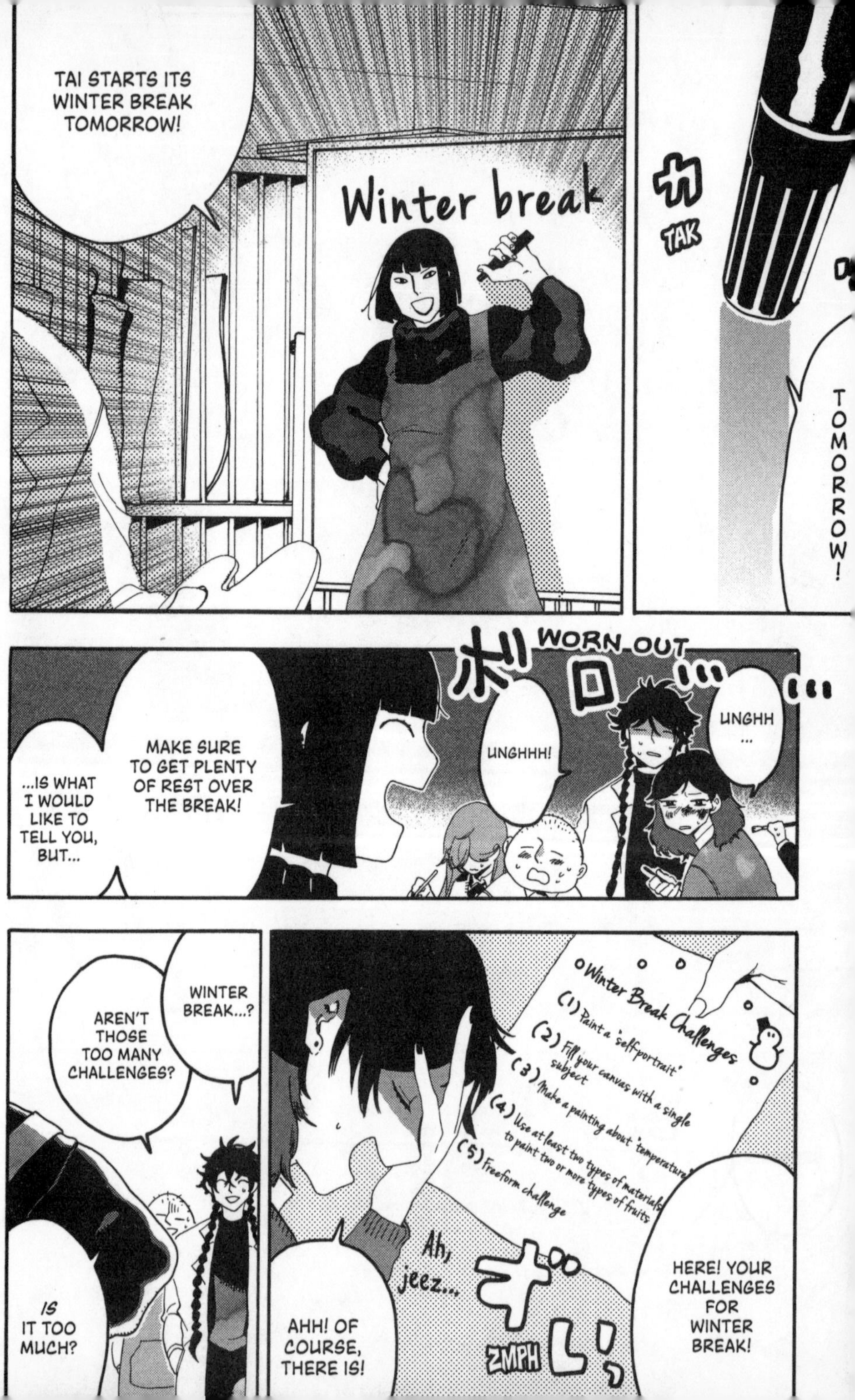
TAK
TOMORROW!
Winter break
TAI STARTS ITS WINTER BREAK TOMORROW!
WORN OUT
UNGHH ...
UNGHHH!
MAKE SURE TO GET PLENTY OF REST OVER THE BREAK!
...IS WHAT I WOULD LIKE TO TELL YOU, BUT...
Winter Break Challenges
(1) Paint a "self-portrait"
(2) Fill your canvas with a single subject
(3) Make a painting about "temperature"
(4) Use at least two types of materials to paint two or more types of fruits
(5) Freeform challenge
HERE! YOUR CHALLENGES FOR WINTER BREAK!
Ah, jeez...
ZMPH
AHH! OF COURSE, THERE IS!
WINTER BREAK...?
AREN'T THOSE TOO MANY CHALLENGES?
IS IT TOO MUCH?

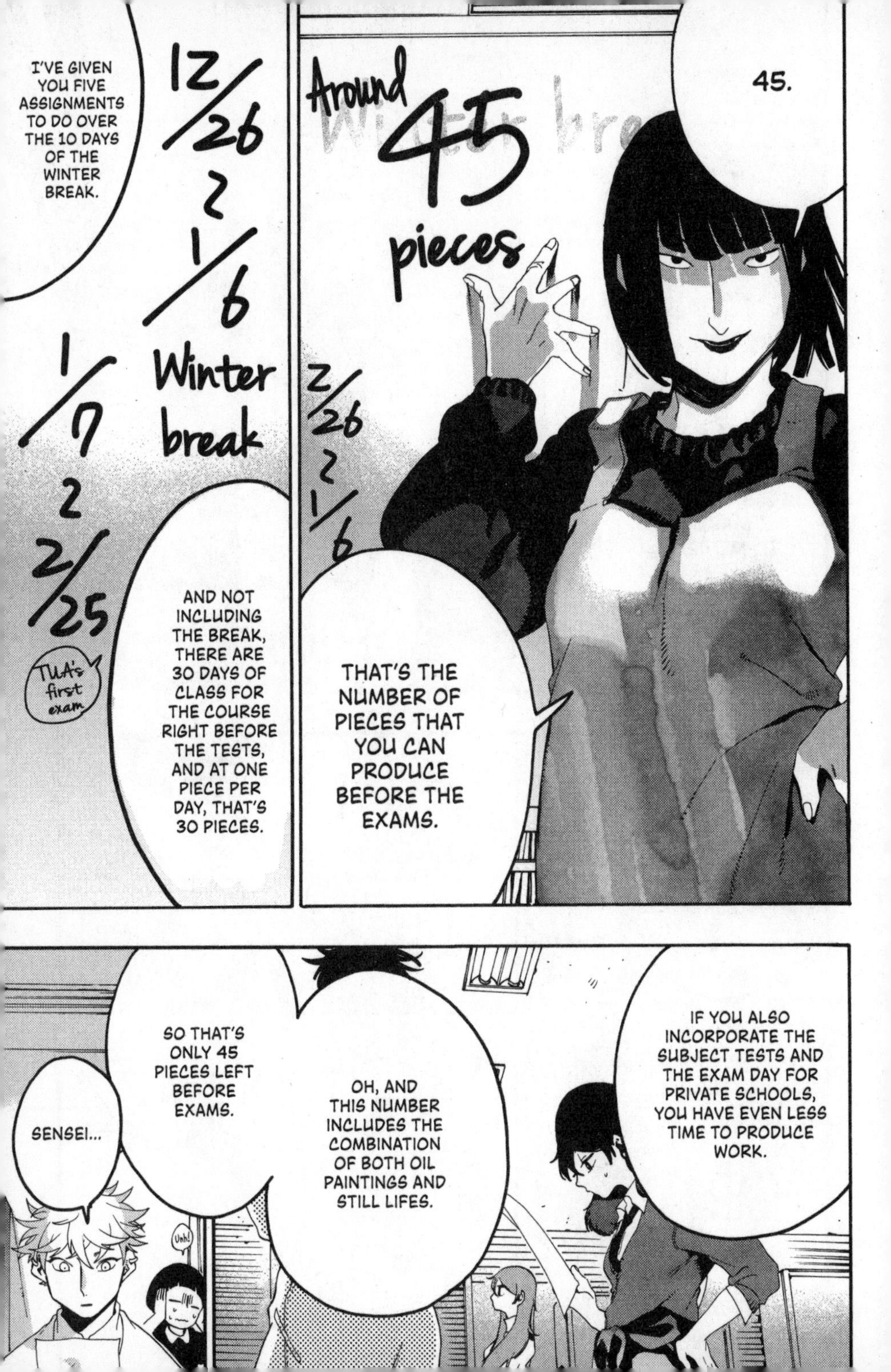
45.
Around 45 pieces
2/26 2 1/6
THAT'S THE NUMBER OF PIECES THAT YOU CAN PRODUCE BEFORE THE EXAMS.
I'VE GIVEN YOU FIVE ASSIGNMENTS TO DO OVER THE 10 DAYS OF THE WINTER BREAK.
12/26 2 1/6
Winter break
1/7 2 2/25
TUA's first exam
AND NOT INCLUDING THE BREAK, THERE ARE 30 DAYS OF CLASS FOR THE COURSE RIGHT BEFORE THE TESTS, AND AT ONE PIECE PER DAY, THAT'S 30 PIECES.
IF YOU ALSO INCORPORATE THE SUBJECT TESTS AND THE EXAM DAY FOR PRIVATE SCHOOLS, YOU HAVE EVEN LESS TIME TO PRODUCE WORK.
OH, AND THIS NUMBER INCLUDES THE COMBINATION OF BOTH OIL PAINTINGS AND STILL LIFES.
SO THAT'S ONLY 45 PIECES LEFT BEFORE EXAMS.
SENSEI...
Unh!

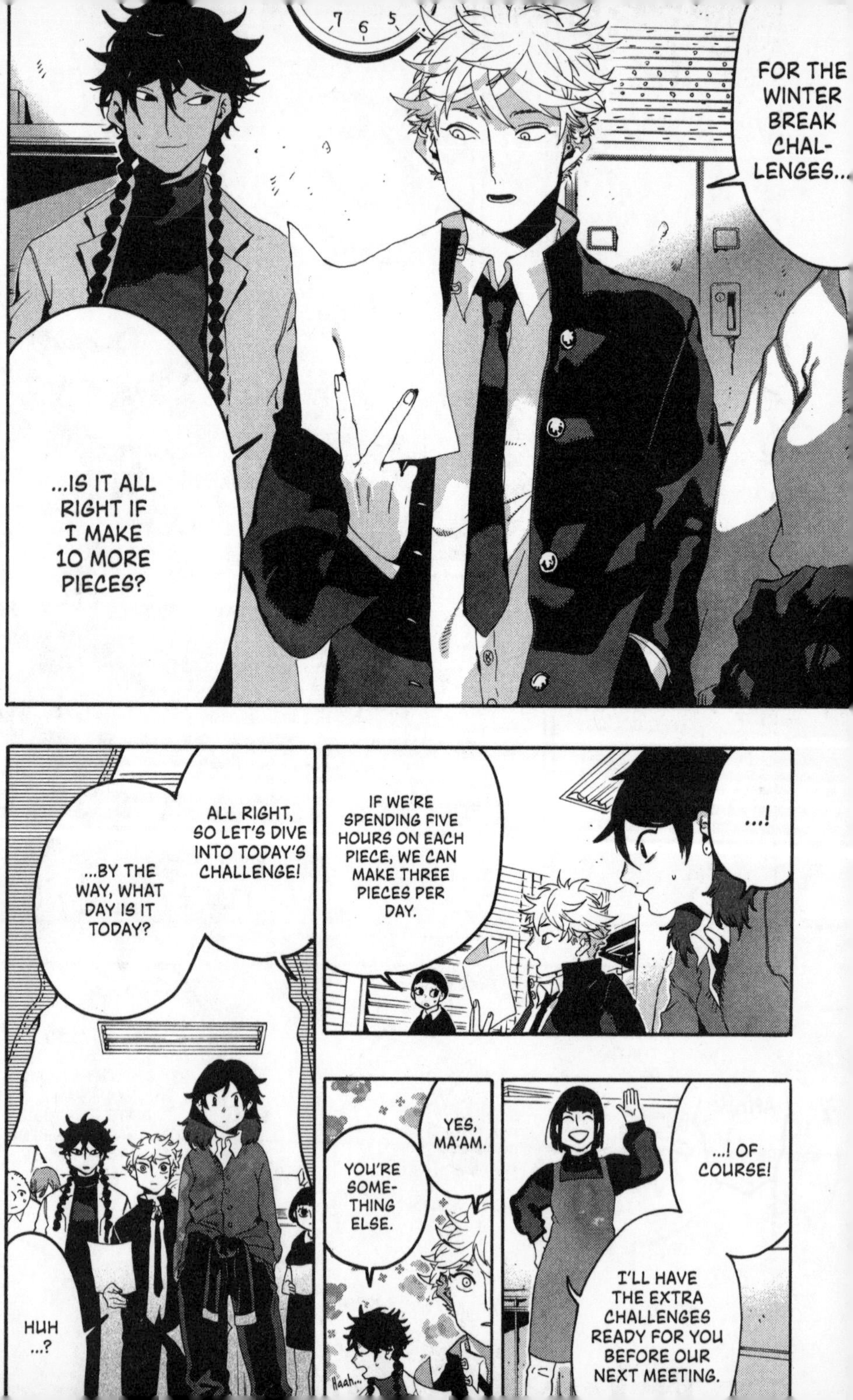
FOR THE WINTER BREAK CHALLENGES...
...IS IT ALL RIGHT IF I MAKE 10 MORE PIECES?
...!
IF WE'RE SPENDING FIVE HOURS ON EACH PIECE, WE CAN MAKE THREE PIECES PER DAY.
...! OF COURSE!
I'LL HAVE THE EXTRA CHALLENGES READY FOR YOU BEFORE OUR NEXT MEETING.
YES, MA'AM.
YOU'RE SOMETHING ELSE.
Haah...
ALL RIGHT, SO LET'S DIVE INTO TODAY'S CHALLENGE!
...BY THE WAY, WHAT DAY IS IT TODAY?
HUH ...?

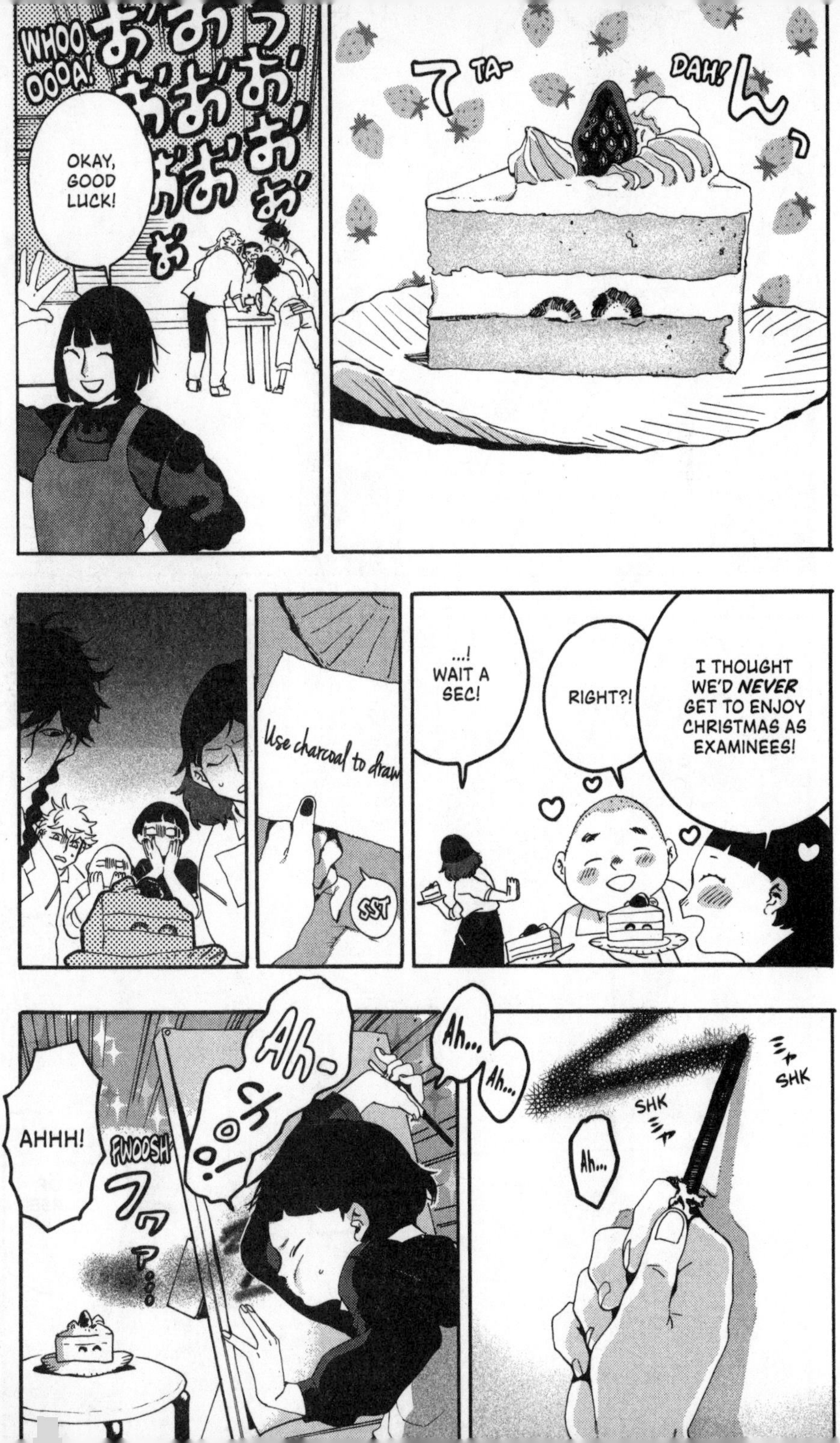

て TA-
DAH! ん
WHOOOOOA!
OKAY, GOOD LUCK!
I THOUGHT WE'D ***NEVER*** GET TO ENJOY CHRISTMAS AS EXAMINEES!
RIGHT?!
...! WAIT A SEC!
Use charcoal to draw
SST
SHK
SHK
Ah...
Ah... Ah...
Ah-choo!
AHHH!
FWOOSH

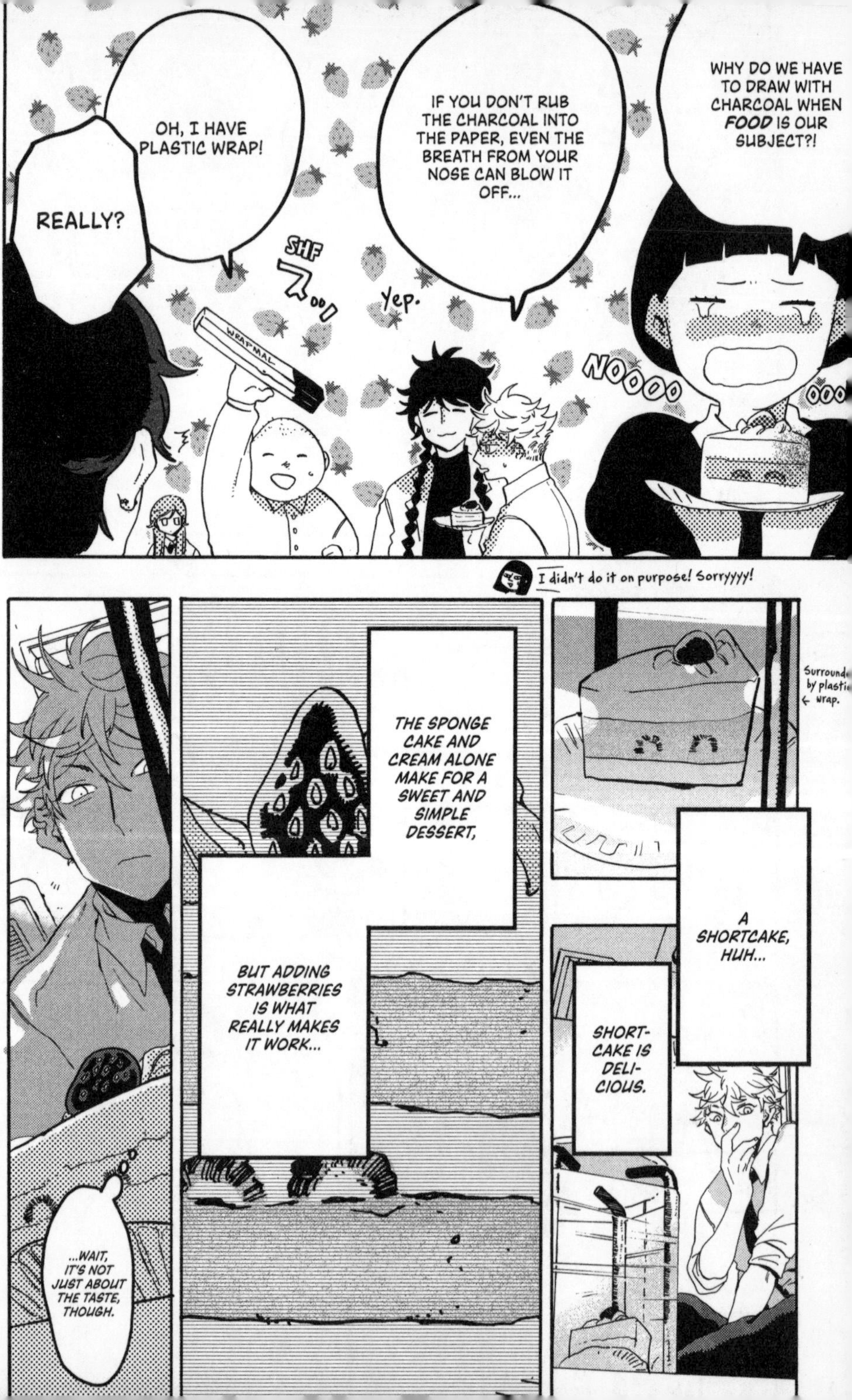
WHY DO WE HAVE TO DRAW WITH CHARCOAL WHEN **FOOD** IS OUR SUBJECT?!
NOOOOOOO
IF YOU DON'T RUB THE CHARCOAL INTO THE PAPER, EVEN THE BREATH FROM YOUR NOSE CAN BLOW IT OFF...
Yep.
SHF
OH, I HAVE PLASTIC WRAP!
WRAPMAL
REALLY?
I didn't do it on purpose! Sorryyyyy!
by plastic
← wrap.
A SHORTCAKE, HUH...
SHORT-CAKE IS DELI-CIOUS.
THE SPONGE CAKE AND CREAM ALONE MAKE FOR A SWEET AND SIMPLE DESSERT,
BUT ADDING STRAWBERRIES IS WHAT REALLY MAKES IT WORK...
...WAIT, IT'S NOT JUST ABOUT THE TASTE, THOUGH.

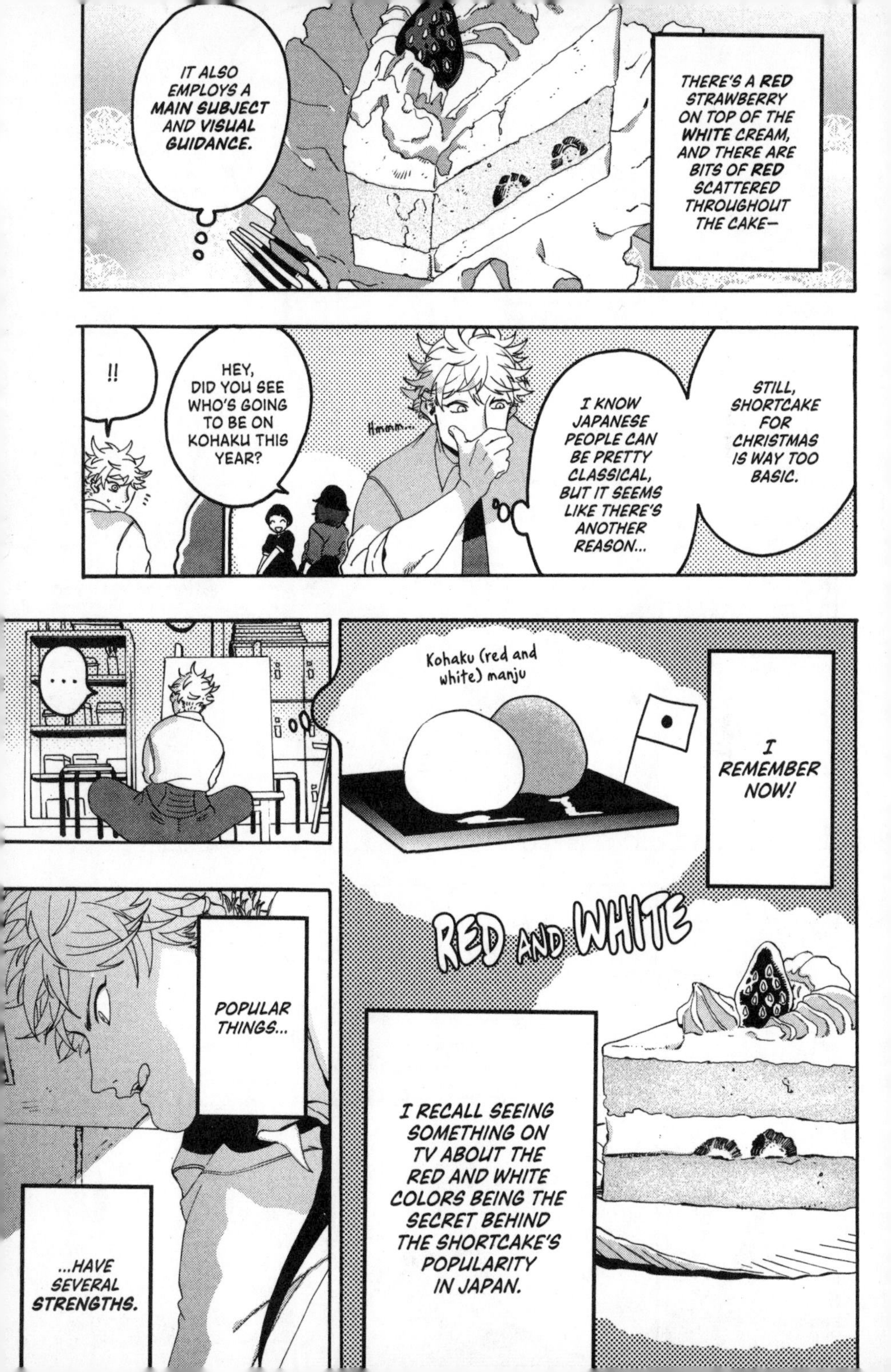
THERE'S A RED STRAWBERRY ON TOP OF THE WHITE CREAM, AND THERE ARE BITS OF RED SCATTERED THROUGHOUT THE CAKE—
IT ALSO EMPLOYS A MAIN SUBJECT AND VISUAL GUIDANCE.
STILL, SHORTCAKE FOR CHRISTMAS IS WAY TOO BASIC.
I KNOW JAPANESE PEOPLE CAN BE PRETTY CLASSICAL, BUT IT SEEMS LIKE THERE'S ANOTHER REASON...
Hmmm...
HEY, DID YOU SEE WHO'S GOING TO BE ON KOHAKU THIS YEAR?
!!
I REMEMBER NOW!
Kohaku (red and white) manju
RED AND WHITE
I RECALL SEEING SOMETHING ON TV ABOUT THE RED AND WHITE COLORS BEING THE SECRET BEHIND THE SHORTCAKE'S POPULARITY IN JAPAN.
...
POPULAR THINGS...
...HAVE SEVERAL STRENGTHS.

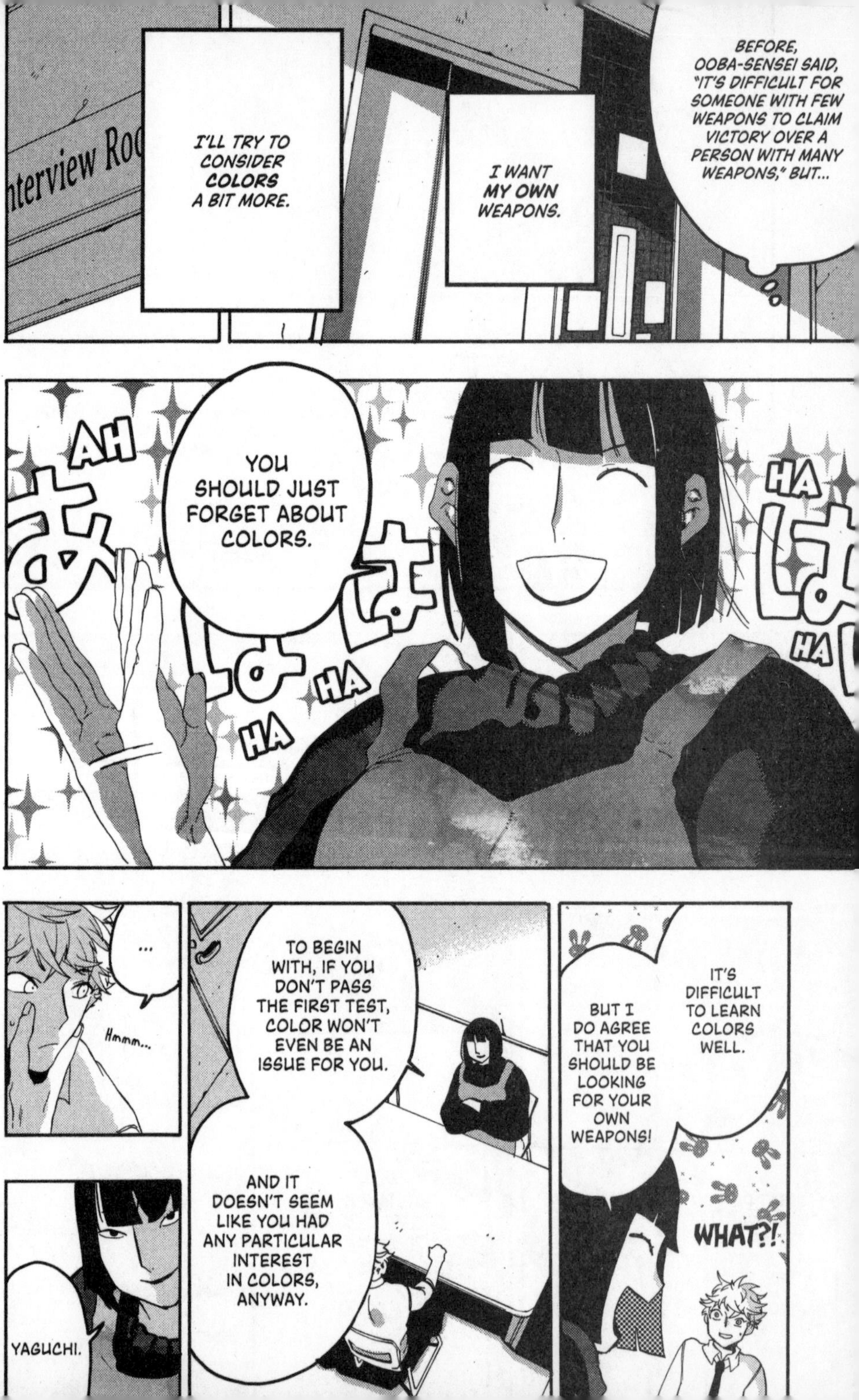
BEFORE, OOBA-SENSEI SAID, "IT'S DIFFICULT FOR SOMEONE WITH FEW WEAPONS TO CLAIM VICTORY OVER A PERSON WITH MANY WEAPONS," BUT...
I WANT MY OWN WEAPONS.
I'LL TRY TO CONSIDER COLORS A BIT MORE.
HA HA
YOU SHOULD JUST FORGET ABOUT COLORS.
AH HA HA
IT'S DIFFICULT TO LEARN COLORS WELL.
BUT I DO AGREE THAT YOU SHOULD BE LOOKING FOR YOUR OWN WEAPONS!
WHAT?!
TO BEGIN WITH, IF YOU DON'T PASS THE FIRST TEST, COLOR WON'T EVEN BE AN ISSUE FOR YOU.
AND IT DOESN'T SEEM LIKE YOU HAD ANY PARTICULAR INTEREST IN COLORS, ANYWAY.
...
Hmmm...
YAGUCHI.

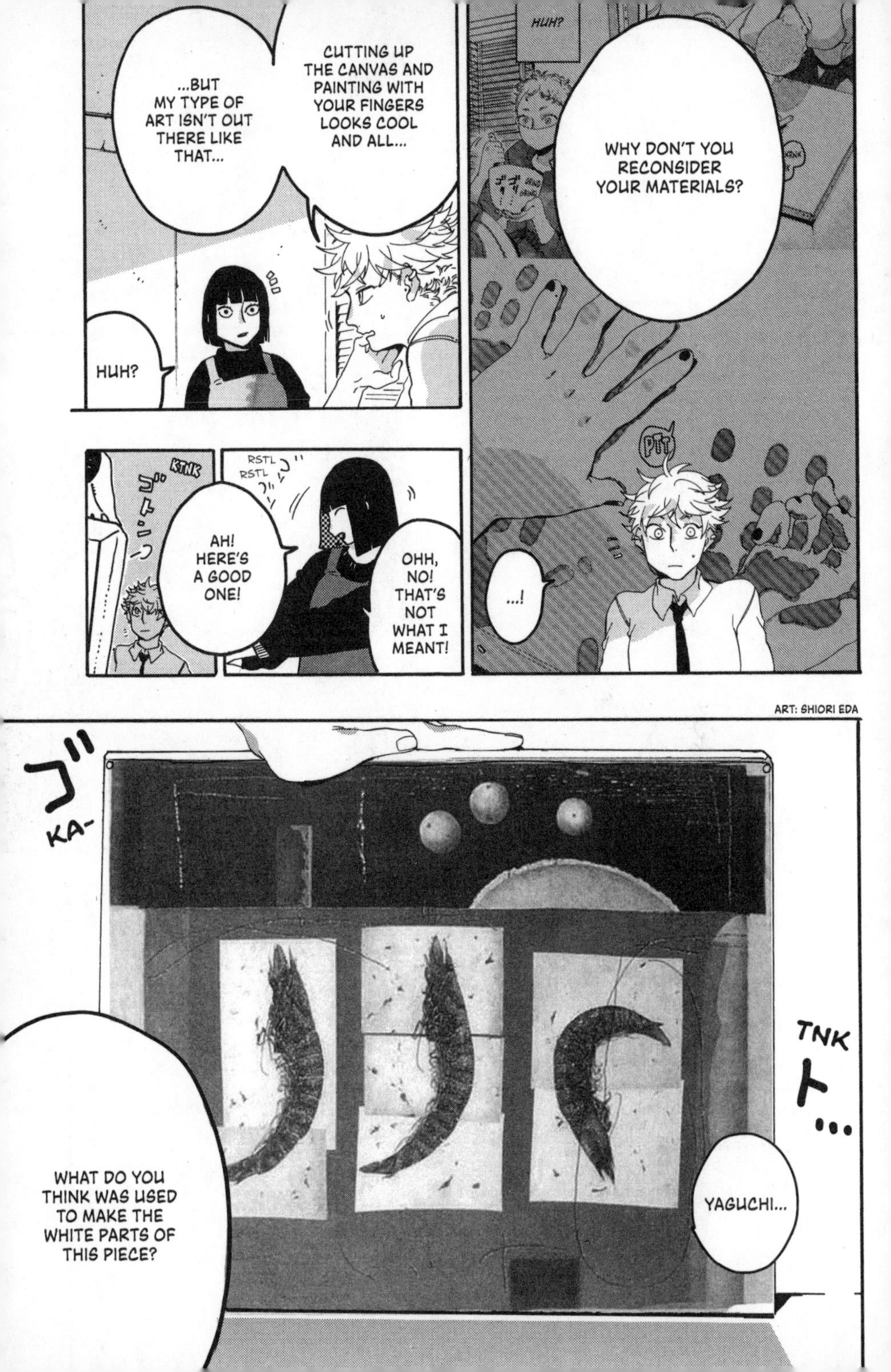
HUH?
WHY DON'T YOU RECONSIDER YOUR MATERIALS?
PUT
...!
CUTTING UP THE CANVAS AND PAINTING WITH YOUR FINGERS LOOKS COOL AND ALL...
...BUT MY TYPE OF ART ISN'T OUT THERE LIKE THAT...
HUH?
RSTL RSTL
AH! HERE'S A GOOD ONE!
OHH, NO! THAT'S NOT WHAT I MEANT!
KTNK
TNK
YAGUCHI...
KA-
WHAT DO YOU THINK WAS USED TO MAKE THE WHITE PARTS OF THIS PIECE?
ART: SHIORI EDA

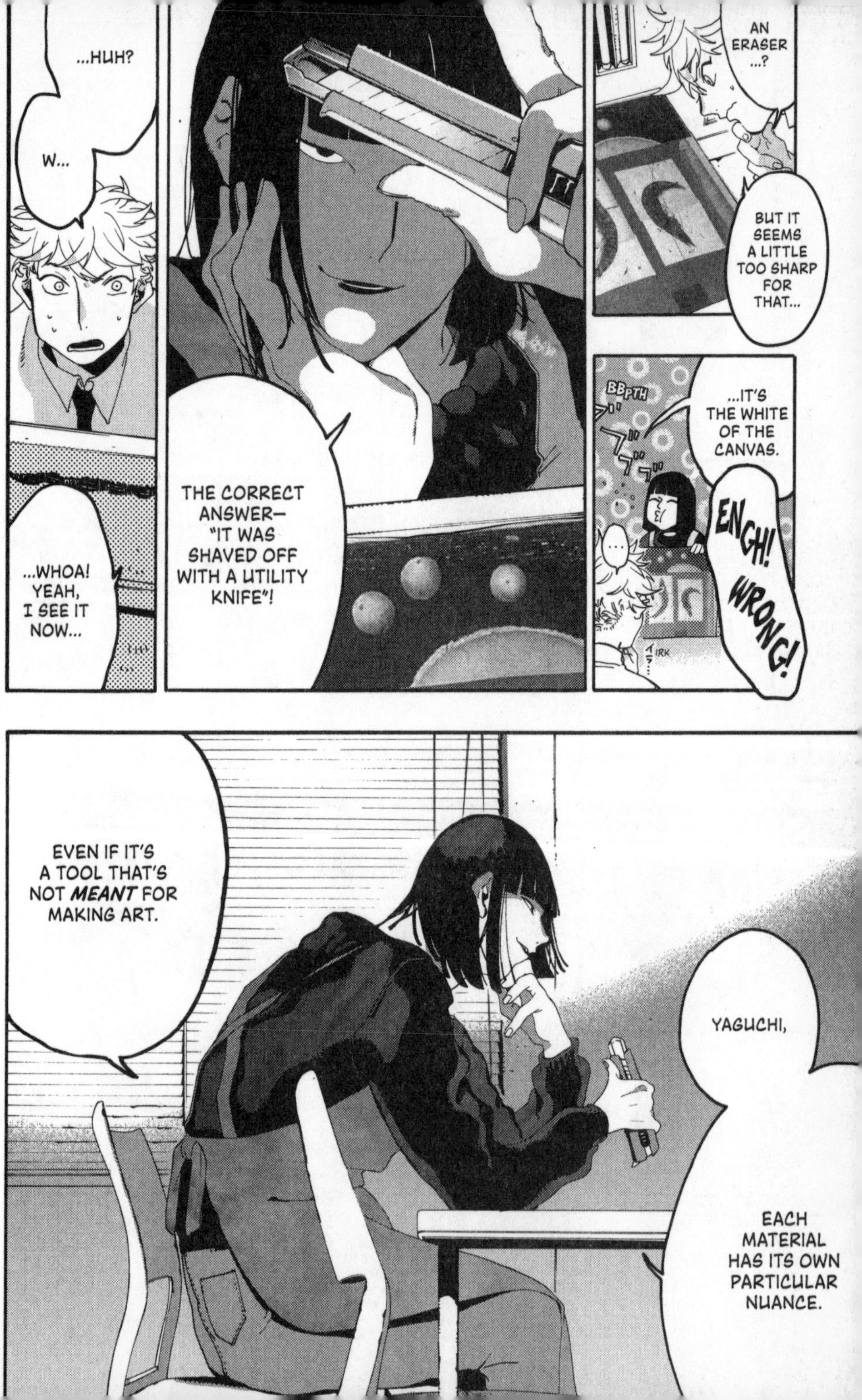
AN ERASER ...?
BUT IT SEEMS A LITTLE TOO SHARP FOR THAT...
...IT'S THE WHITE OF THE CANVAS.
BBPTH
ENGH! WRONG!
...
IRK
THE CORRECT ANSWER— "IT WAS SHAVED OFF WITH A UTILITY KNIFE"!
...HUH?
W...
...WHOA! YEAH, I SEE IT NOW...
YAGUCHI,
EACH MATERIAL HAS ITS OWN PARTICULAR NUANCE.
EVEN IF IT'S A TOOL THAT'S NOT *MEANT* FOR MAKING ART.

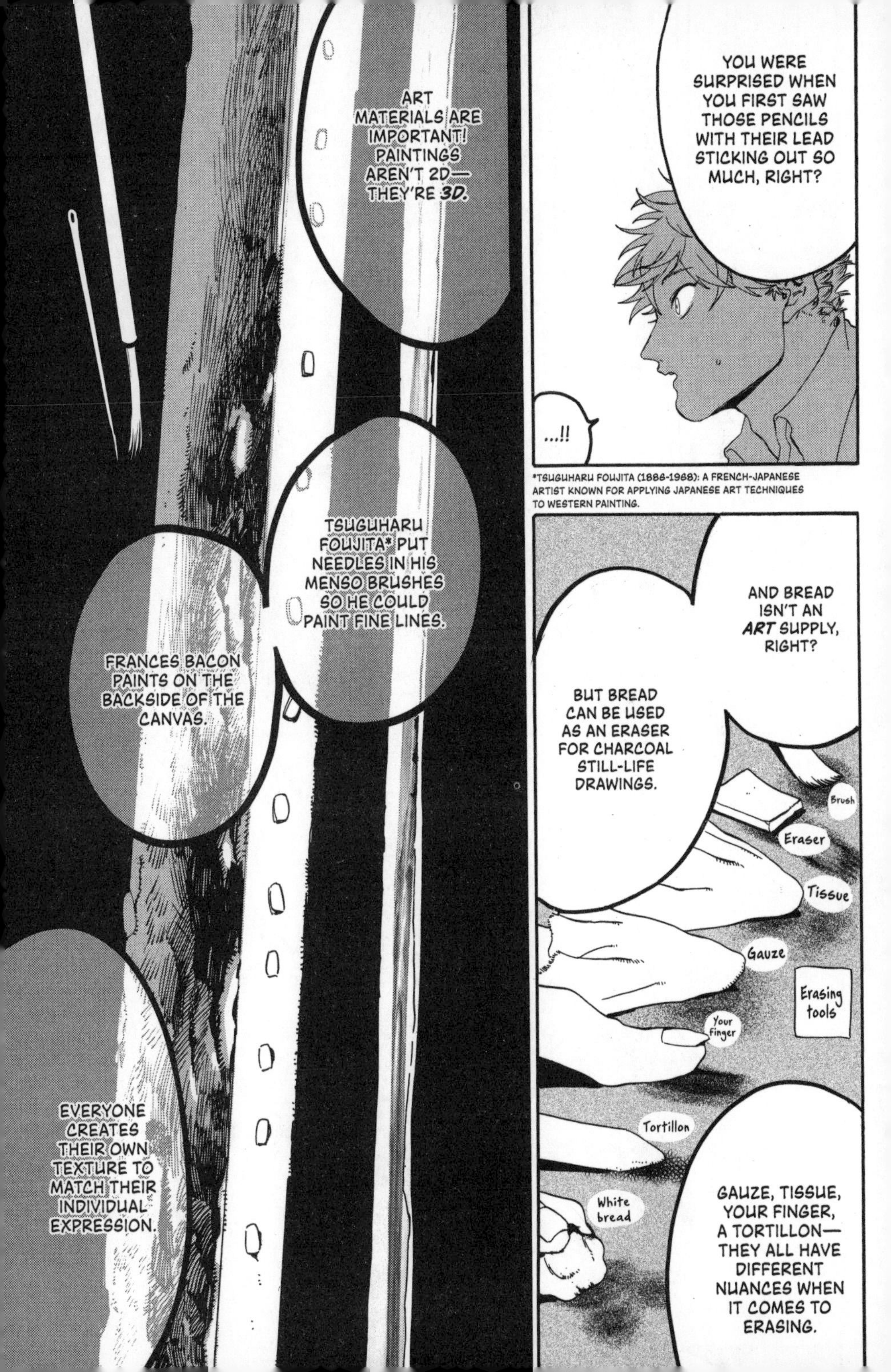
YOU WERE SURPRISED WHEN YOU FIRST SAW THOSE PENCILS WITH THEIR LEAD STICKING OUT SO MUCH, RIGHT?
...!!
AND BREAD ISN'T AN ***ART*** SUPPLY, RIGHT?
BUT BREAD CAN BE USED AS AN ERASER FOR CHARCOAL STILL-LIFE DRAWINGS.
Brush
Eraser
Tissue
Gauze
Erasing tools
Your Finger
Tortillon
White bread
GAUZE, TISSUE, YOUR FINGER, A TORTILLON—THEY ALL HAVE DIFFERENT NUANCES WHEN IT COMES TO ERASING.
ART MATERIALS ARE IMPORTANT! PAINTINGS AREN'T 2D—THEY'RE ***3D.***
TSUGUHARU FOUJITA* PUT NEEDLES IN HIS MENSO BRUSHES SO HE COULD PAINT FINE LINES.
FRANCES BACON PAINTS ON THE BACKSIDE OF THE CANVAS.
EVERYONE CREATES THEIR OWN TEXTURE TO MATCH THEIR INDIVIDUAL EXPRESSION.

*TSUGUHARU FOUJITA (1886-1968): A FRENCH-JAPANESE ARTIST KNOWN FOR APPLYING JAPANESE ART TECHNIQUES TO WESTERN PAINTING.

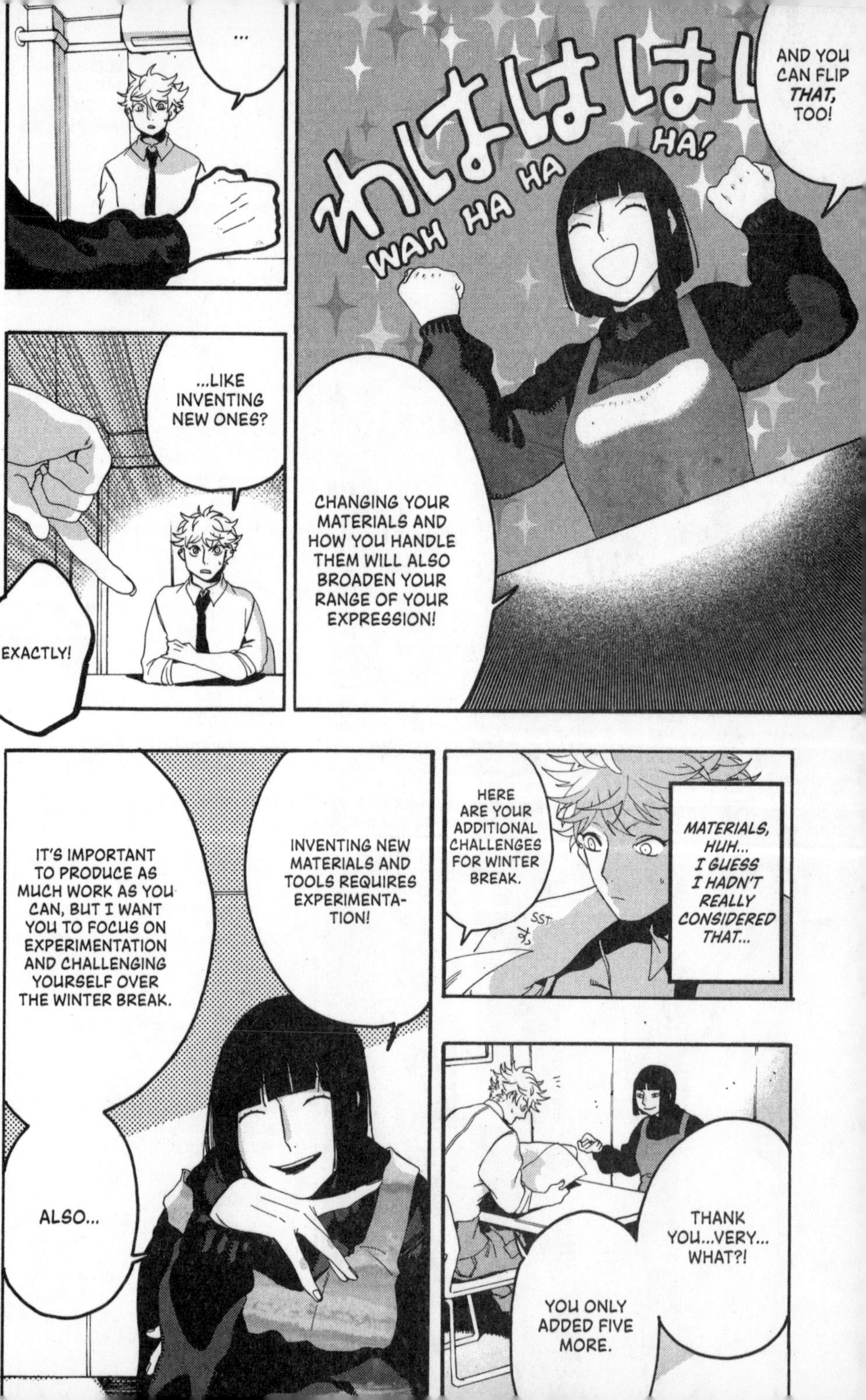
AND YOU CAN FLIP *THAT,* TOO!
わはははは
WAH HA HA HA!
CHANGING YOUR MATERIALS AND HOW YOU HANDLE THEM WILL ALSO BROADEN YOUR RANGE OF YOUR EXPRESSION!
...
...LIKE INVENTING NEW ONES?
EXACTLY!
MATERIALS, HUH... I GUESS I HADN'T REALLY CONSIDERED THAT...
HERE ARE YOUR ADDITIONAL CHALLENGES FOR WINTER BREAK.
SST
THANK YOU...VERY... WHAT?!
YOU ONLY ADDED FIVE MORE.
INVENTING NEW MATERIALS AND TOOLS REQUIRES EXPERIMENTA-TION!
IT'S IMPORTANT TO PRODUCE AS MUCH WORK AS YOU CAN, BUT I WANT YOU TO FOCUS ON EXPERIMENTATION AND CHALLENGING YOURSELF OVER THE WINTER BREAK.
ALSO...

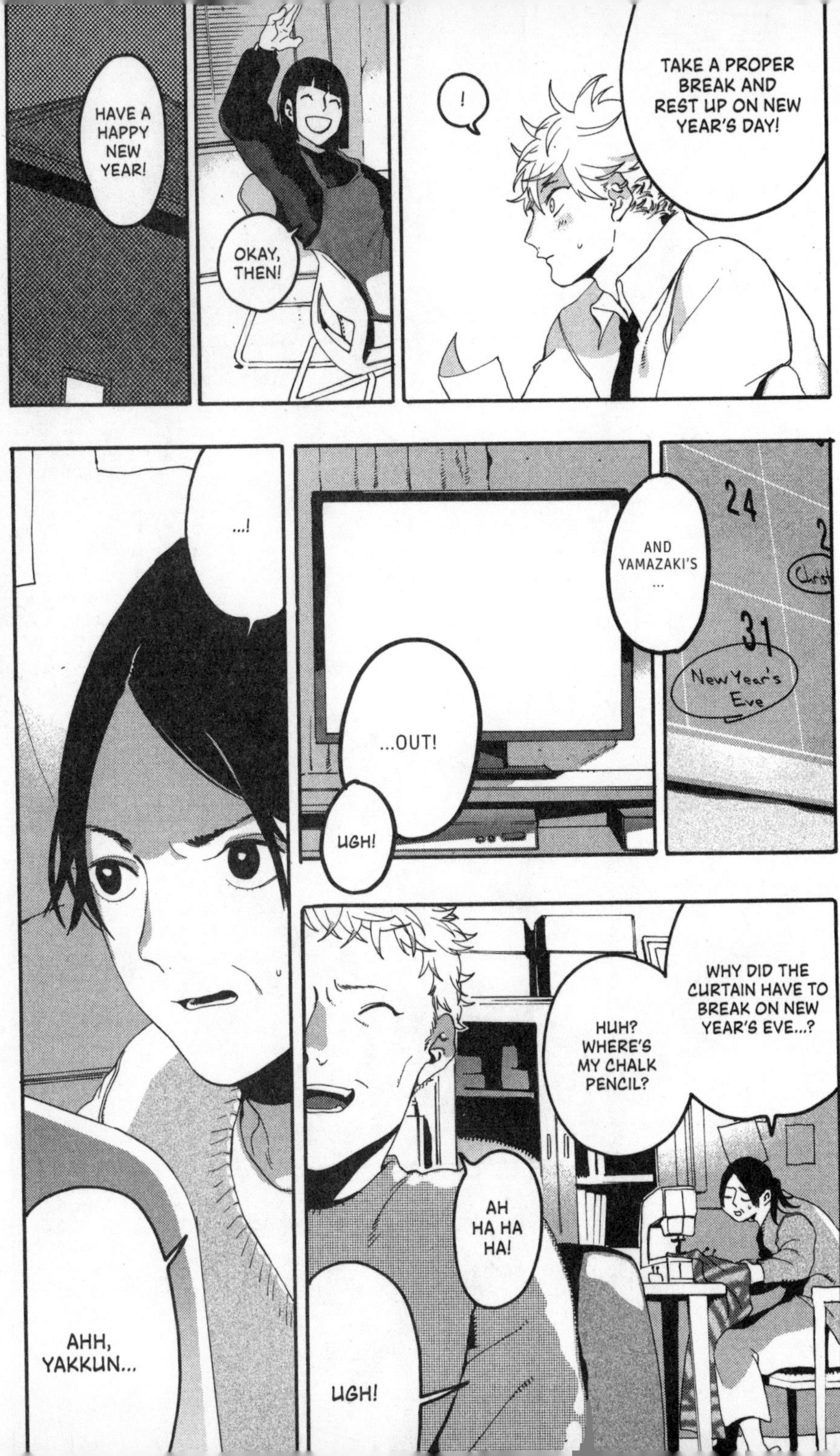
TAKE A PROPER BREAK AND REST UP ON NEW YEAR'S DAY!
!
OKAY, THEN!
HAVE A HAPPY NEW YEAR!
24
31
New Year's Eve
AND YAMAZAKI'S ...
...OUT!
UGH!
WHY DID THE CURTAIN HAVE TO BREAK ON NEW YEAR'S EVE...?
HUH? WHERE'S MY CHALK PENCIL?
AH HA HA HA!
UGH!
...!
AHH, YAKKUN...

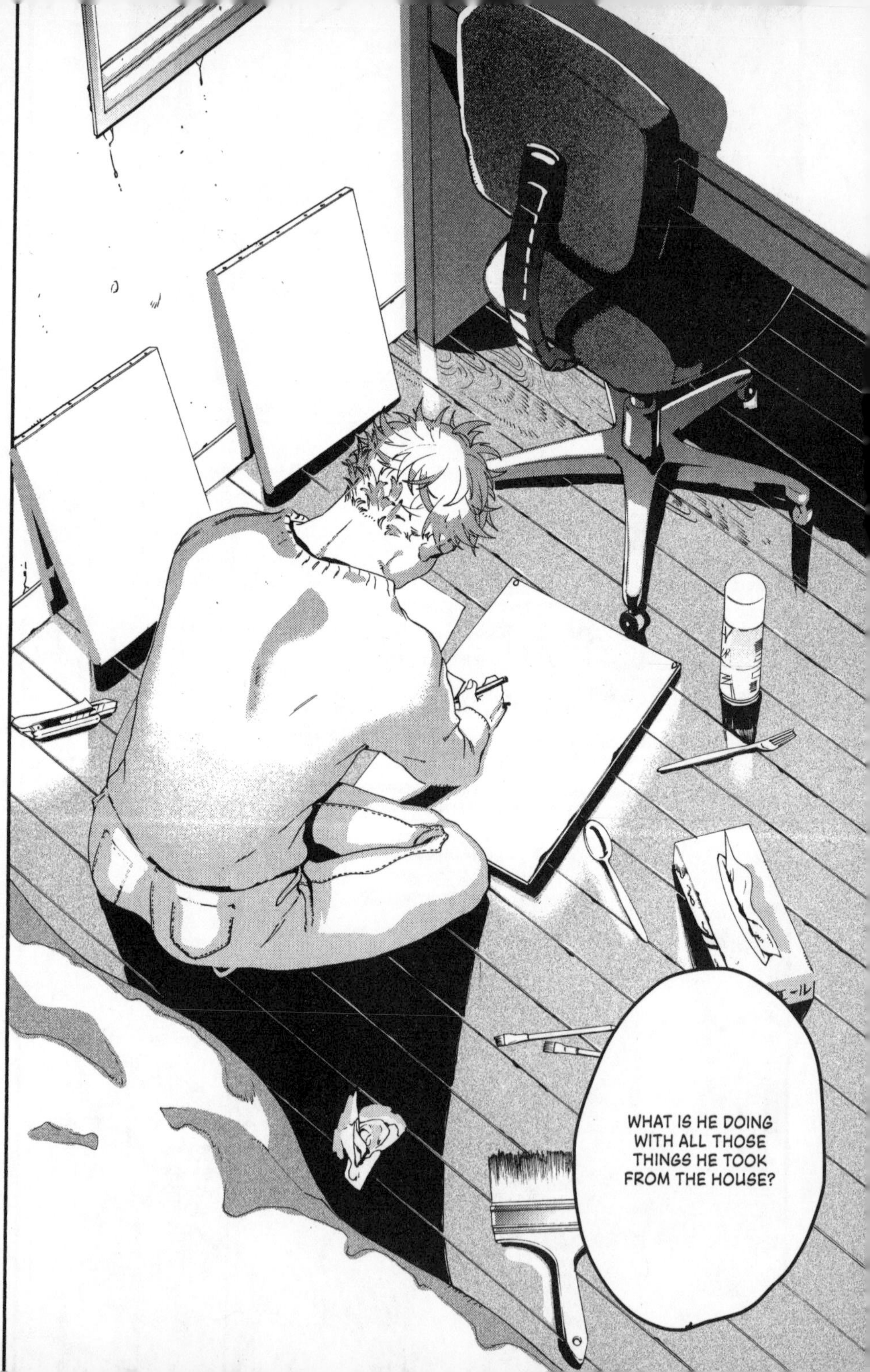
WHAT IS HE DOING WITH ALL THOSE THINGS HE TOOK FROM THE HOUSE?

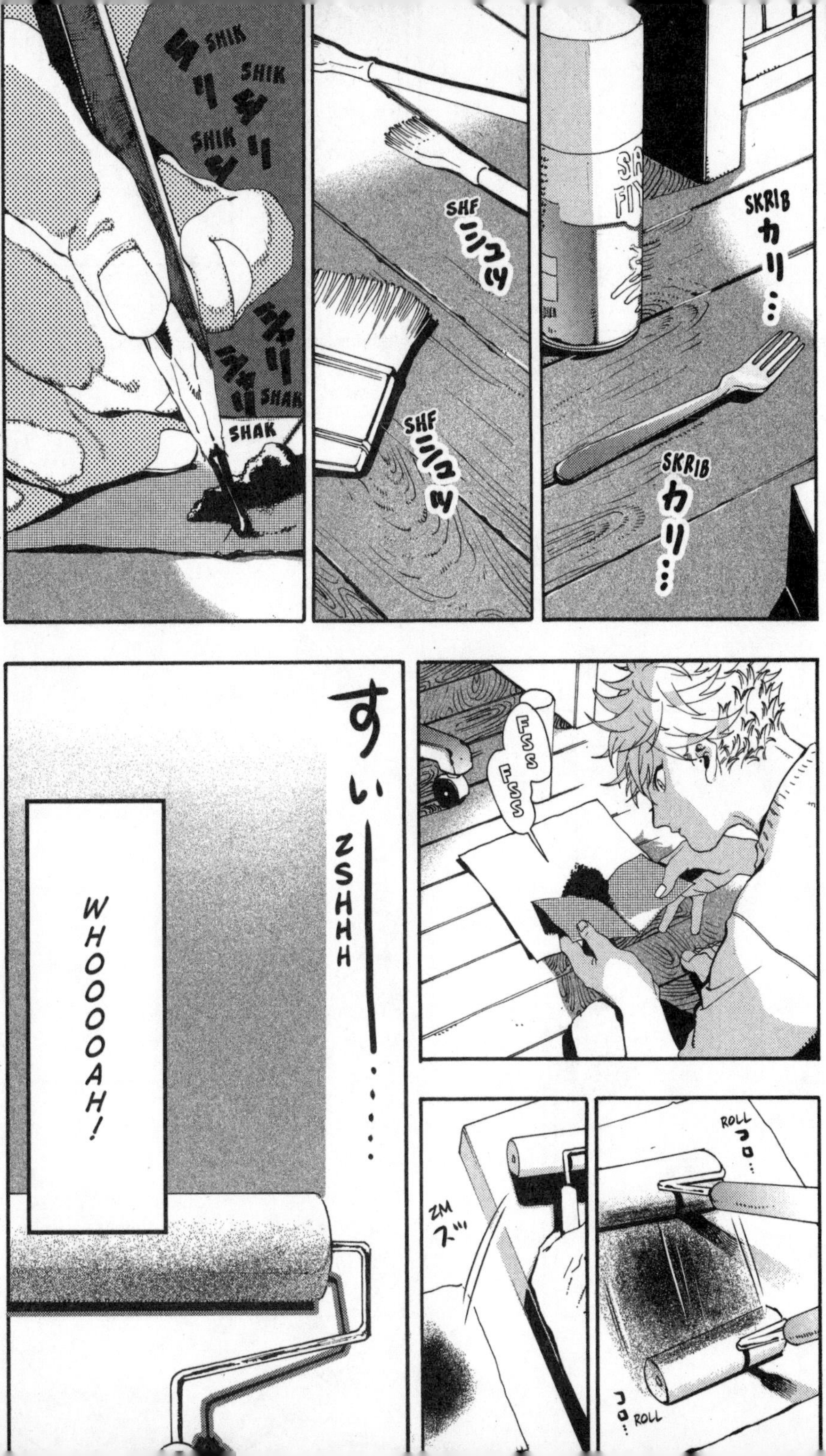

SKRIB カリ…
SKRIB カリ…
SHF シュッ
SHF シュッ
SHIK シリ
SHIK シリ
SHIK シリ
SHAK シャリ
SHAK シャリ
FSS FSS
ROLL コロ…
ZM ズッ
ROLL コロ…
すいーー……
ZSHHH
WHOOOOOAH!

Using sandpaper to grind the pencil lead into powder.

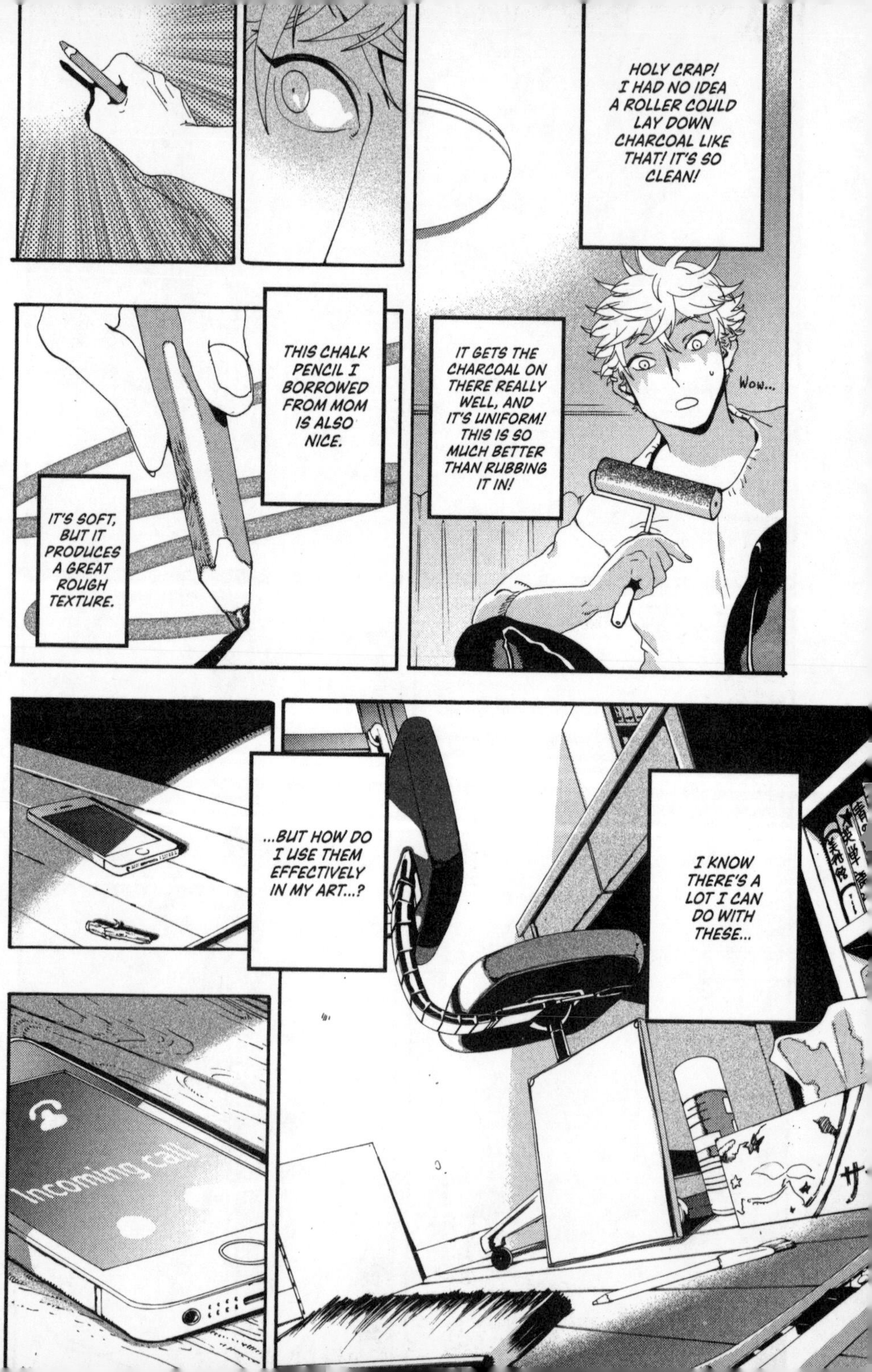
HOLY CRAP! I HAD NO IDEA A ROLLER COULD LAY DOWN CHARCOAL LIKE THAT! IT'S SO CLEAN!
IT GETS THE CHARCOAL ON THERE REALLY WELL, AND IT'S UNIFORM! THIS IS SO MUCH BETTER THAN RUBBING IT IN!
Wow...
THIS CHALK PENCIL I BORROWED FROM MOM IS ALSO NICE.
IT'S SOFT, BUT IT PRODUCES A GREAT ROUGH TEXTURE.
I KNOW THERE'S A LOT I CAN DO WITH THESE...
...BUT HOW DO I USE THEM EFFECTIVELY IN MY ART...?
サ
Incoming call

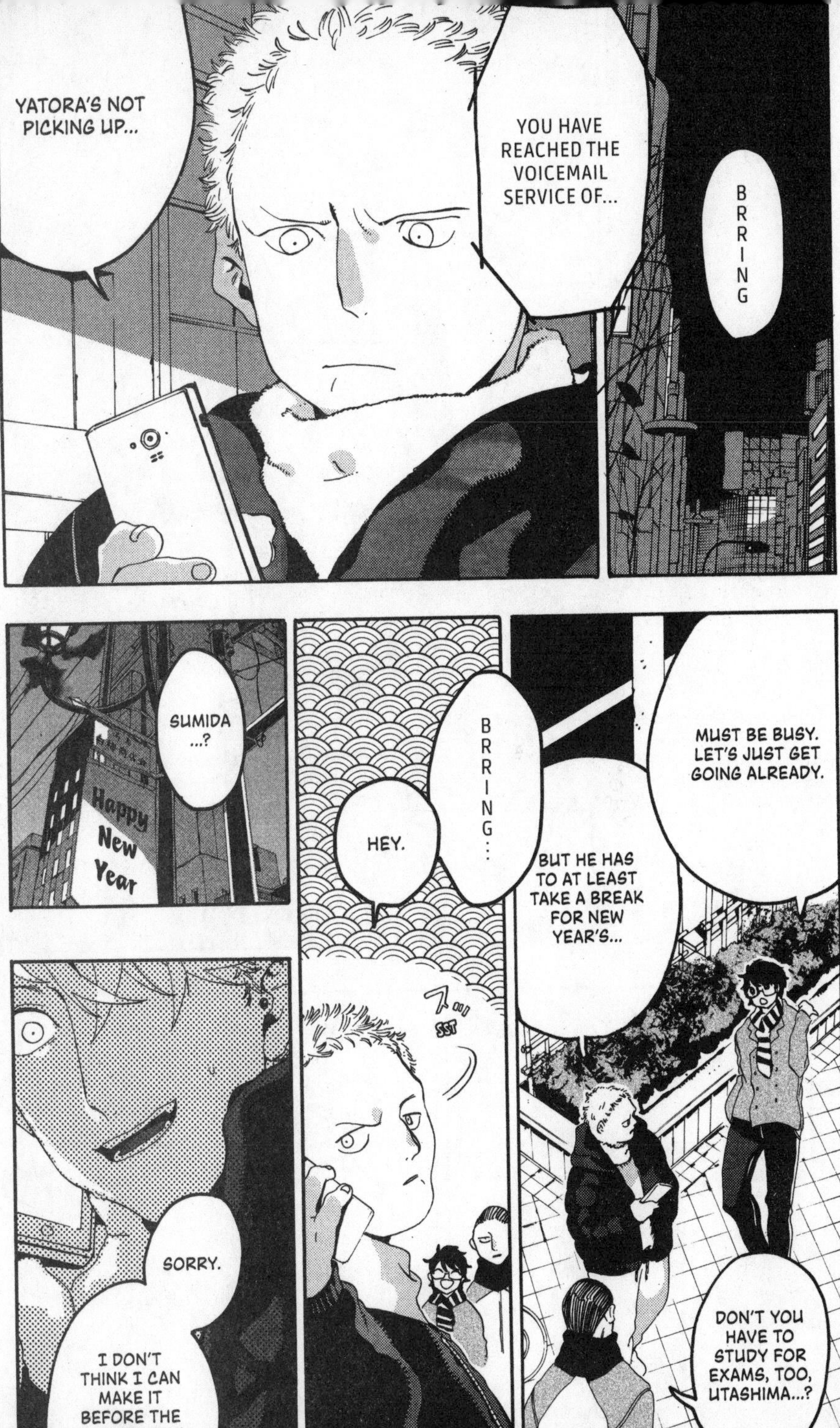

BRRING
YOU HAVE REACHED THE VOICEMAIL SERVICE OF...
YATORA'S NOT PICKING UP...
MUST BE BUSY. LET'S JUST GET GOING ALREADY.
BUT HE HAS TO AT LEAST TAKE A BREAK FOR NEW YEAR'S...
DON'T YOU HAVE TO STUDY FOR EXAMS, TOO, UTASHIMA...?
BRRING...
HEY.
SUMIDA ...?
Happy New Year
SST
SORRY.
I DON'T THINK I CAN MAKE IT BEFORE THE COUNTDOWN THIS YEAR.

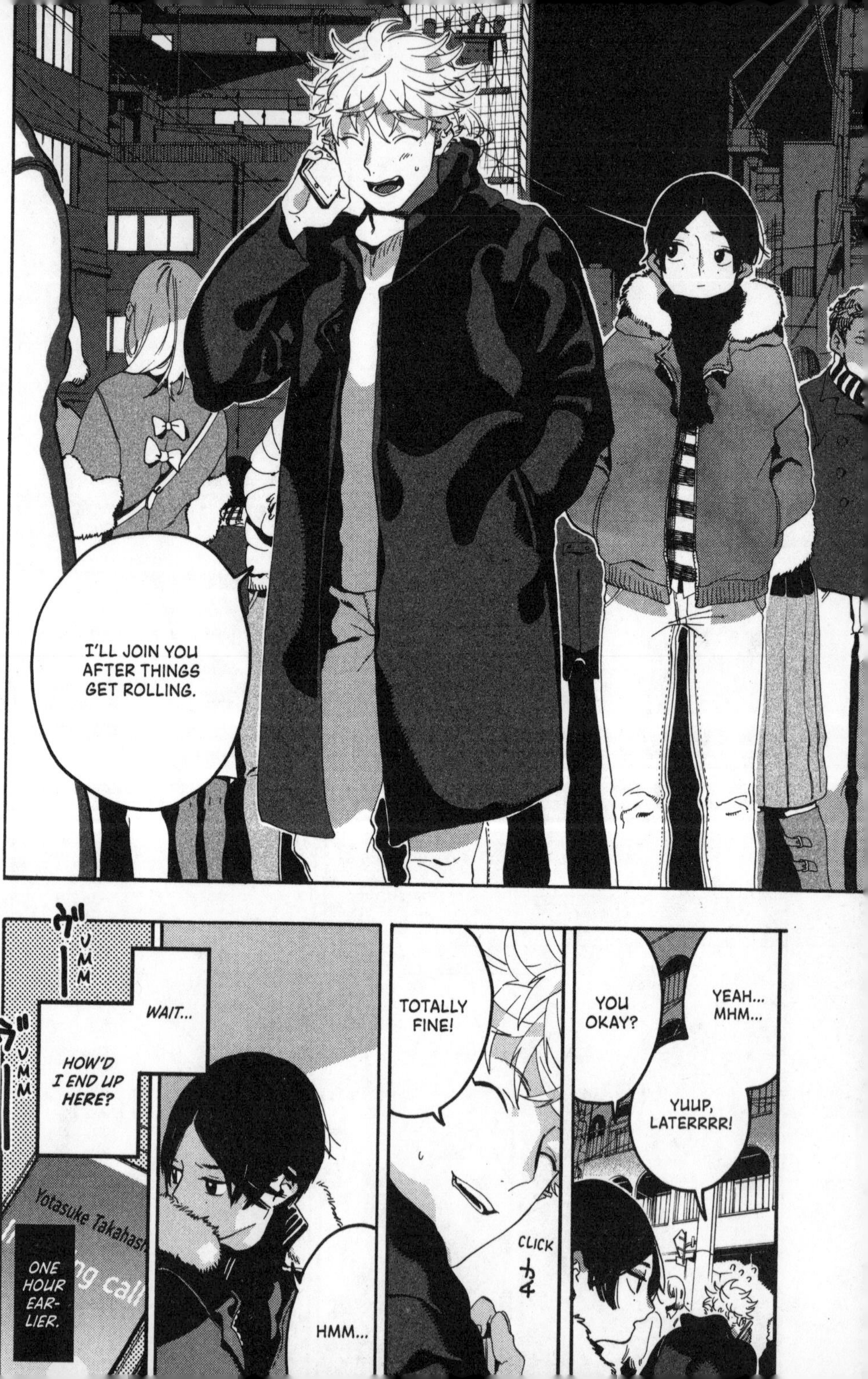
I'LL JOIN YOU AFTER THINGS GET ROLLING.
YEAH... MHM...
YOU OKAY?
YUUP, LATERRRR!
TOTALLY FINE!
CLICK
カチ
HMM...
ヴー
UMM
ヴー
UMM
WAIT...
HOW'D I END UP HERE?
Yotasuke Takahash
ONE HOUR EAR-LIER.

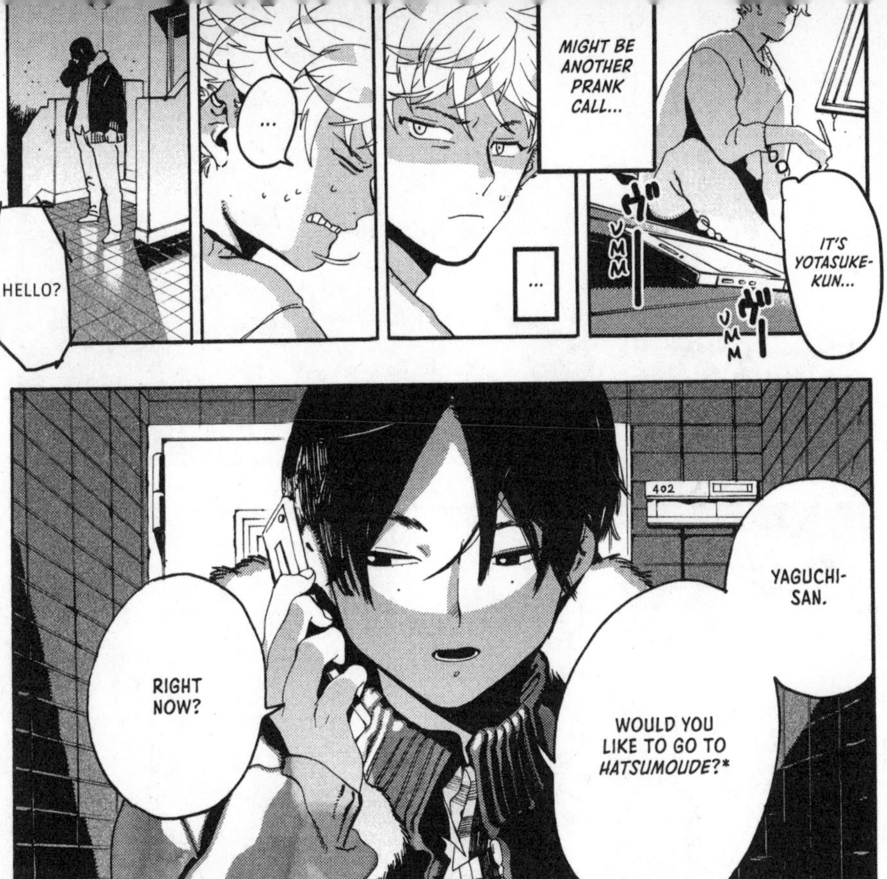
VMM
VMM
IT'S YOTASUKE-KUN...
MIGHT BE ANOTHER PRANK CALL...
...
...
HELLO?
YAGUCHI-SAN.
WOULD YOU LIKE TO GO TO HATSUMOUDE?*
RIGHT NOW?

*HATSUMOUDE = THE FIRST SHRINE VISIT OF THE NEW YEAR.

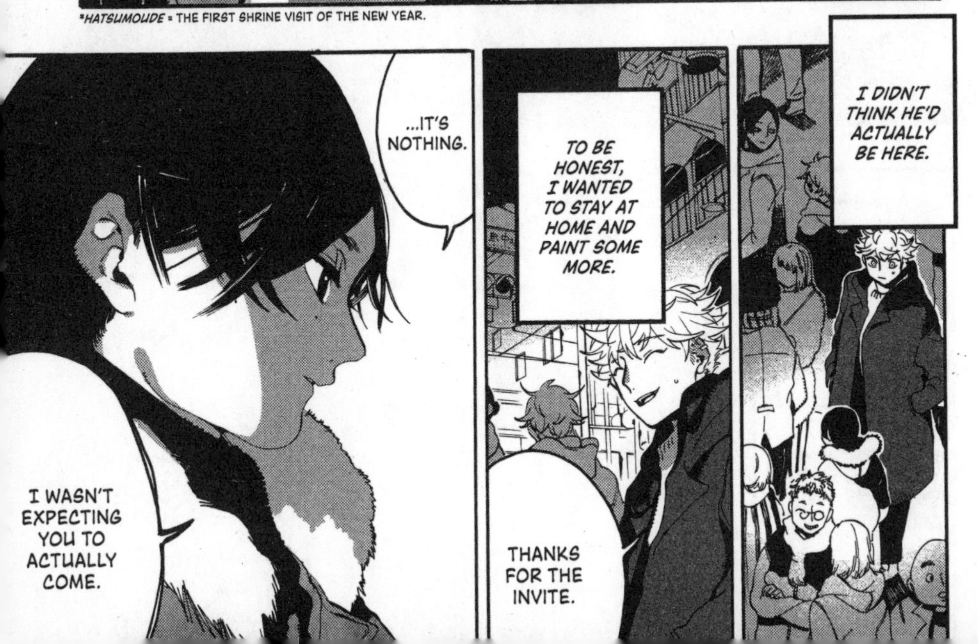
I DIDN'T THINK HE'D ACTUALLY BE HERE.
TO BE HONEST, I WANTED TO STAY AT HOME AND PAINT SOME MORE.
THANKS FOR THE INVITE.
...IT'S NOTHING.
I WASN'T EXPECTING YOU TO ACTUALLY COME.

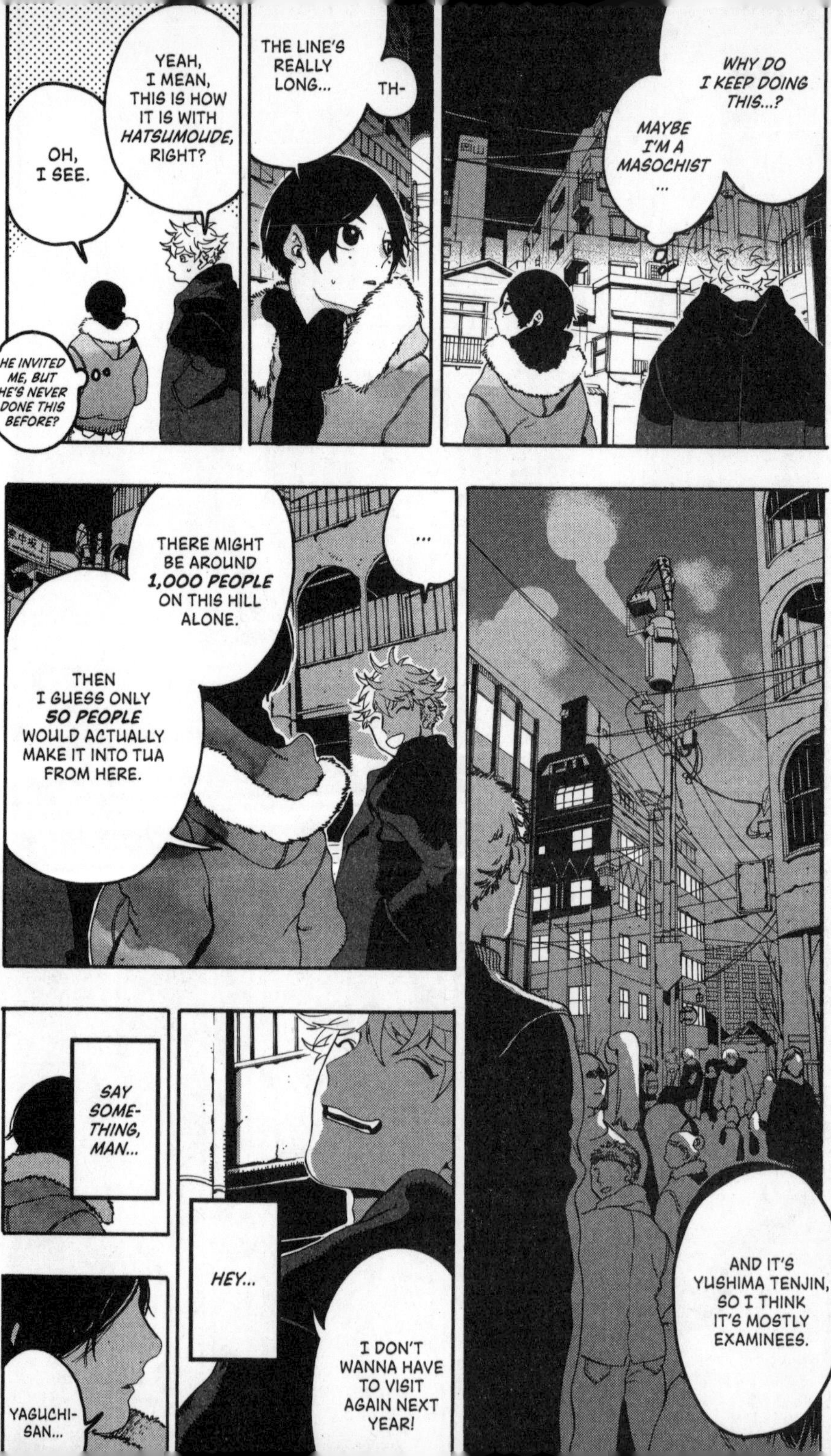
WHY DO I KEEP DOING THIS...?
MAYBE I'M A MASOCHIST ...
THE LINE'S REALLY LONG...
TH-
YEAH, I MEAN, THIS IS HOW IT IS WITH HATSUMOUDE, RIGHT?
OH, I SEE.
HE INVITED ME, BUT HE'S NEVER DONE THIS BEFORE?
AND IT'S YUSHIMA TENJIN, SO I THINK IT'S MOSTLY EXAMINEES.
...
THERE MIGHT BE AROUND 1,000 PEOPLE ON THIS HILL ALONE.
THEN I GUESS ONLY 50 PEOPLE WOULD ACTUALLY MAKE IT INTO TUA FROM HERE.
HEY...
I DON'T WANNA HAVE TO VISIT AGAIN NEXT YEAR!
SAY SOME-THING, MAN...
YAGUCHI-SAN...

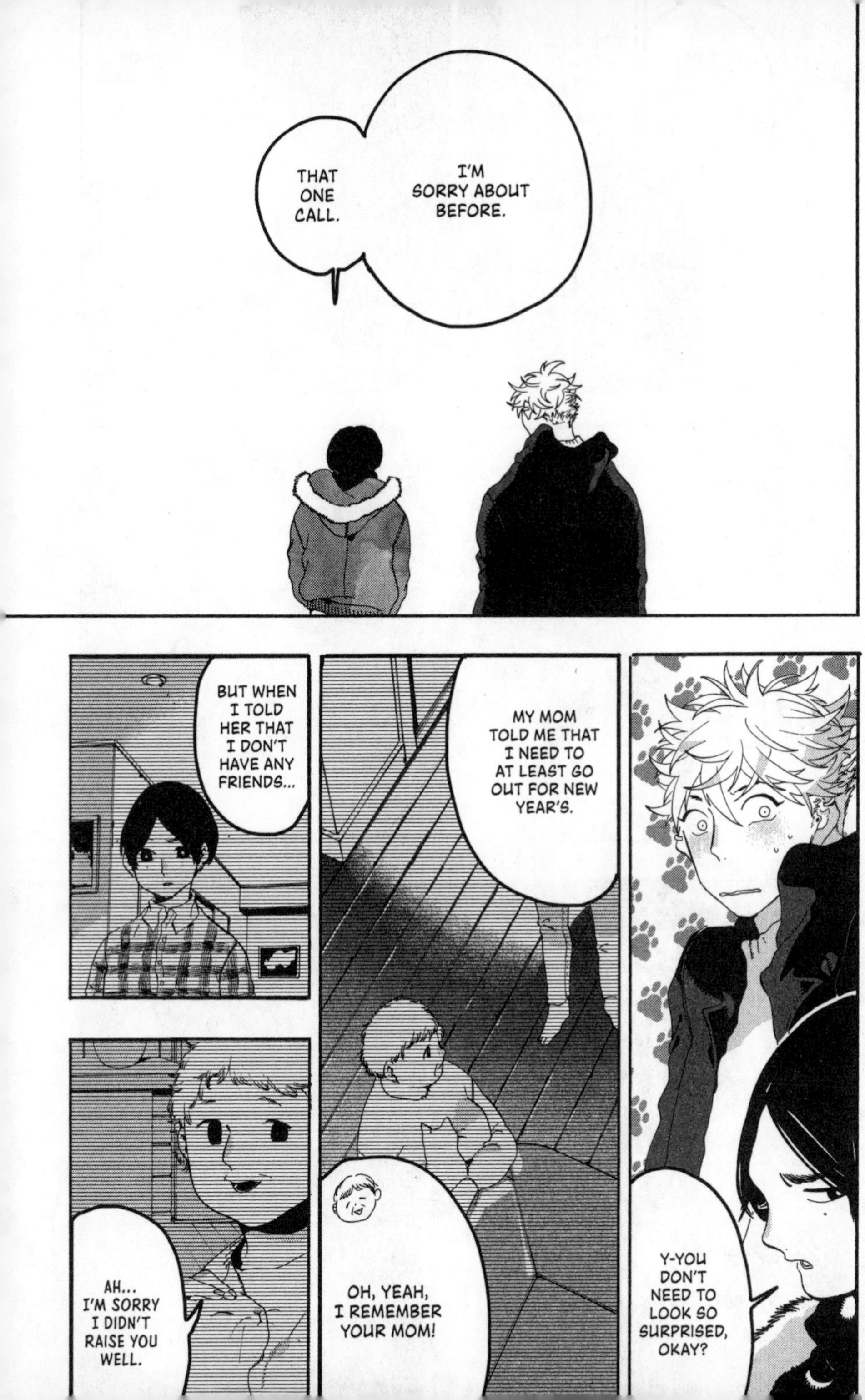
I'M SORRY ABOUT BEFORE.
THAT ONE CALL.
Y-YOU DON'T NEED TO LOOK SO SURPRISED, OKAY?
MY MOM TOLD ME THAT I NEED TO AT LEAST GO OUT FOR NEW YEAR'S.
OH, YEAH, I REMEMBER YOUR MOM!
BUT WHEN I TOLD HER THAT I DON'T HAVE ANY FRIENDS...
AH... I'M SORRY I DIDN'T RAISE YOU WELL.

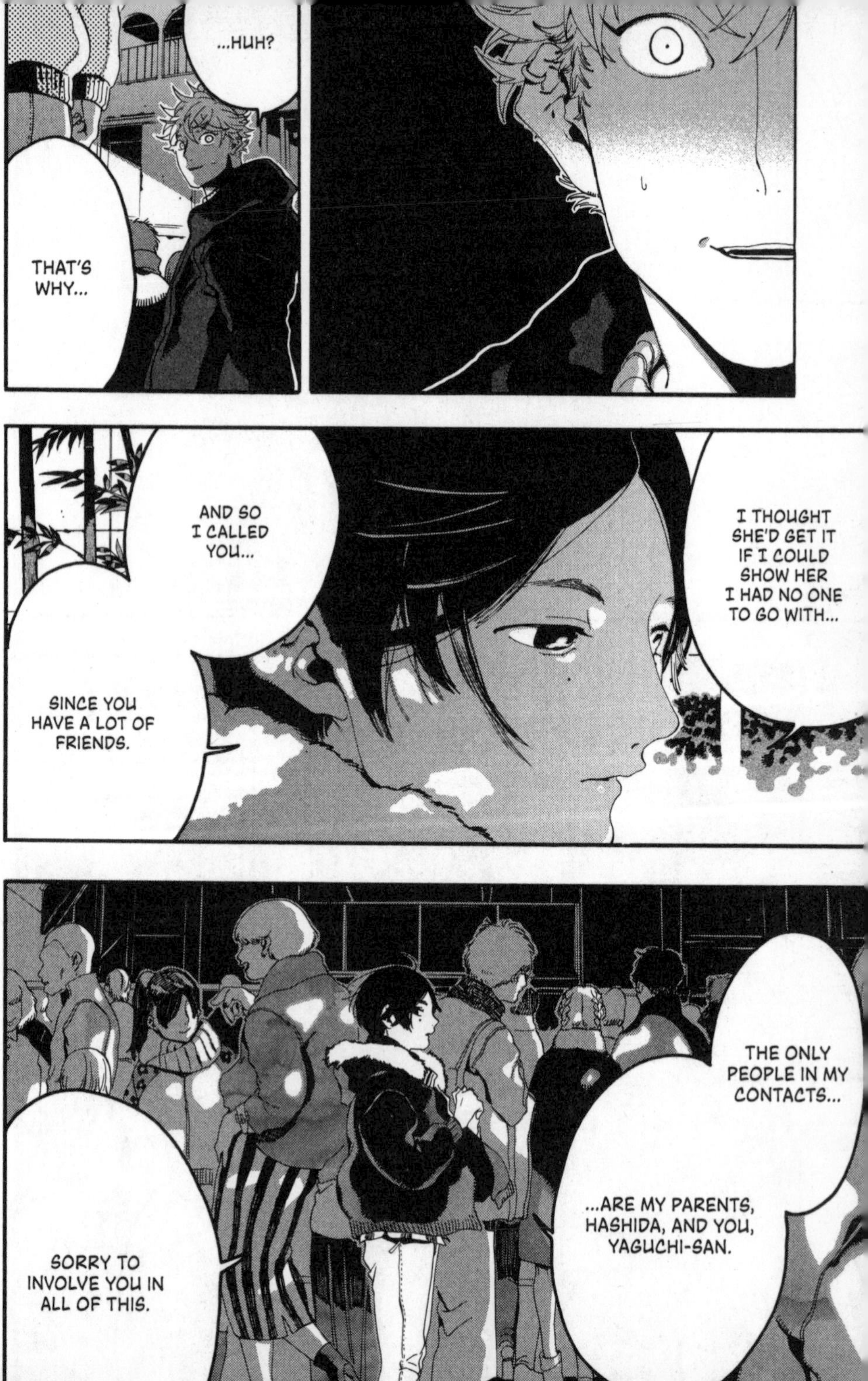
...HUH?
THAT'S WHY...
I THOUGHT SHE'D GET IT IF I COULD SHOW HER I HAD NO ONE TO GO WITH...
AND SO I CALLED YOU...
SINCE YOU HAVE A LOT OF FRIENDS.
THE ONLY PEOPLE IN MY CONTACTS...
...ARE MY PARENTS, HASHIDA, AND YOU, YAGUCHI-SAN.
SORRY TO INVOLVE YOU IN ALL OF THIS.

HUH?

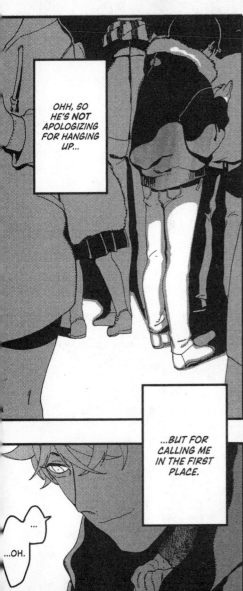

OHH, SO HE'S NOT APOLOGIZING FOR HANGING UP...

...BUT FOR CALLING ME IN THE FIRST PLACE.

...

...OH.

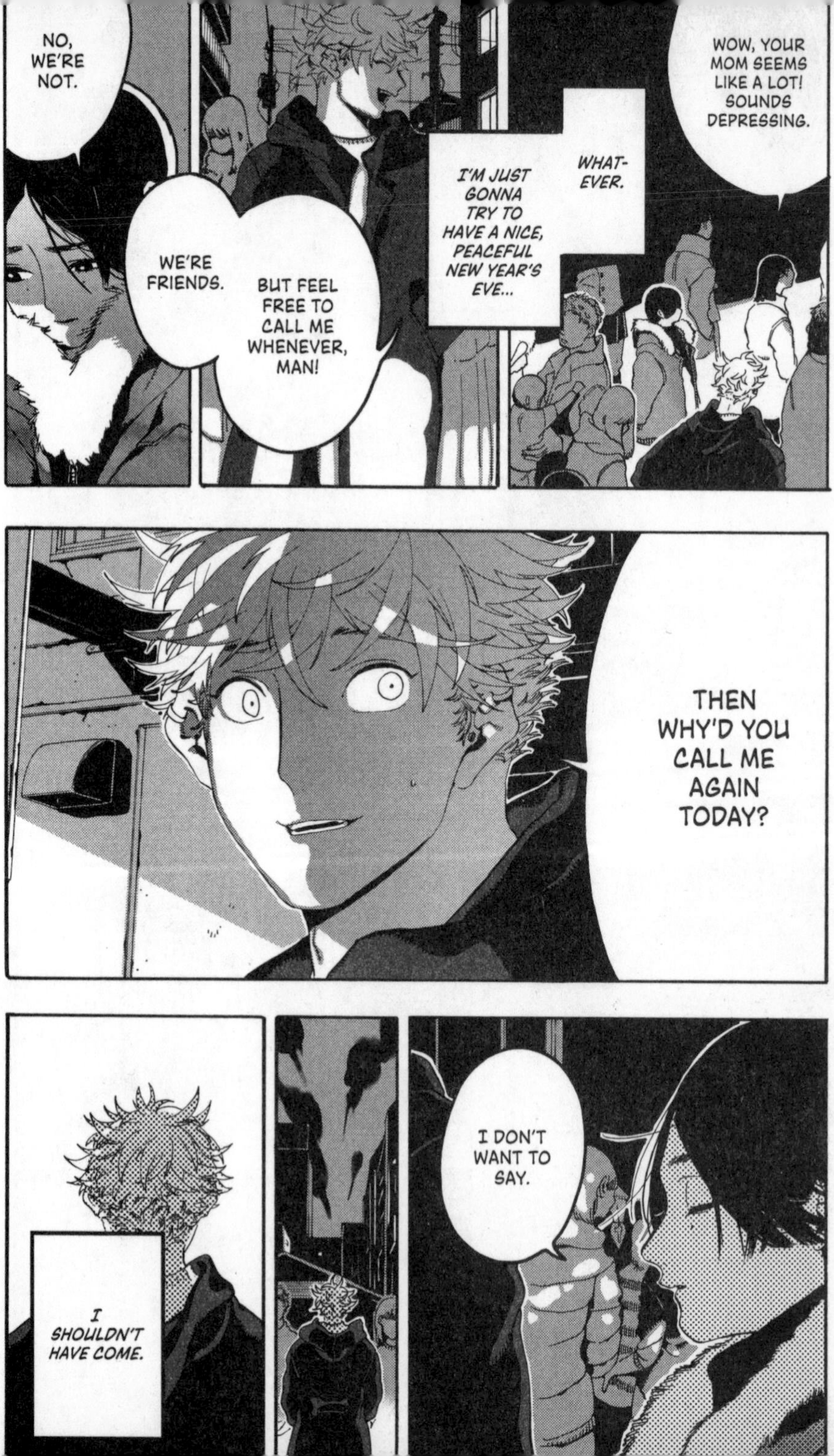
WOW, YOUR MOM SEEMS LIKE A LOT! SOUNDS DEPRESSING.
WHAT-EVER.
I'M JUST GONNA TRY TO HAVE A NICE, PEACEFUL NEW YEAR'S EVE...
BUT FEEL FREE TO CALL ME WHENEVER, MAN!
WE'RE FRIENDS.
NO, WE'RE NOT.
THEN WHY'D YOU CALL ME AGAIN TODAY?
I DON'T WANT TO SAY.
I SHOULDN'T HAVE COME.

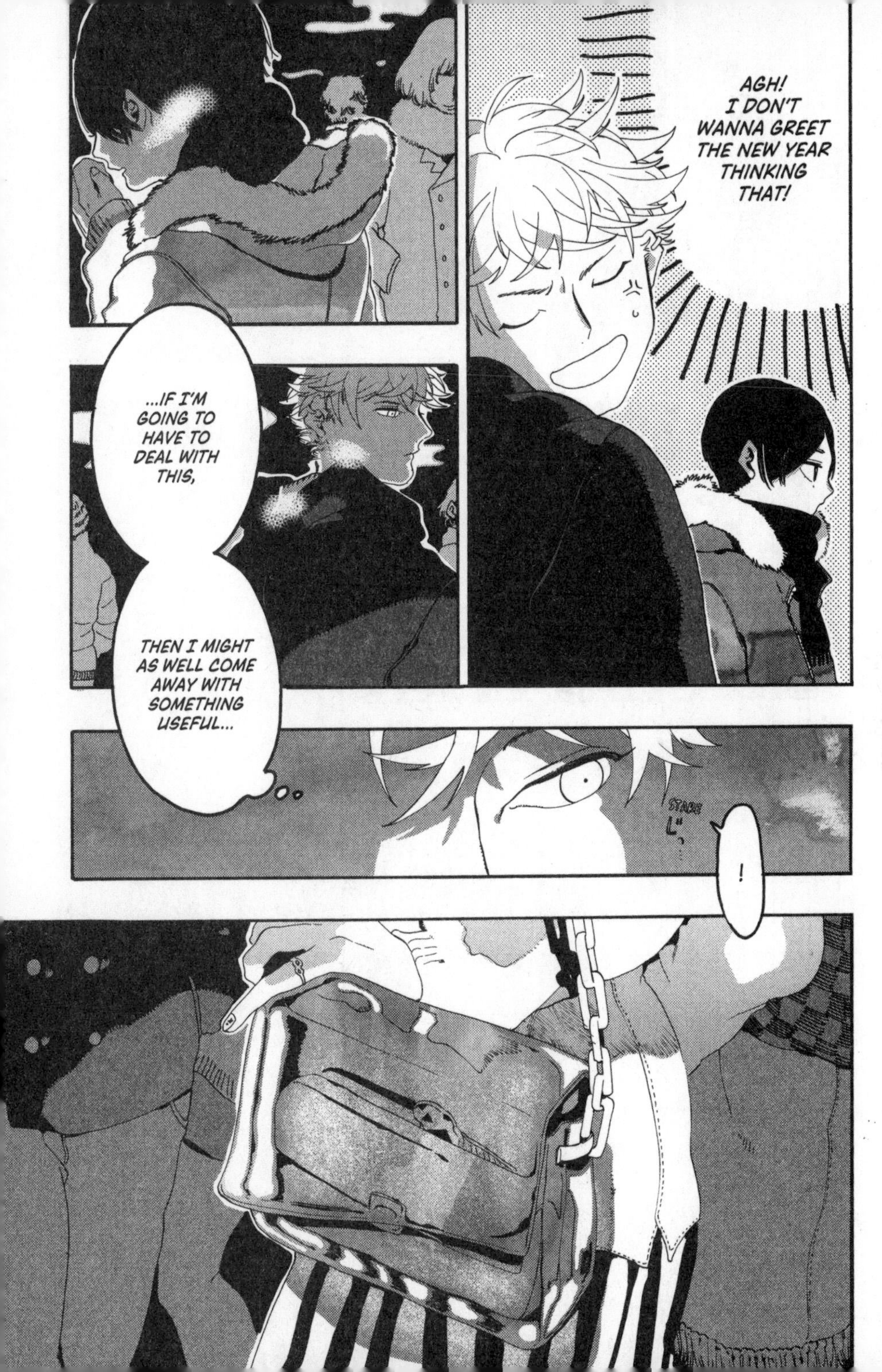
AGH! I DON'T WANNA GREET THE NEW YEAR THINKING THAT!
...IF I'M GOING TO HAVE TO DEAL WITH THIS,
THEN I MIGHT AS WELL COME AWAY WITH SOMETHING USEFUL...
STARE
!

FOR PLASTIC MATERIAL...

KWK
KWK
KWK

Your Ad Here

Contact us at:
03-8888-0088

I CAN USE A HARD H PENCIL...

...AND THEN I CAN USE BOTH A UTILITY KNIFE AND AN ERASER TO PULL OUT THE HIGHLIGHTS...

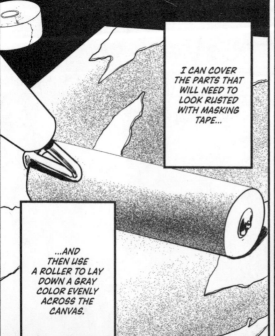

I CAN COVER THE PARTS THAT WILL NEED TO LOOK RUSTED WITH MASKING TAPE...

...AND THEN USE A ROLLER TO LAY DOWN A GRAY COLOR EVENLY ACROSS THE CANVAS.

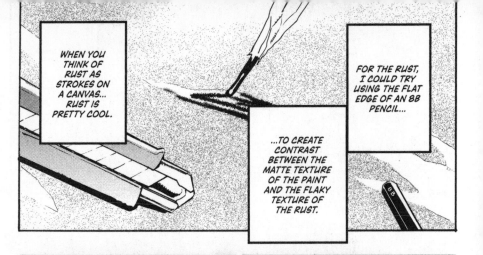

FOR THE RUST, I COULD TRY USING THE FLAT EDGE OF AN 8B PENCIL...
...TO CREATE CONTRAST BETWEEN THE MATTE TEXTURE OF THE PAINT AND THE FLAKY TEXTURE OF THE RUST.
WHEN YOU THINK OF RUST AS STROKES ON A CANVAS... RUST IS PRETTY COOL.
8B
I NEVER IMAGINED THERE'D COME A DAY WHEN I'D THINK **RUST** WAS COOL.
...IT'S SOMETHING I'VE NOTICED BECAUSE I'VE BEEN MAKING ART.
New
Year
BUT...
...I COULDN'T HAVE NOTICED SOMETHING LIKE THAT **JUST** FROM MAKING ART.

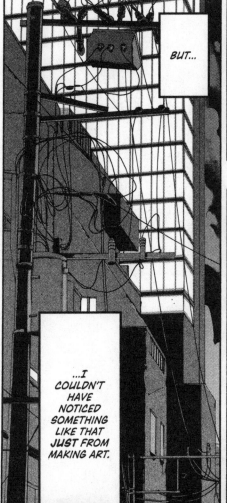

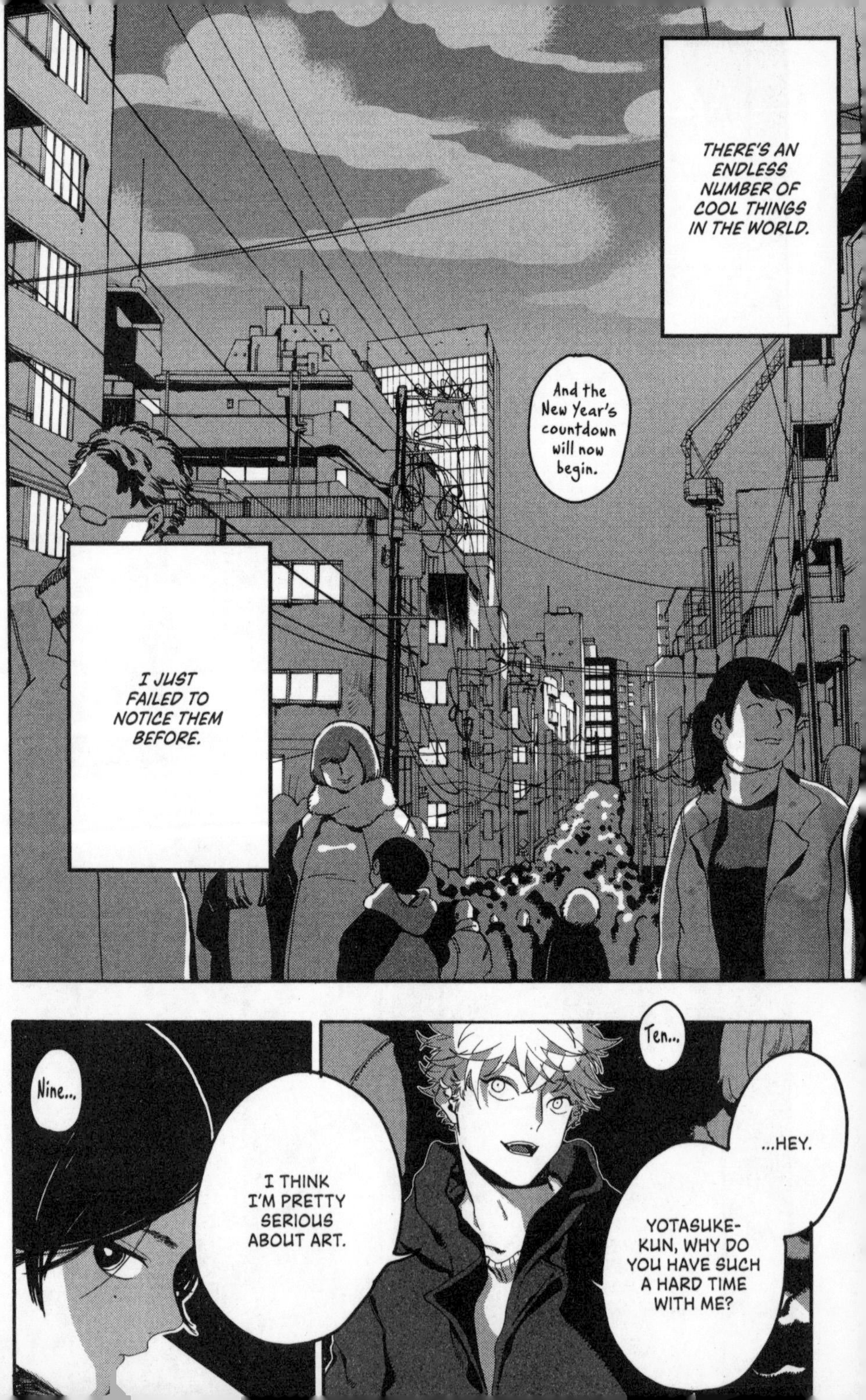
THERE'S AN ENDLESS NUMBER OF COOL THINGS IN THE WORLD.
And the New Year's countdown will now begin.
I JUST FAILED TO NOTICE THEM BEFORE.
Ten...
...HEY.
YOTASUKE-KUN, WHY DO YOU HAVE SUCH A HARD TIME WITH ME?
I THINK I'M PRETTY SERIOUS ABOUT ART.
Nine...

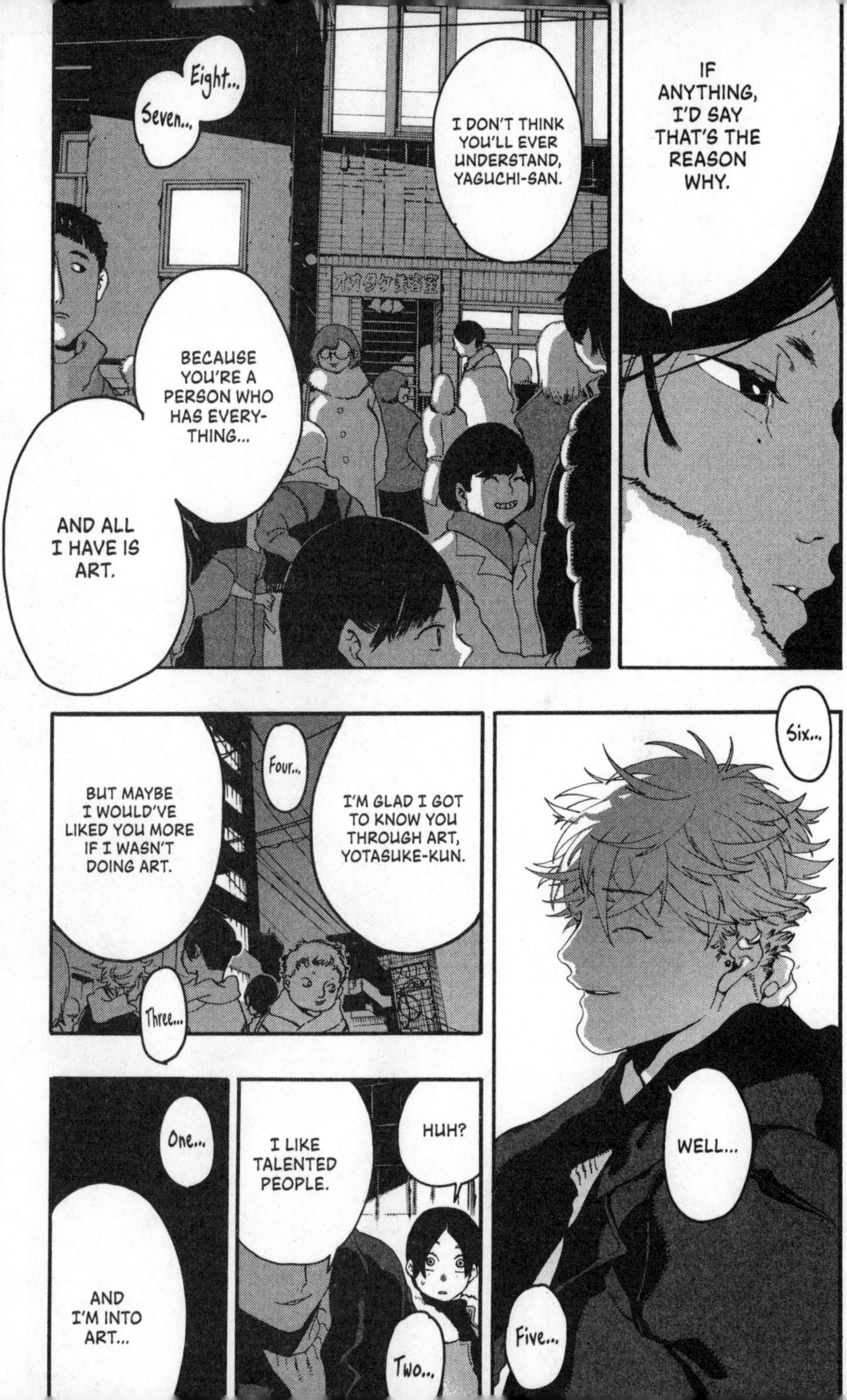
IF ANYTHING, I'D SAY THAT'S THE REASON WHY.
I DON'T THINK YOU'LL EVER UNDERSTAND, YAGUCHI-SAN.
Eight...
Seven...
BECAUSE YOU'RE A PERSON WHO HAS EVERY-THING...
AND ALL I HAVE IS ART.
Six...
WELL...
Five...
Four...
I'M GLAD I GOT TO KNOW YOU THROUGH ART, YOTASUKE-KUN.
BUT MAYBE I WOULD'VE LIKED YOU MORE IF I WASN'T DOING ART.
Three...
HUH?
I LIKE TALENTED PEOPLE.
Two...
One...
AND I'M INTO ART...

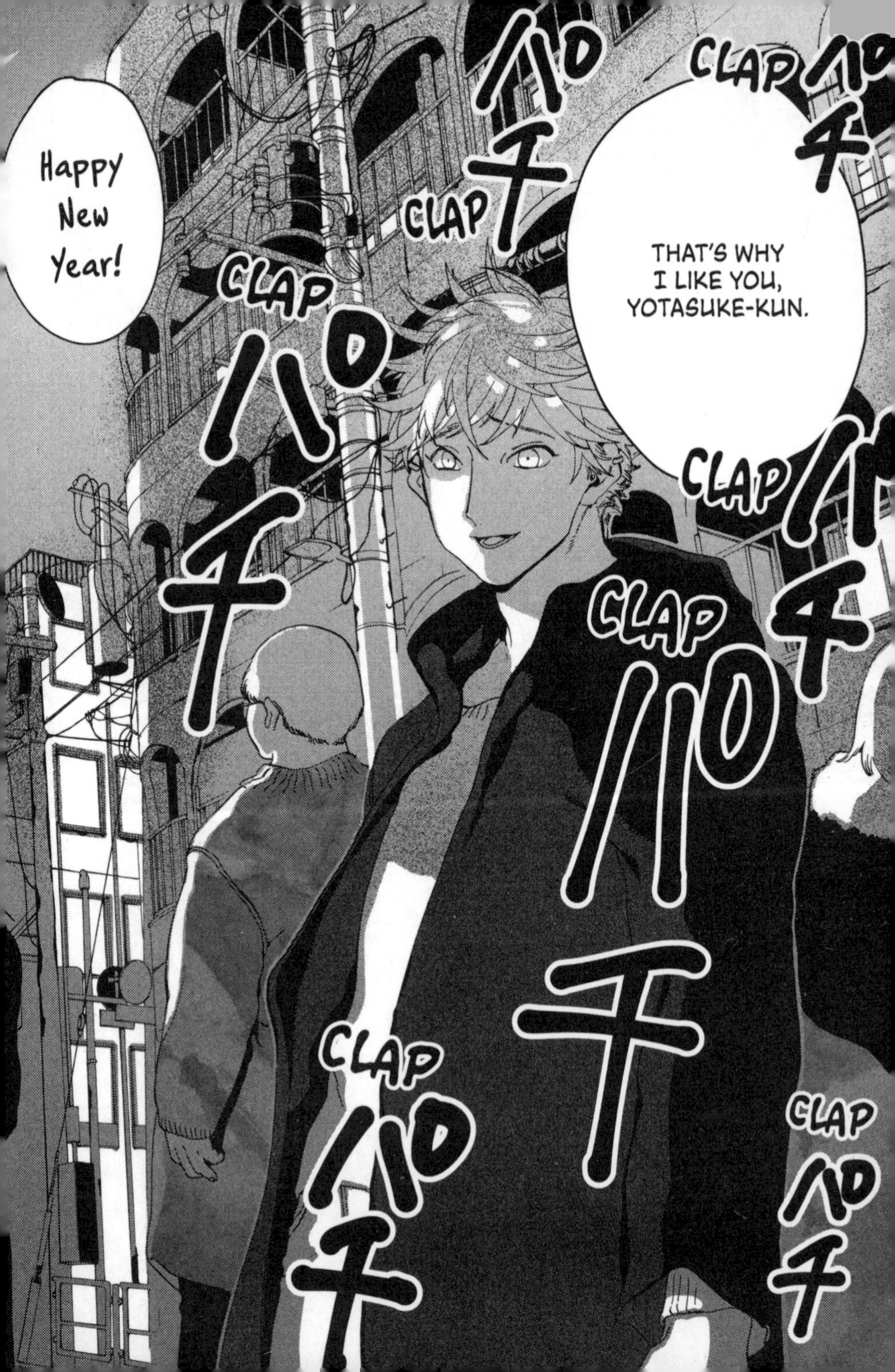
CLAP
THAT'S WHY I LIKE YOU, YOTASUKE-KUN.
CLAP
CLAP
CLAP
CLAP
CLAP
CLAP
CLAP
Happy New Year!

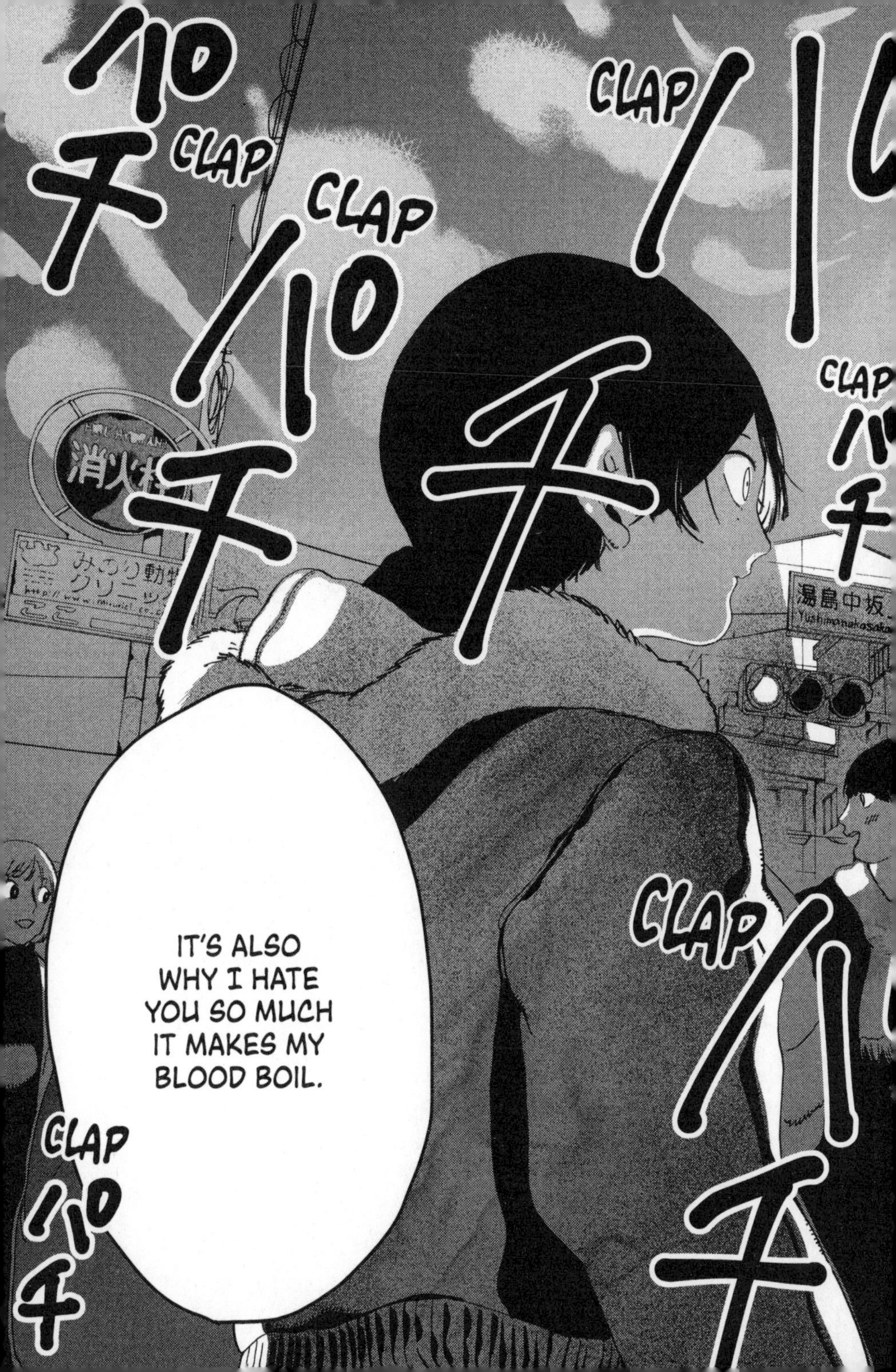
CLAP
CLAP
パチ
CLAP
パチ
CLAP
パチ
湯島中坂
消火栓
IT'S ALSO WHY I HATE YOU SO MUCH IT MAKES MY BLOOD BOIL.
CLAP
パチ
CLAP
パチ

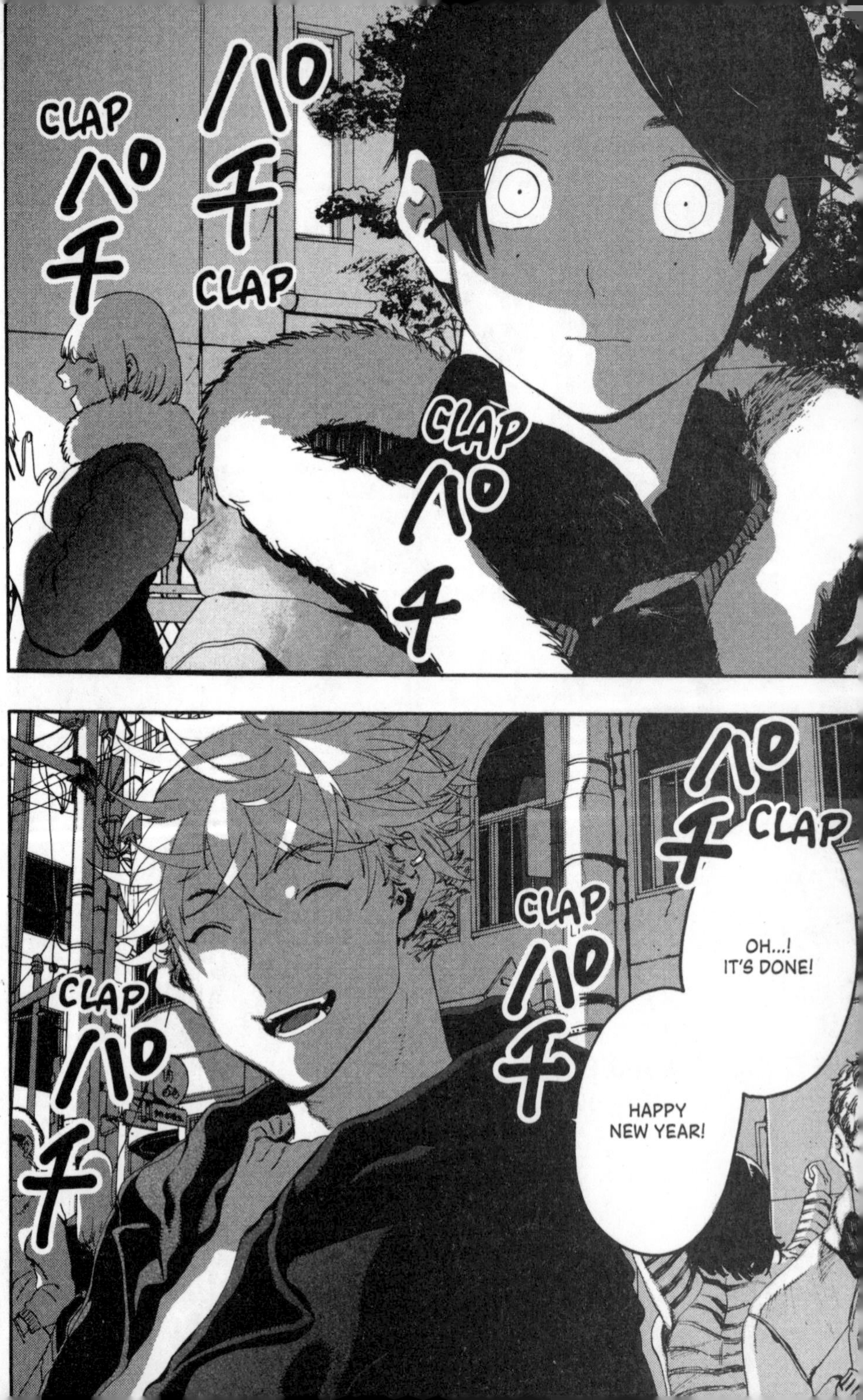
パチ
CLAP
パチ
CLAP
パチ
CLAP
パチ
CLAP
パチ
CLAP
OH...! IT'S DONE!
HAPPY NEW YEAR!
パチ
CLAP

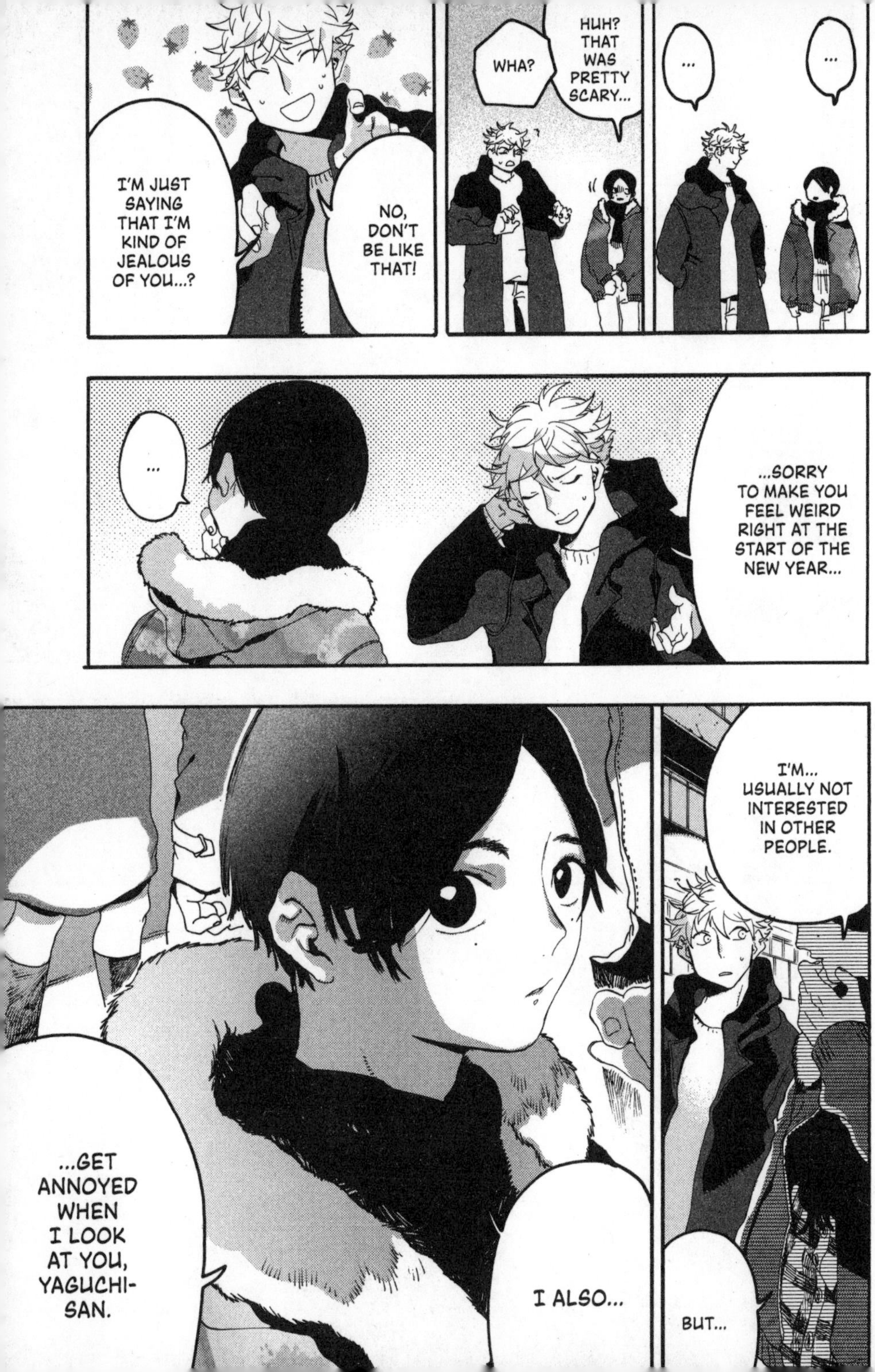
...
...
HUH? THAT WAS PRETTY SCARY...
WHA?
NO, DON'T BE LIKE THAT!
I'M JUST SAYING THAT I'M KIND OF JEALOUS OF YOU...?
...SORRY TO MAKE YOU FEEL WEIRD RIGHT AT THE START OF THE NEW YEAR...
...
I'M... USUALLY NOT INTERESTED IN OTHER PEOPLE.
BUT...
I ALSO...
...GET ANNOYED WHEN I LOOK AT YOU, YAGUCHI-SAN.

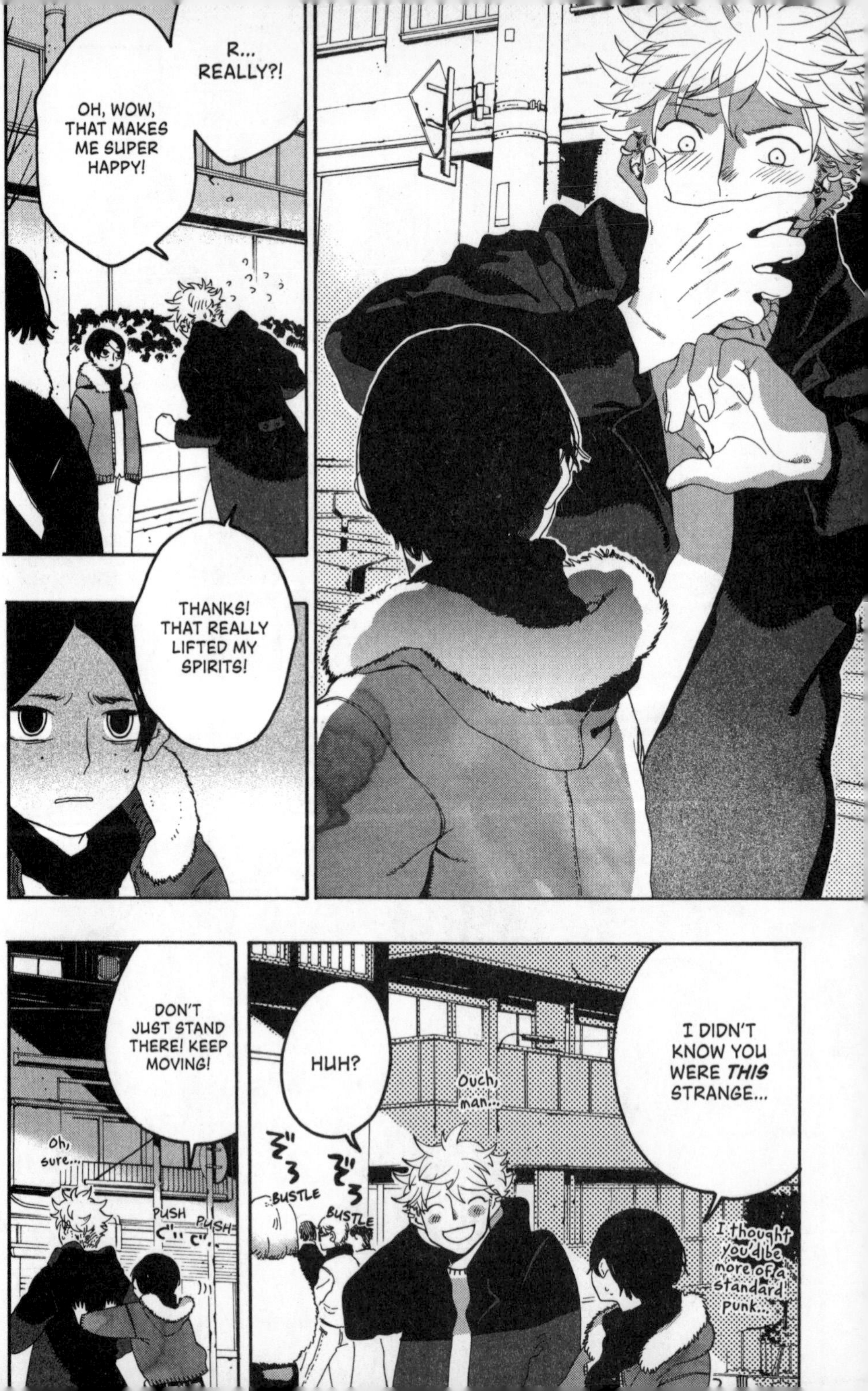
R... REALLY?!
OH, WOW, THAT MAKES ME SUPER HAPPY!
THANKS! THAT REALLY LIFTED MY SPIRITS!
I DIDN'T KNOW YOU WERE *THIS* STRANGE...
I thought you'd be more of a standard punk...
Ouch, man...
HUH?
ぞろ BUSTLE
ぞろ BUSTLE
DON'T JUST STAND THERE! KEEP MOVING!
Oh, sure...
PUSH
PUSH

SHIT...

I'M SO FREAKIN' HAPPY.

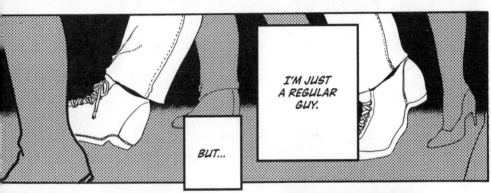

I'M JUST A REGULAR GUY.

BUT...

...TO THIS GENIUS...

...I'M SPECIAL.

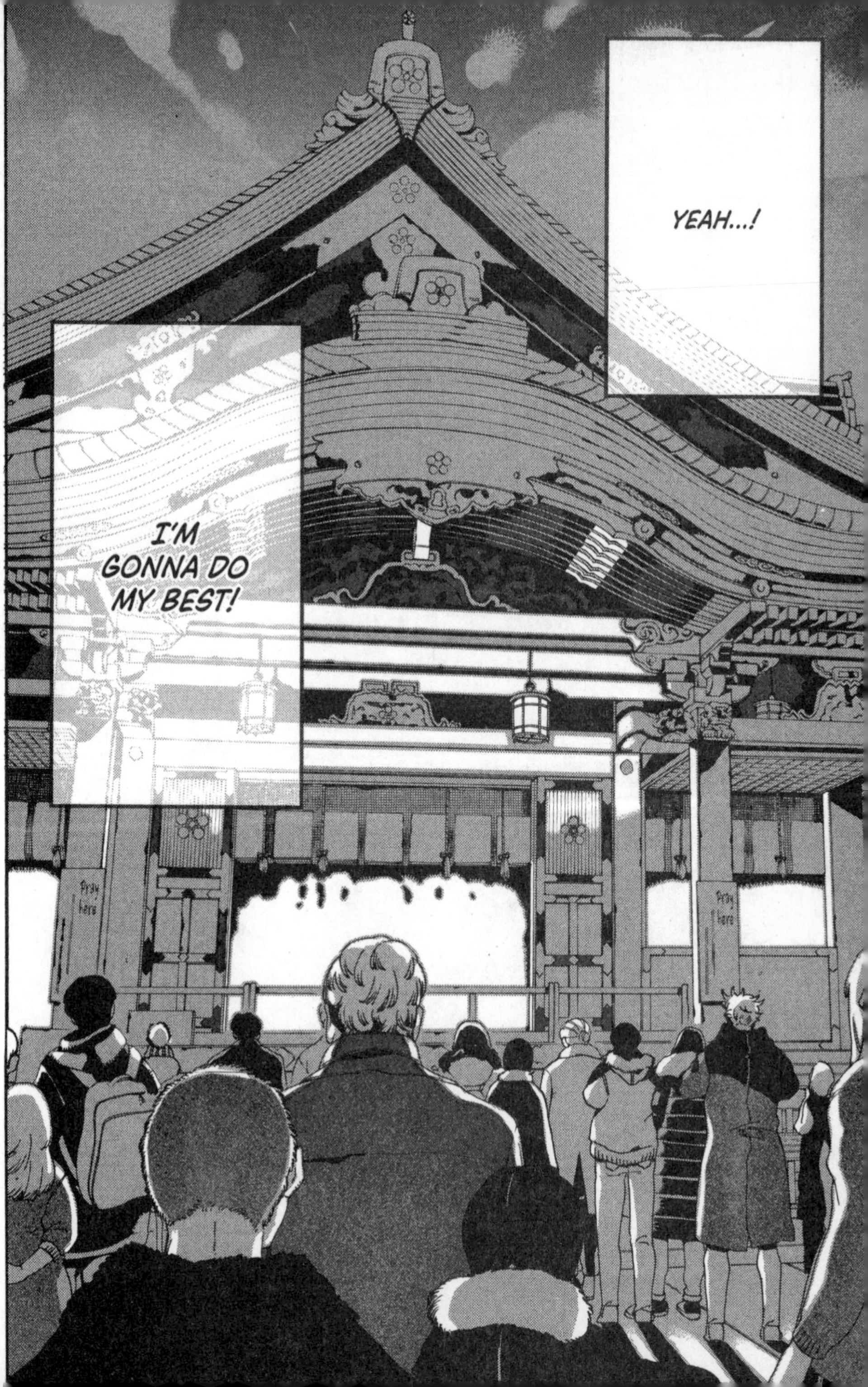
YEAH...!
I'M GONNA DO MY BEST!
Pray here
Pray here

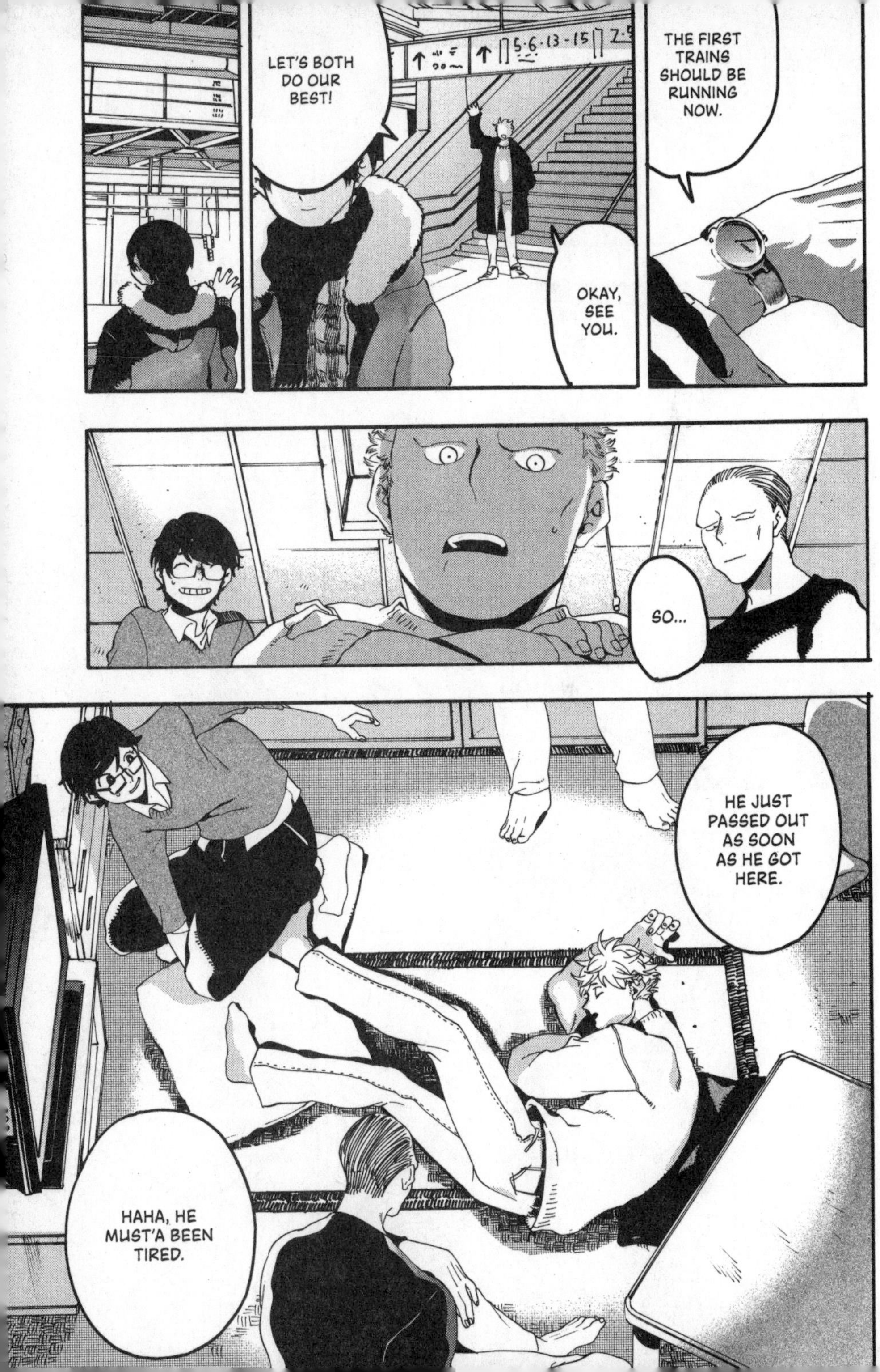

THE FIRST TRAINS SHOULD BE RUNNING NOW.
LET'S BOTH DO OUR BEST!
OKAY, SEE YOU.
SO...
HE JUST PASSED OUT AS SOON AS HE GOT HERE.
HAHA, HE MUST'A BEEN TIRED.

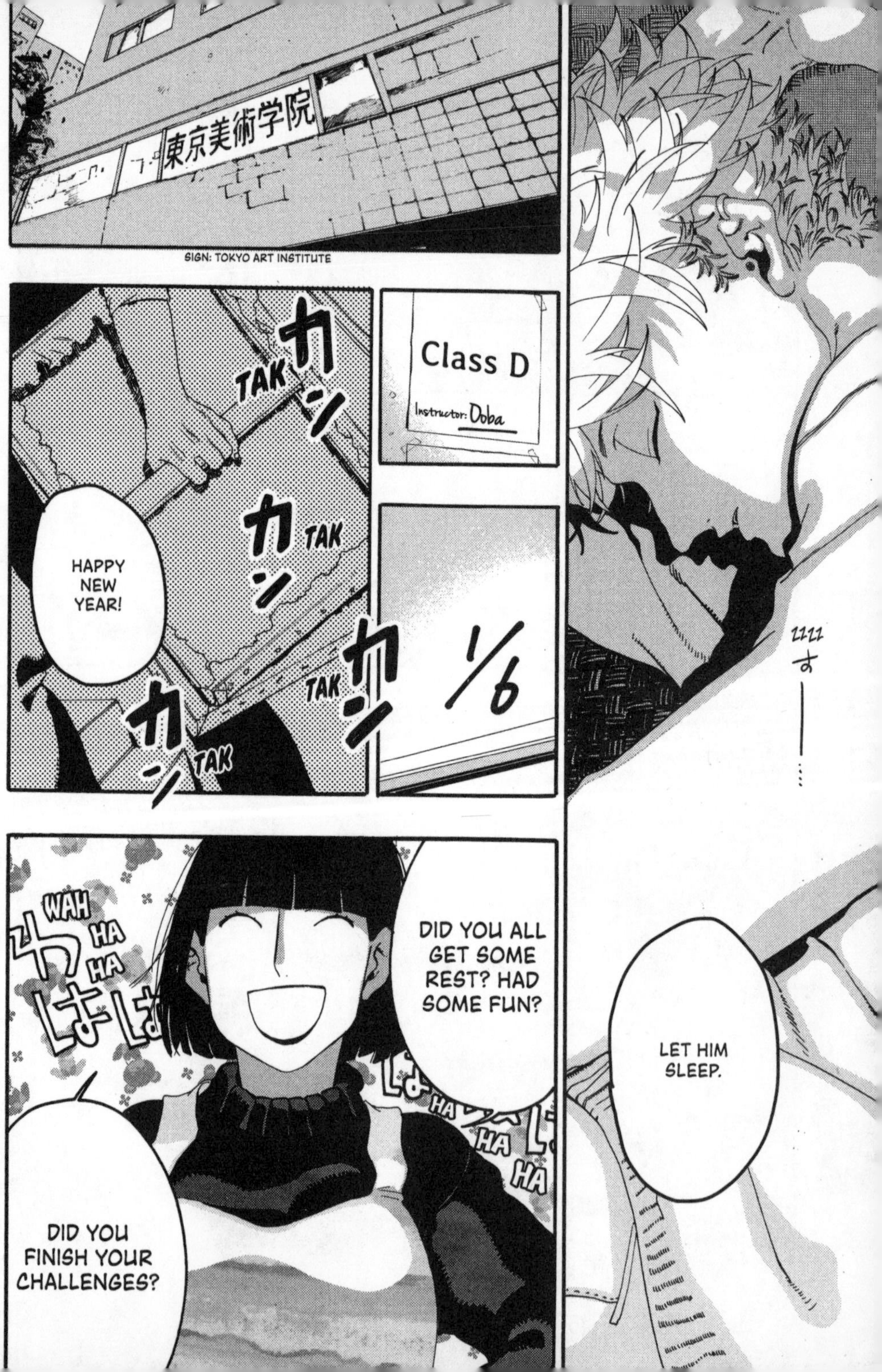
ZZZZ
す—…
LET HIM SLEEP.
東京美術学院
SIGN: TOKYO ART INSTITUTE
Class D
Instructor: Doba
1/6
カン TAK
カン TAK
カン TAK
カン TAK
HAPPY NEW YEAR!
DID YOU ALL GET SOME REST? HAD SOME FUN?
WAH HA HA
HA HA HA
DID YOU FINISH YOUR CHALLENGES?

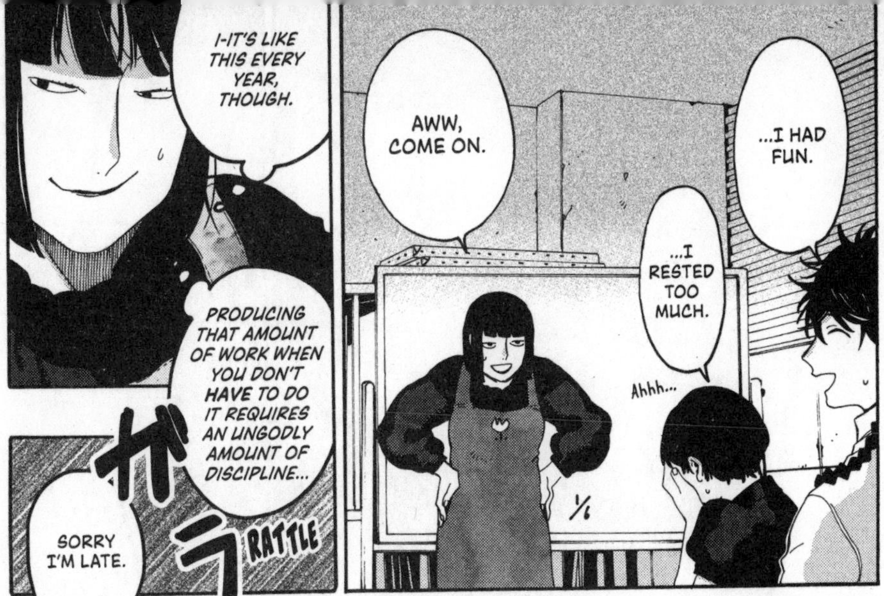
...I HAD FUN.
...I RESTED TOO MUCH.
Ahhh...
AWW, COME ON.
I-IT'S LIKE THIS EVERY YEAR, THOUGH.
PRODUCING THAT AMOUNT OF WORK WHEN YOU DON'T HAVE TO DO IT REQUIRES AN UNGODLY AMOUNT OF DISCIPLINE...
ガラ
RATTLE
SORRY I'M LATE.

ART: SHOTA YAMAMICHI

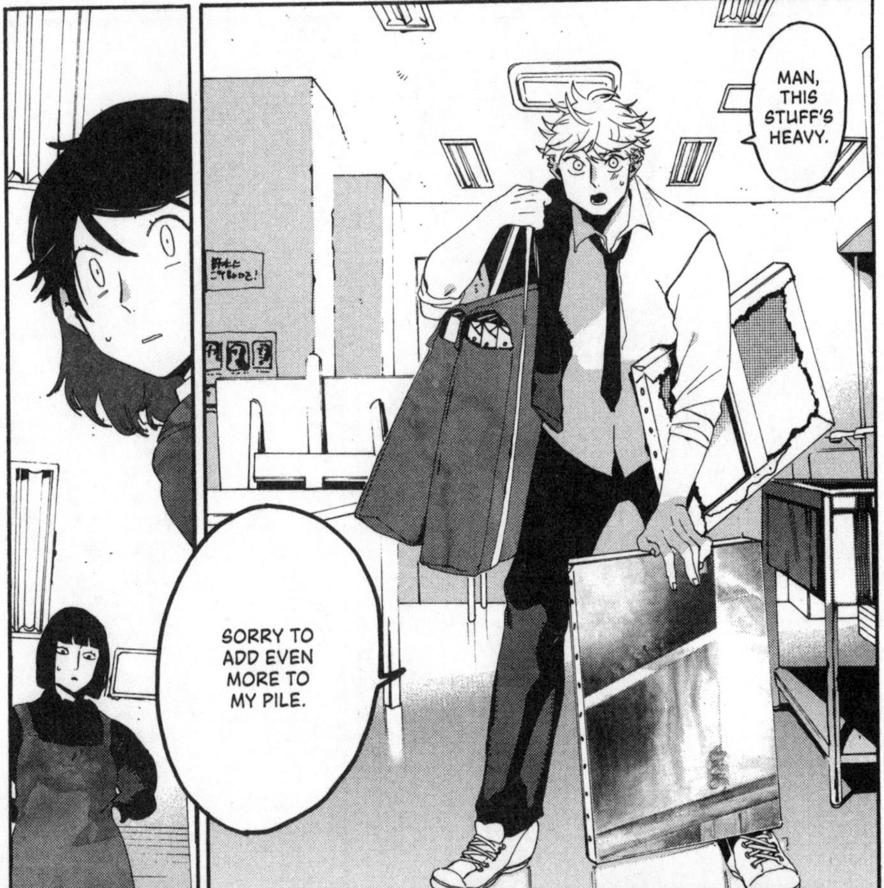
MAN, THIS STUFF'S HEAVY.
SORRY TO ADD EVEN MORE TO MY PILE.

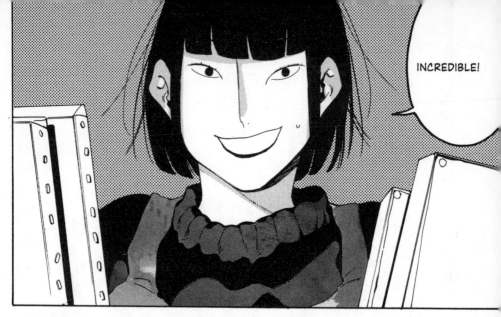

INCREDIBLE!
THANK YOU VERY MUCH.
YUP! JUST GREAT!
TNK
KA-
YOU SEEM TO HAVE HAD TROUBLE WITH YOUR MATERIALS ON SOME OF THESE PIECES, BUT YOU REALLY CHALLENGED YOURSELF IN MANY WAYS.
Really! These are great!
THIS ONE IN PARTICULAR HAS SOME POTENTIAL.
HOW'D YOU GET THIS ROUGH TEXTURE?
A CHALK PENCIL.

ART: SHOTA YAMAMICHI

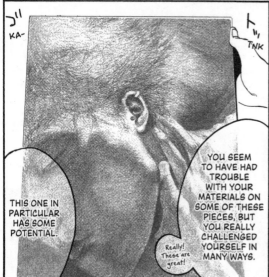

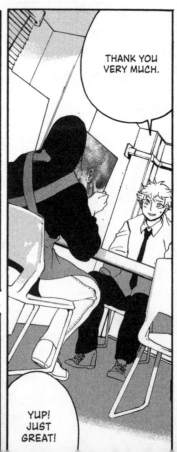

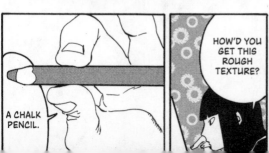

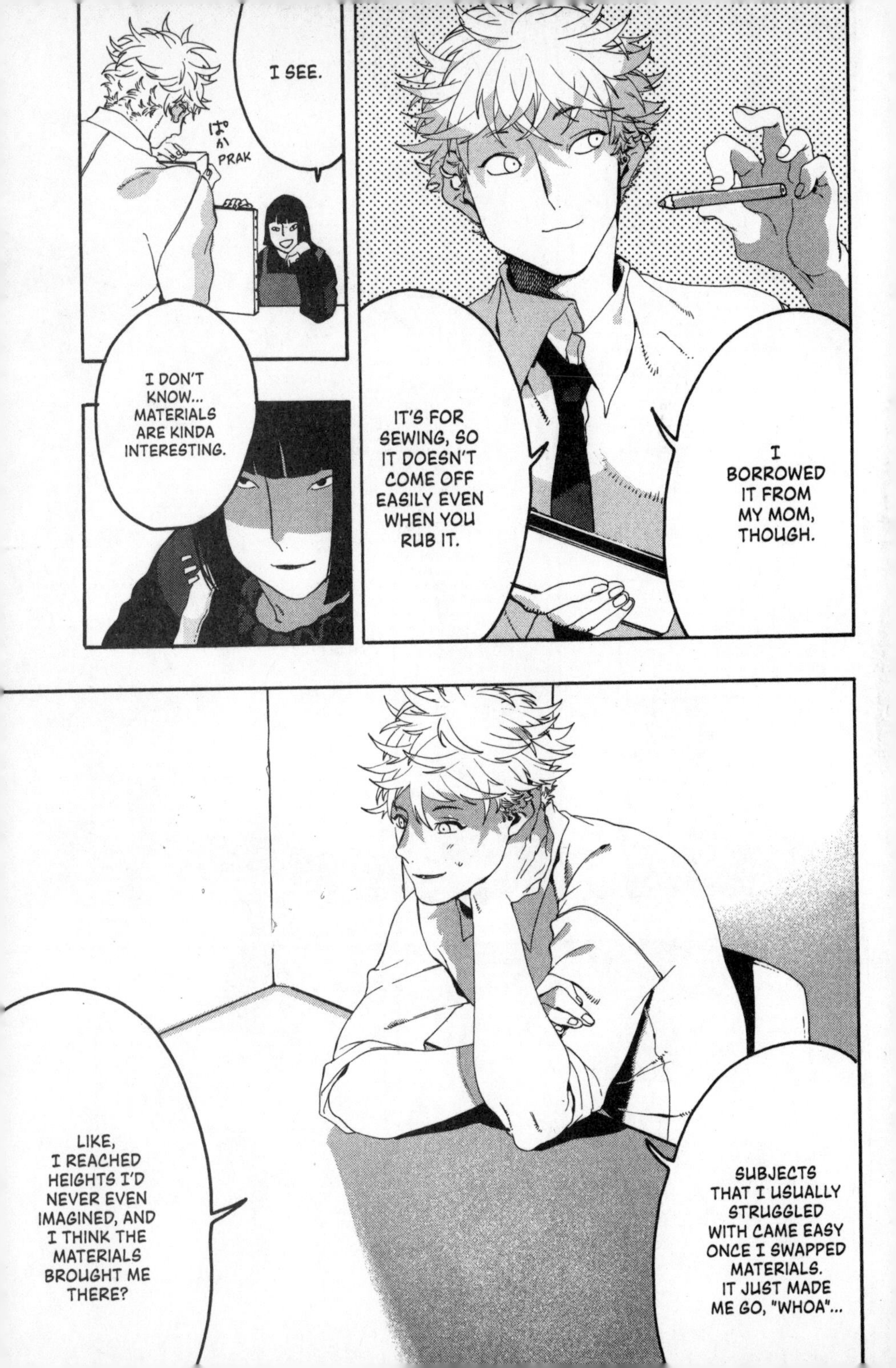

I BORROWED IT FROM MY MOM, THOUGH.
IT'S FOR SEWING, SO IT DOESN'T COME OFF EASILY EVEN WHEN YOU RUB IT.
I SEE.
ぱか
PRAK
I DON'T KNOW... MATERIALS ARE KINDA INTERESTING.
SUBJECTS THAT I USUALLY STRUGGLED WITH CAME EASY ONCE I SWAPPED MATERIALS. IT JUST MADE ME GO, "WHOA"...
LIKE, I REACHED HEIGHTS I'D NEVER EVEN IMAGINED, AND I THINK THE MATERIALS BROUGHT ME THERE?

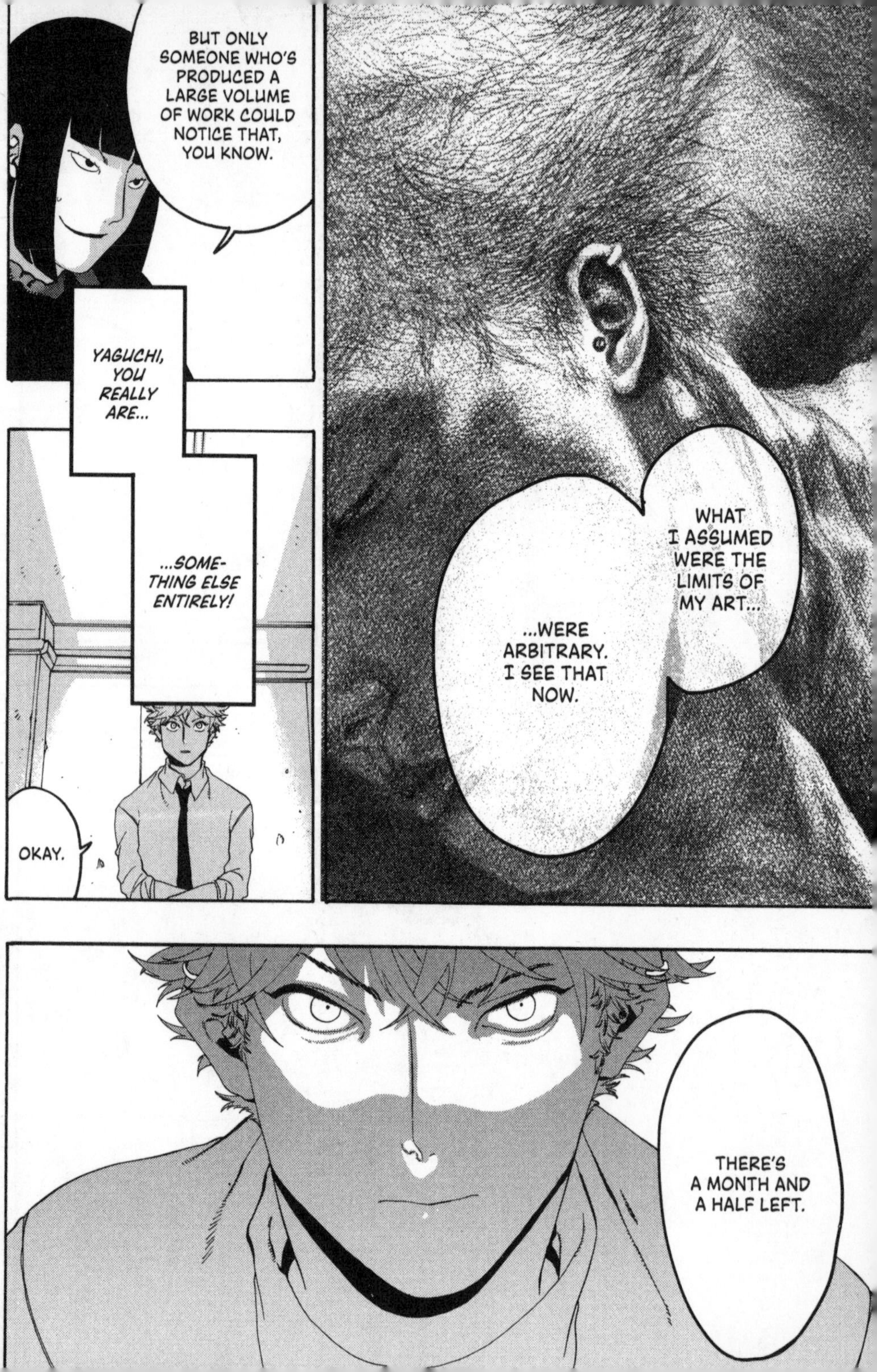
WHAT I ASSUMED WERE THE LIMITS OF MY ART...
...WERE ARBITRARY. I SEE THAT NOW.
BUT ONLY SOMEONE WHO'S PRODUCED A LARGE VOLUME OF WORK COULD NOTICE THAT, YOU KNOW.
YAGUCHI, YOU REALLY ARE...
...SOME-THING ELSE ENTIRELY!
OKAY.
THERE'S A MONTH AND A HALF LEFT.

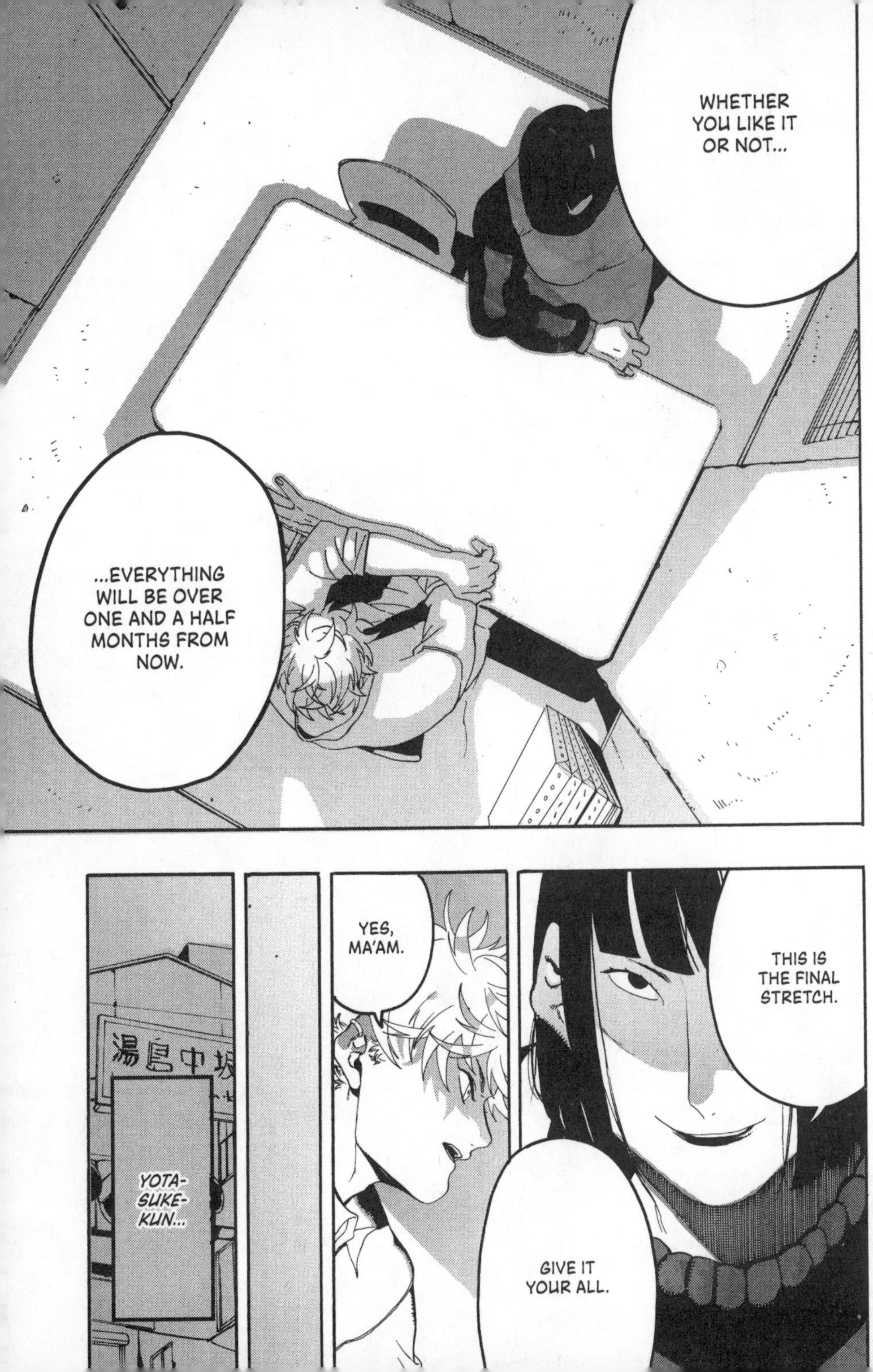
WHETHER YOU LIKE IT OR NOT...
...EVERYTHING WILL BE OVER ONE AND A HALF MONTHS FROM NOW.
THIS IS THE FINAL STRETCH.
GIVE IT YOUR ALL.
YES, MA'AM.
YOTA-SUKE-KUN...

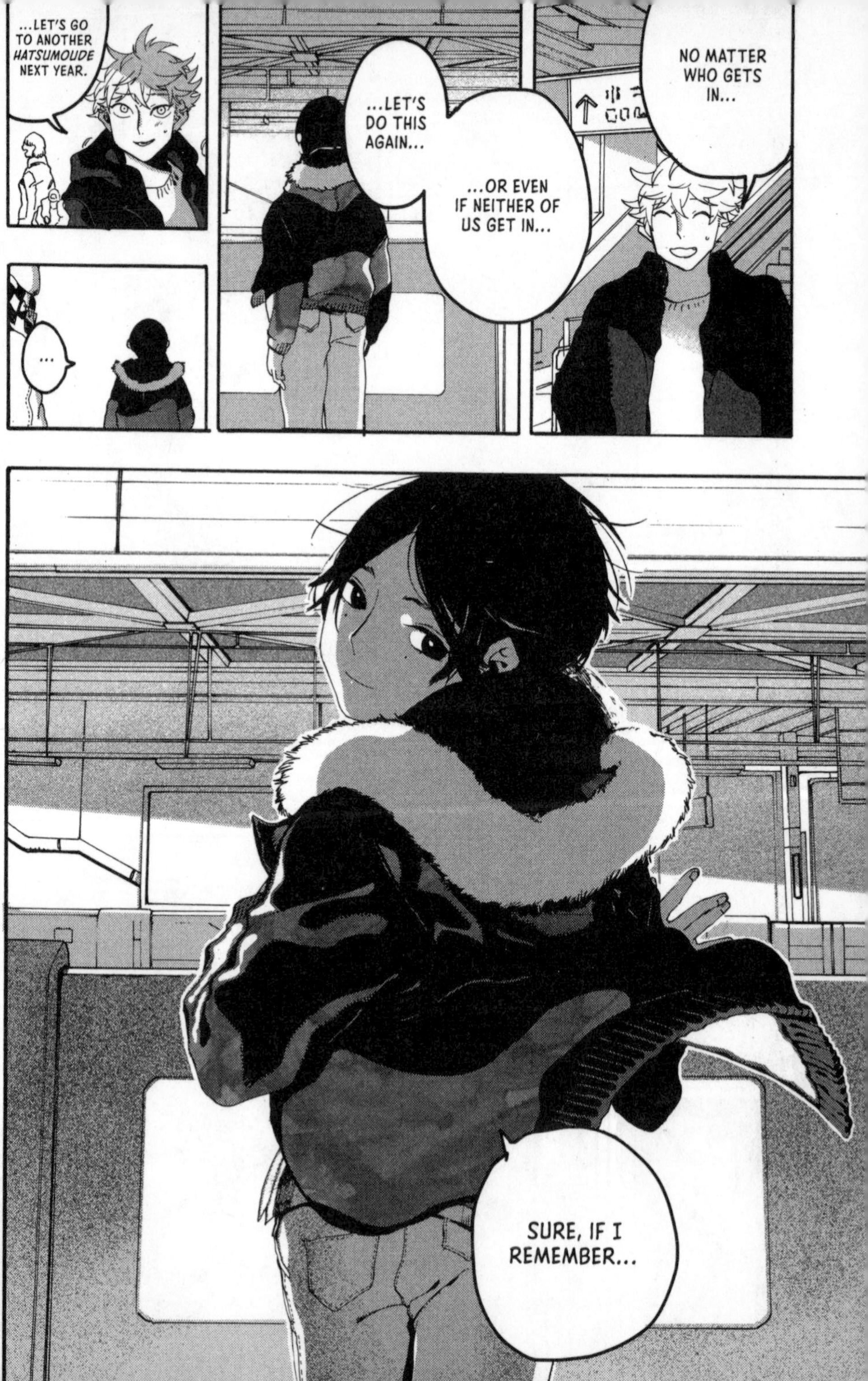
NO MATTER WHO GETS IN...
...OR EVEN IF NEITHER OF US GET IN...
...LET'S DO THIS AGAIN...
...LET'S GO TO ANOTHER *HATSUMOUDE* NEXT YEAR.
...
SURE, IF I REMEMBER...

STROKE 12 END

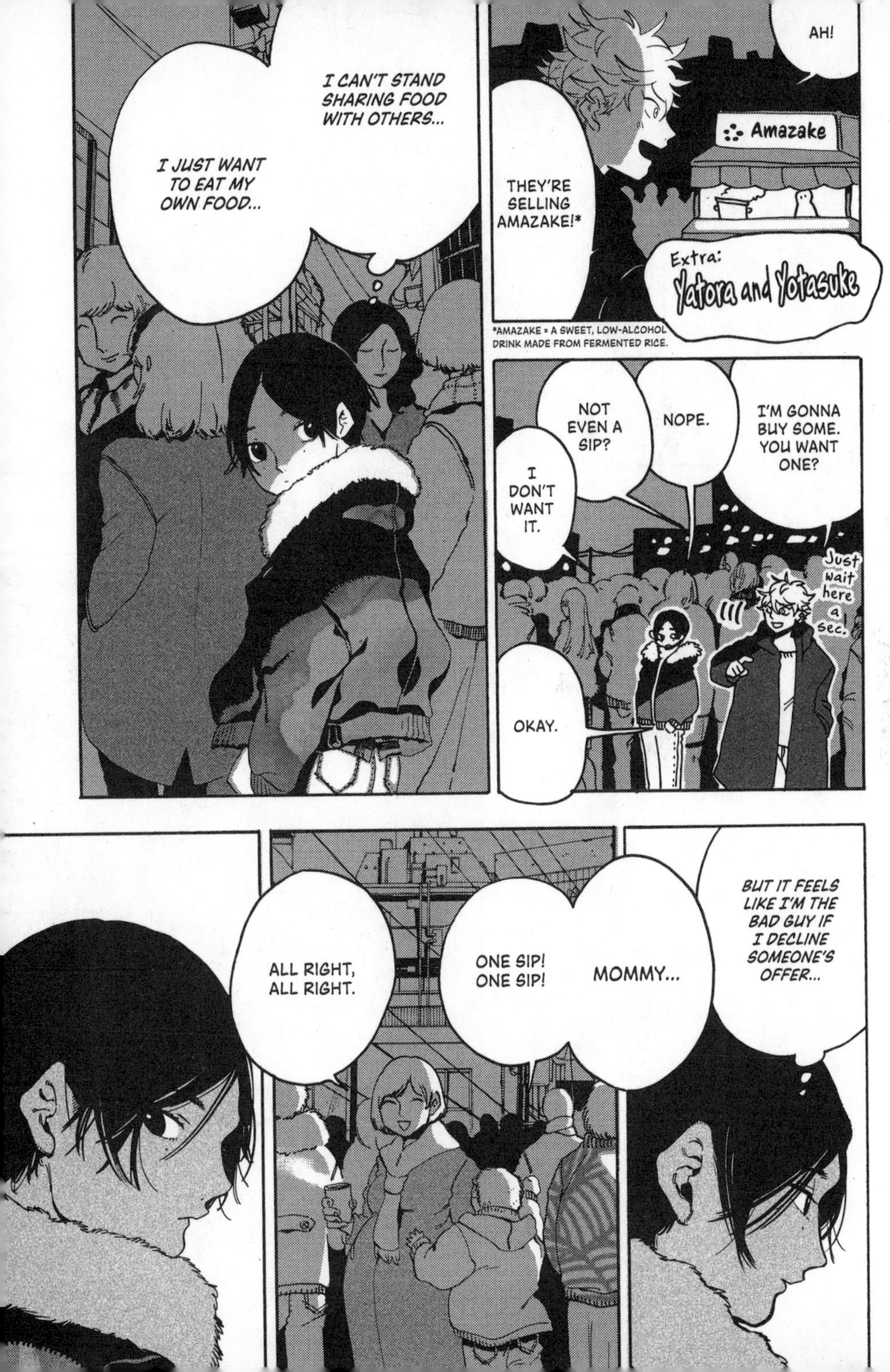
AH!
Amazake
THEY'RE SELLING AMAZAKE!*
Extra: Yatora and Yotasuke
*AMAZAKE = A SWEET, LOW-ALCOHOL DRINK MADE FROM FERMENTED RICE.
I'M GONNA BUY SOME. YOU WANT ONE?
NOPE.
NOT EVEN A SIP?
I DON'T WANT IT.
Just wait here a sec.
OKAY.
I CAN'T STAND SHARING FOOD WITH OTHERS...
I JUST WANT TO EAT MY OWN FOOD...
BUT IT FEELS LIKE I'M THE BAD GUY IF I DECLINE SOMEONE'S OFFER...
MOMMY...
ONE SIP! ONE SIP!
ALL RIGHT, ALL RIGHT.

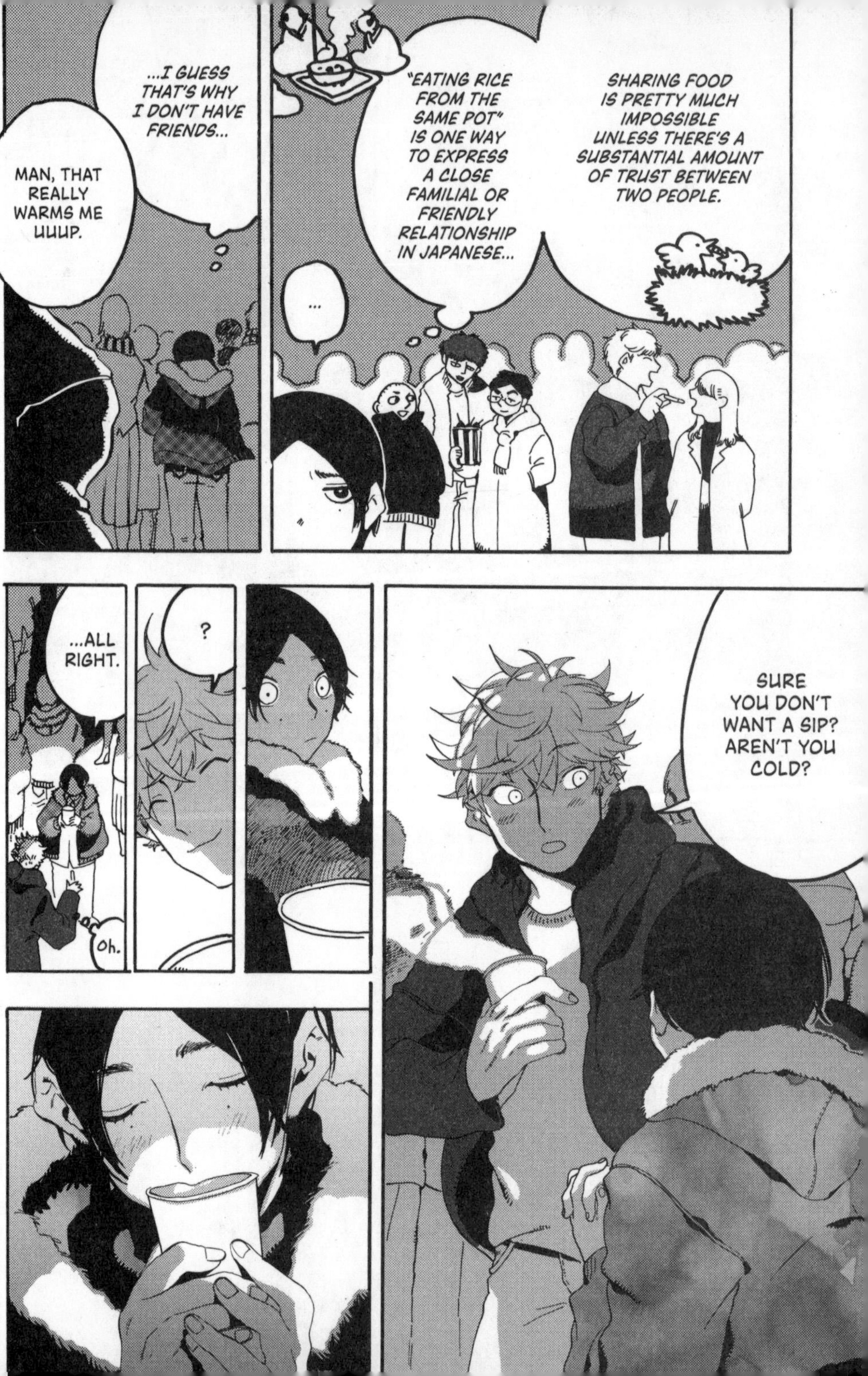

SHARING FOOD IS PRETTY MUCH IMPOSSIBLE UNLESS THERE'S A SUBSTANTIAL AMOUNT OF TRUST BETWEEN TWO PEOPLE.
"EATING RICE FROM THE SAME POT" IS ONE WAY TO EXPRESS A CLOSE FAMILIAL OR FRIENDLY RELATIONSHIP IN JAPANESE...
...
...I GUESS THAT'S WHY I DON'T HAVE FRIENDS...
MAN, THAT REALLY WARMS ME UUUP.
SURE YOU DON'T WANT A SIP? AREN'T YOU COLD?
?
...ALL RIGHT.
Oh.

SOUNDS BAD!

AMAZAKE'S ONE OF THOSE THINGS YOU EITHER LOVE OR HATE.

UGHHHH!

NGHHHHHH...

Blue Period was created with the support of many people!

Special Thanks

Thank you so very much!

Shota Yamamichi-san
Thank you so much this time, too! I can have a lot of fun drawing thanks to you, Yamamichi-san...!

Aya Morita-san
Morita-saaan! Thank you for your precious work! The impact of the real thing is incredible, so I hope that the readers can see it in an exhibition.

Hazuki Suzuki-san
Thank you for letting me borrow your valuable work...! Let's grab some brain curry again sometime...!

Marimo Tomori-san
Congrats on getting published! I'm looking forward to "Hansuke's Gourmet Album"! Let's both do our best...and exercise...!

Shiori Eda-san
Thank you for your precious work! This was a really impactful piece during exams, so I'm glad that I could use it here.

Assistants: Marimo Tomori-san, Maiko Saki-san, Nishi Aikawa-san, Asuma Sato-san
Editors: Y. Kawamura-san, S. Furihata-san

TRANSLATION NOTES

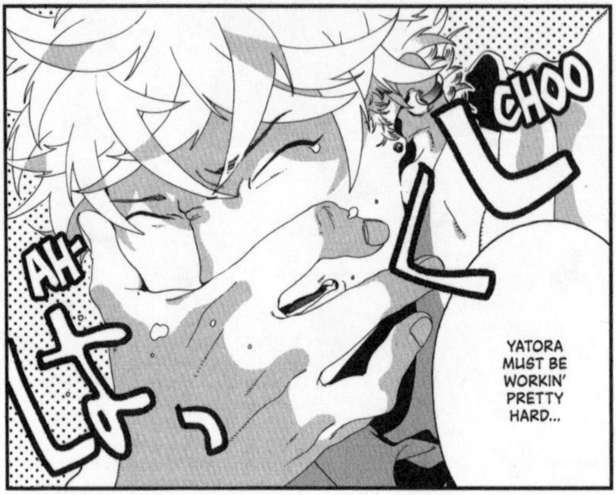
CHOO
YATORA MUST BE WORKIN' PRETTY HARD...
AH-

Sneezing, page 3
In Japan, a common superstition associated with sneezing is that doing so signifies someone talking or gossiping about you. Depending on how many times you sneeze, the contents of that chatter could be good or bad, but beyond the specifics, in manga, it can also be used to transition from one scene to another.

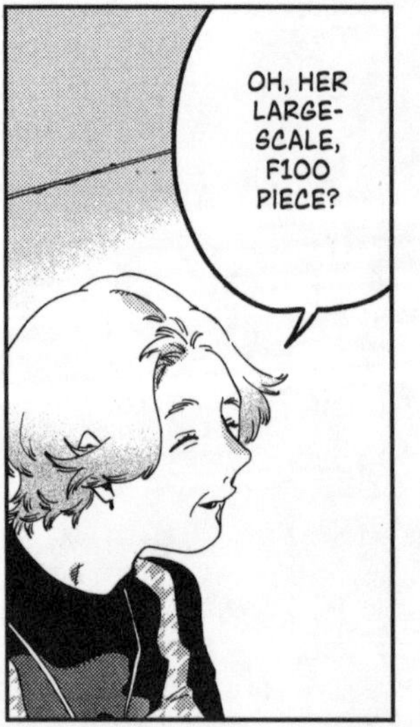
OH, HER LARGE-SCALE, F100 PIECE?

F100, page 42
F100 refers to one of several painting sizes that were standard in the art world in the time of Van Gogh (the 19th century). The sizes run from size 0 to 120, and the letter in front of the size represents a different width and subject that the painting will be used for—F for figure, P for landscapes (*paysage*), M for marines, and S for square, which seems to be an addition exclusive to Japan. When this system was brought to Japan, the measurements were expressed in Japanese *shaku*, and after being converted back to centimeters, the current sizes are slightly different from the original French sizes. A Japanese F100 is 162 cm x 130.3 cm.

Hydrogen water, page 71
Hydrogen water is regular water that has been infused with extra hydrogen, hence the chemistry association to "bonds." There are claims that this water has health benefits that may improve one's quality of life, and for that reason, hydrogen water has enjoyed some popularity in Japan. Hydrogen water has also been associated with multi-level marketing schemes and can connote people who are into "alternative" medicine, which is why the invitation to reconsider their "bonds" also makes Maki suspect that Yatora might be into hydrogen water.

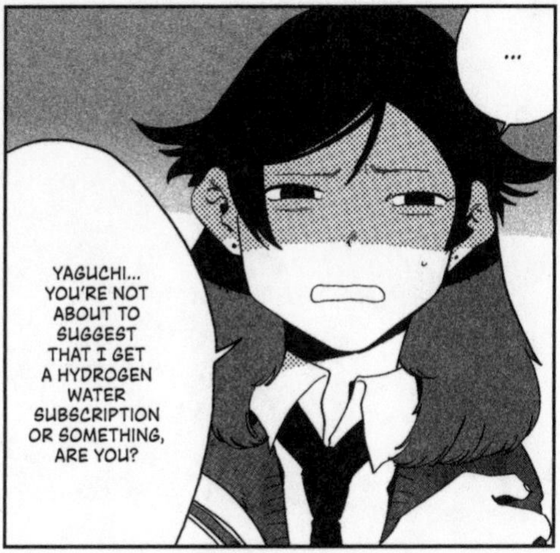
...
YAGUCHI... YOU'RE NOT ABOUT TO SUGGEST THAT I GET A HYDROGEN WATER SUBSCRIPTION OR SOMETHING, ARE YOU?

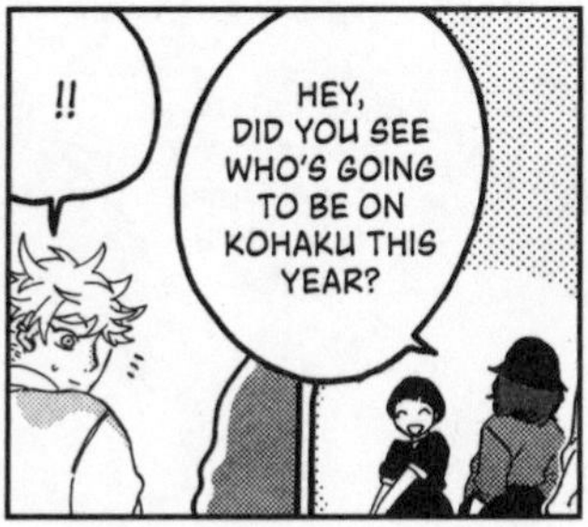
HEY, DID YOU SEE WHO'S GOING TO BE ON KOHAKU THIS YEAR?
!!

Kohaku, page 155
Kohaku refers to *NHK Kohaku Uta Gassen*, a long-running television special that is broadcast on NHK (Japan's PBS) on New Year's Eve. It features musical performances from the most popular musical artists in Japan at the time, and the artists on the show compete to be the best performers on one of two teams: the red team or the white team.

◄ KAMOME ►
SHIRAHAMA

Witch Hat Atelier

A magical manga
adventure for
fans of Disney
and Studio
Ghibli!

Witch Hat Atelier © Kamome Shirahama/Kodansha Ltd.

The magical adventure that took Japan by storm is finally here, from acclaimed DC and Marvel cover artist Kamome Shirahama!

In a world where everyone takes wonders like magic spells and dragons for granted, Coco is a girl with a simple dream: She wants to be a witch. But everybody knows magicians are born, not made, and Coco was not born with a gift for magic. Resigned to her un-magical life, Coco is about to give up on her dream to become a witch…until the day she meets Qifrey, a mysterious, traveling magician. After secretly seeing Qifrey perform magic in a way she's never seen before, Coco soon learns what everybody "knows" might not be the truth, and discovers that her magical dream may not be as far away as it may seem…

SAINT ☆ YOUNG MEN

A LONG AWAITED ARRIVAL IN PREMIUM 2-IN-1 HARDCOVER

After centuries of hard work, Jesus and Buddha take a break from their
heavenly duties to relax among the people of Japan, and their adventures in this
lighthearted buddy comedy are sure to bring mirth and merriment to all!

"Brilliant…the physical comedy
and facial expressions will
make you literally LOL."
—Sam Humphries
(host of *DC Daily*;
writer, *Green Lanterns,
Legendary Star-Lord*)

KC
KODANSHA
COMICS

complex age

yui sakuma

26-year-old Nagisa Kataura has a secret. Transforming into her favorite anime and manga characters is her passion in life, and she's earned great respect amongst her fellow cospayers. But to the rest of society, her hobby is a silly fantasy. As demands from both her office job and cosplaying begin to increase, she may one day have to make a tough choice— what's more important to her, cosplay or being "normal"?

PERFECT WORLD

Rie Aruga

A TOUCHING NEW SERIES ABOUT LOVE AND COPING WITH DISABILITY

An office party reunites Tsugumi with her high school crush Itsuki. He's realized his dream of becoming an architect, but along the way, he experienced a spinal injury that put him in a wheelchair. Now Tsugumi's rekindled feelings will butt up against prejudices she never considered — and Itsuki will have to decide if he's ready to let someone into his heart...

"Depicts with great delicacy and courage the difficulties some with disabilities experience getting involved in romantic relationships... Rie Aruga refuses to romanticize, pushing her heroine to face the reality of disability. She invites her readers to the same tasks of empathy, knowledge and recognition."
—Slate.fr

"An important entry [in manga romance]... The emotional core of both plot and characters indicates thoughtfulness... [Aruga's] research is readily apparent in the text and artwork, making this feel like a real story."
—Anime News Network

Princess Jellyfish

Akiko Higashimura

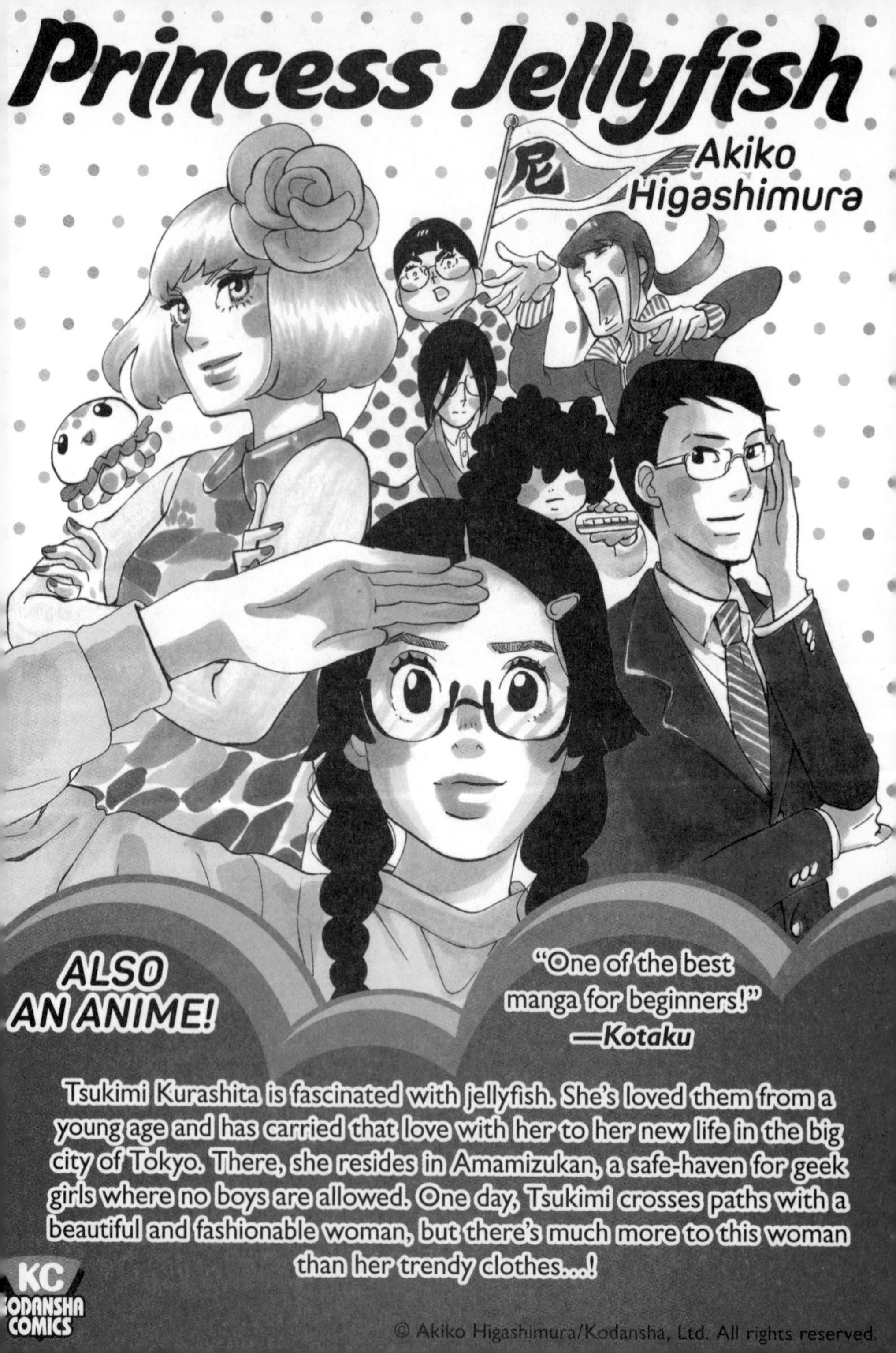

ALSO AN ANIME!

"One of the best manga for beginners!"
—*Kotaku*

Tsukimi Kurashita is fascinated with jellyfish. She's loved them from a young age and has carried that love with her to her new life in the big city of Tokyo. There, she resides in Amamizukan, a safe-haven for geek girls where no boys are allowed. One day, Tsukimi crosses paths with a beautiful and fashionable woman, but there's much more to this woman than her trendy clothes...!

KC KODANSHA COMICS

OTOMO 大友克洋

A GLOBAL TRIBUTE TO THE MIND BEHIND AKIRA

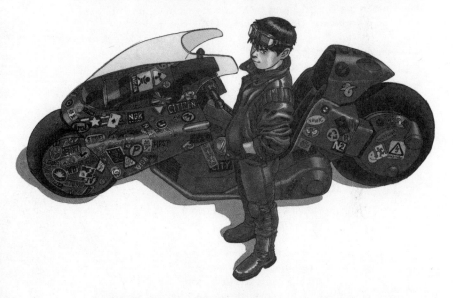

A celebration of manga legend Katsuhiro Otomo from more than 80
world-renowned fine artists and comics legends
With contributions from:
- Stan Sakai
- Tomer and Asaf Hanuka
- Sara Pichelli
- Range Murata
- Aleksi Briclot
And more!
168 pages of stunning, full-color art

A Kodansha Comics Trade Paperback Original
Blue Period 3 copyright © 2018 Tsubasa Yamaguchi
English translation copyright © 2021 Tsubasa Yamaguchi

Published in the United States by Kodansha Comics, an imprint of Kodansha USA Publishing, LLC, New York.

Publication rights for this English edition arranged through Kodansha Ltd., Tokyo.

First published in Japan in 2018 by Kodansha Ltd., Tokyo.

ISBN 978-1-64651-125-9

Original cover design by Yohei Okashita (Inazuma Onsen)

Printed in the United States of America.

www.kodanshacomics.com

9 8 7 6 5 4 3 2 1
Translation: Ajani Oloye
Lettering: Lys Blakeslee
Editing: Haruko Hashimoto
Kodansha Comics edition cover design by Matthew Akuginow

Publisher: Kiichiro Sugawara

Director of publishing services: Ben Applegate
Associate director of operations: Stephen Pakula
Publishing services managing editor: Noelle Webster
Assistant production manager: Emi Lotto, Angela Zurlo
Logo and character art ©Kodansha USA Publishing, LLC

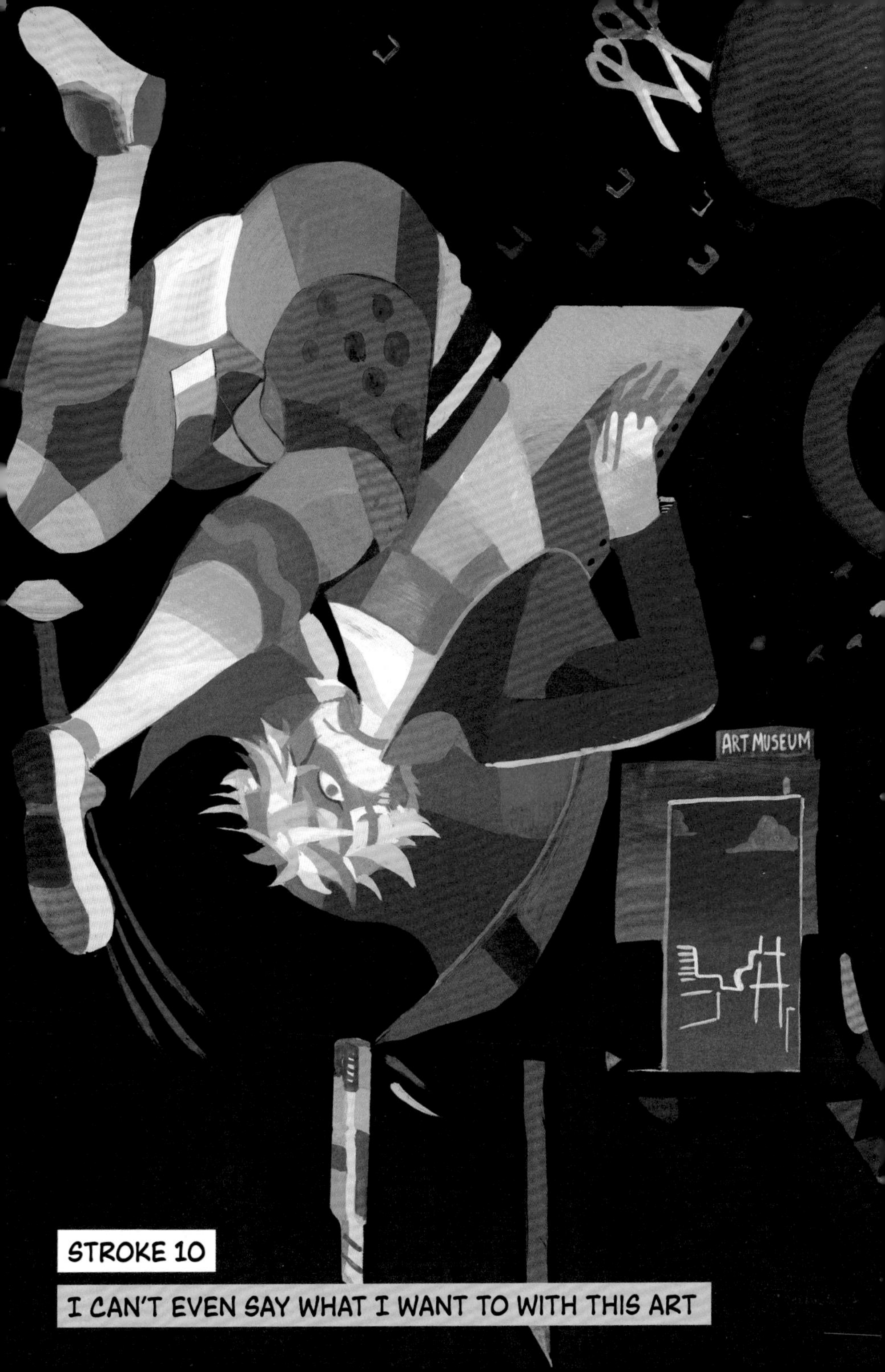
ART MUSEUM

STROKE 10

I CAN'T EVEN SAY WHAT I WANT TO WITH THIS ART

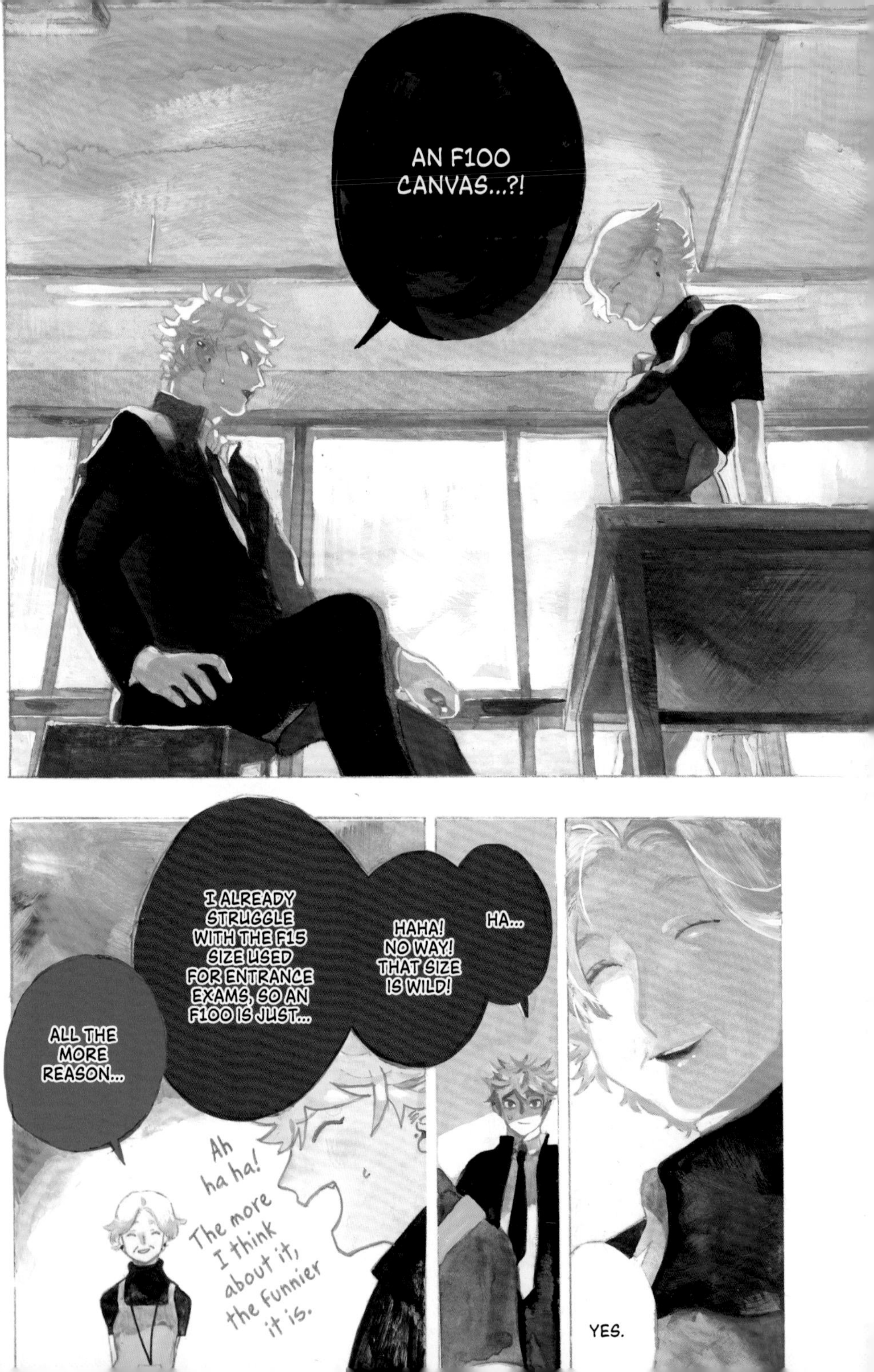
AN F100 CANVAS...?!
YES.
HA...
HAHA! NO WAY! THAT SIZE IS WILD!
I ALREADY STRUGGLE WITH THE F15 SIZE USED FOR ENTRANCE EXAMS, SO AN F100 IS JUST...
ALL THE MORE REASON...
Ah ha ha! The more I think about it, the funnier it is.

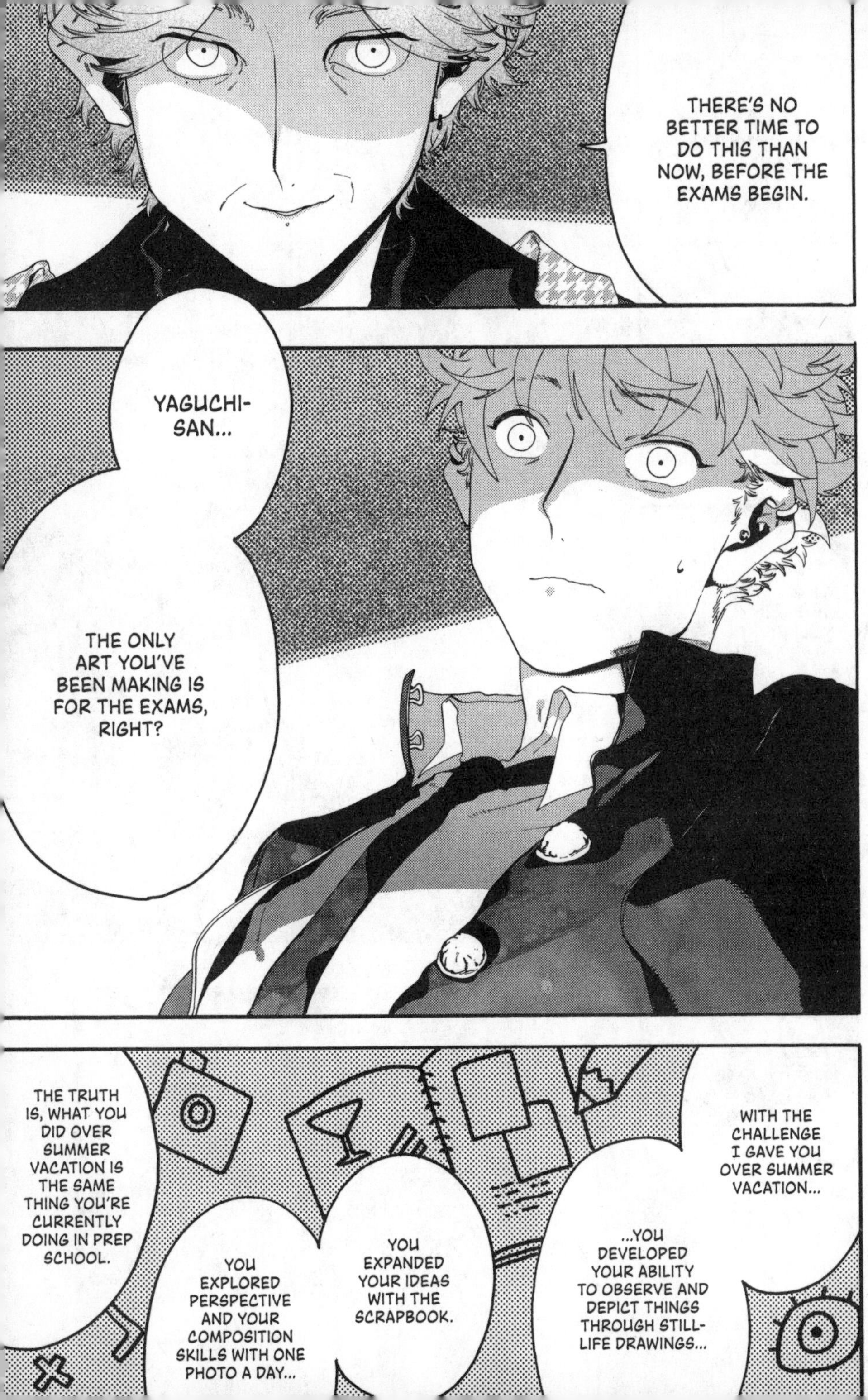
THERE'S NO BETTER TIME TO DO THIS THAN NOW, BEFORE THE EXAMS BEGIN.
YAGUCHI-SAN...
THE ONLY ART YOU'VE BEEN MAKING IS FOR THE EXAMS, RIGHT?
WITH THE CHALLENGE I GAVE YOU OVER SUMMER VACATION...
...YOU DEVELOPED YOUR ABILITY TO OBSERVE AND DEPICT THINGS THROUGH STILL-LIFE DRAWINGS...
YOU EXPANDED YOUR IDEAS WITH THE SCRAPBOOK.
YOU EXPLORED PERSPECTIVE AND YOUR COMPOSITION SKILLS WITH ONE PHOTO A DAY...
THE TRUTH IS, WHAT YOU DID OVER SUMMER VACATION IS THE SAME THING YOU'RE CURRENTLY DOING IN PREP SCHOOL.

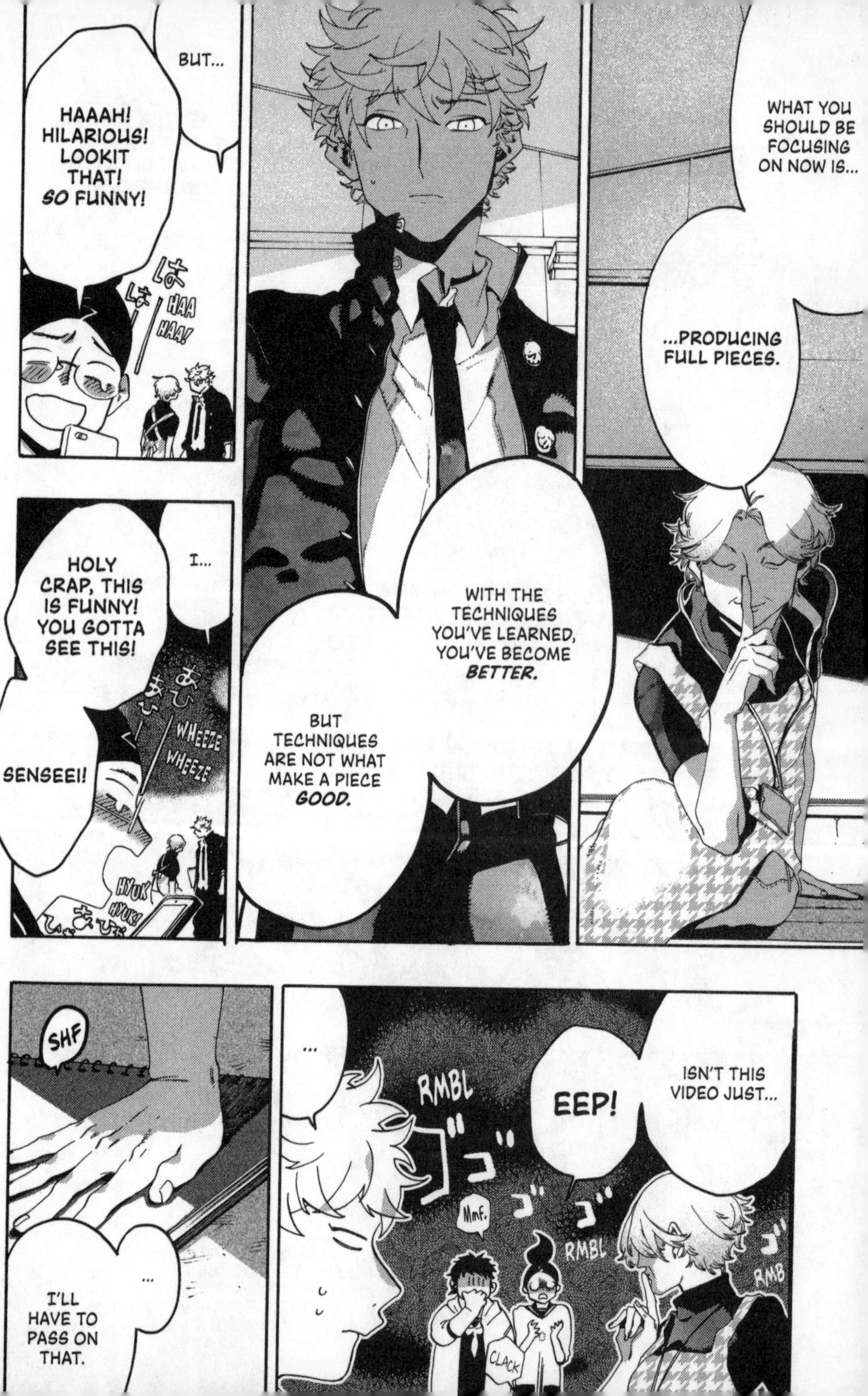
WHAT YOU SHOULD BE FOCUSING ON NOW IS...
...PRODUCING FULL PIECES.
WITH THE TECHNIQUES YOU'VE LEARNED, YOU'VE BECOME *BETTER.*
BUT TECHNIQUES ARE NOT WHAT MAKE A PIECE *GOOD.*
BUT...
HAAAH! HILARIOUS! LOOKIT THAT! *SO* FUNNY!
HAA HAA!
I...
HOLY CRAP, THIS IS FUNNY! YOU GOTTA SEE THIS!
SENSEI!
WHEEZE WHEEZE
HYUK HYUK!
ISN'T THIS VIDEO JUST...
EEP!
RMBL
...
Mmf.
RMBL
RMB
CLACK
SHF
...
I'LL HAVE TO PASS ON THAT.

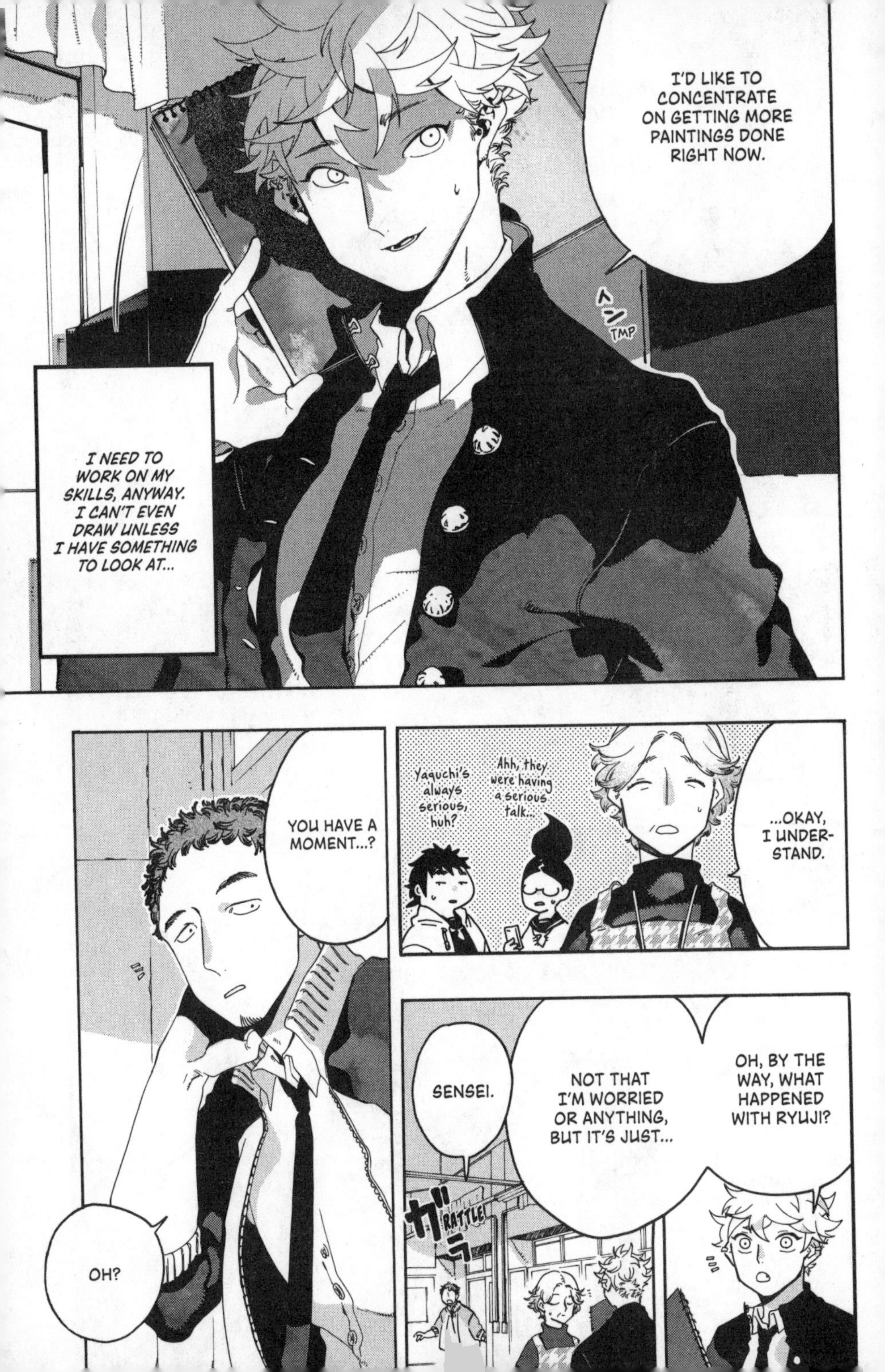
I'D LIKE TO CONCENTRATE ON GETTING MORE PAINTINGS DONE RIGHT NOW.
TMP
I NEED TO WORK ON MY SKILLS, ANYWAY. I CAN'T EVEN DRAW UNLESS I HAVE SOMETHING TO LOOK AT...
...OKAY, I UNDERSTAND.
Ahh, they were having a serious talk...
Yaguchi's always serious, huh?
OH, BY THE WAY, WHAT HAPPENED WITH RYUJI?
NOT THAT I'M WORRIED OR ANYTHING, BUT IT'S JUST...
SENSEI.
RATTLE
YOU HAVE A MOMENT...?
OH?

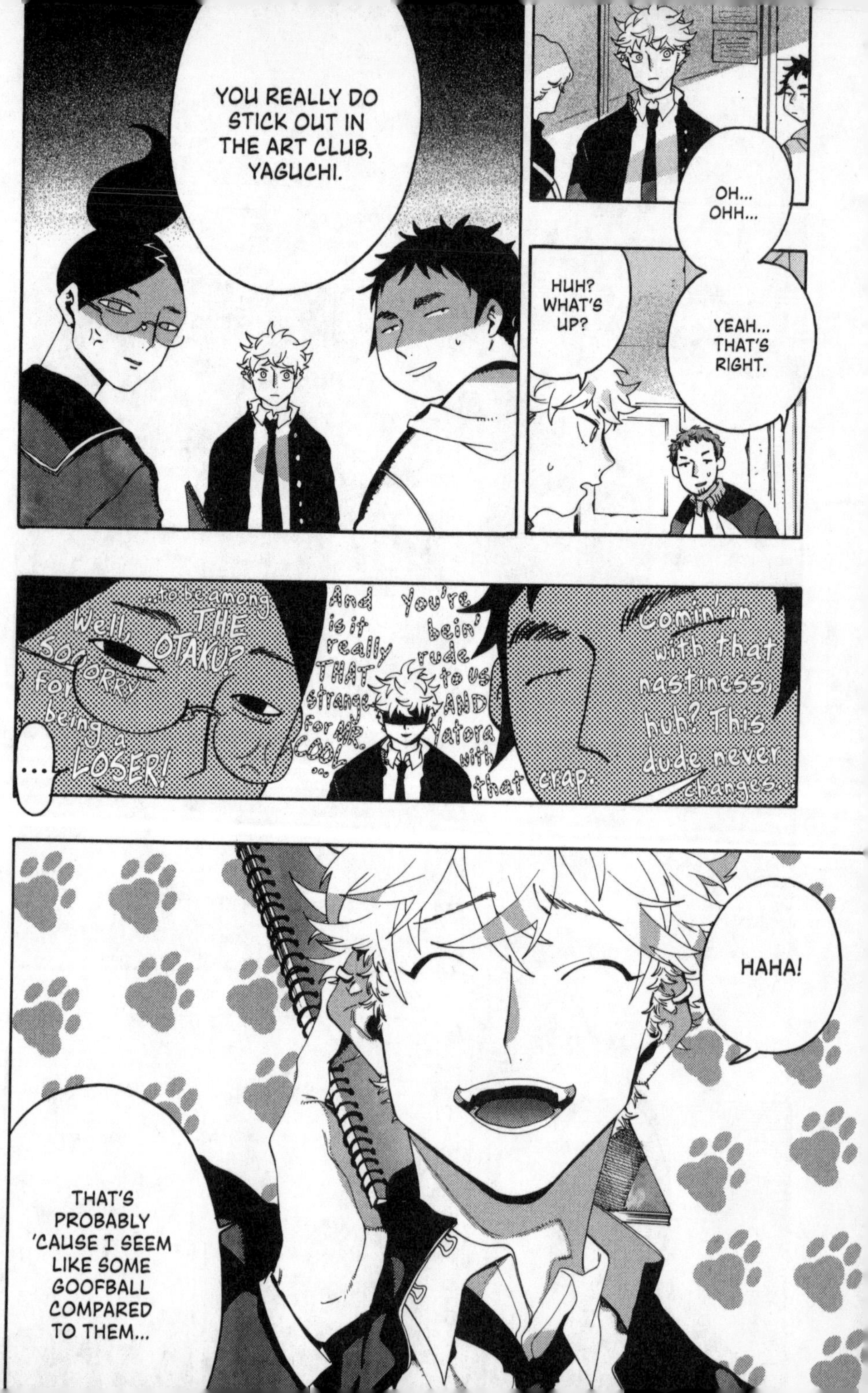
OH... OHH... YEAH... THAT'S RIGHT.
HUH? WHAT'S UP?
YOU REALLY DO STICK OUT IN THE ART CLUB, YAGUCHI.
Comin' in with that nastiness, huh? This dude never changes...
You're bein' rude to us AND Yatora with that crap.
And is it really THAT strange for MR. COOL...
...to be among THE OTAKU?
Well, SOOORRY for being a LOSER!
...
HAHA!
THAT'S PROBABLY 'CAUSE I SEEM LIKE SOME GOOFBALL COMPARED TO THEM...

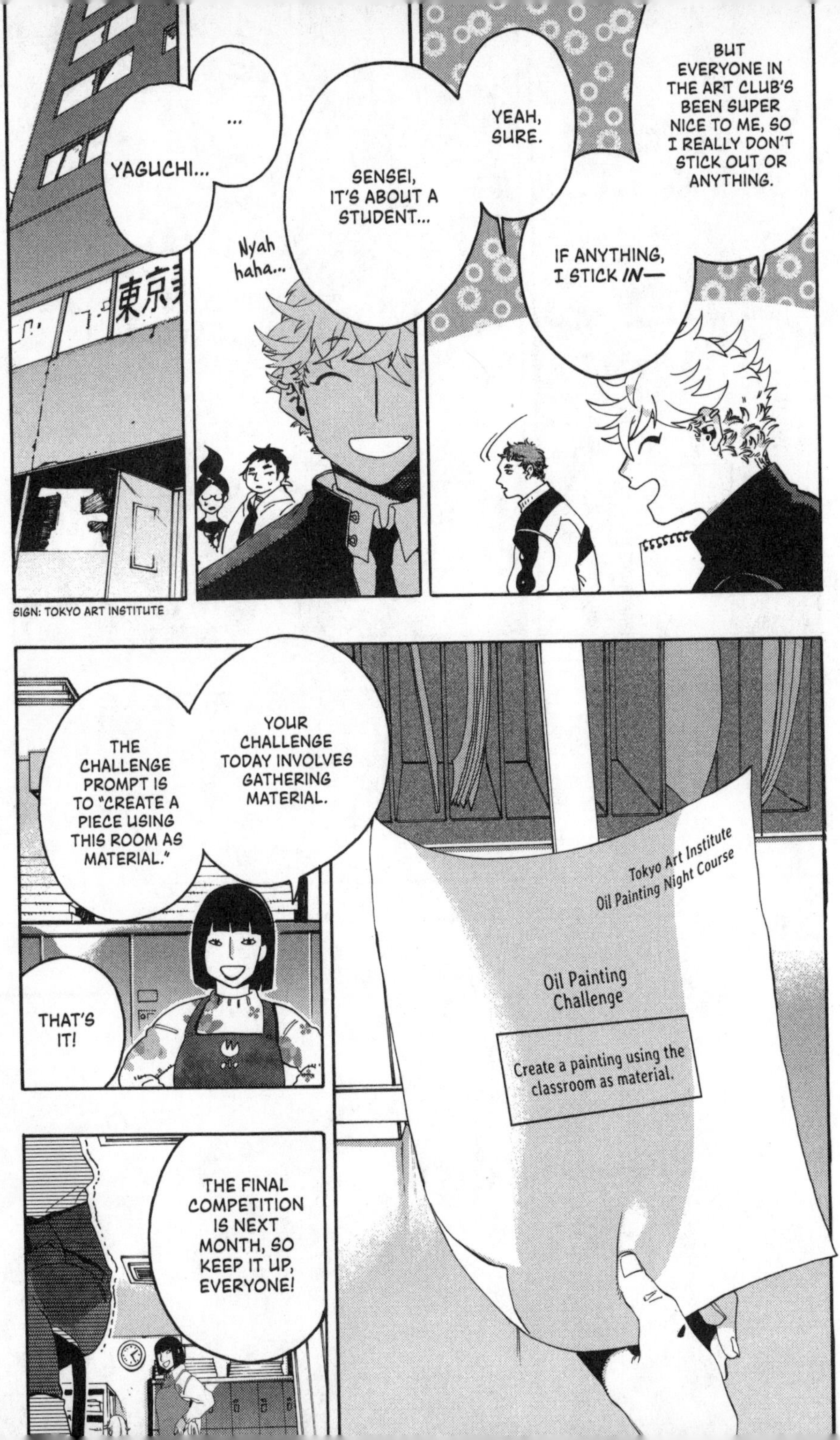
BUT EVERYONE IN THE ART CLUB'S BEEN SUPER NICE TO ME, SO I REALLY DON'T STICK OUT OR ANYTHING.
IF ANYTHING, I STICK *IN*—
YEAH, SURE.
SENSEI, IT'S ABOUT A STUDENT...
Nyah haha...
...
YAGUCHI...
東京美
SIGN: TOKYO ART INSTITUTE
Tokyo Art Institute
Oil Painting Night Course
Oil Painting Challenge
Create a painting using the classroom as material.
YOUR CHALLENGE TODAY INVOLVES GATHERING MATERIAL.
THE CHALLENGE PROMPT IS TO "CREATE A PIECE USING THIS ROOM AS MATERIAL."
THAT'S IT!
THE FINAL COMPETITION IS NEXT MONTH, SO KEEP IT UP, EVERYONE!

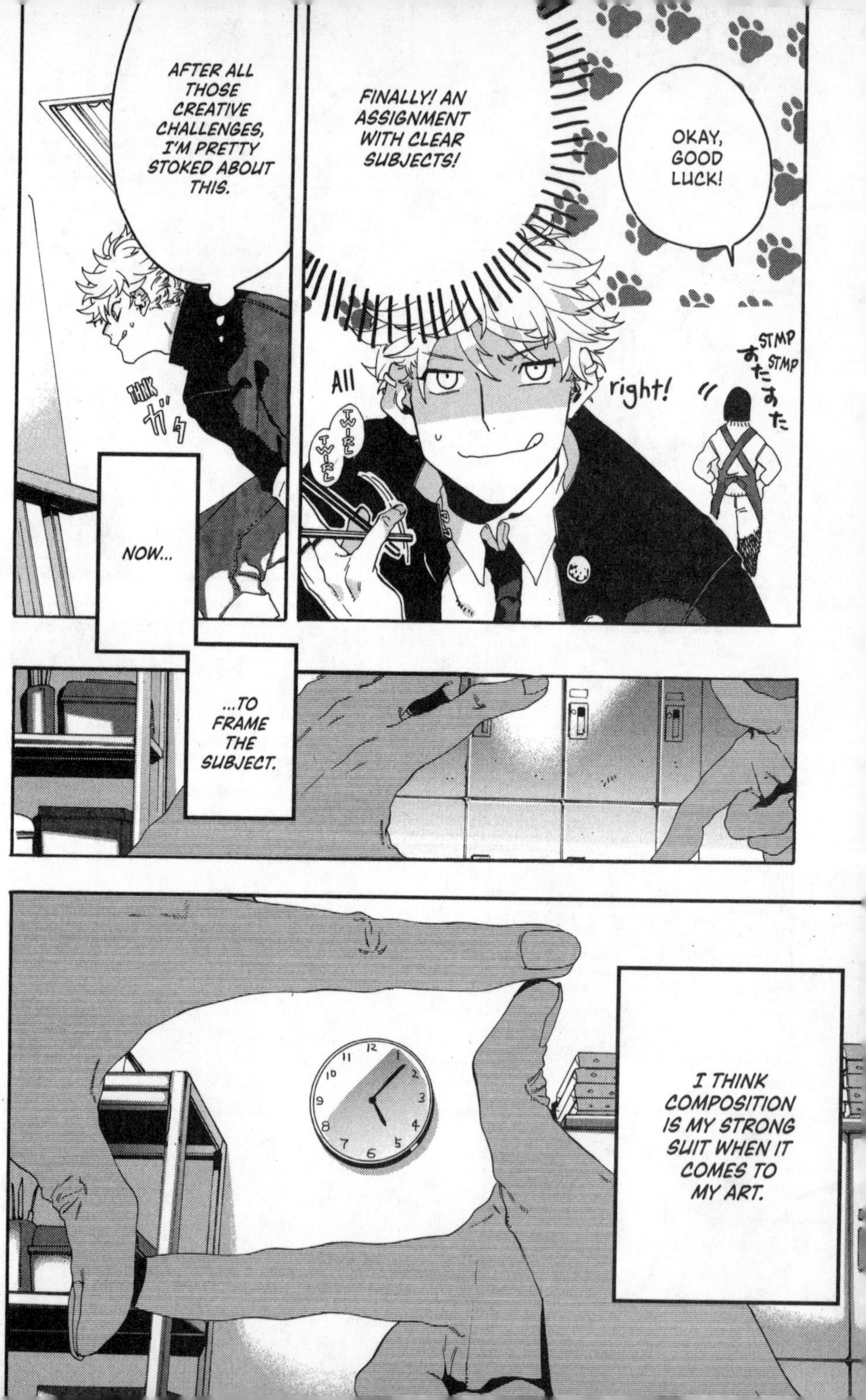
OKAY, GOOD LUCK!
STMP STMP
すたすた
FINALLY! AN ASSIGNMENT WITH CLEAR SUBJECTS!
All right!
TWIRL TWIRL
AFTER ALL THOSE CREATIVE CHALLENGES, I'M PRETTY STOKED ABOUT THIS.
THK
ガタ
NOW...
...TO FRAME THE SUBJECT.
I THINK COMPOSITION IS MY STRONG SUIT WHEN IT COMES TO MY ART.

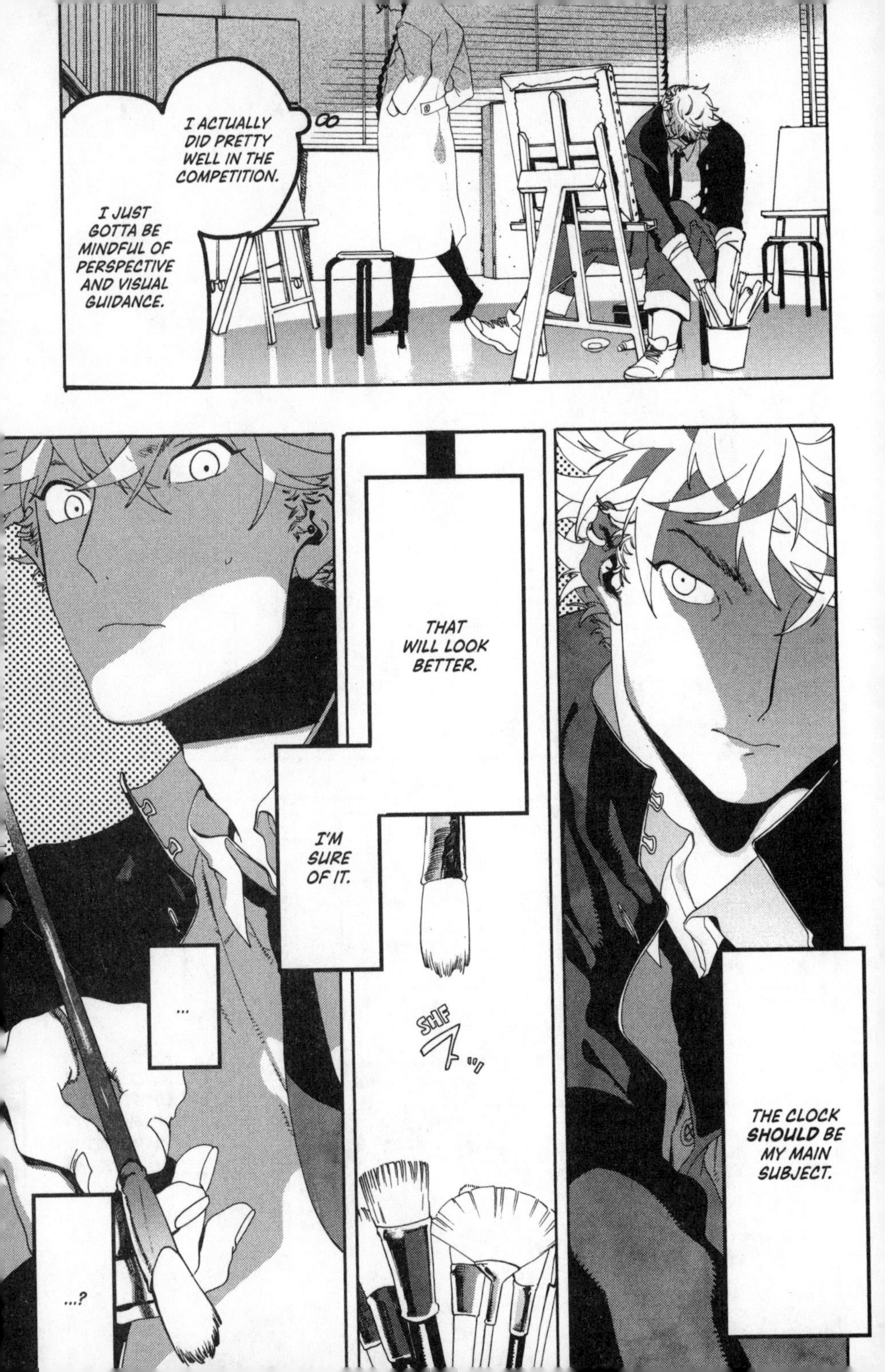
I ACTUALLY DID PRETTY WELL IN THE COMPETITION.
I JUST GOTTA BE MINDFUL OF PERSPECTIVE AND VISUAL GUIDANCE.
THE CLOCK SHOULD BE MY MAIN SUBJECT.
THAT WILL LOOK BETTER.
I'M SURE OF IT.
SHF
...
...?

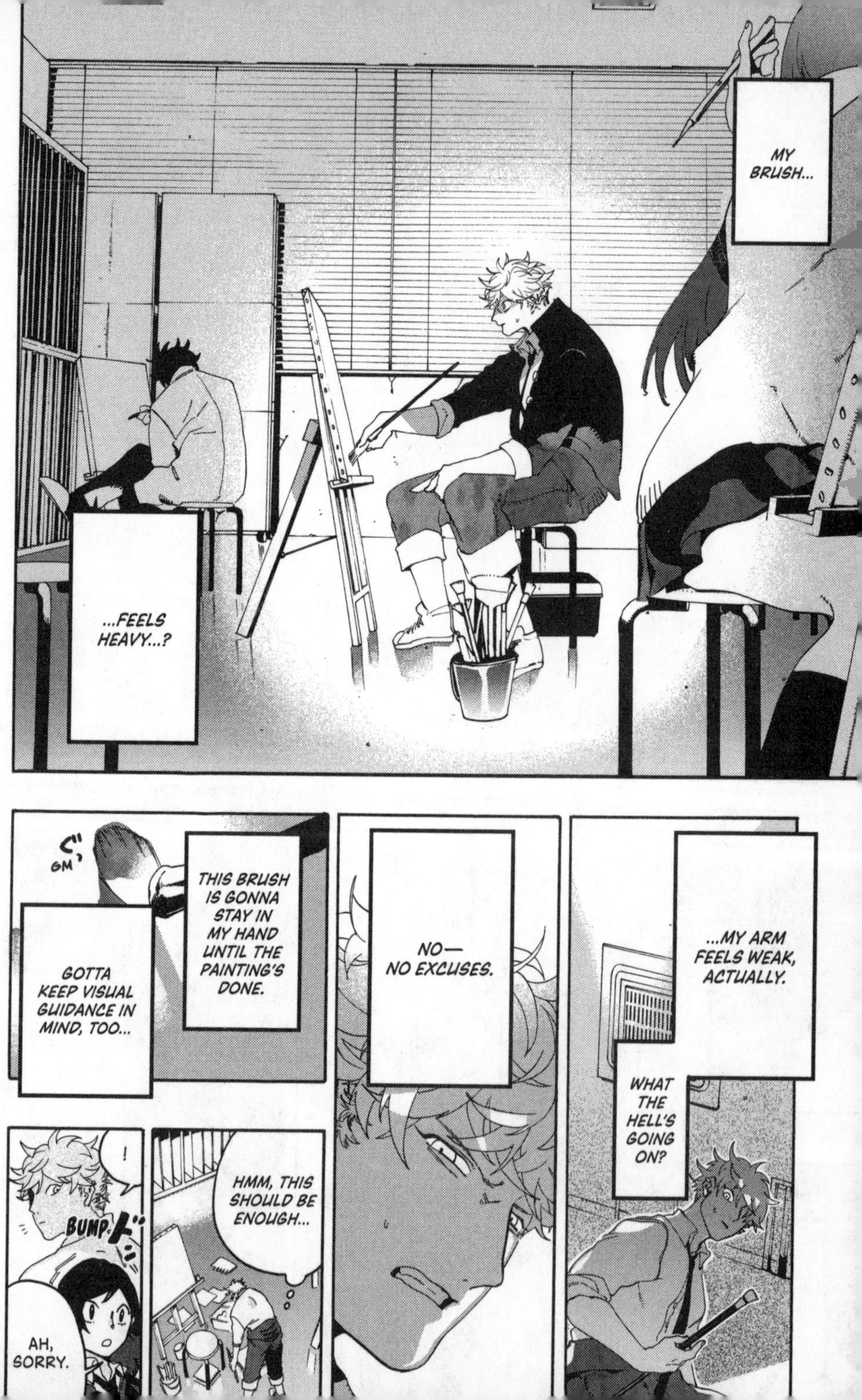
MY BRUSH...
...FEELS HEAVY...?
...MY ARM FEELS WEAK, ACTUALLY.
WHAT THE HELL'S GOING ON?
NO— NO EXCUSES.
GM
THIS BRUSH IS GONNA STAY IN MY HAND UNTIL THE PAINTING'S DONE.
GOTTA KEEP VISUAL GUIDANCE IN MIND, TOO...
HMM, THIS SHOULD BE ENOUGH...
!
BUMP
AH, SORRY.

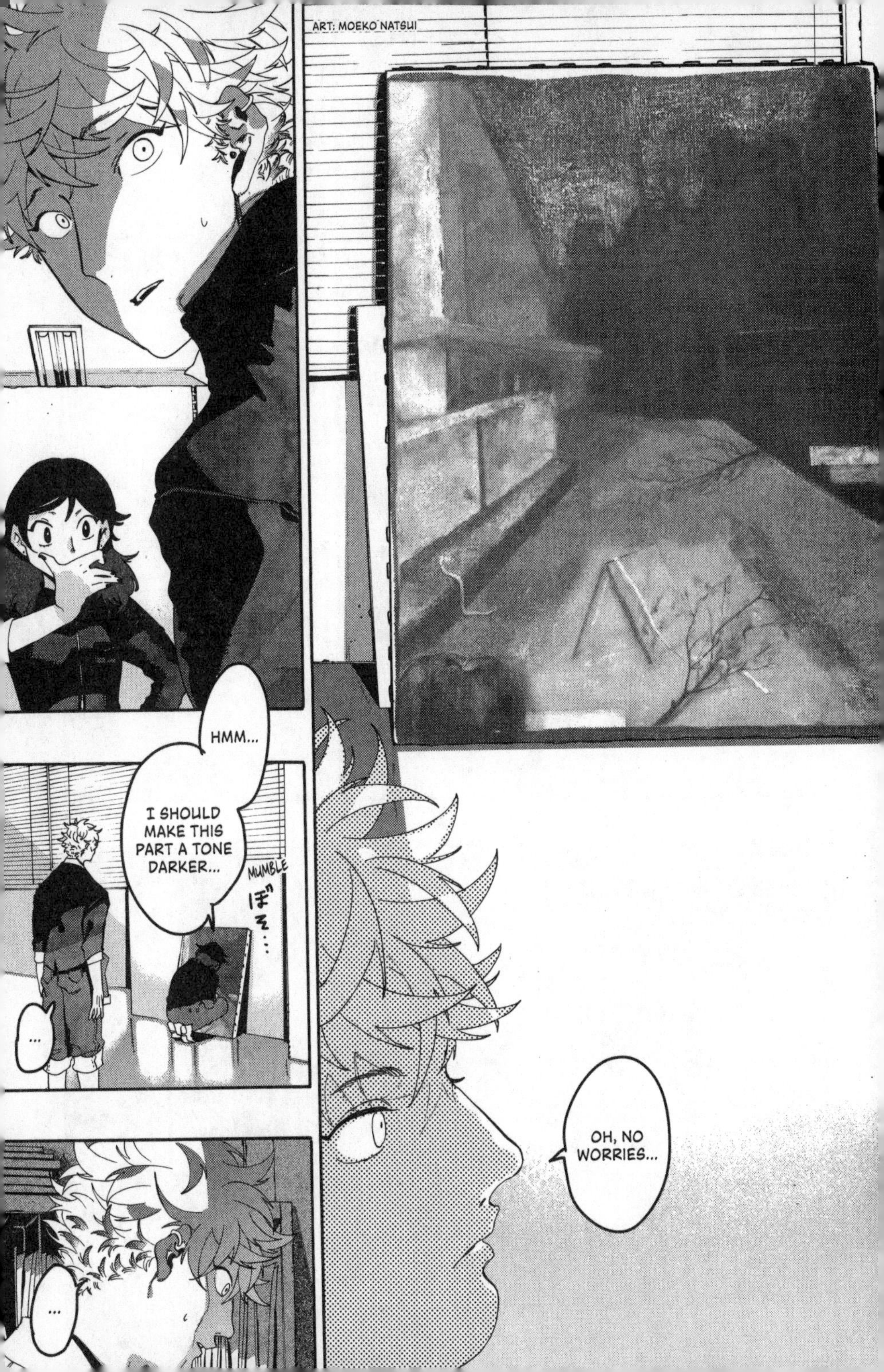
ART: MOEKO NATSUI
OH, NO WORRIES...
HMM...
I SHOULD MAKE THIS PART A TONE DARKER...
MUMBLE
ぼそ…
...
...

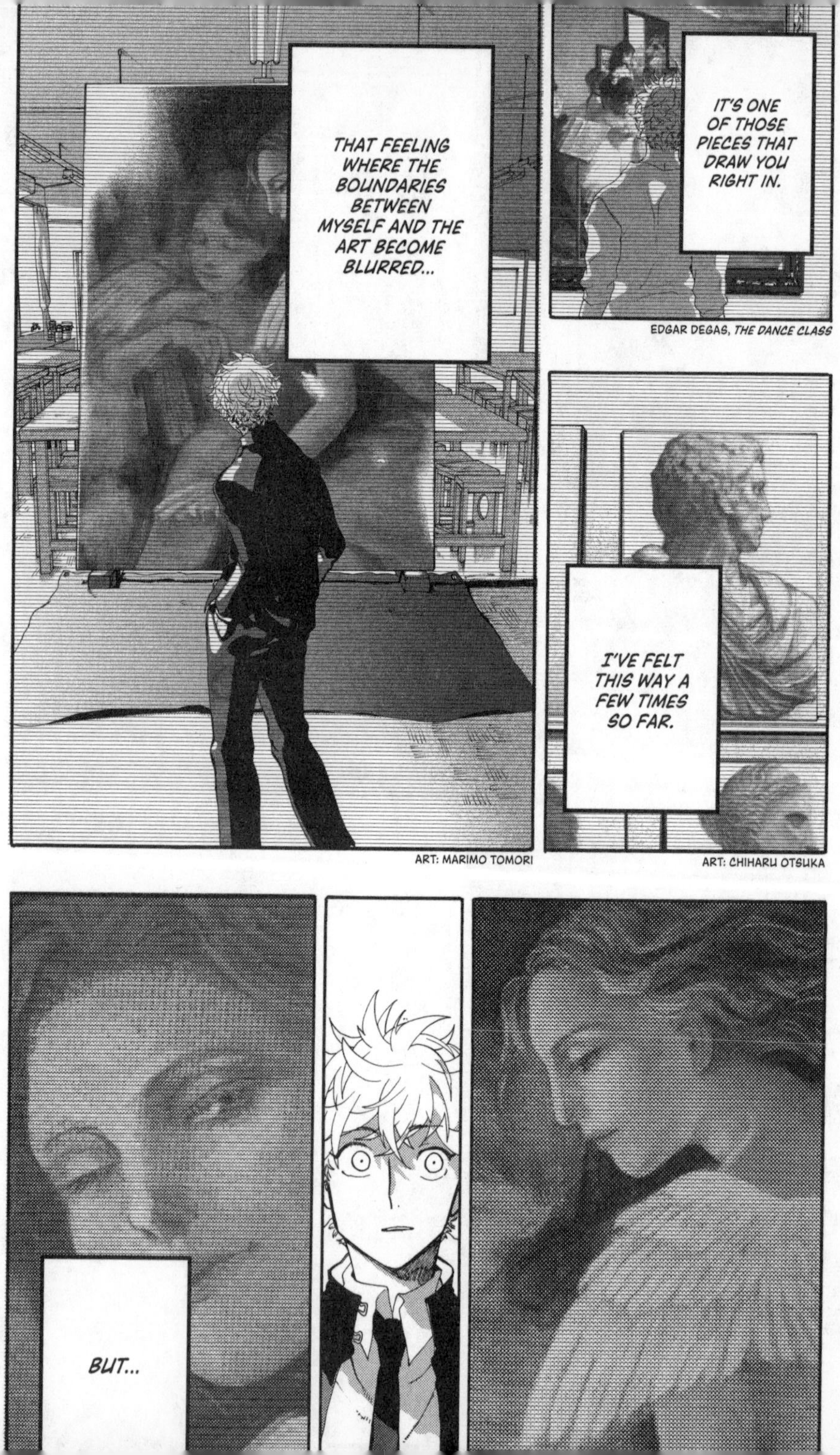
IT'S ONE OF THOSE PIECES THAT DRAW YOU RIGHT IN.
EDGAR DEGAS, THE DANCE CLASS
I'VE FELT THIS WAY A FEW TIMES SO FAR.
ART: CHIHARU OTSUKA
THAT FEELING WHERE THE BOUNDARIES BETWEEN MYSELF AND THE ART BECOME BLURRED...
ART: MARIMO TOMORI
BUT...

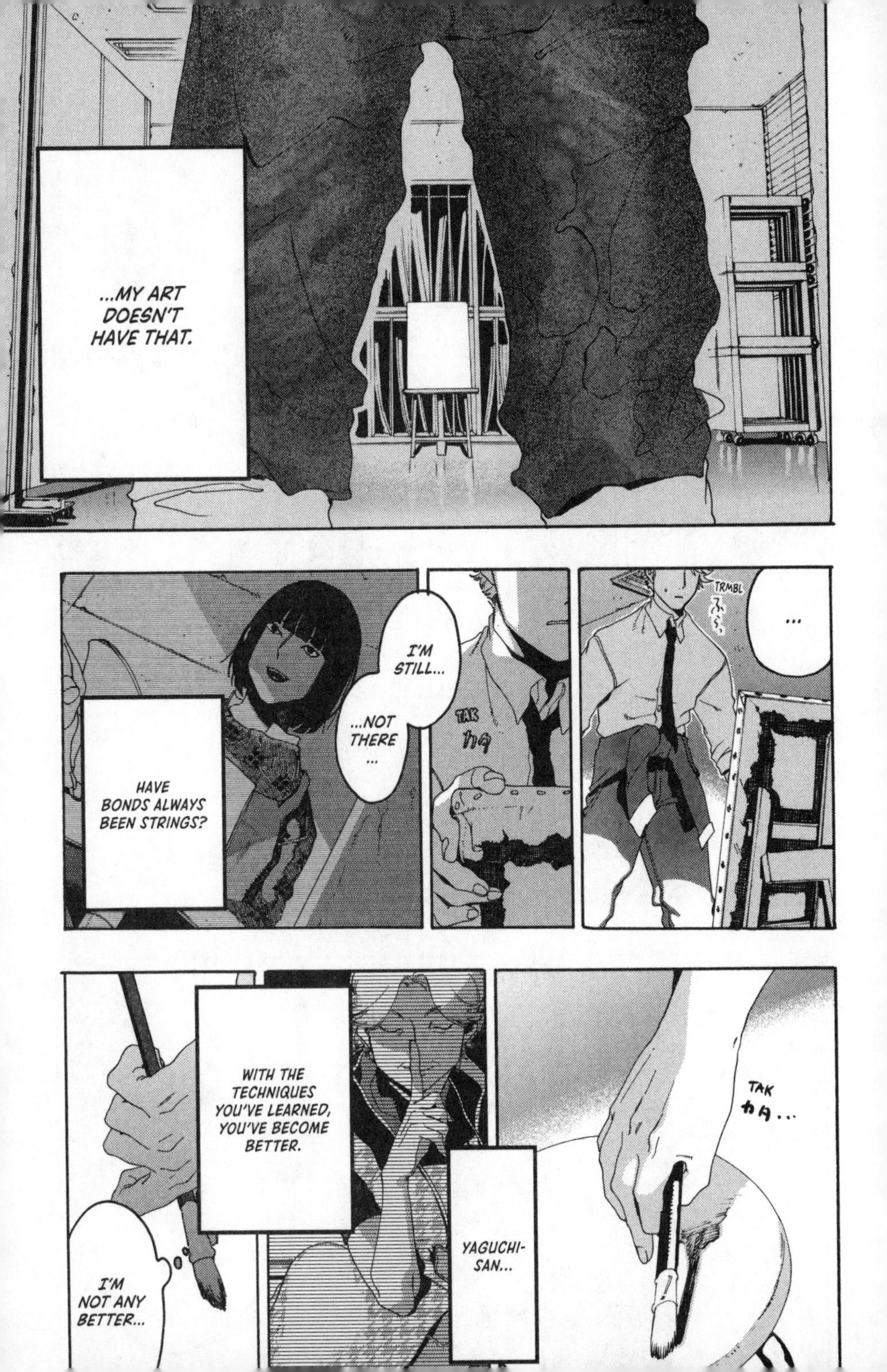
...MY ART DOESN'T HAVE THAT.
...
TRMBL
ふら
TAK
カタ
I'M STILL...
...NOT THERE ...
HAVE BONDS ALWAYS BEEN STRINGS?
TAK
カタ...
YAGUCHI-SAN...
WITH THE TECHNIQUES YOU'VE LEARNED, YOU'VE BECOME BETTER.
I'M NOT ANY BETTER...

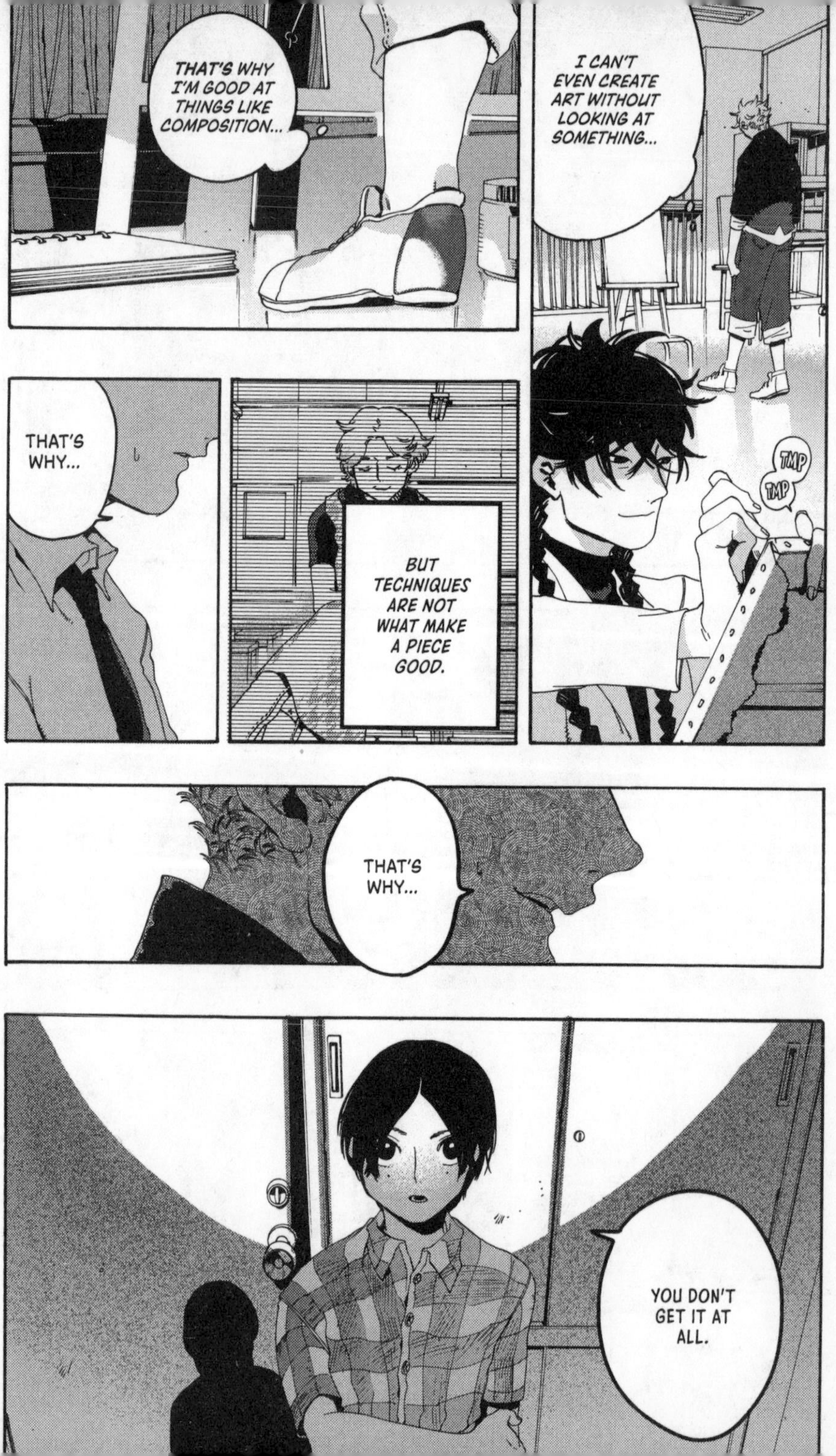
I CAN'T EVEN CREATE ART WITHOUT LOOKING AT SOMETHING...
TMP
TMP
THAT'S WHY I'M GOOD AT THINGS LIKE COMPOSITION...
BUT TECHNIQUES ARE NOT WHAT MAKE A PIECE GOOD.
THAT'S WHY...
THAT'S WHY...
YOU DON'T GET IT AT ALL.

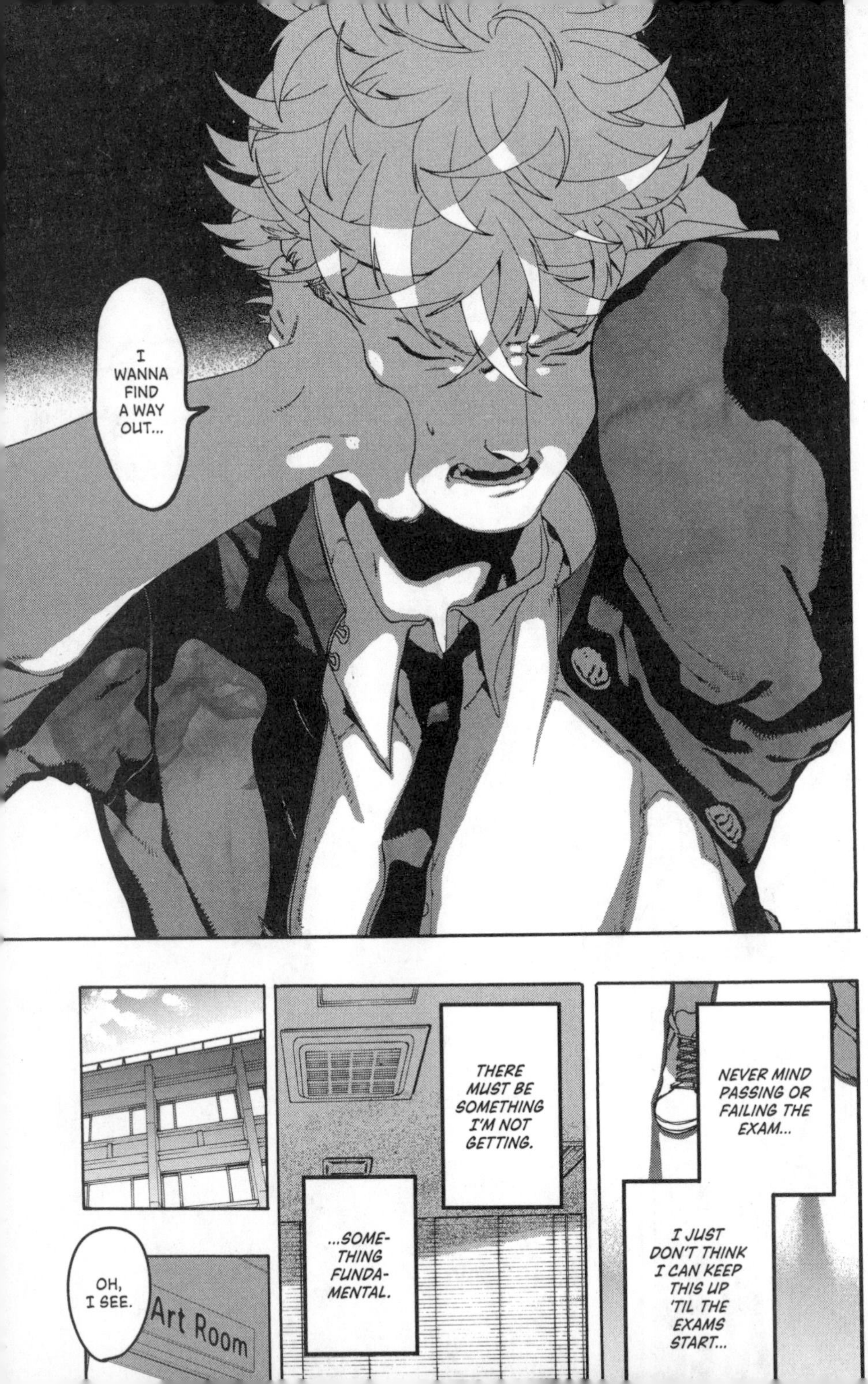
I WANNA FIND A WAY OUT...
NEVER MIND PASSING OR FAILING THE EXAM...
I JUST DON'T THINK I CAN KEEP THIS UP 'TIL THE EXAMS START...
THERE MUST BE SOMETHING I'M NOT GETTING.
...SOME-THING FUNDA-MENTAL.
OH, I SEE.
Art Room

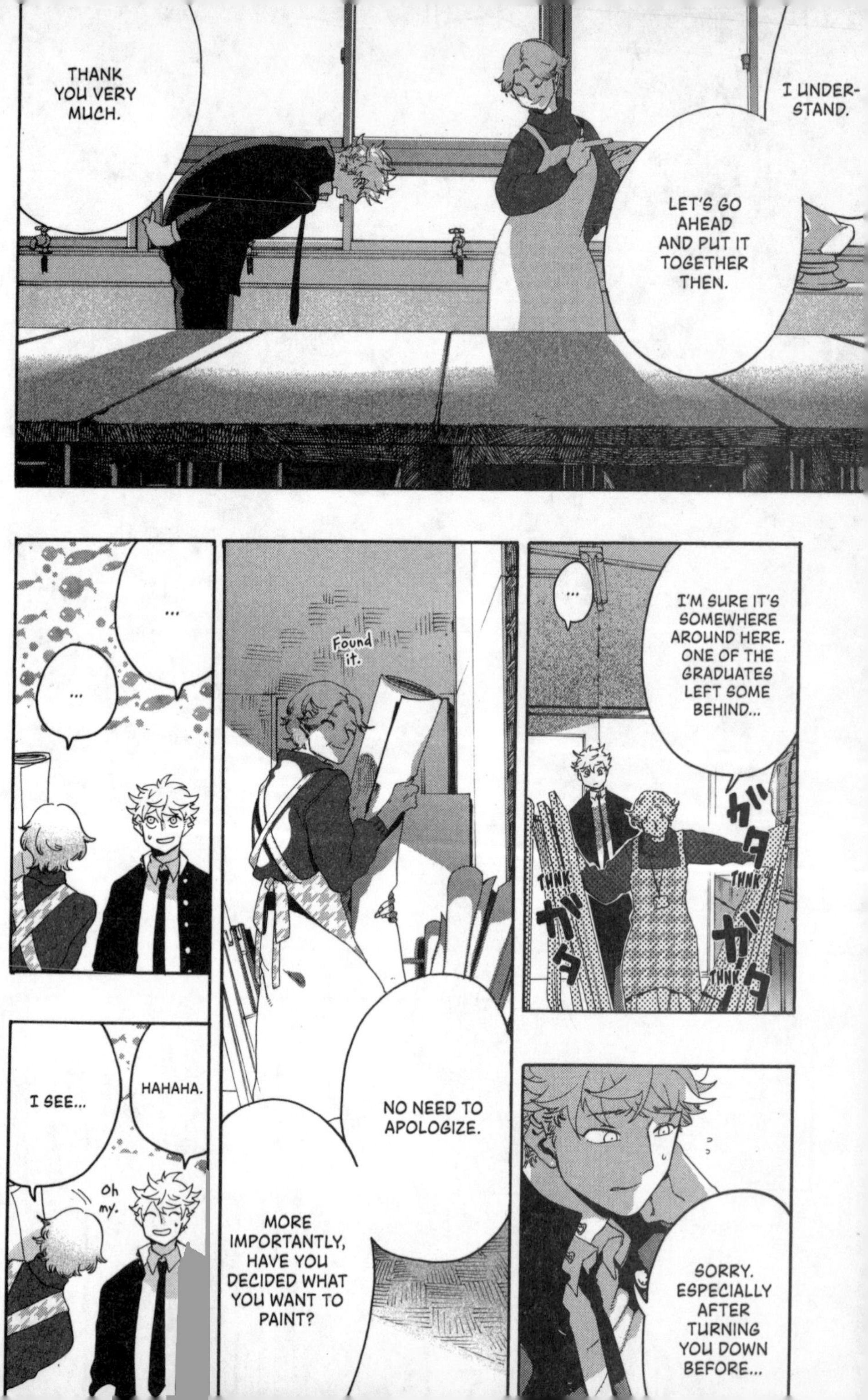
I UNDERSTAND.
LET'S GO AHEAD AND PUT IT TOGETHER THEN.
THANK YOU VERY MUCH.
I'M SURE IT'S SOMEWHERE AROUND HERE. ONE OF THE GRADUATES LEFT SOME BEHIND...
...
ガタ
THNK
ガタ
THNK
ガタ
THNK
SORRY. ESPECIALLY AFTER TURNING YOU DOWN BEFORE...
Found it.
NO NEED TO APOLOGIZE.
MORE IMPORTANTLY, HAVE YOU DECIDED WHAT YOU WANT TO PAINT?
...
...
HAHAHA.
I SEE...
Oh my.

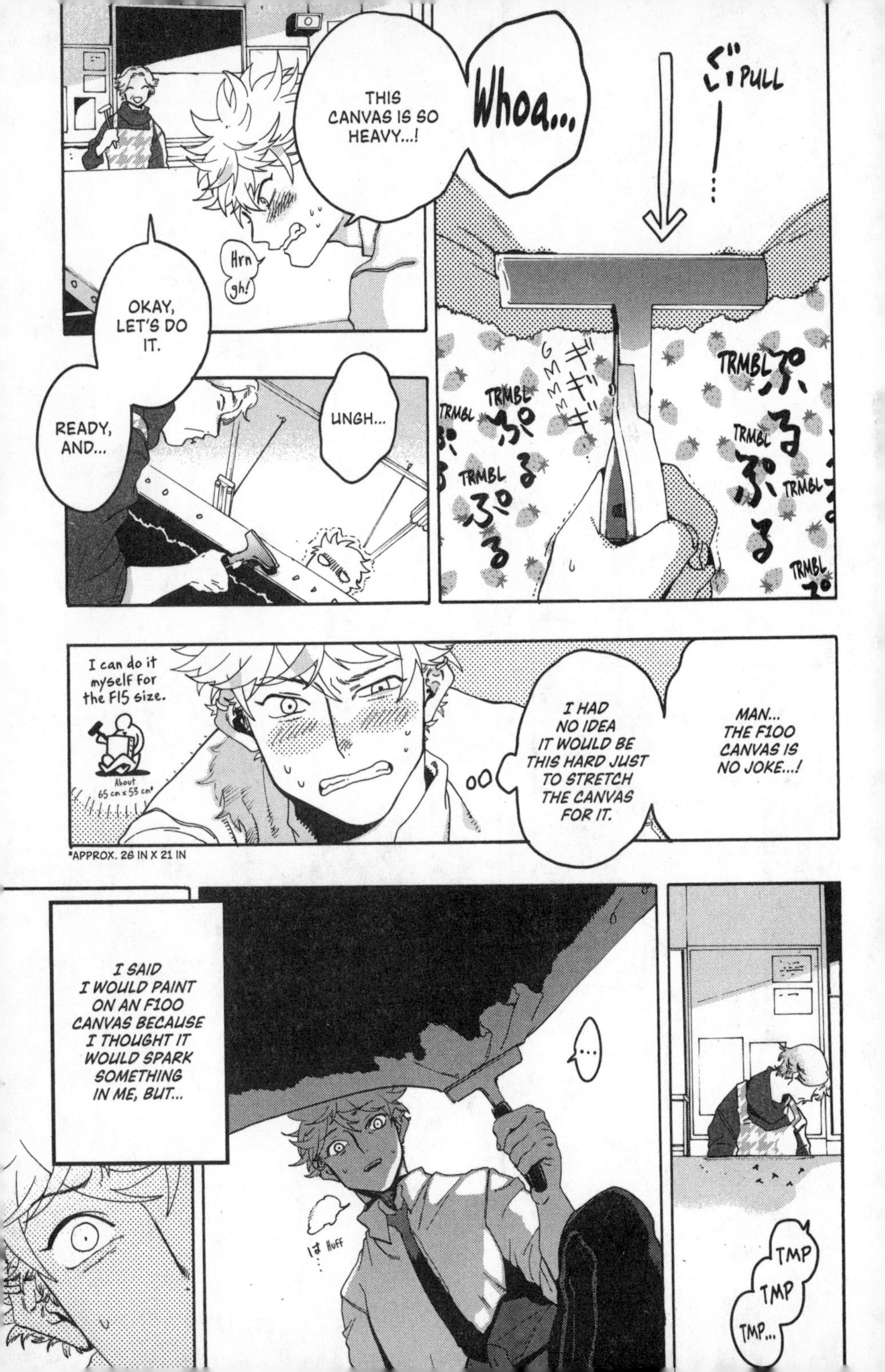

ぐい PULL
GMMMM ギギギ
TRMBL ぷる
TRMBL ぷる
TRMBL ぷる
TRMBL ぷる
TRMBL ぷる
TRMBL ぷる
TRMBL
TRMBL ぷ
Whoa...
THIS CANVAS IS SO HEAVY...!
Hrngh!
OKAY, LET'S DO IT.
READY, AND...
UNGH...
MAN... THE F100 CANVAS IS NO JOKE...!
I HAD NO IDEA IT WOULD BE THIS HARD JUST TO STRETCH THE CANVAS FOR IT.
I can do it myself for the F15 size.
About 65 cm x 53 cm*
*APPROX. 26 IN X 21 IN
TMP
TMP
TMP...
...
は Huff
I SAID I WOULD PAINT ON AN F100 CANVAS BECAUSE I THOUGHT IT WOULD SPARK SOMETHING IN ME, BUT...

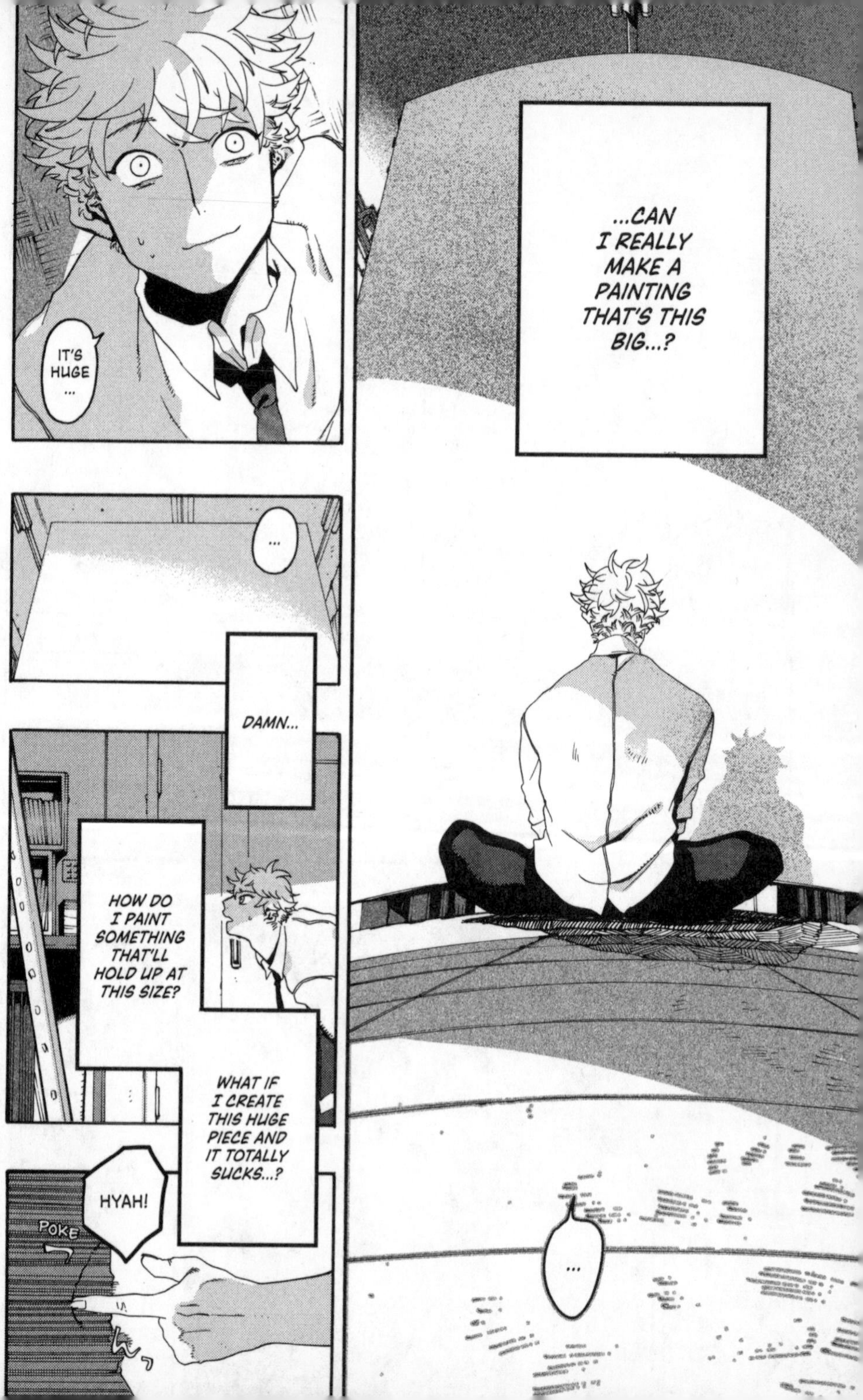
...CAN I REALLY MAKE A PAINTING THAT'S THIS BIG...?
...
IT'S HUGE ...
...
DAMN...
HOW DO I PAINT SOMETHING THAT'LL HOLD UP AT THIS SIZE?
WHAT IF I CREATE THIS HUGE PIECE AND IT TOTALLY SUCKS...?
HYAH!
POKE

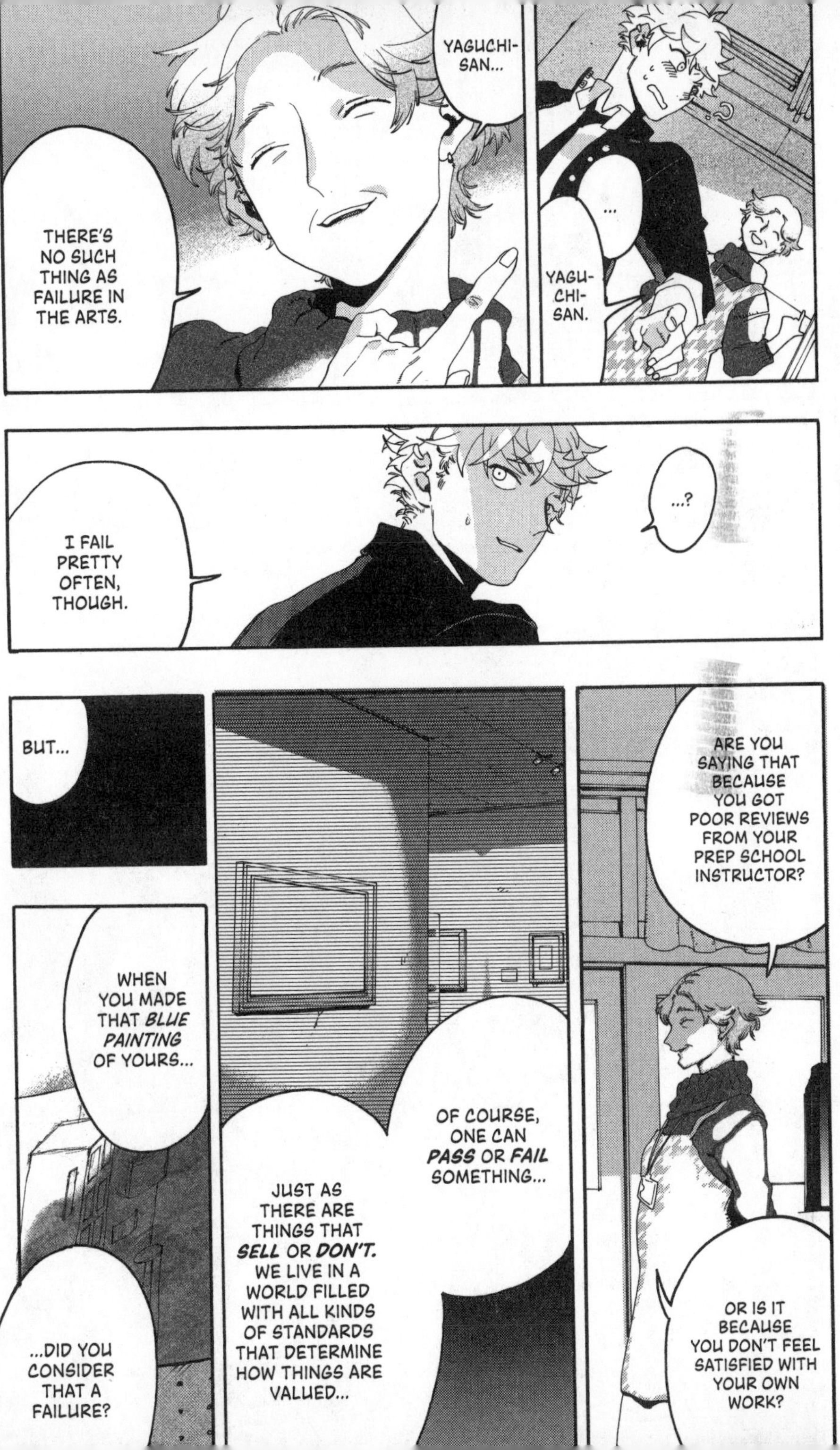
...
YAGU-CHI-SAN.
YAGUCHI-SAN...
THERE'S NO SUCH THING AS FAILURE IN THE ARTS.
...?
I FAIL PRETTY OFTEN, THOUGH.
ARE YOU SAYING THAT BECAUSE YOU GOT POOR REVIEWS FROM YOUR PREP SCHOOL INSTRUCTOR?
OR IS IT BECAUSE YOU DON'T FEEL SATISFIED WITH YOUR OWN WORK?
OF COURSE, ONE CAN *PASS* OR *FAIL* SOMETHING...
JUST AS THERE ARE THINGS THAT *SELL* OR *DON'T.* WE LIVE IN A WORLD FILLED WITH ALL KINDS OF STANDARDS THAT DETERMINE HOW THINGS ARE VALUED...
BUT...
WHEN YOU MADE THAT *BLUE PAINTING* OF YOURS...
...DID YOU CONSIDER THAT A FAILURE?

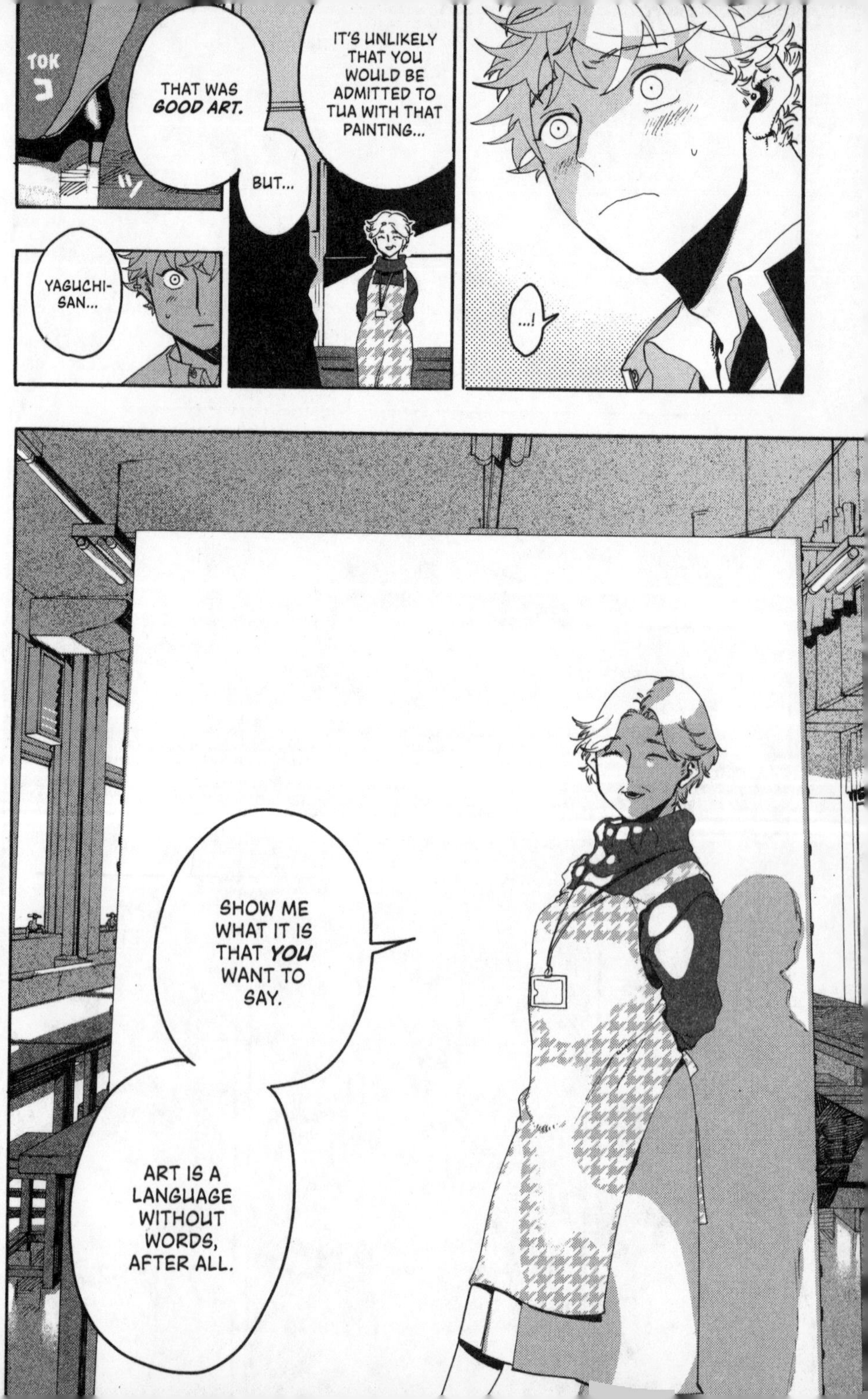
...!
IT'S UNLIKELY THAT YOU WOULD BE ADMITTED TO TUA WITH THAT PAINTING...
BUT...
TOK
THAT WAS *GOOD ART.*
YAGUCHI-SAN...
SHOW ME WHAT IT IS THAT *YOU* WANT TO SAY.
ART IS A LANGUAGE WITHOUT WORDS, AFTER ALL.

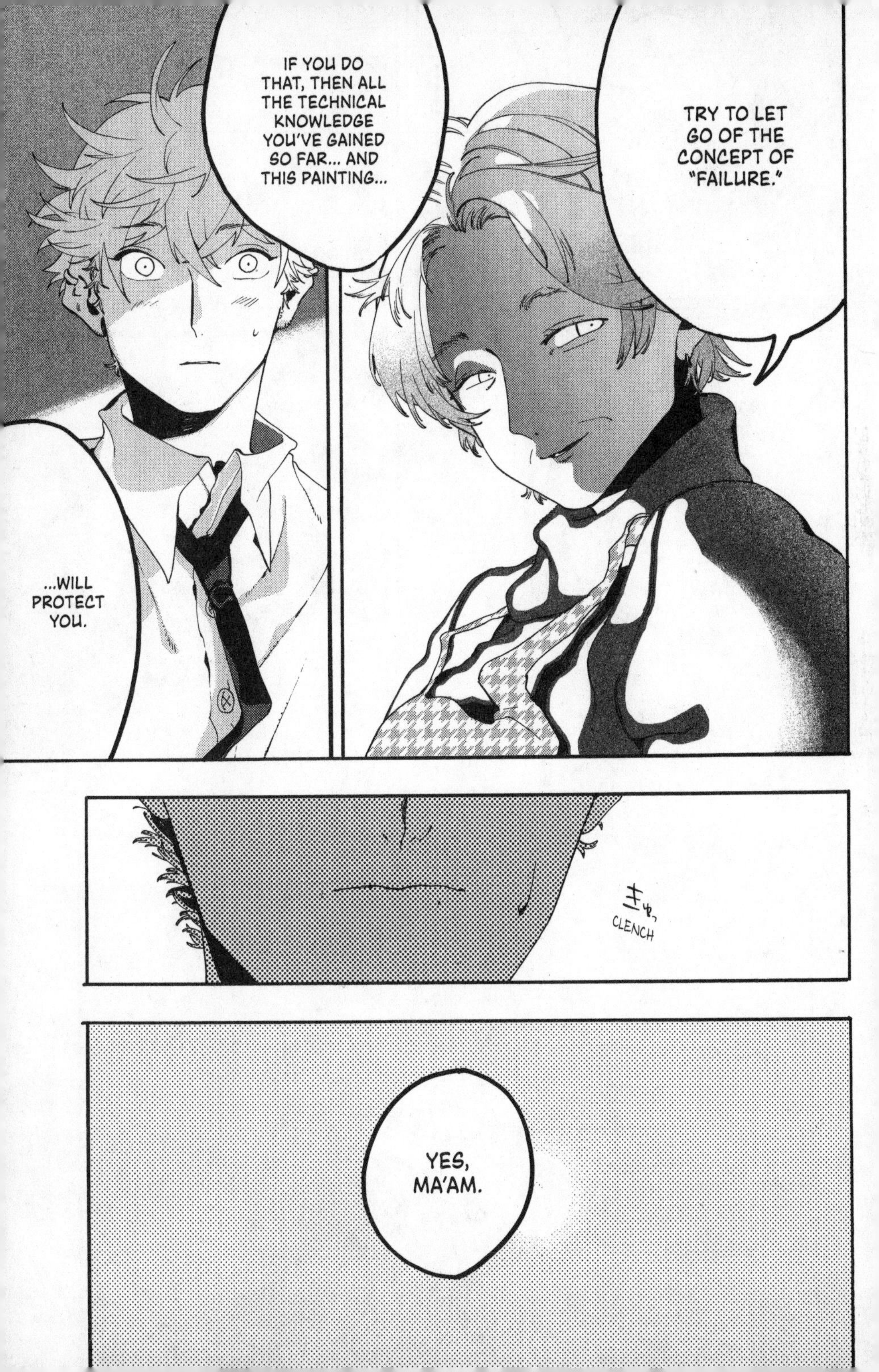
TRY TO LET GO OF THE CONCEPT OF "FAILURE."
IF YOU DO THAT, THEN ALL THE TECHNICAL KNOWLEDGE YOU'VE GAINED SO FAR... AND THIS PAINTING...
...WILL PROTECT YOU.
きゅっ
CLENCH
YES, MA'AM.

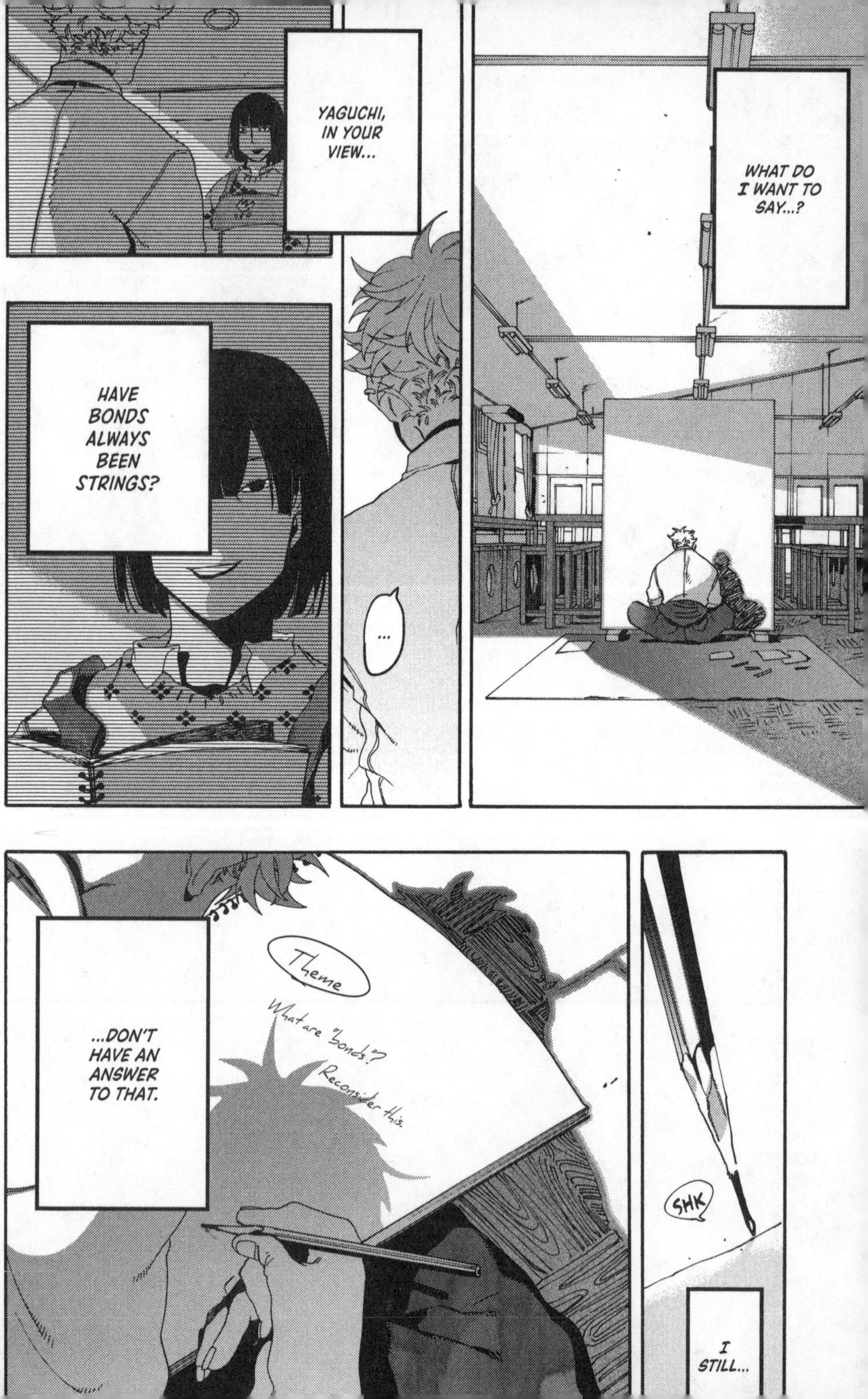
WHAT DO I WANT TO SAY...?
...
YAGUCHI, IN YOUR VIEW...
HAVE BONDS ALWAYS BEEN STRINGS?
SHK
I STILL...
...DON'T HAVE AN ANSWER TO THAT.
Theme
What are "bonds"?
Reconsider this.

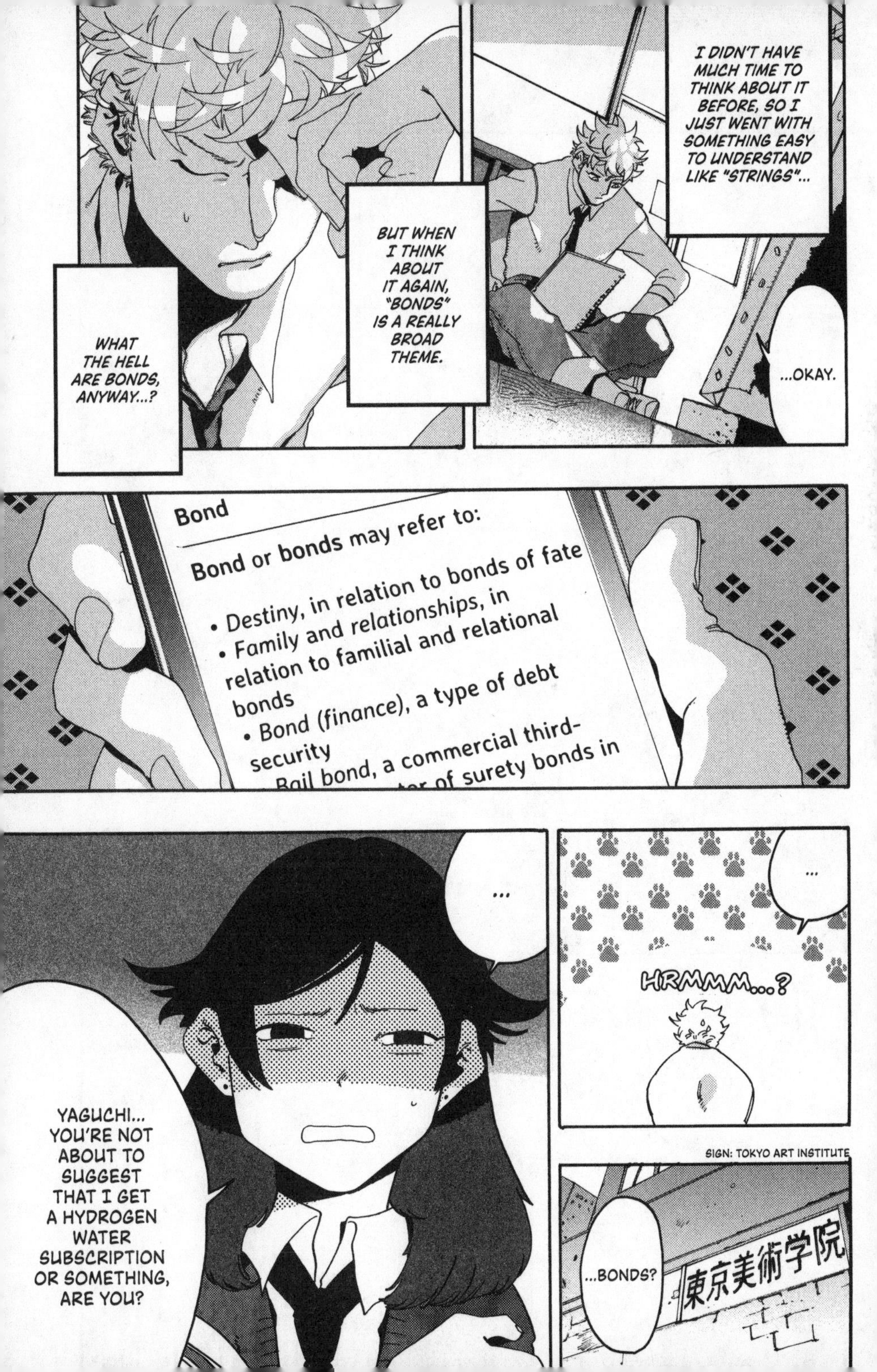
I DIDN'T HAVE MUCH TIME TO THINK ABOUT IT BEFORE, SO I JUST WENT WITH SOMETHING EASY TO UNDERSTAND LIKE "STRINGS"...
BUT WHEN I THINK ABOUT IT AGAIN, "BONDS" IS A REALLY BROAD THEME.
...OKAY.
WHAT THE HELL ARE BONDS, ANYWAY...?
Bond
Bond or bonds may refer to:
Bond or bonds may refer to:
• Destiny, in relation to bonds of fate
• Family and relationships, in relation to familial and relational bonds
• Bond (finance), a type of debt security
Bail bond, a commercial third-
surety bonds in
...
HRMMM...?
SIGN: TOKYO ART INSTITUTE
東京美術学院
...BONDS?
...
YAGUCHI... YOU'RE NOT ABOUT TO SUGGEST THAT I GET A HYDROGEN WATER SUBSCRIPTION OR SOMETHING, ARE YOU?

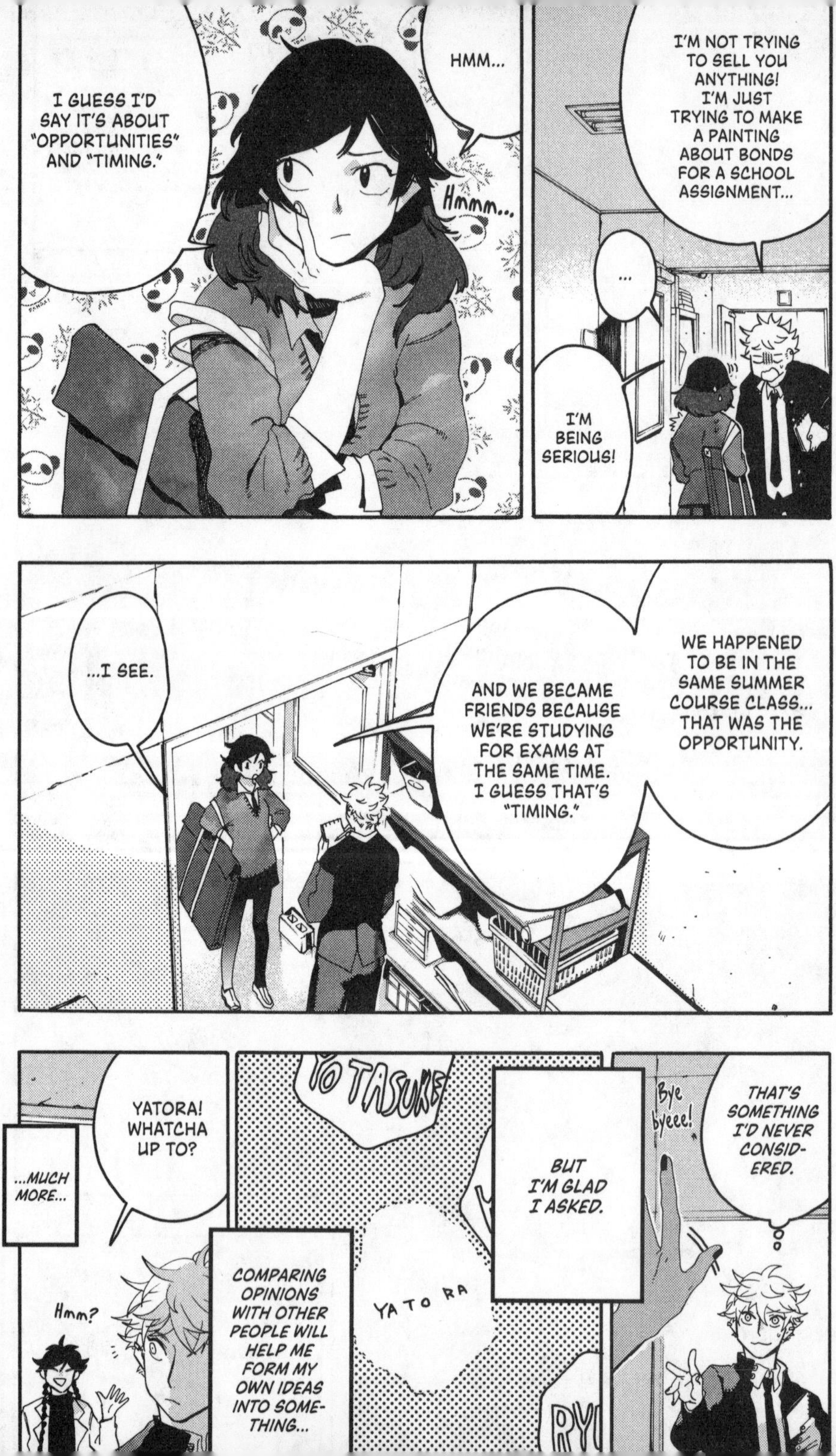
I'M NOT TRYING TO SELL YOU ANYTHING! I'M JUST TRYING TO MAKE A PAINTING ABOUT BONDS FOR A SCHOOL ASSIGNMENT...
...
I'M BEING SERIOUS!
HMM...
Hmmm...
I GUESS I'D SAY IT'S ABOUT "OPPORTUNITIES" AND "TIMING."
WE HAPPENED TO BE IN THE SAME SUMMER COURSE CLASS... THAT WAS THE OPPORTUNITY.
AND WE BECAME FRIENDS BECAUSE WE'RE STUDYING FOR EXAMS AT THE SAME TIME. I GUESS THAT'S "TIMING."
...I SEE.
THAT'S SOMETHING I'D NEVER CONSIDERED.
Bye byeee!
BUT I'M GLAD I ASKED.
YO TASUKE
YA TO RA
COMPARING OPINIONS WITH OTHER PEOPLE WILL HELP ME FORM MY OWN IDEAS INTO SOMETHING...
RYU
YATORA! WHATCHA UP TO?
...MUCH MORE...
Hmm?

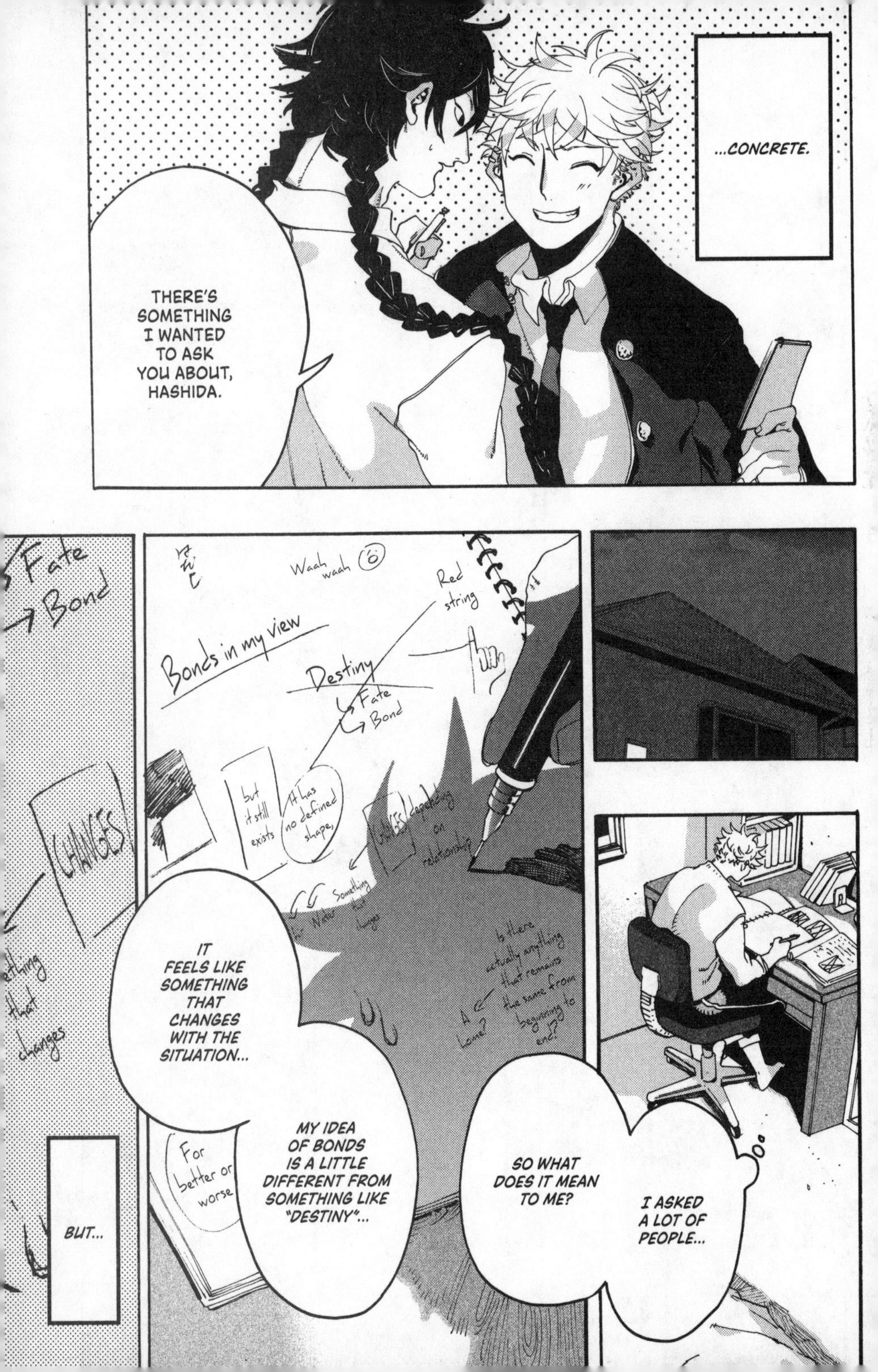
...CONCRETE.
THERE'S SOMETHING I WANTED TO ASK YOU ABOUT, HASHIDA.
I ASKED A LOT OF PEOPLE...
Waah waah
Red string
Bonds in my view
Destiny
Fate
Bond
It has no defined shape,
but it still exists
changes depending on relationship
Something that changes
Water
Is there actually anything that remains the same from beginning to end?
A Lover?
SO WHAT DOES IT MEAN TO ME?
MY IDEA OF BONDS IS A LITTLE DIFFERENT FROM SOMETHING LIKE "DESTINY"...
IT FEELS LIKE SOMETHING THAT CHANGES WITH THE SITUATION...
For better or worse
CHANGES
BUT...

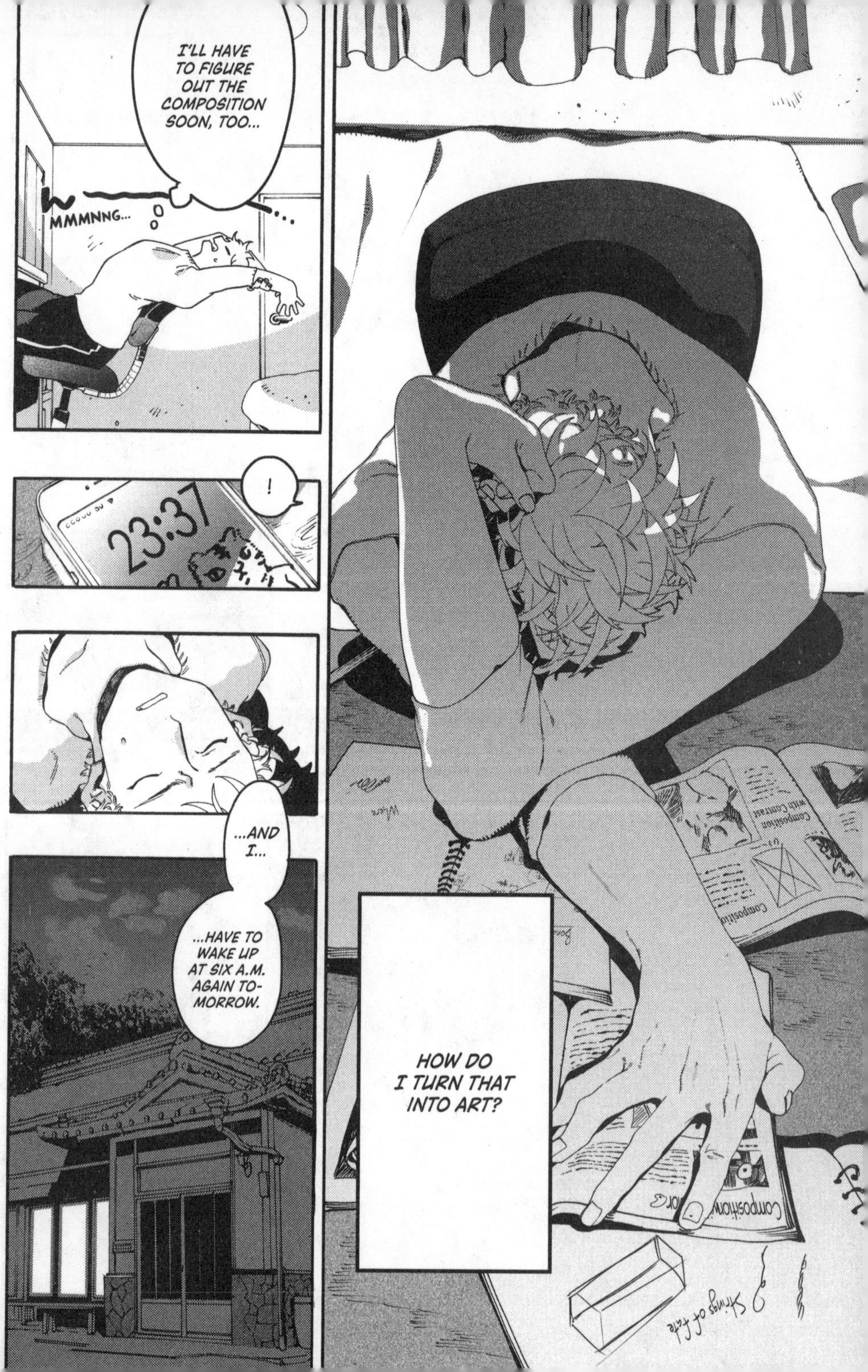
HOW DO I TURN THAT INTO ART?
I'LL HAVE TO FIGURE OUT THE COMPOSITION SOON, TOO...
MMMNNG...
!
23:37
...AND I...
...HAVE TO WAKE UP AT SIX A.M. AGAIN TO-MORROW.

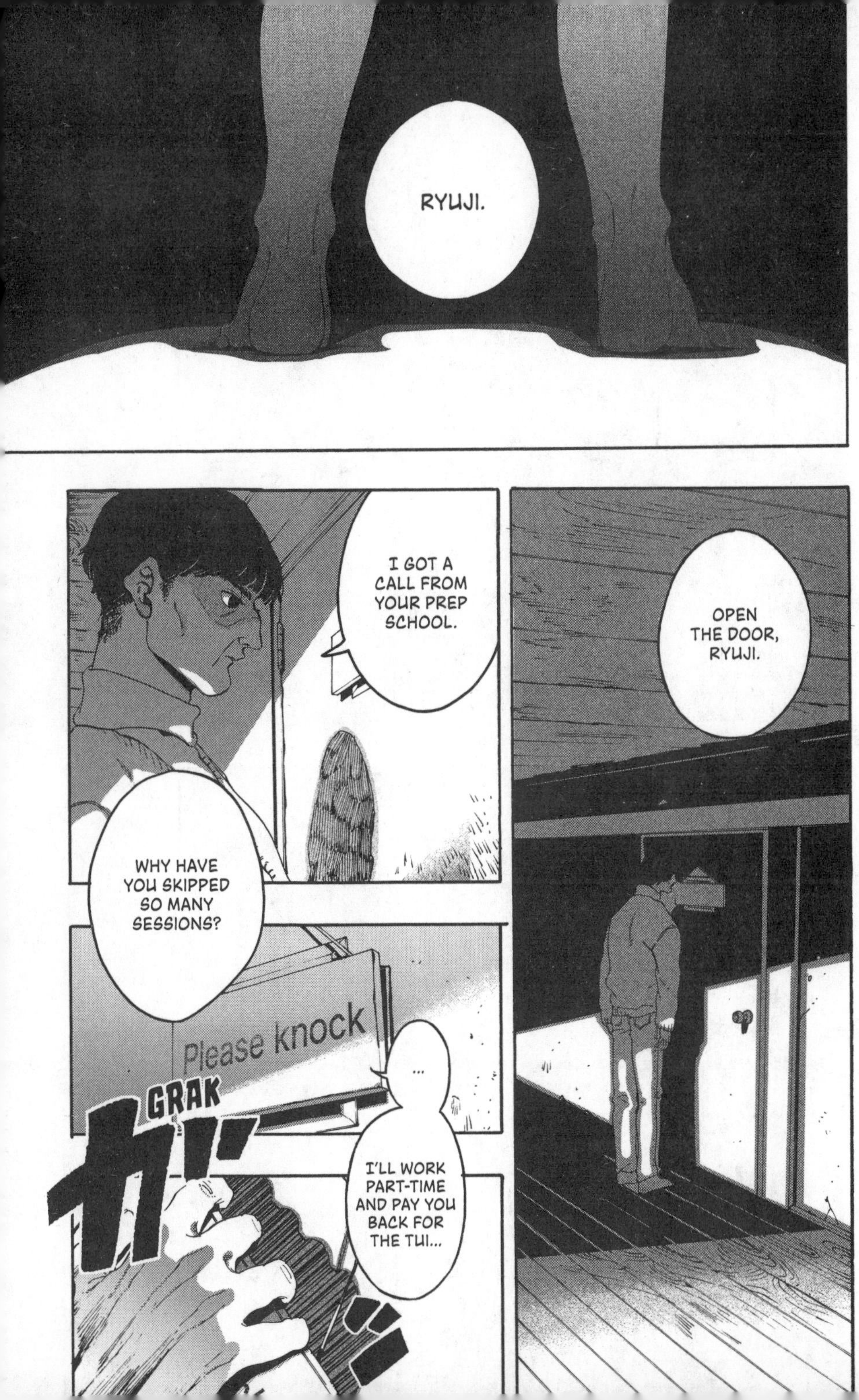
RYUJI.
OPEN THE DOOR, RYUJI.
I GOT A CALL FROM YOUR PREP SCHOOL.
WHY HAVE YOU SKIPPED SO MANY SESSIONS?
Please knock
...
I'LL WORK PART-TIME AND PAY YOU BACK FOR THE TUI...
GRAK

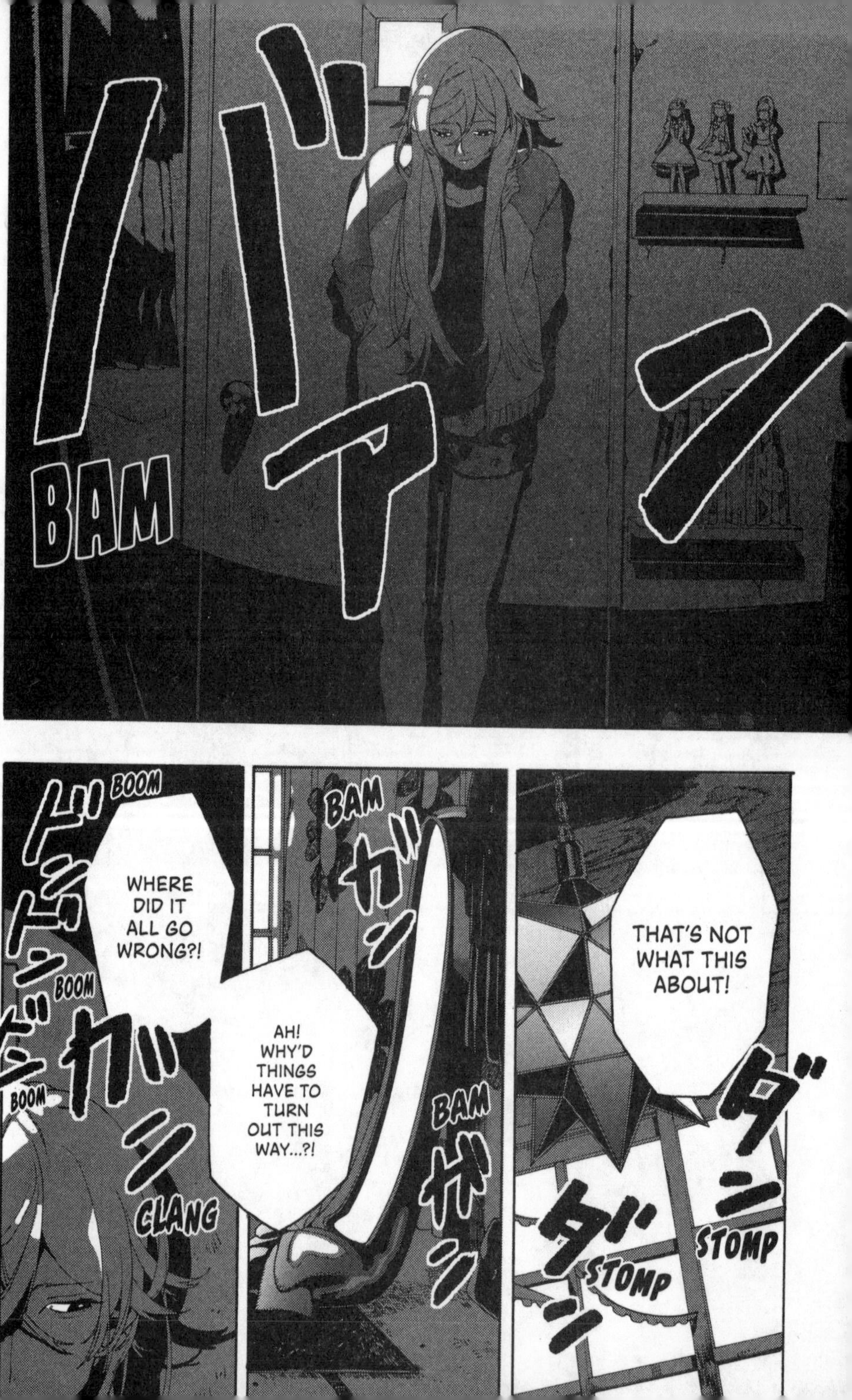
BAM
THAT'S NOT WHAT THIS ABOUT!
STOMP
STOMP
BAM
AH! WHY'D THINGS HAVE TO TURN OUT THIS WAY...?!
BAM
BOOM
WHERE DID IT ALL GO WRONG?!
BOOM
BOOM
CLANG

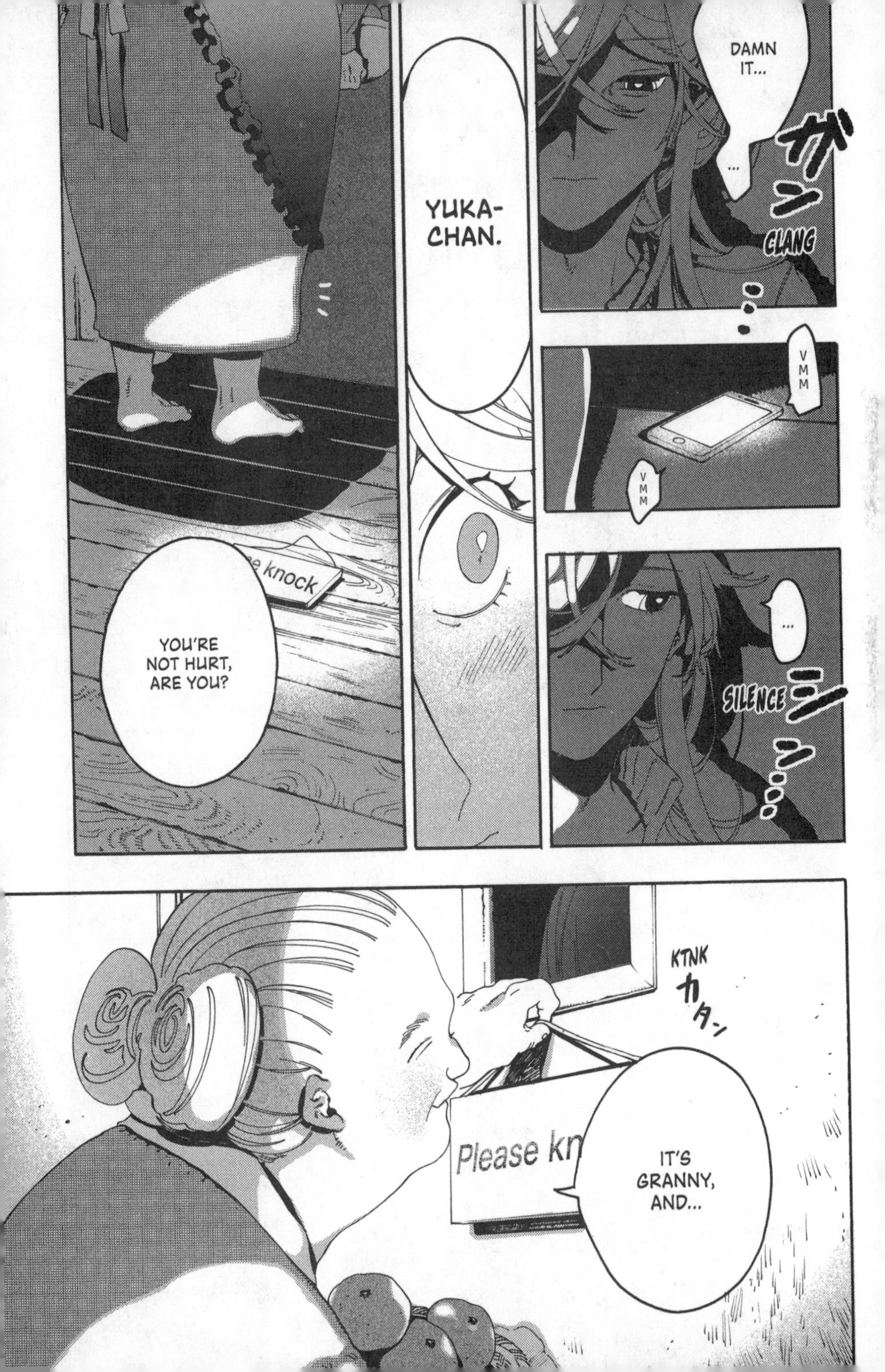
DAMN IT...
...
CLANG
...
VMM
VMM
...
SILENCE
...
YUKA-CHAN.
e knock
YOU'RE NOT HURT, ARE YOU?
KTNK
カタン
Please kn
IT'S GRANNY, AND...

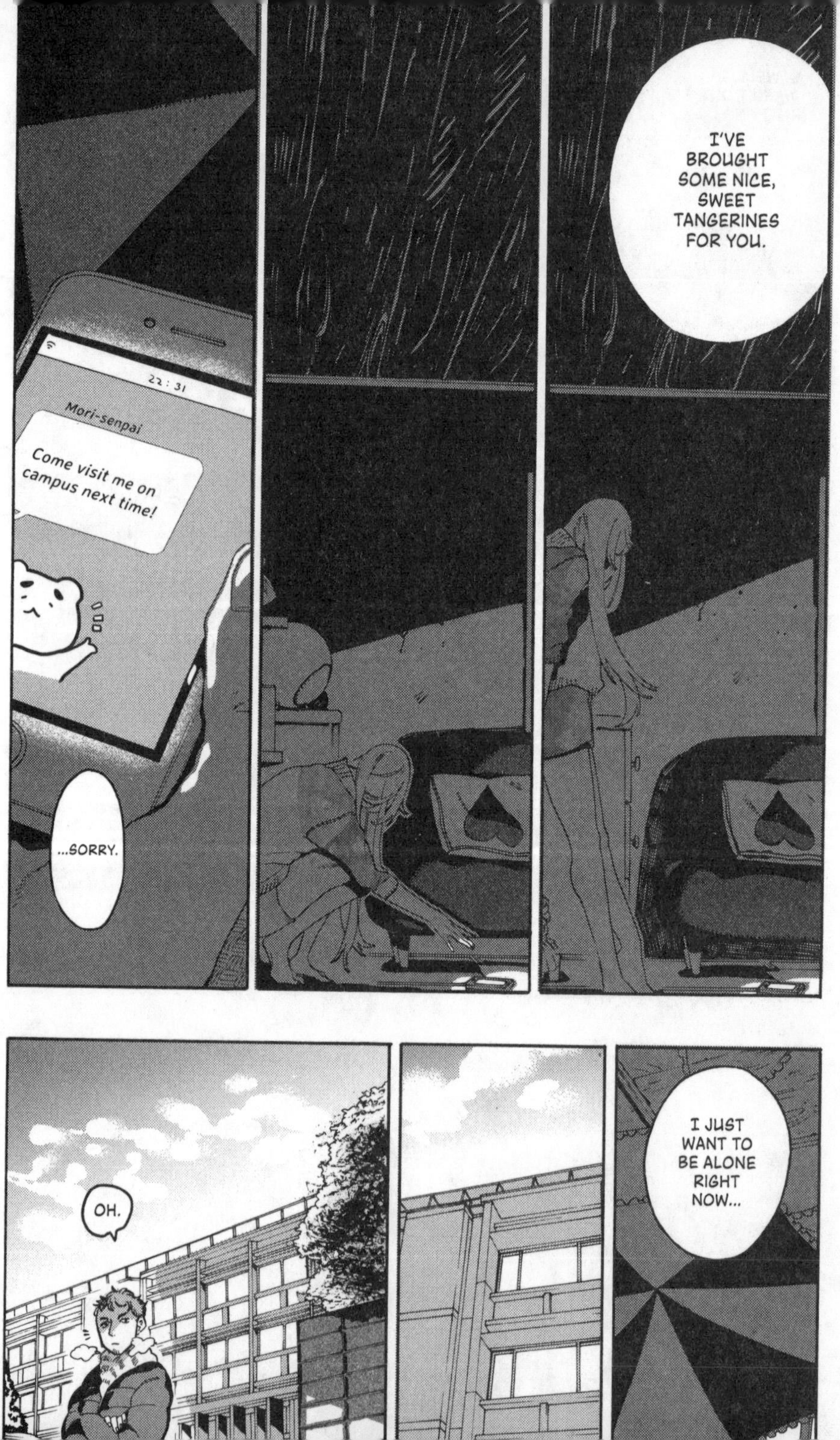
I'VE BROUGHT SOME NICE, SWEET TANGERINES FOR YOU.
22:31
Mori-senpai
Come visit me on campus next time!
...SORRY.
I JUST WANT TO BE ALONE RIGHT NOW...
OH.

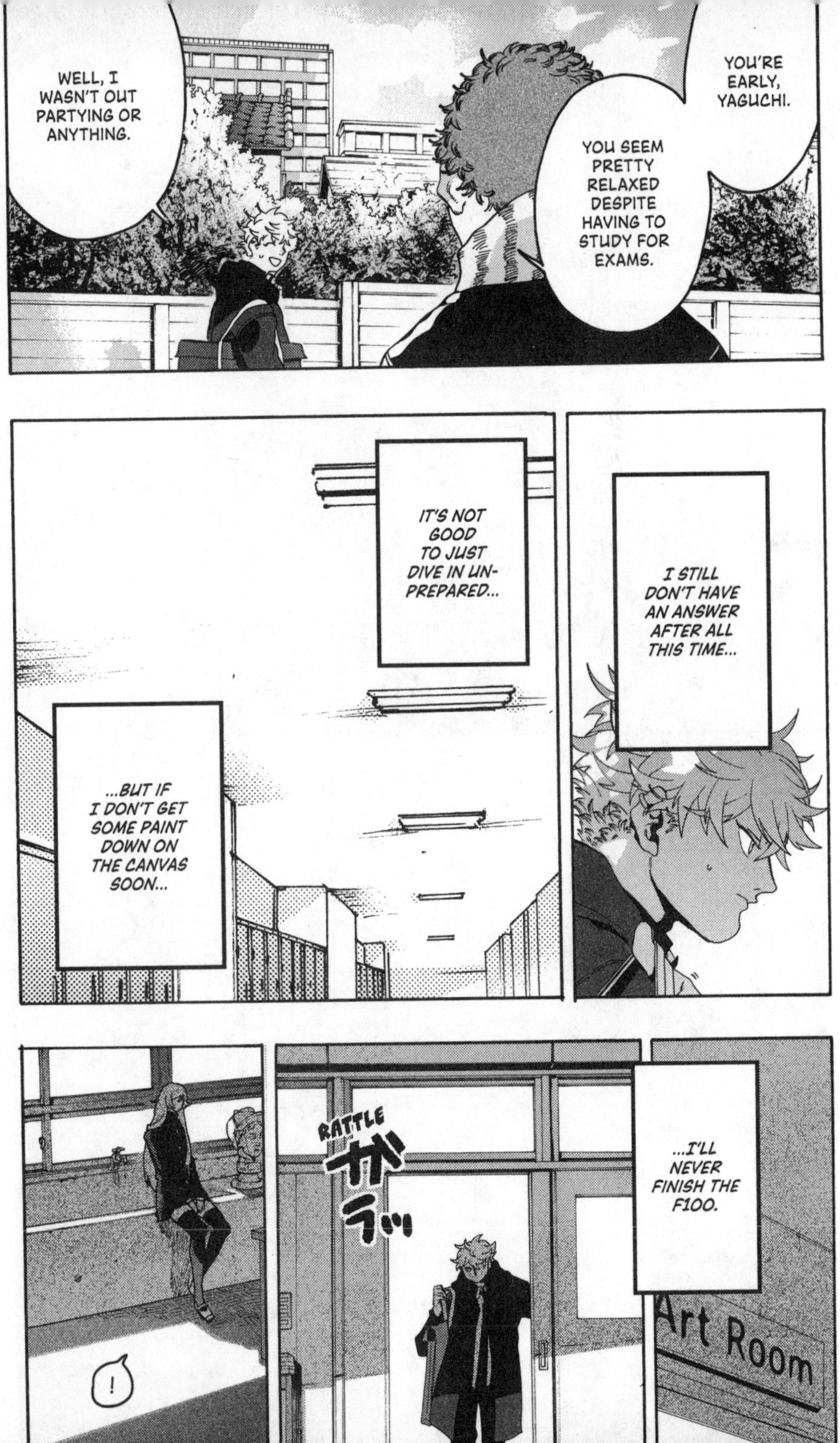
YOU'RE EARLY, YAGUCHI.
YOU SEEM PRETTY RELAXED DESPITE HAVING TO STUDY FOR EXAMS.
WELL, I WASN'T OUT PARTYING OR ANYTHING.
I STILL DON'T HAVE AN ANSWER AFTER ALL THIS TIME...
IT'S NOT GOOD TO JUST DIVE IN UN-PREPARED...
...BUT IF I DON'T GET SOME PAINT DOWN ON THE CANVAS SOON...
...I'LL NEVER FINISH THE F100.
Art Room
RATTLE
ガラッ
!

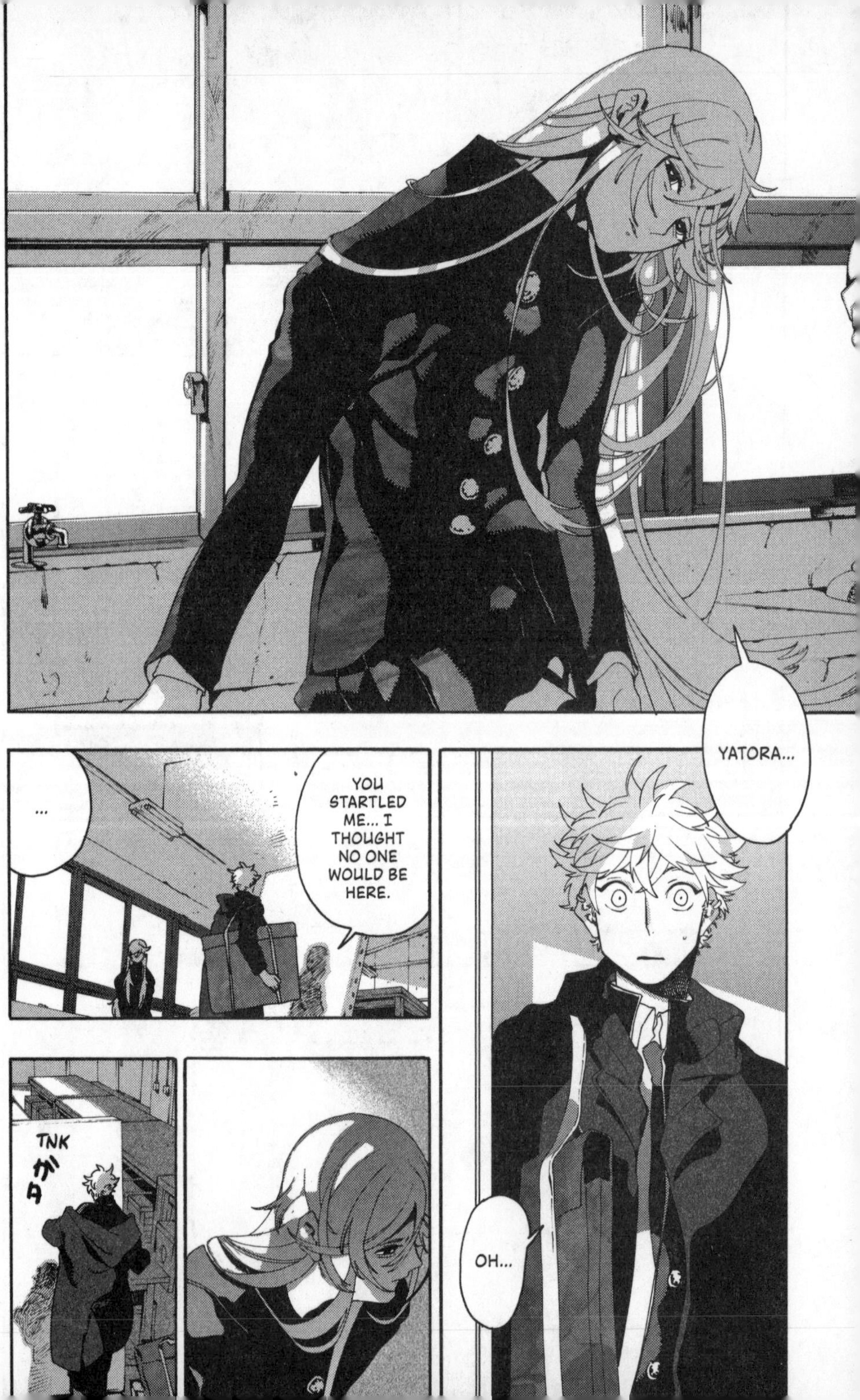
YATORA...
OH...
YOU STARTLED ME... I THOUGHT NO ONE WOULD BE HERE.
...
TNK
ガタ

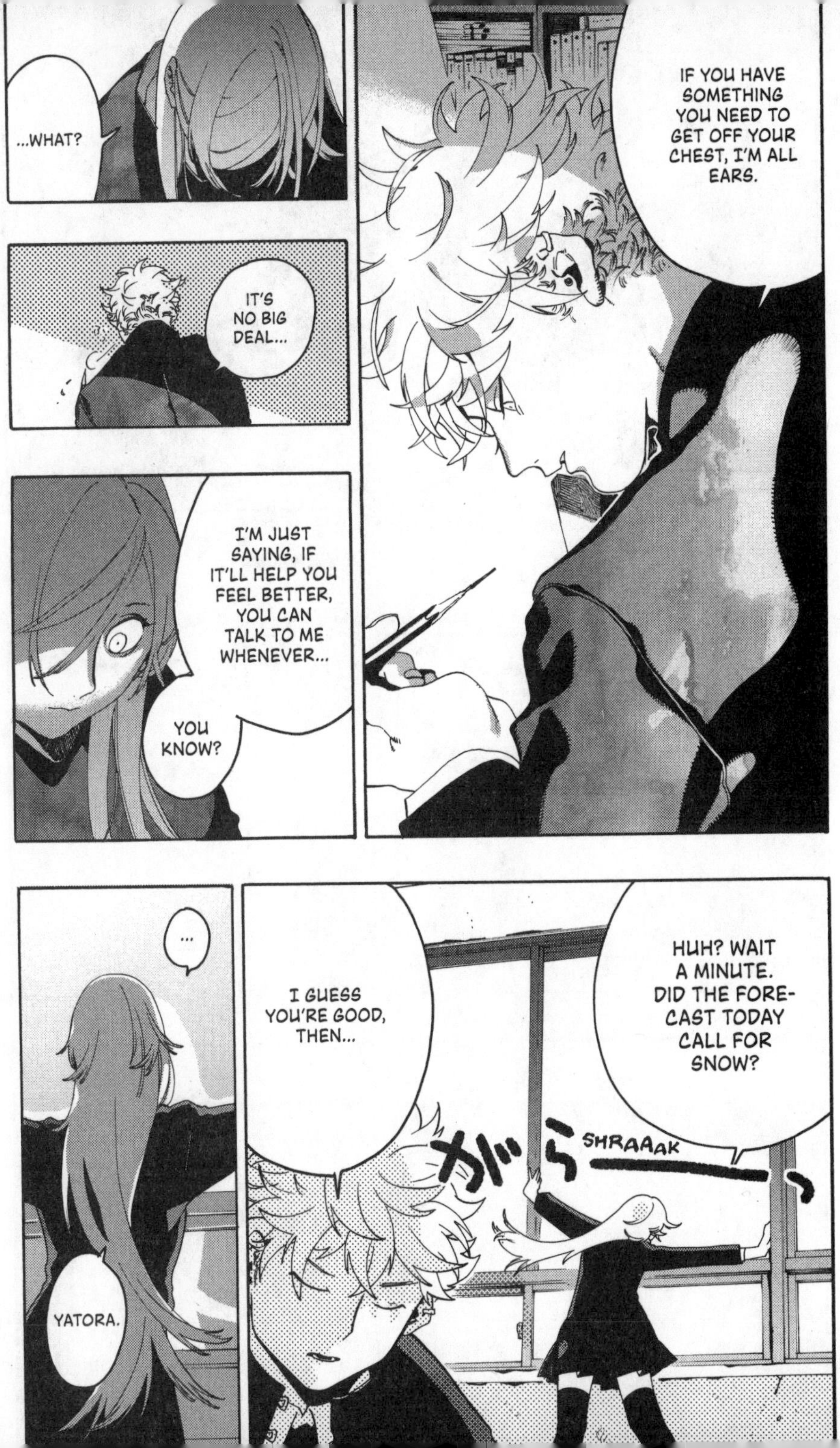
IF YOU HAVE SOMETHING YOU NEED TO GET OFF YOUR CHEST, I'M ALL EARS.
...WHAT?
IT'S NO BIG DEAL...
I'M JUST SAYING, IF IT'LL HELP YOU FEEL BETTER, YOU CAN TALK TO ME WHENEVER...
YOU KNOW?
HUH? WAIT A MINUTE. DID THE FORE-CAST TODAY CALL FOR SNOW?
I GUESS YOU'RE GOOD, THEN...
SHRAAAK
...
YATORA.

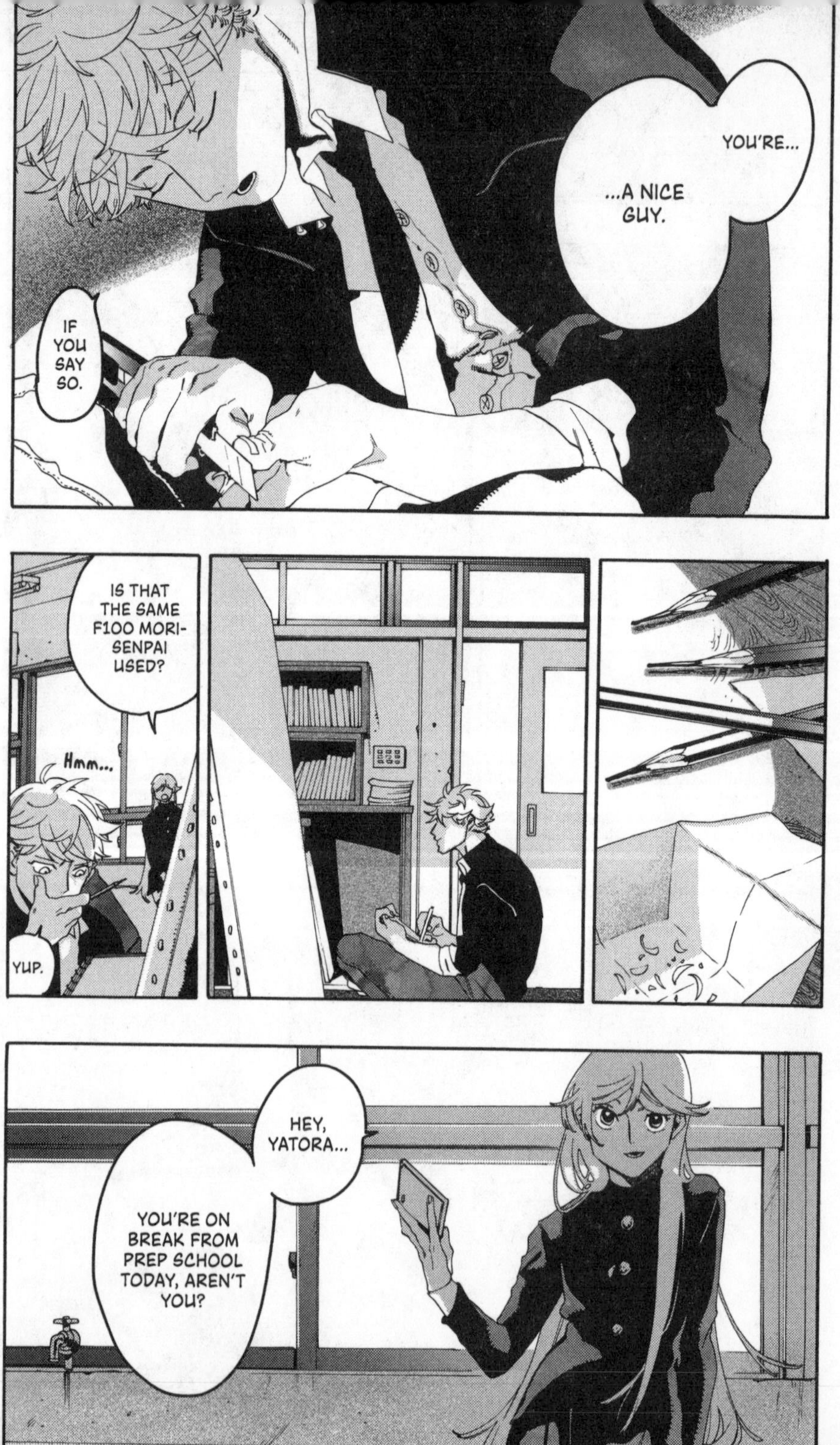
YOU'RE...
...A NICE GUY.
IF YOU SAY SO.
IS THAT THE SAME F100 MORI-SENPAI USED?
Hmm...
YUP.
HEY, YATORA...
YOU'RE ON BREAK FROM PREP SCHOOL TODAY, AREN'T YOU?

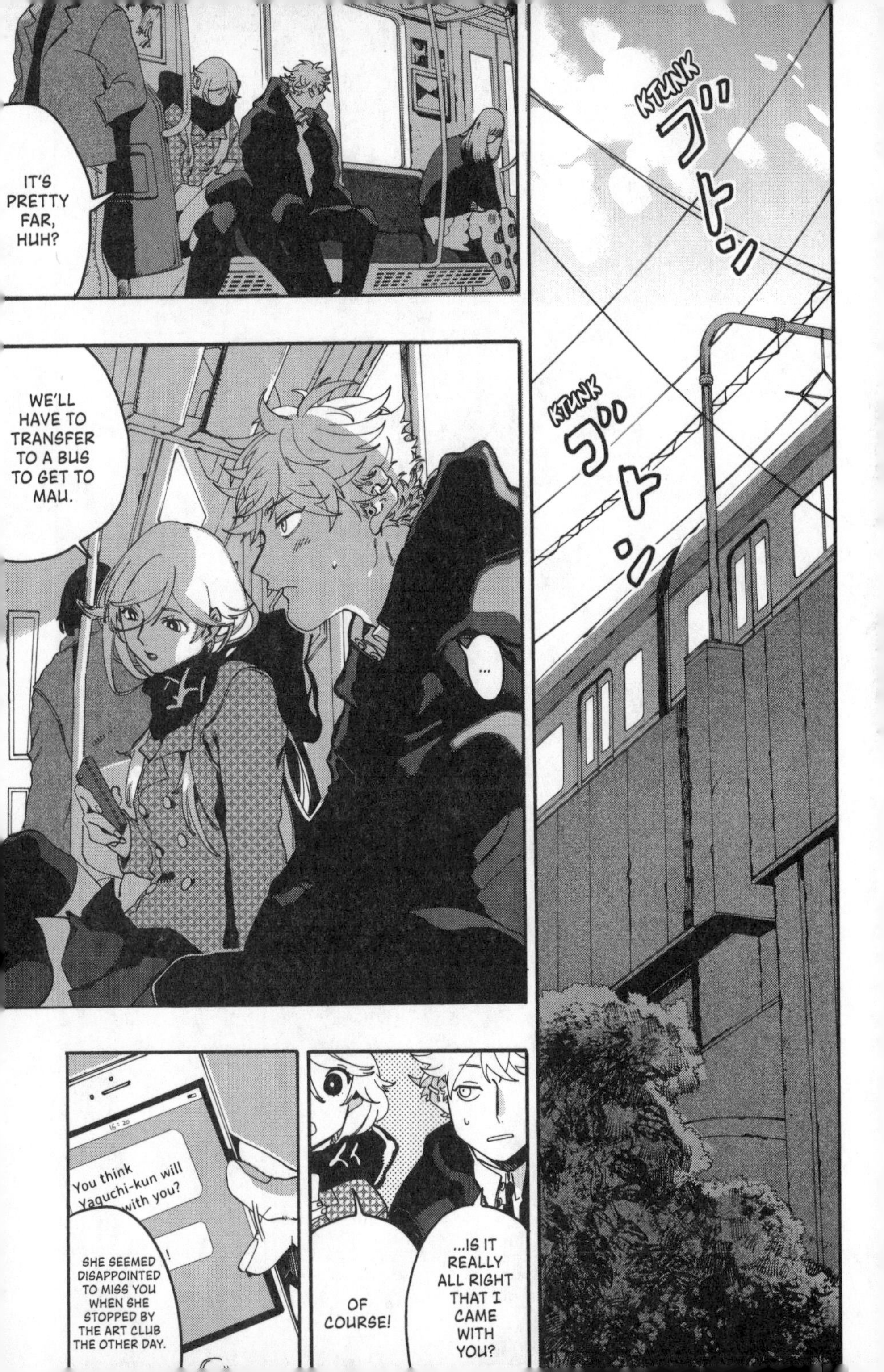
KTUNK
ゴトッ
KTUNK
ゴトン
IT'S PRETTY FAR, HUH?
WE'LL HAVE TO TRANSFER TO A BUS TO GET TO MAU.
...
...IS IT REALLY ALL RIGHT THAT I CAME WITH YOU?
OF COURSE!
16:20
You think Yaguchi-kun will
with you?
!
SHE SEEMED DISAPPOINTED TO MISS YOU WHEN SHE STOPPED BY THE ART CLUB THE OTHER DAY.

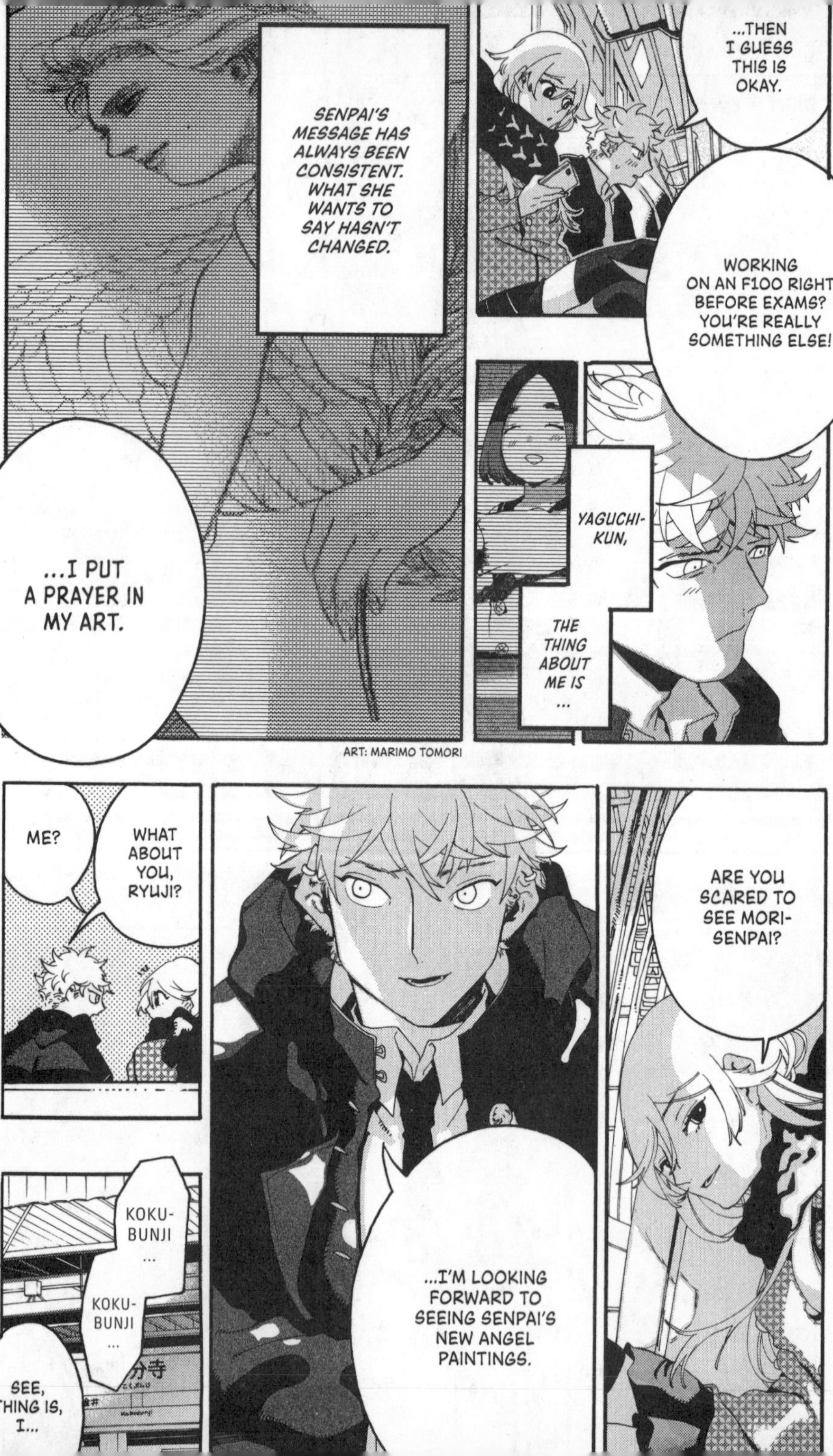
...THEN I GUESS THIS IS OKAY.
WORKING ON AN F100 RIGHT BEFORE EXAMS? YOU'RE REALLY SOMETHING ELSE!
YAGUCHI-KUN,
THE THING ABOUT ME IS ...
SENPAI'S MESSAGE HAS ALWAYS BEEN CONSISTENT. WHAT SHE WANTS TO SAY HASN'T CHANGED.
...I PUT A PRAYER IN MY ART.
ART: MARIMO TOMORI
ARE YOU SCARED TO SEE MORI-SENPAI?
...I'M LOOKING FORWARD TO SEEING SENPAI'S NEW ANGEL PAINTINGS.
WHAT ABOUT YOU, RYUJI?
ME?
KOKU-BUNJI ...
KOKU-BUNJI ...
SEE, THING IS, I...

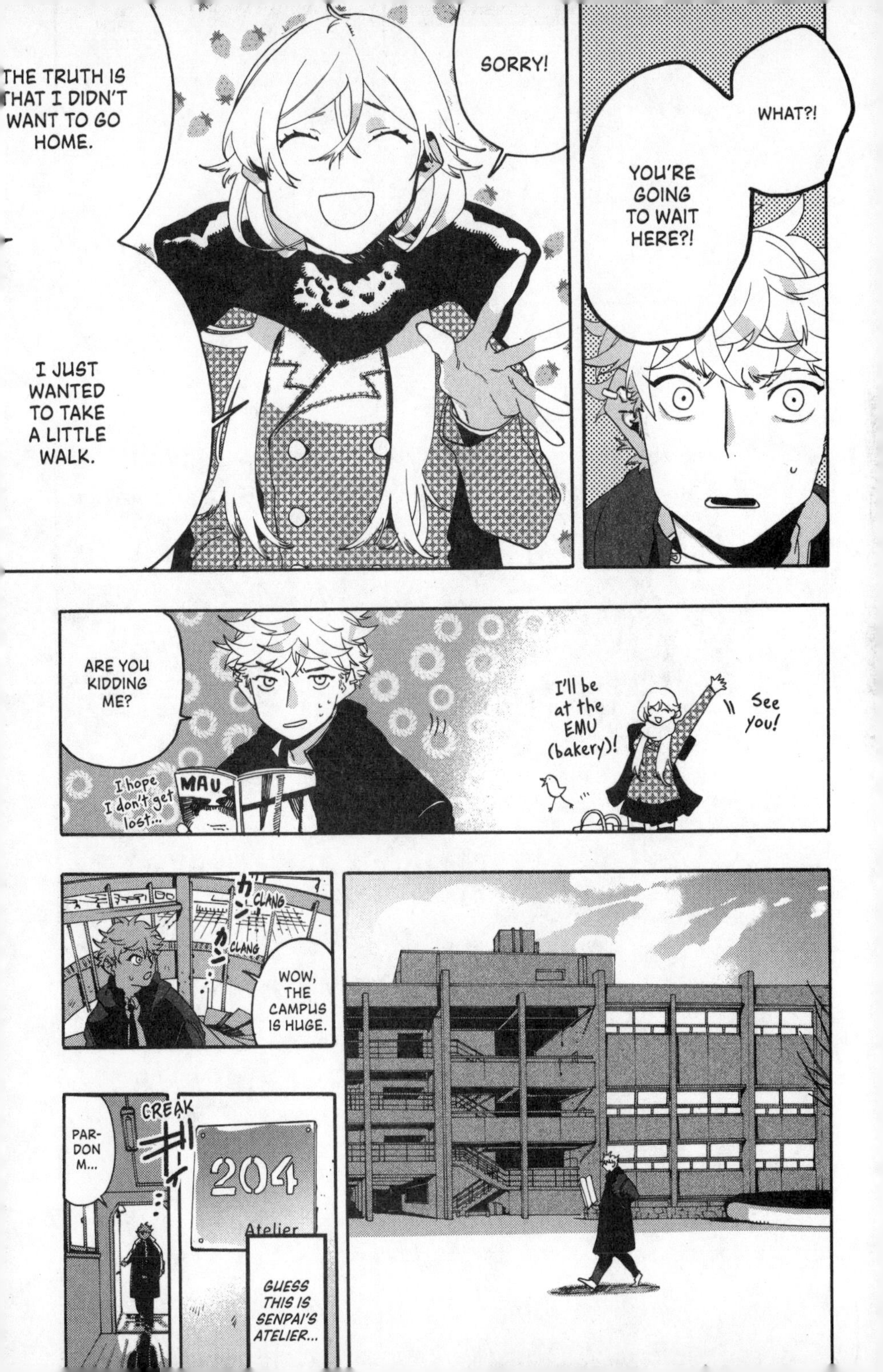
WHAT?!
YOU'RE GOING TO WAIT HERE?!
SORRY!
THE TRUTH IS THAT I DIDN'T WANT TO GO HOME.
I JUST WANTED TO TAKE A LITTLE WALK.
See you!
I'll be at the EMU (bakery)!
ARE YOU KIDDING ME?
MAU
I hope I don't get lost...
CLANG
CLANG
WOW, THE CAMPUS IS HUGE.
CREAK
PAR-DON M...
204
Atelier
GUESS THIS IS SENPAI'S ATELIER...

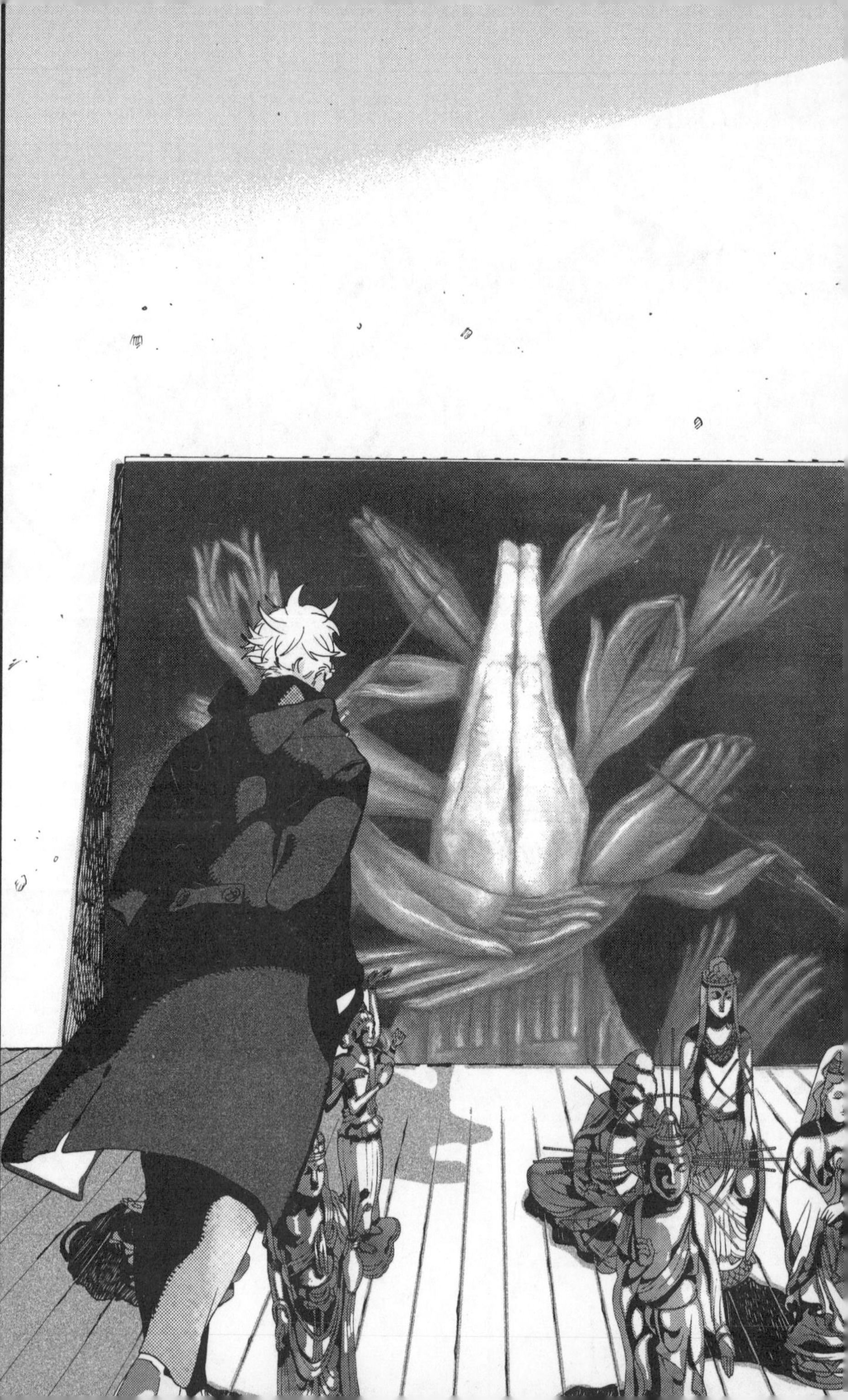

ART: MARIMO TOMORI

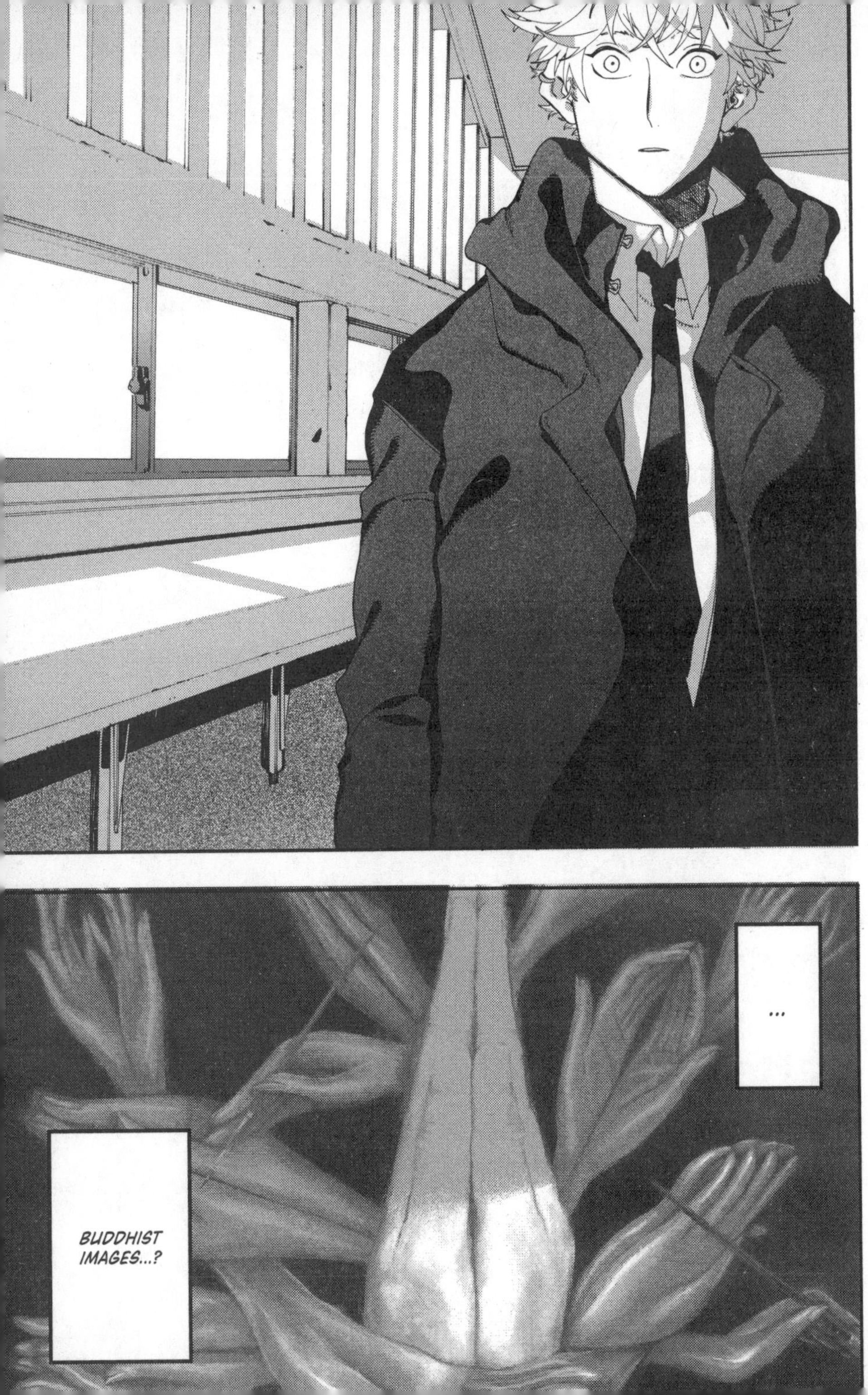
...
BUDDHIST IMAGES...?

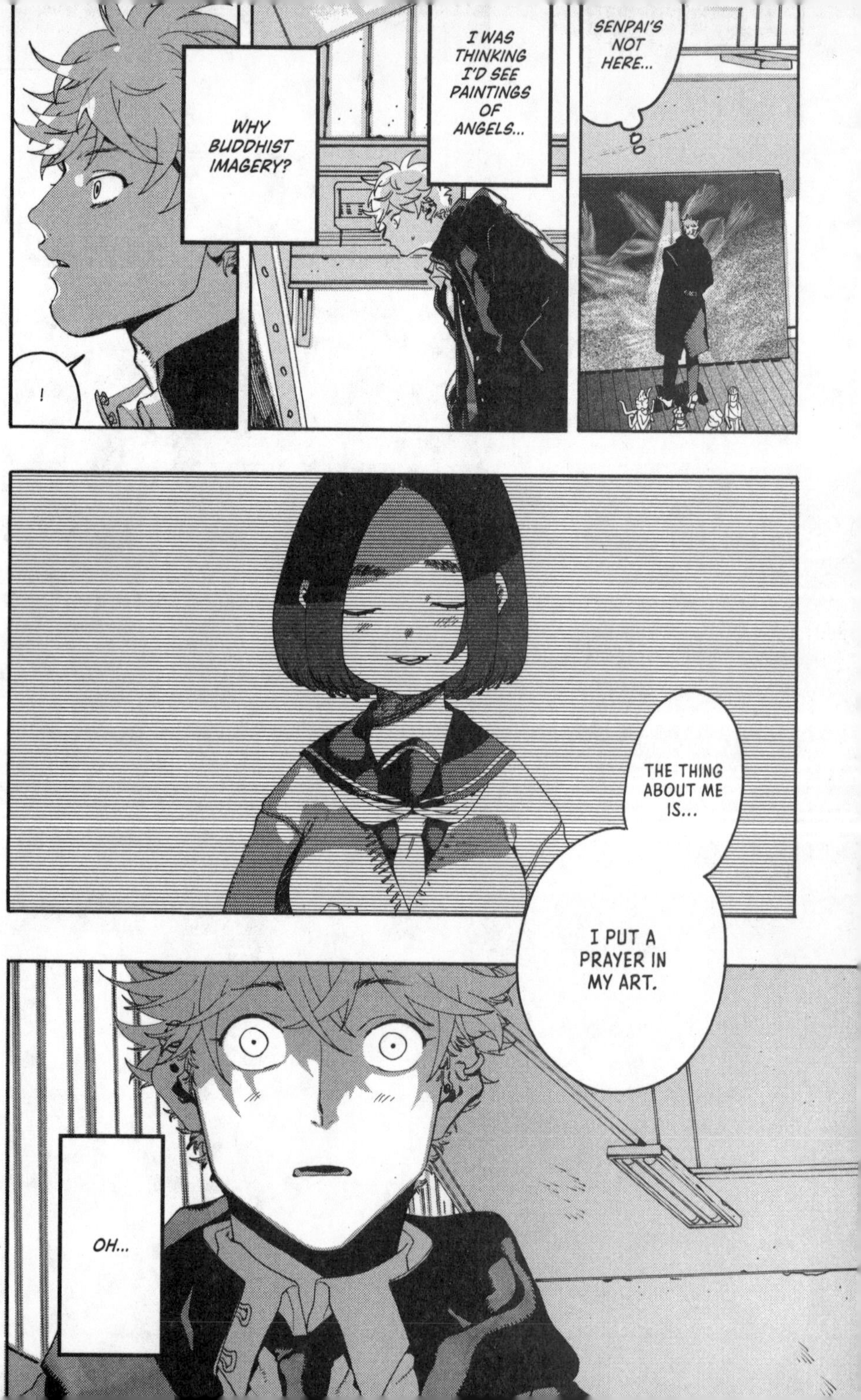
SENPAI'S NOT HERE...
I WAS THINKING I'D SEE PAINTINGS OF ANGELS...
WHY BUDDHIST IMAGERY?
!
THE THING ABOUT ME IS...
I PUT A PRAYER IN MY ART.
OH...

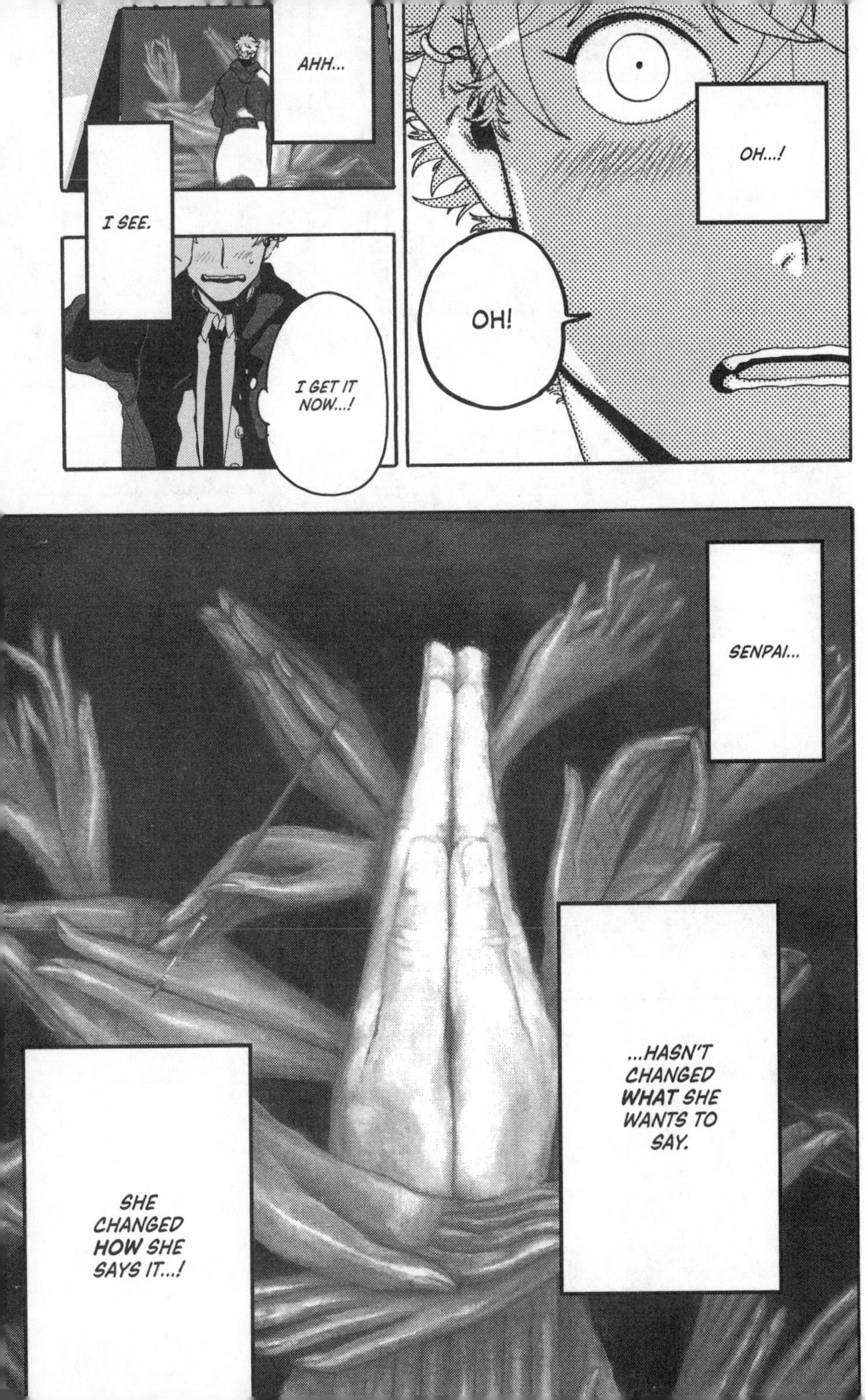
OH...!
OH!
AHH...
I SEE.
I GET IT NOW...!
SENPAI...
...HASN'T CHANGED WHAT SHE WANTS TO SAY.
SHE CHANGED HOW SHE SAYS IT...!

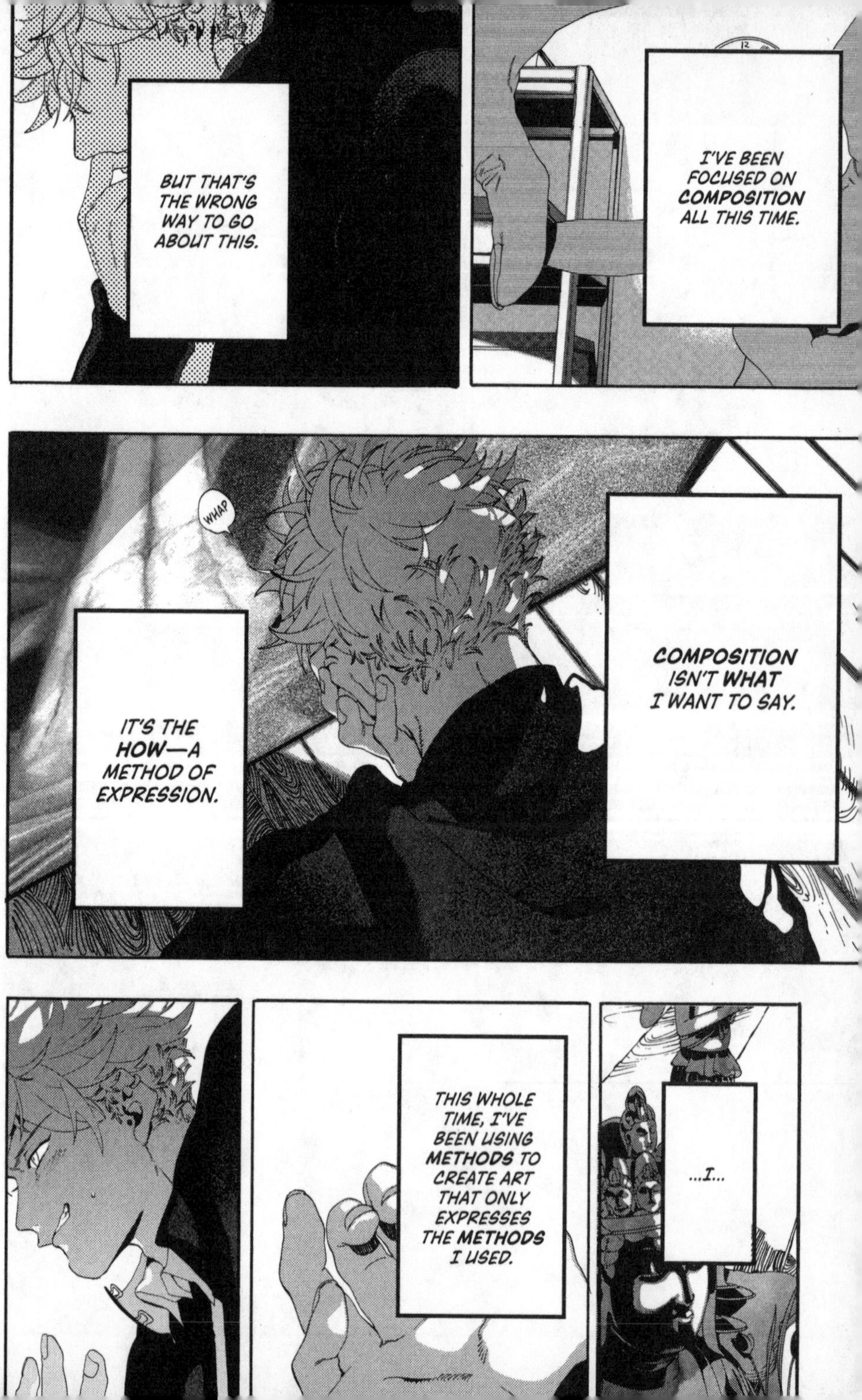
I'VE BEEN FOCUSED ON COMPOSITION ALL THIS TIME.
BUT THAT'S THE WRONG WAY TO GO ABOUT THIS.
COMPOSITION ISN'T WHAT I WANT TO SAY.
WHAP
IT'S THE HOW—A METHOD OF EXPRESSION.
...I...
THIS WHOLE TIME, I'VE BEEN USING METHODS TO CREATE ART THAT ONLY EXPRESSES THE METHODS I USED.

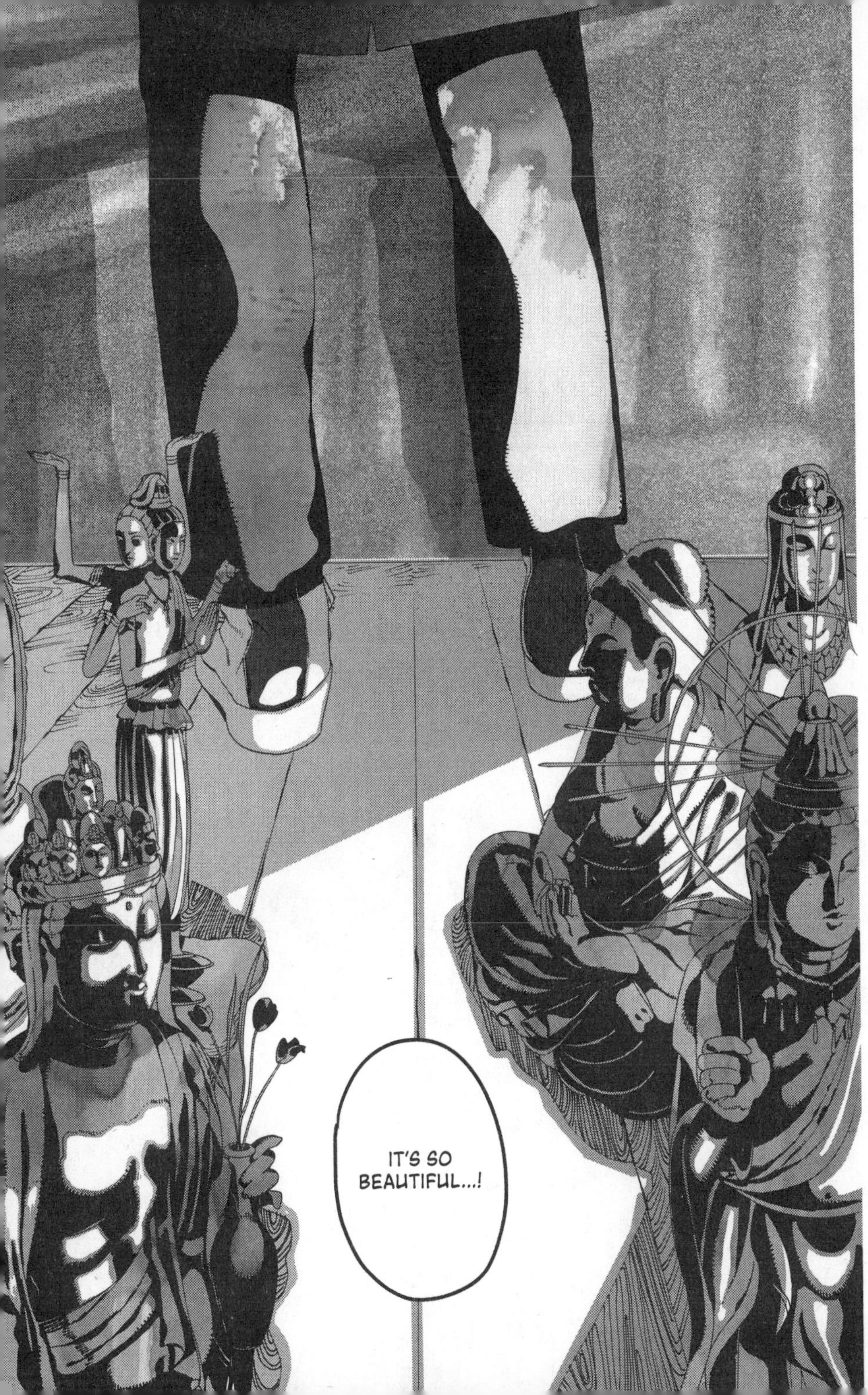
IT'S SO BEAUTIFUL...!

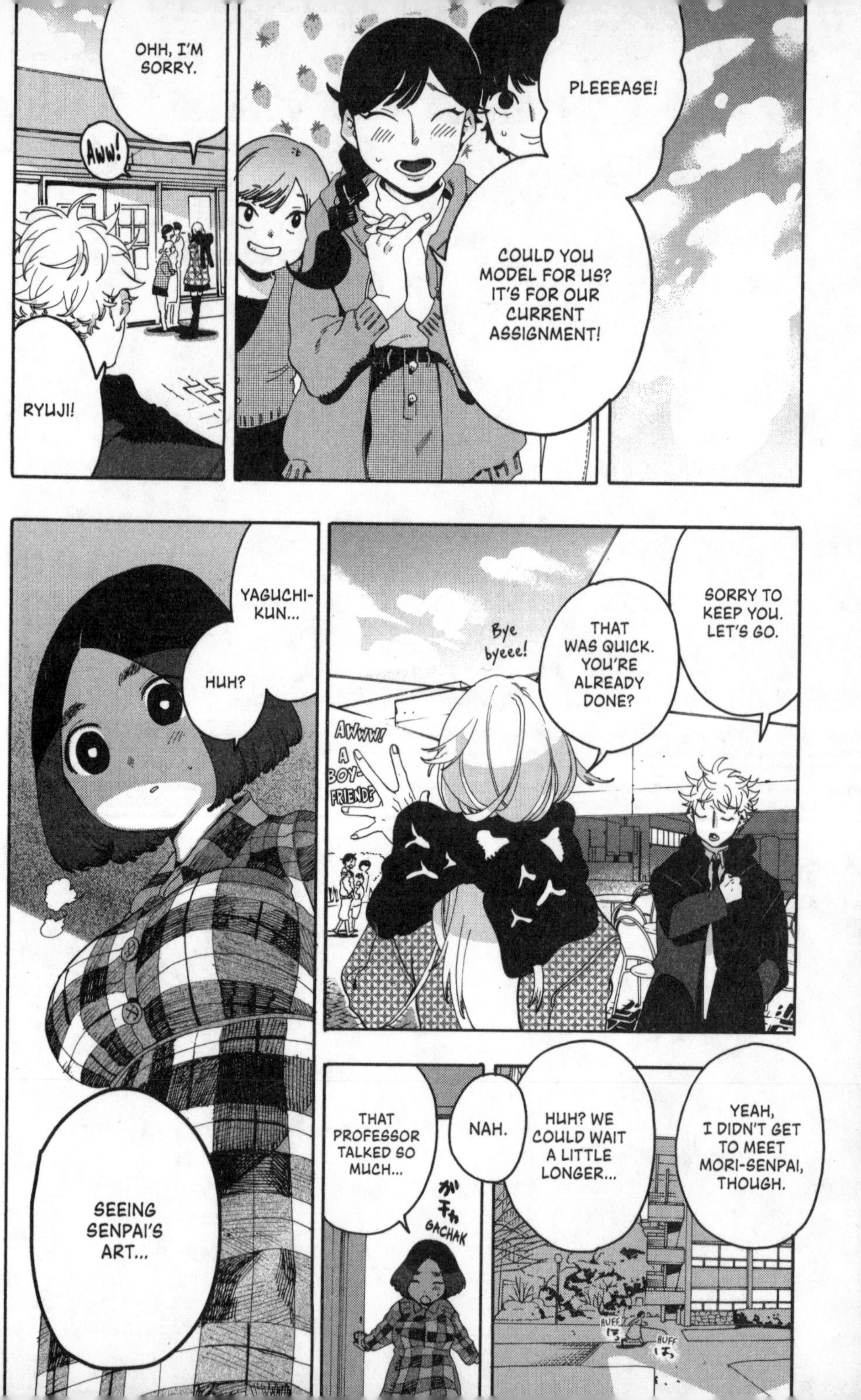

PLEEEASE!
COULD YOU MODEL FOR US? IT'S FOR OUR CURRENT ASSIGNMENT!
OHH, I'M SORRY.
Aww!
RYUJI!
SORRY TO KEEP YOU. LET'S GO.
THAT WAS QUICK. YOU'RE ALREADY DONE?
Bye byeee!
AWWW! A BOY-FRIEND?
YEAH, I DIDN'T GET TO MEET MORI-SENPAI, THOUGH.
HUH? WE COULD WAIT A LITTLE LONGER...
NAH.
HUFF
HUFF
THAT PROFESSOR TALKED SO MUCH...
GACHAK
YAGUCHI-KUN...
HUH?
SEEING SENPAI'S ART...

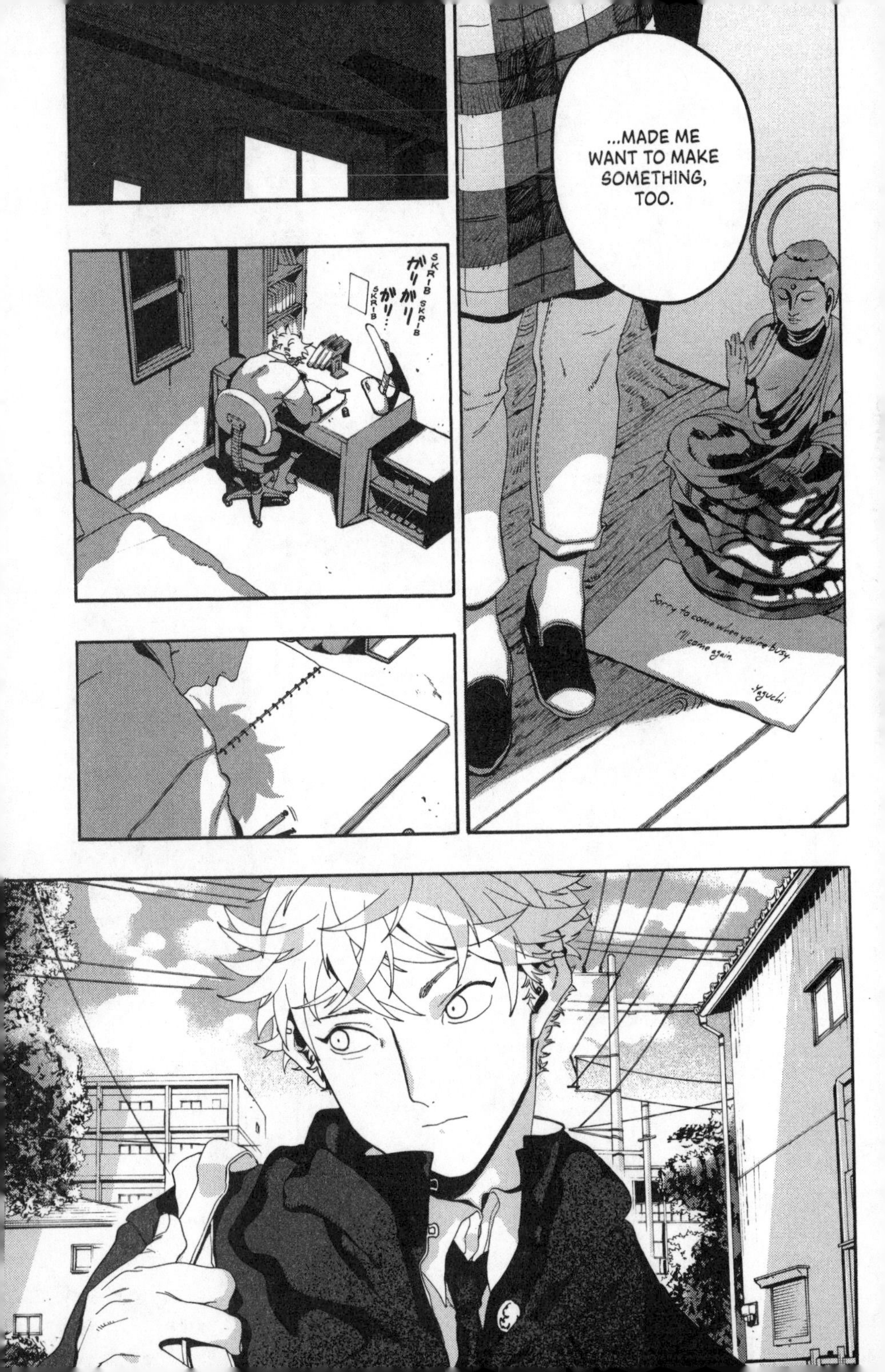
...MADE ME WANT TO MAKE SOMETHING, TOO.
Sorry to come when you're busy.
I'll come again.
-Yaguchi
ガリガリ
SKRIB SKRIB
ガリ…
SKRIB

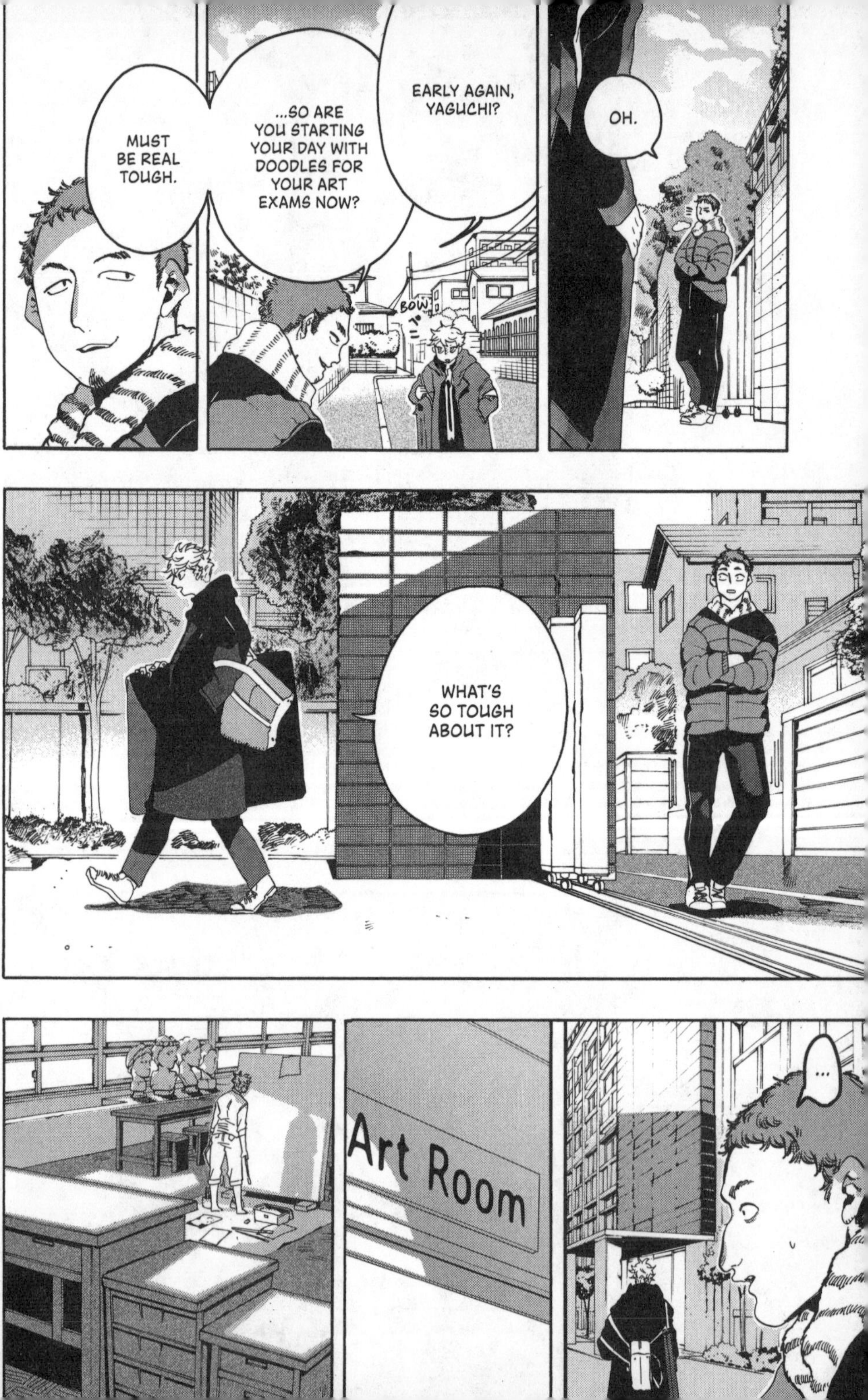
OH.
EARLY AGAIN, YAGUCHI?
...SO ARE YOU STARTING YOUR DAY WITH DOODLES FOR YOUR ART EXAMS NOW?
BOW
MUST BE REAL TOUGH.
WHAT'S SO TOUGH ABOUT IT?
...
Art Room

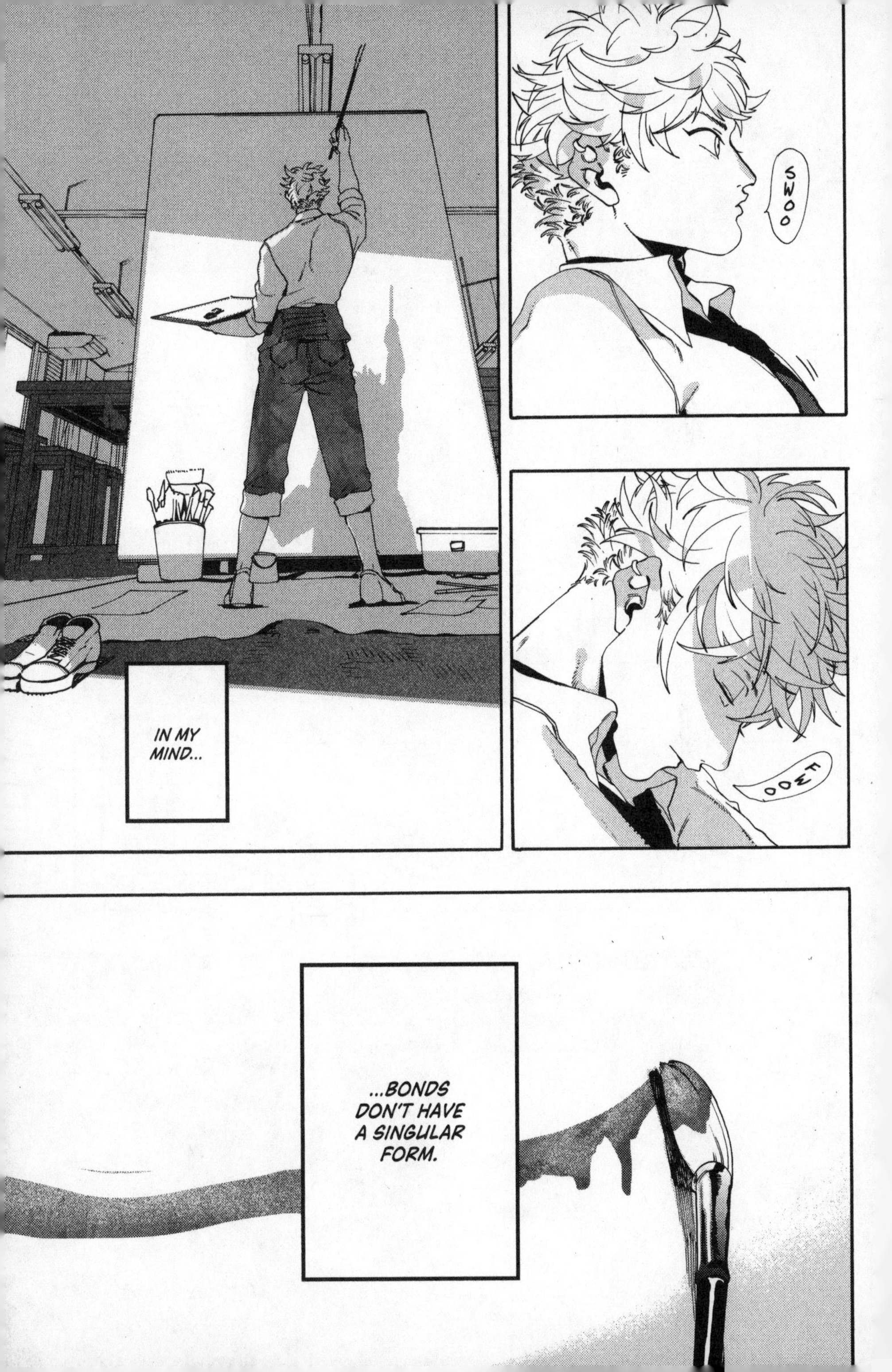
SWOO
FWOO
IN MY MIND...
...BONDS DON'T HAVE A SINGULAR FORM.

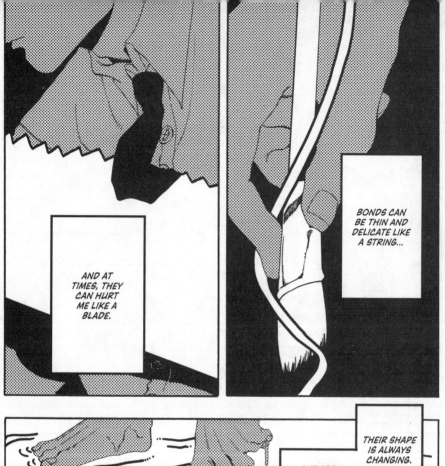

BONDS CAN
BE THIN AND
DELICATE LIKE
A STRING...

AND AT
TIMES, THEY
CAN HURT
ME LIKE A
BLADE.

THEIR SHAPE
IS ALWAYS
CHANGING.

AND WITH
HEAT, THEIR
SHAPE CAN
ALSO CHANGE
WITH THEIR
SURROUND-
INGS.

WITH EVERY
HIT, EVERY
BLOW, THEY
BECOME
STRONGER.

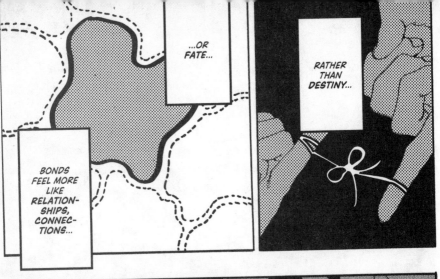

RATHER THAN DESTINY...
...OR FATE...
BONDS FEEL MORE LIKE RELATION-SHIPS, CONNEC-TIONS...
BUT THIS IS MY REALITY...
IT'S MINE...
MY VIEW OF THINGS...
IN MY VIEW, BONDS...

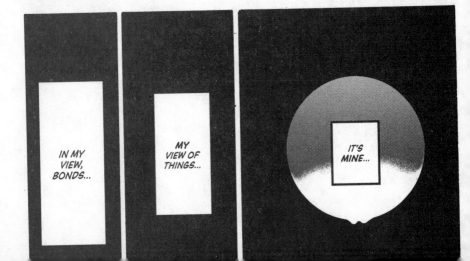

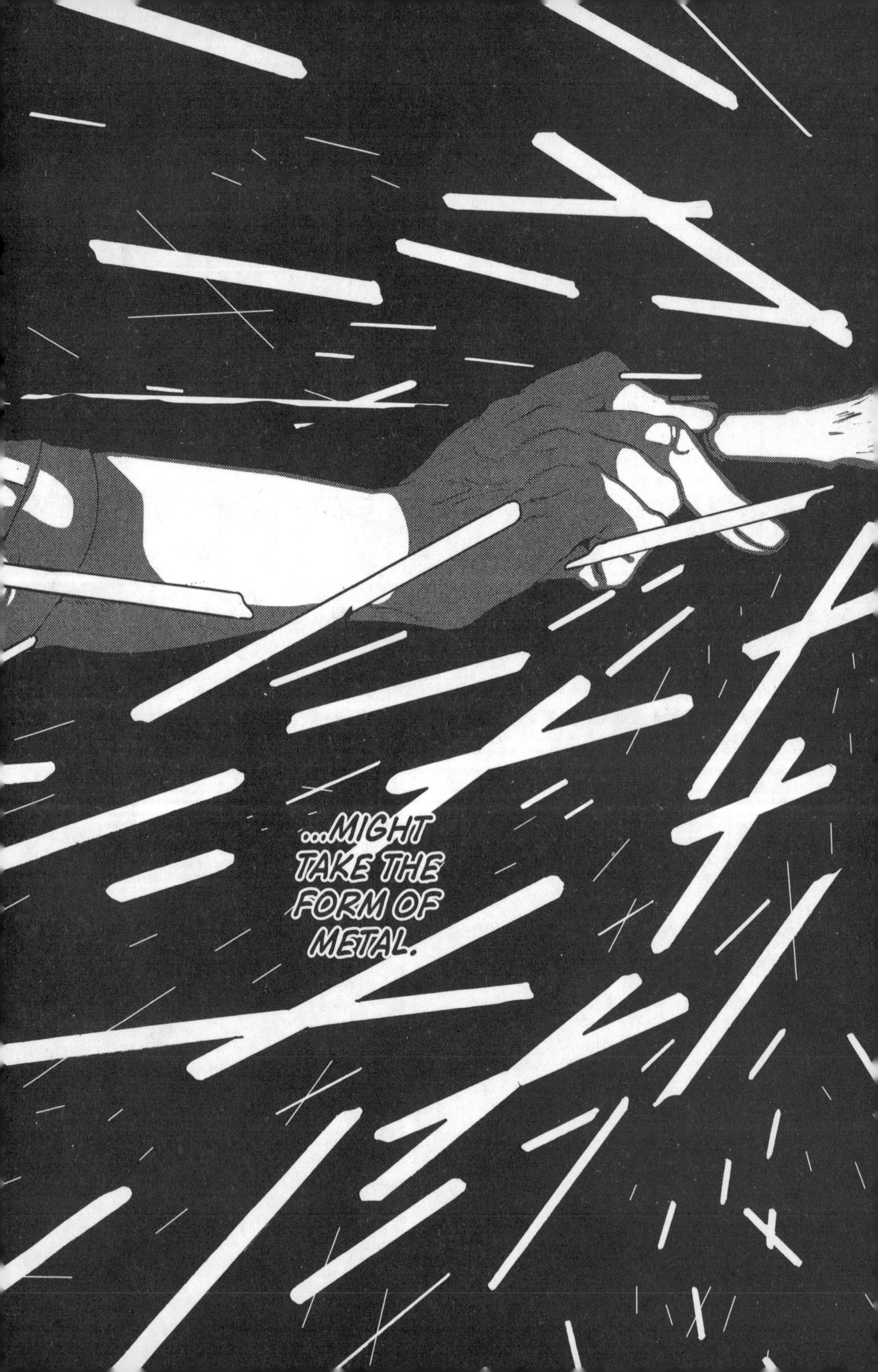
...MIGHT TAKE THE FORM OF METAL.

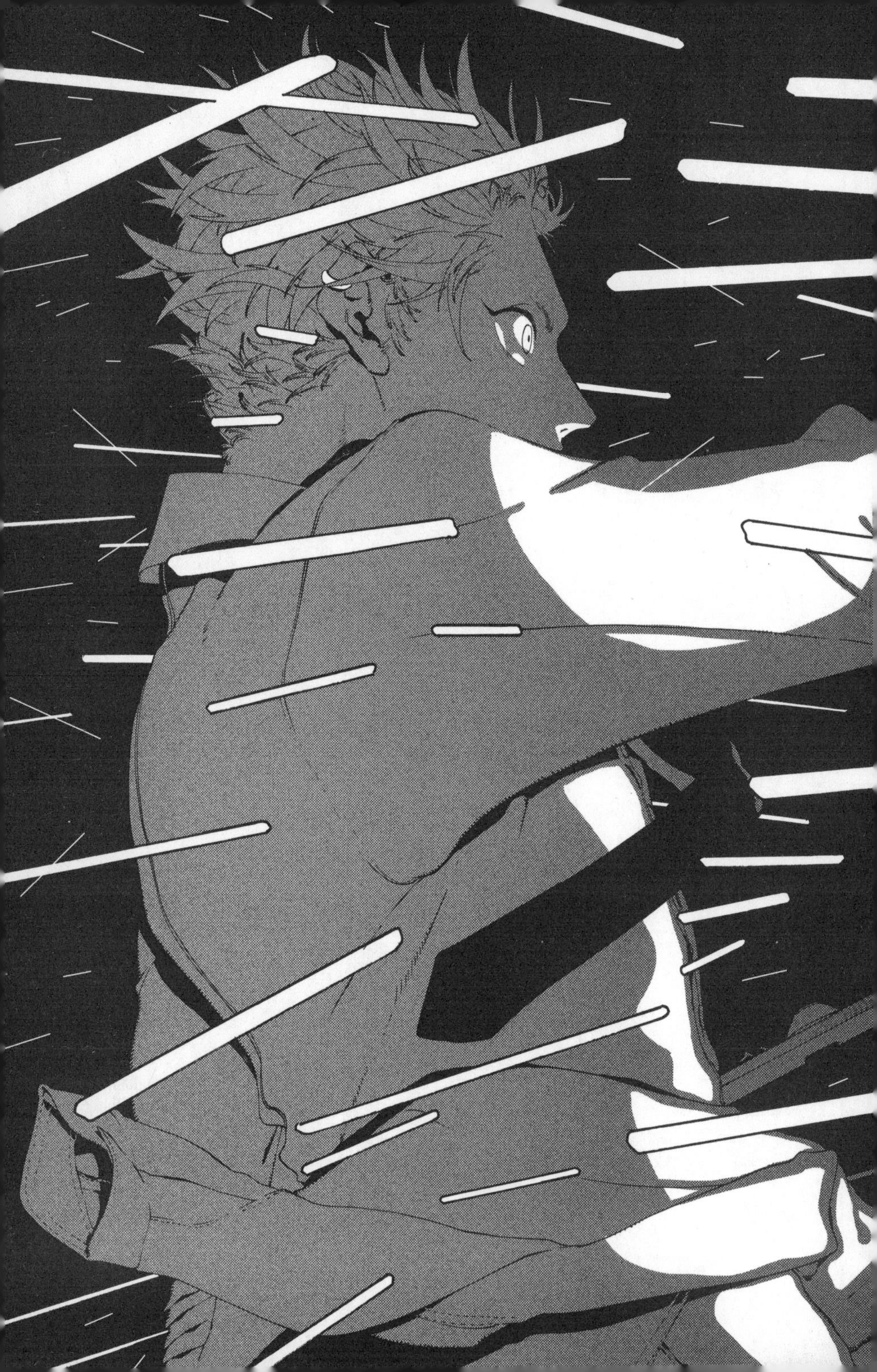

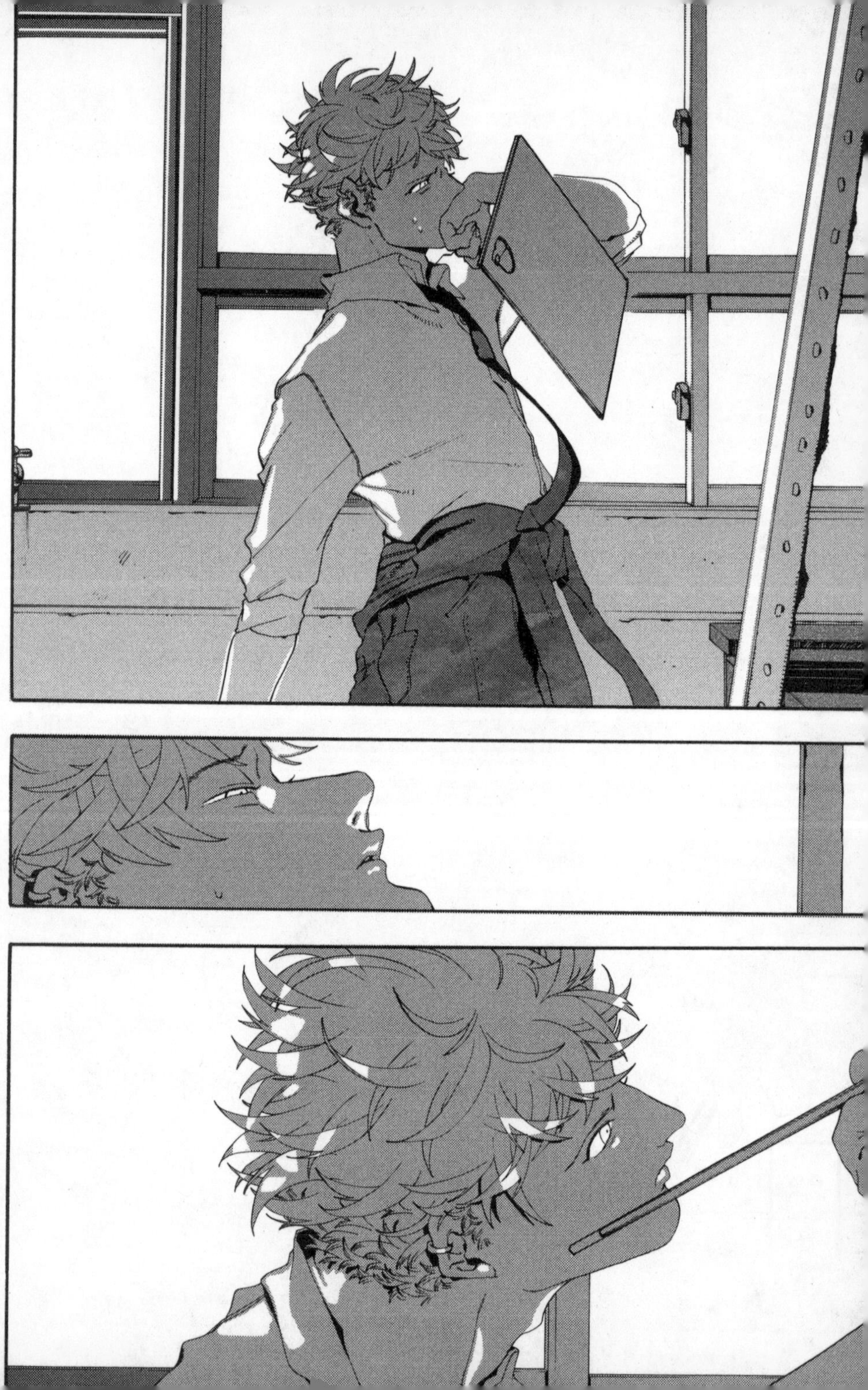

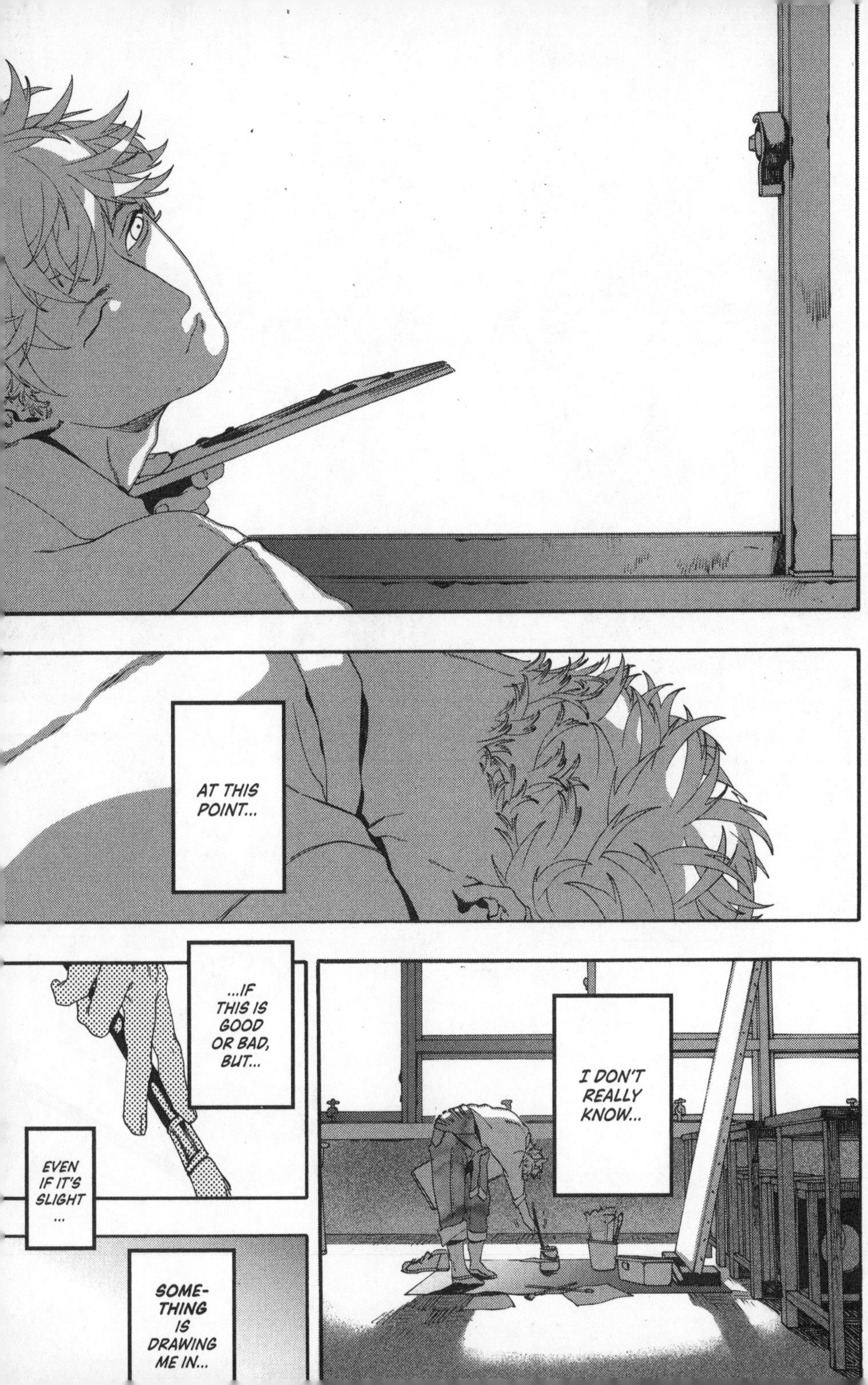
AT THIS POINT...
I DON'T REALLY KNOW...
...IF THIS IS GOOD OR BAD, BUT...
EVEN IF IT'S SLIGHT...
SOME-THING IS DRAWING ME IN...

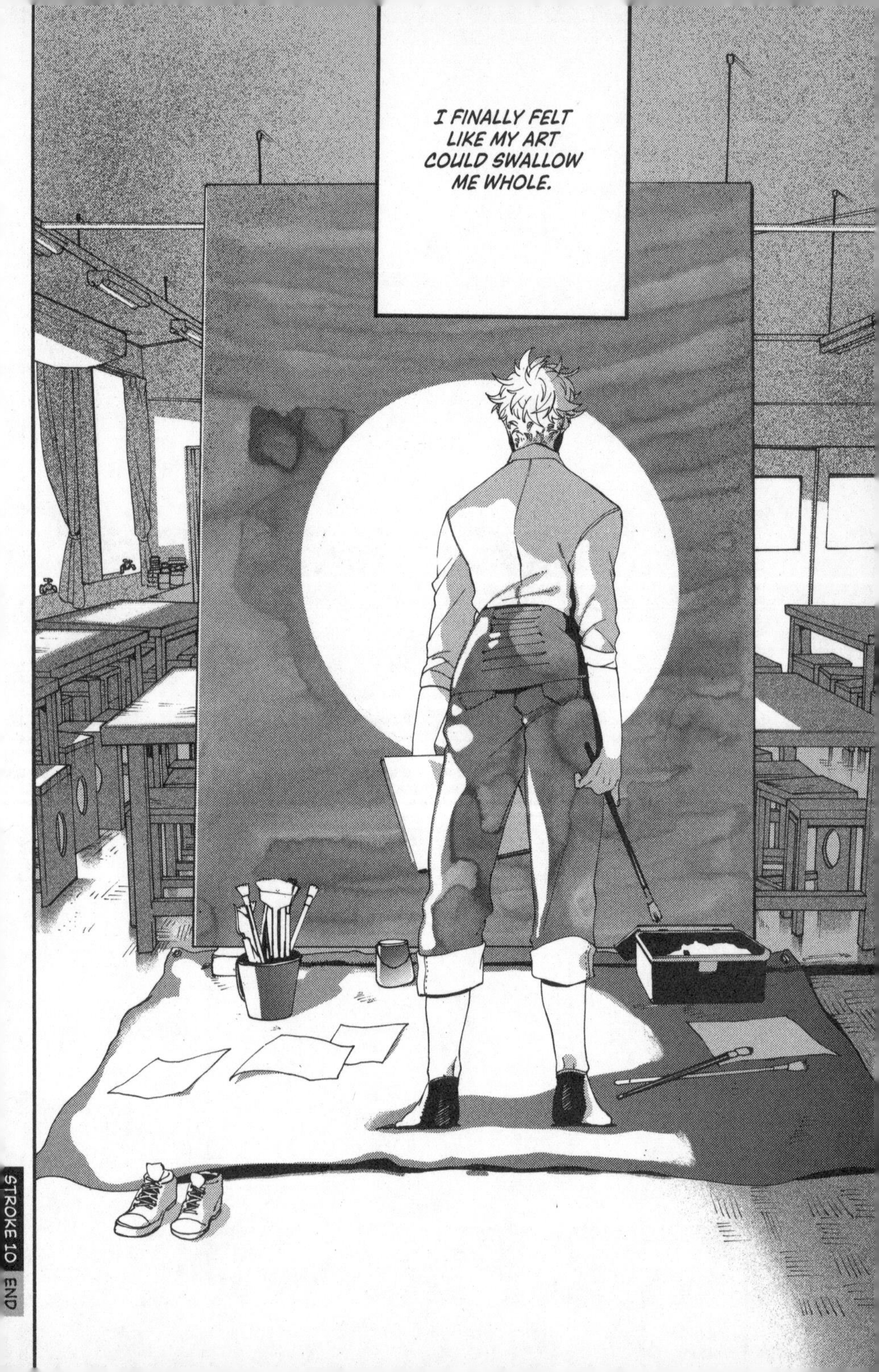
I FINALLY FELT LIKE MY ART COULD SWALLOW ME WHOLE.
STROKE 10 END

BLUE PERIOD

ABOUT THE MEMBERS OF THE ART CLUB (1)

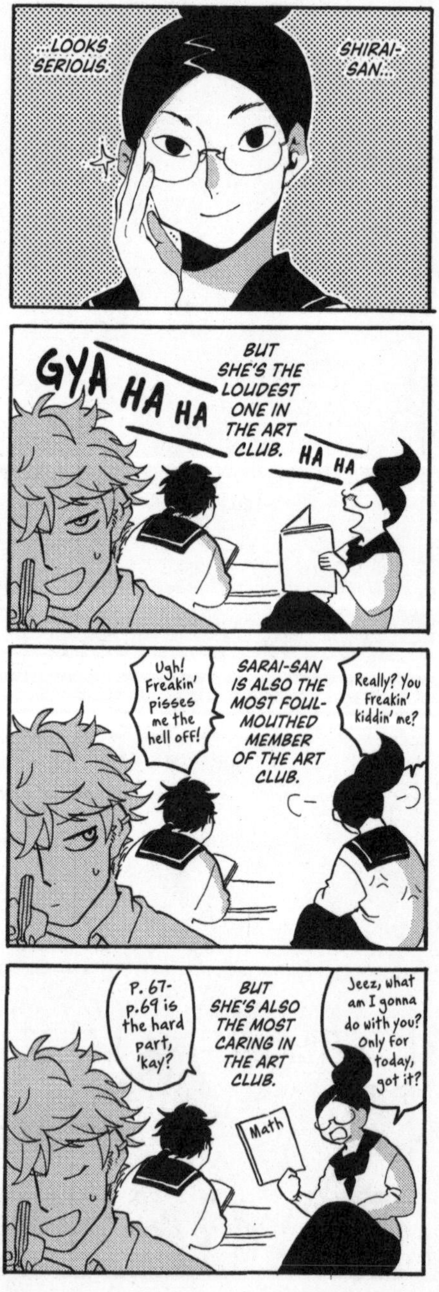
SHIRAI-SAN...
...LOOKS SERIOUS.
GYA HA HA
BUT SHE'S THE LOUDEST ONE IN THE ART CLUB.
HA HA
Really? You Freakin' kiddin' me?
SARAI-SAN IS ALSO THE MOST FOUL-MOUTHED MEMBER OF THE ART CLUB.
Ugh! Freakin' pisses me the hell off!
Jeez, what am I gonna do with you? Only for today, got it?
BUT SHE'S ALSO THE MOST CARING IN THE ART CLUB.
P. 67-p.69 is the hard part, 'kay?
Math

ABOUT THE PREP SCHOOL INSTRUCTOR

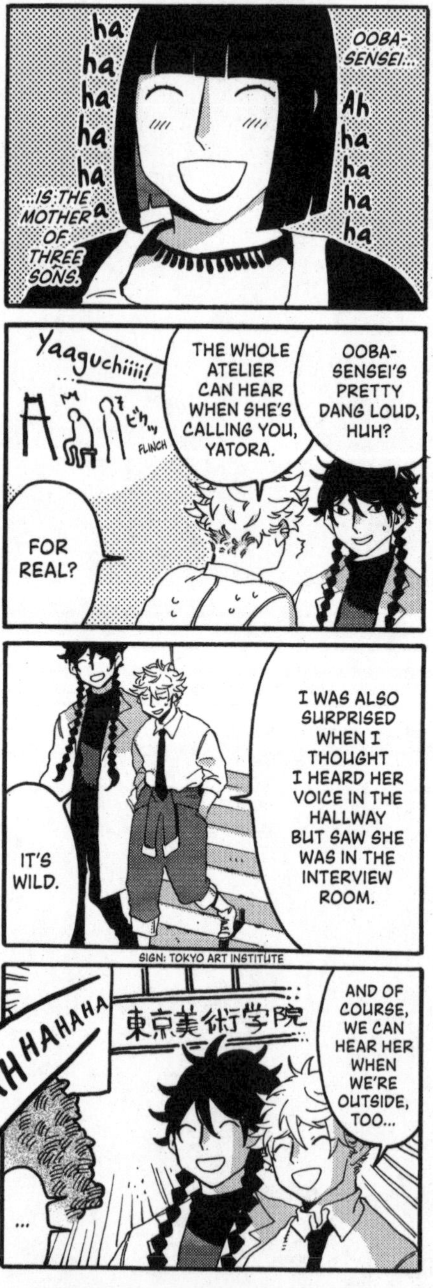
OOBA-SENSEI...
Ah ha ha ha ha ha
ha ha ha ha ha a
...IS THE MOTHER OF THREE SONS.
OOBA-SENSEI'S PRETTY DANG LOUD, HUH?
THE WHOLE ATELIER CAN HEAR WHEN SHE'S CALLING YOU, YATORA.
Yaaguchiiii!
FLINCH
FOR REAL?
I WAS ALSO SURPRISED WHEN I THOUGHT I HEARD HER VOICE IN THE HALLWAY BUT SAW SHE WAS IN THE INTERVIEW ROOM.
IT'S WILD.
SIGN: TOKYO ART INSTITUTE
AND OF COURSE, WE CAN HEAR HER WHEN WE'RE OUTSIDE, TOO...
東京美術学院
AHHAHAHA
...

ABOUT THE MEMBERS OF THE ART CLUB (2)

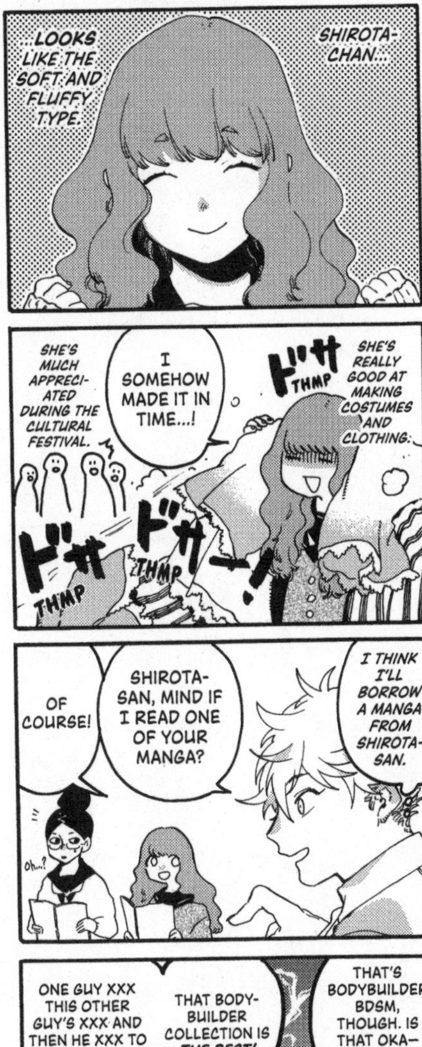
SHIROTA-CHAN...
...LOOKS LIKE THE SOFT AND FLUFFY TYPE.
SHE'S REALLY GOOD AT MAKING COSTUMES AND CLOTHING.
ドサ THMP
I SOMEHOW MADE IT IN TIME...!
SHE'S MUCH APPRECIATED DURING THE CULTURAL FESTIVAL.
ドサー! THMP
ドサ THMP
I THINK I'LL BORROW A MANGA FROM SHIROTA-SAN.
SHIROTA-SAN, MIND IF I READ ONE OF YOUR MANGA?
OF COURSE!
Oh...?
THAT'S BODYBUILDER BDSM, THOUGH. IS THAT OKA— AND TOO LATE!
THAT BODY-BUILDER COLLECTION IS *THE BEST!*
ONE GUY XXX THIS OTHER GUY'S XXX AND THEN HE XXX TO HIS XXX AND UP HIS XXX.

ABOUT THE FRIEND WITH BRAIDED PIGTAILS

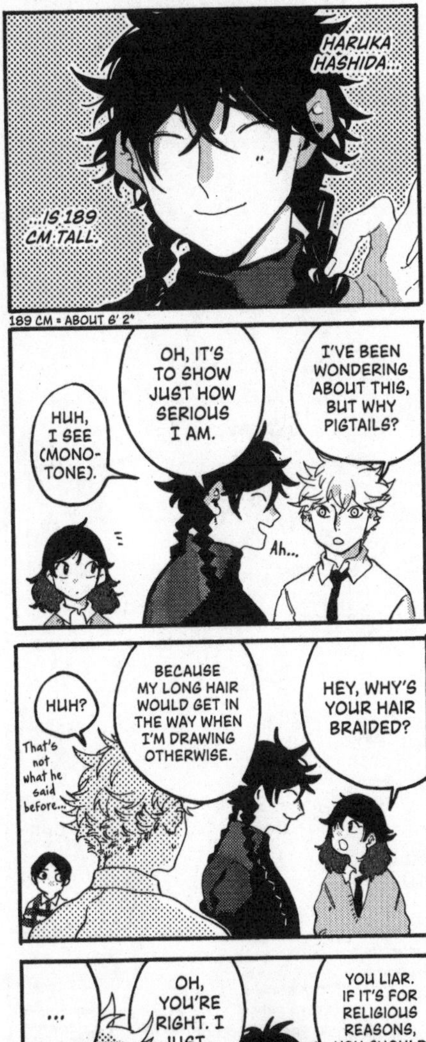
HARUKA HASHIDA...
...IS 189 CM TALL.
I'VE BEEN WONDERING ABOUT THIS, BUT WHY PIGTAILS?
OH, IT'S TO SHOW JUST HOW SERIOUS I AM.
Ah...
HUH, I SEE (MONOTONE).
HEY, WHY'S YOUR HAIR BRAIDED?
BECAUSE MY LONG HAIR WOULD GET IN THE WAY WHEN I'M DRAWING OTHERWISE.
HUH?
That's not what he said before...
YOU LIAR. IF IT'S FOR RELIGIOUS REASONS, YOU SHOULD JUST SAY SO.
OH, YOU'RE RIGHT. I JUST...
...

189 CM = ABOUT 6' 2"

Relatable Content ②

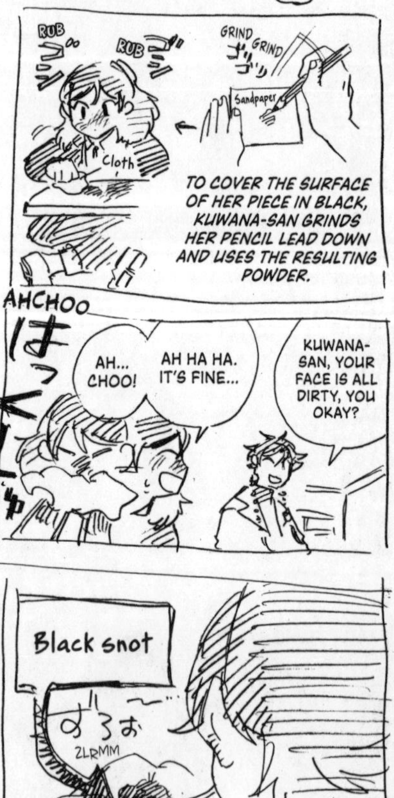
RUB
RUB
GRIND
GRIND
Sandpaper
Cloth
TO COVER THE SURFACE OF HER PIECE IN BLACK, KUWANA-SAN GRINDS HER PENCIL LEAD DOWN AND USES THE RESULTING POWDER.
AHCHOO
KUWANA-SAN, YOUR FACE IS ALL DIRTY, YOU OKAY?
AH HA HA. IT'S FINE...
AH... CHOO!
Black snot
ZLRMM

BLUE PERIOD

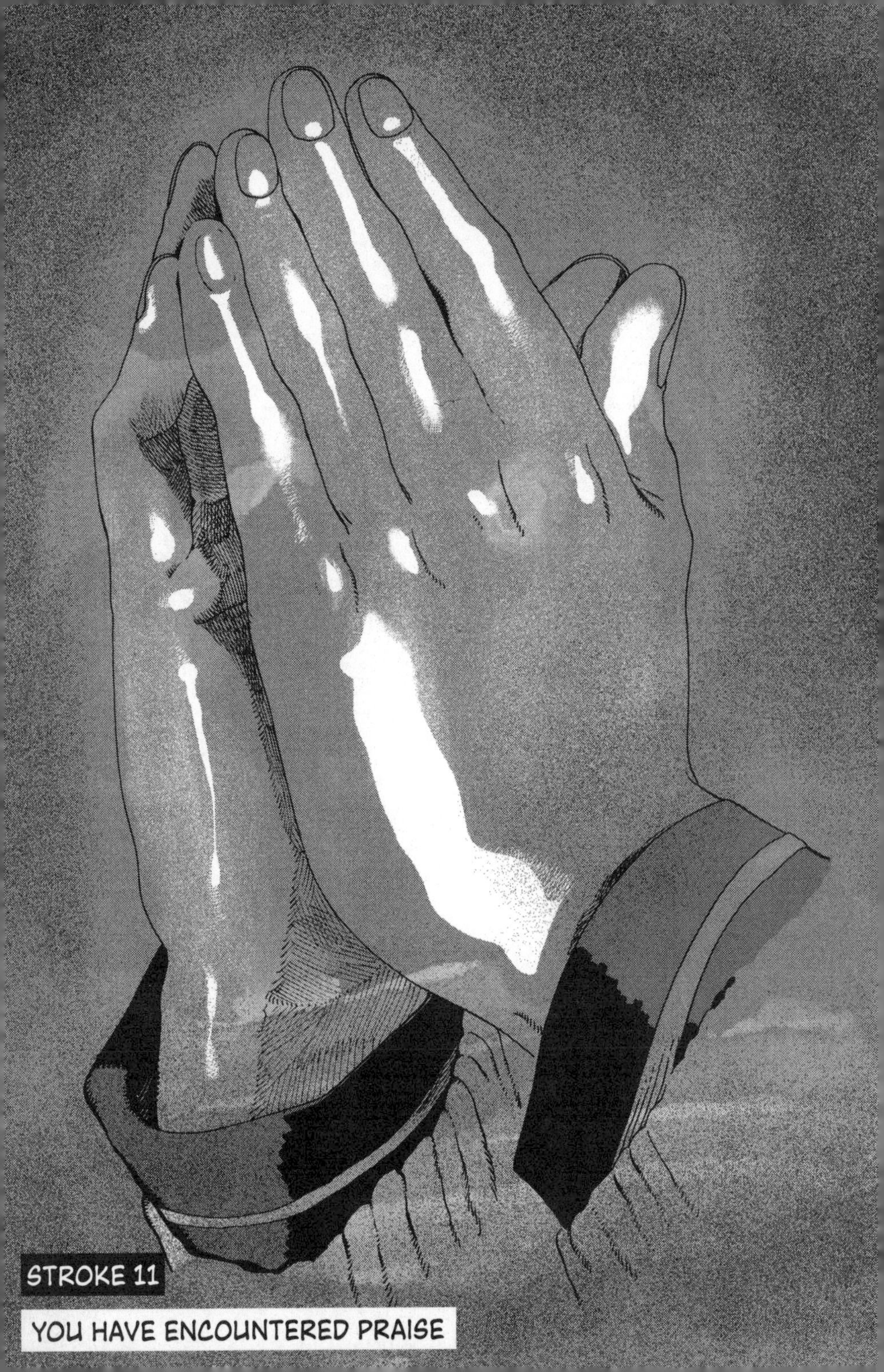

STROKE 11

YOU HAVE ENCOUNTERED PRAISE

ガリ…
SCRIB
がり…
SCRIB
SCRIB
ガリ…
ガリ…
SCRIB
SCRIB
ガリ…
SCRIB
がり…
SCRIB
ガッリ…
SCRIB
ガリ…
SCRIB
ガリ…
がり…
SCRIB
SCRIB
ガリ…

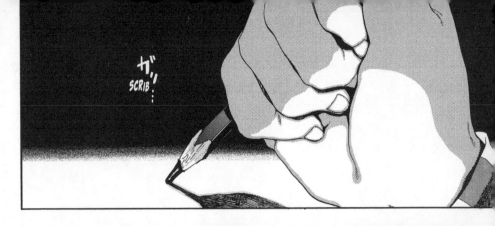

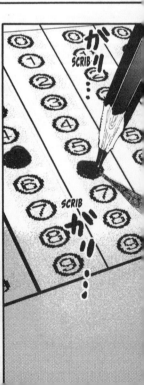

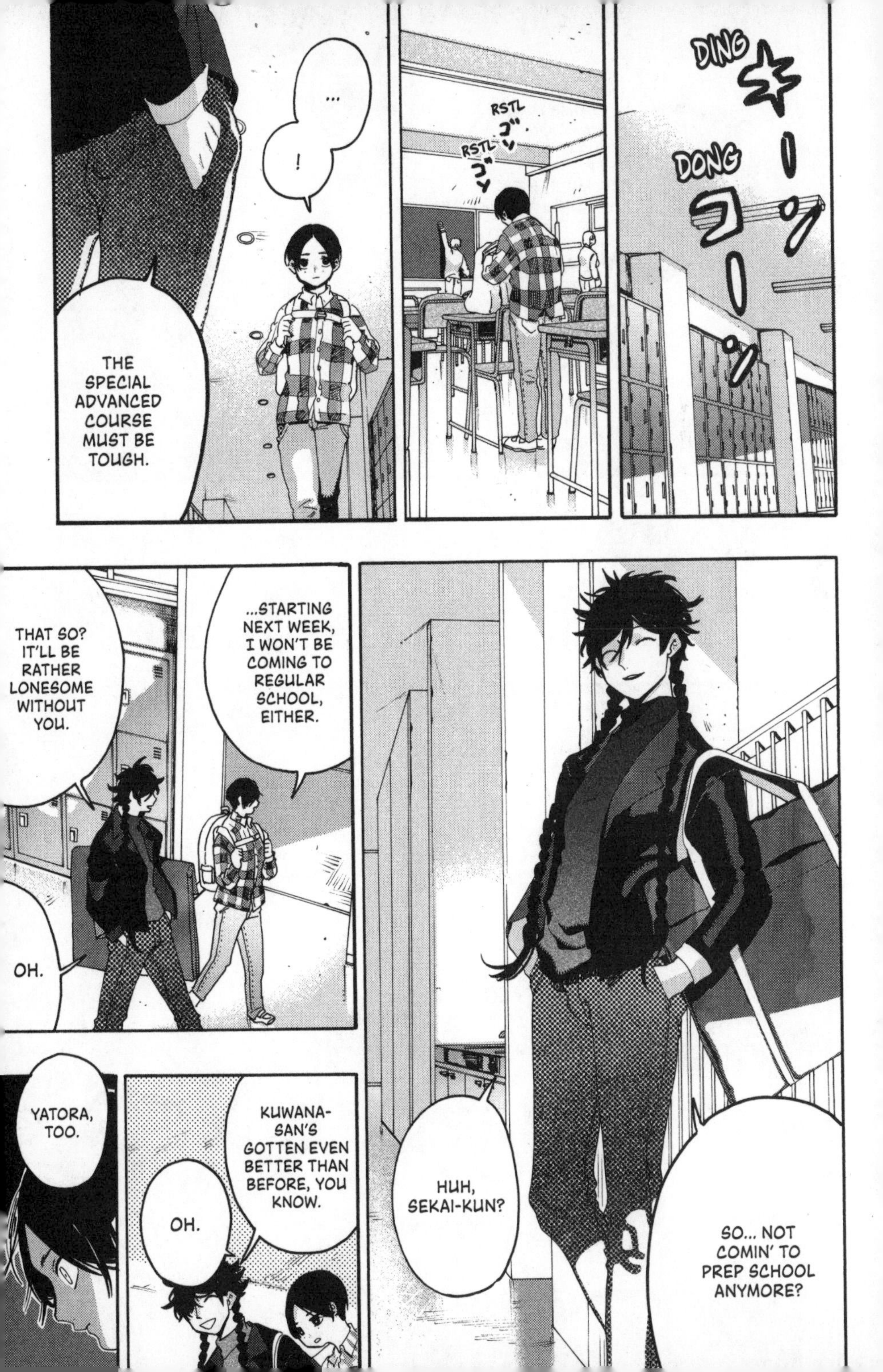
DING
DONG
RSTL
RSTL
...
!
THE SPECIAL ADVANCED COURSE MUST BE TOUGH.
HUH, SEKAI-KUN?
SO... NOT COMIN' TO PREP SCHOOL ANYMORE?
...STARTING NEXT WEEK, I WON'T BE COMING TO REGULAR SCHOOL, EITHER.
THAT SO? IT'LL BE RATHER LONESOME WITHOUT YOU.
OH.
KUWANA-SAN'S GOTTEN EVEN BETTER THAN BEFORE, YOU KNOW.
OH.
YATORA, TOO.

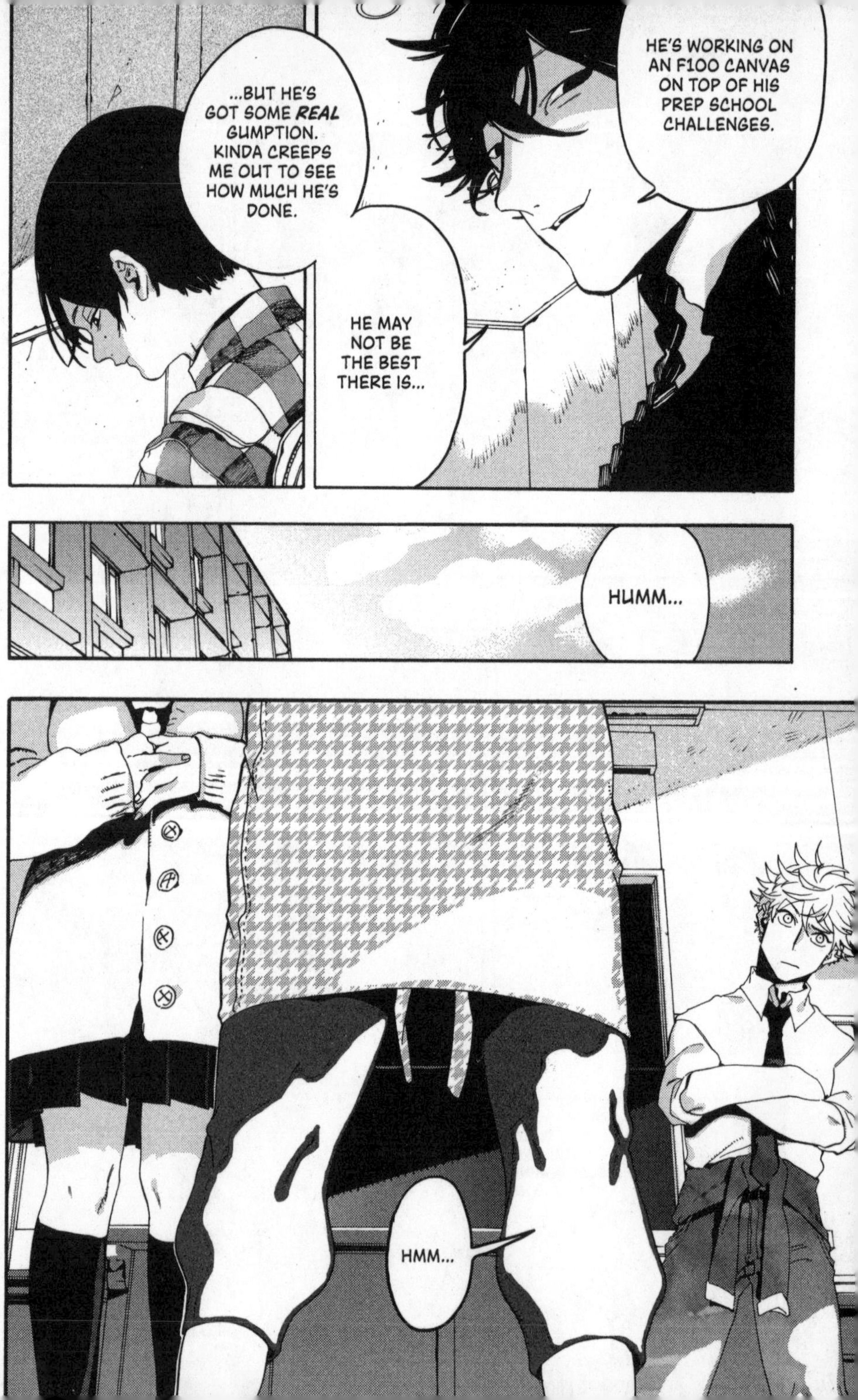
HE'S WORKING ON AN F100 CANVAS ON TOP OF HIS PREP SCHOOL CHALLENGES.
HE MAY NOT BE THE BEST THERE IS...
...BUT HE'S GOT SOME *REAL* GUMPTION. KINDA CREEPS ME OUT TO SEE HOW MUCH HE'S DONE.
HUMM...
HMM...

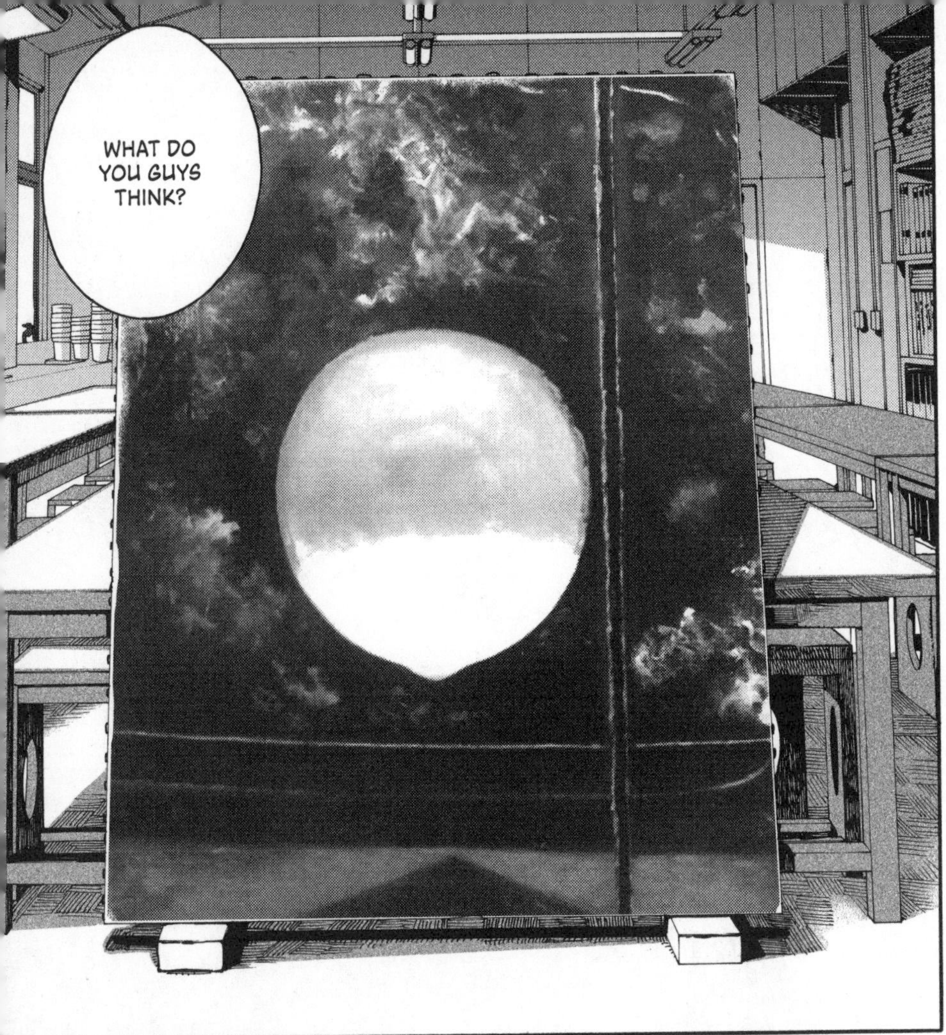
WHAT DO YOU GUYS THINK?

ART: SHOTA YAMAMICHI

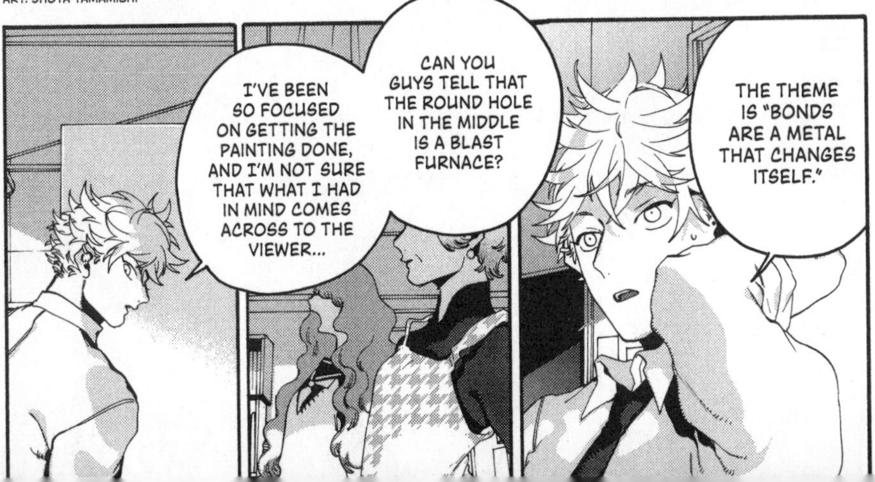
THE THEME IS "BONDS ARE A METAL THAT CHANGES ITSELF."
CAN YOU GUYS TELL THAT THE ROUND HOLE IN THE MIDDLE IS A BLAST FURNACE?
I'VE BEEN SO FOCUSED ON GETTING THE PAINTING DONE, AND I'M NOT SURE THAT WHAT I HAD IN MIND COMES ACROSS TO THE VIEWER...

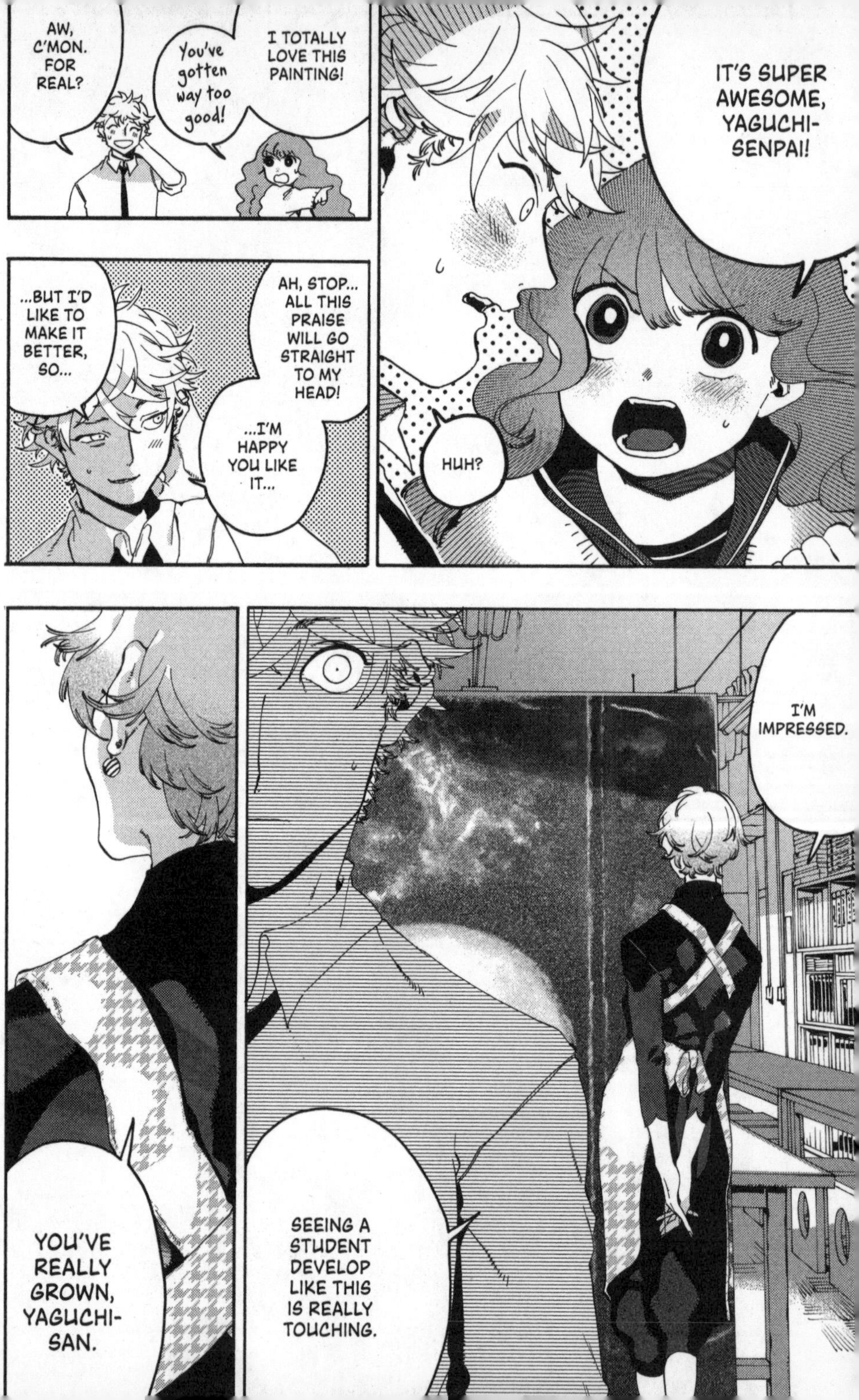
IT'S SUPER AWESOME, YAGUCHI-SENPAI!
HUH?
I TOTALLY LOVE THIS PAINTING!
You've gotten way too good!
AW, C'MON. FOR REAL?
AH, STOP... ALL THIS PRAISE WILL GO STRAIGHT TO MY HEAD!
...I'M HAPPY YOU LIKE IT...
...BUT I'D LIKE TO MAKE IT BETTER, SO...
I'M IMPRESSED.
SEEING A STUDENT DEVELOP LIKE THIS IS REALLY TOUCHING.
YOU'VE REALLY GROWN, YAGUCHI-SAN.

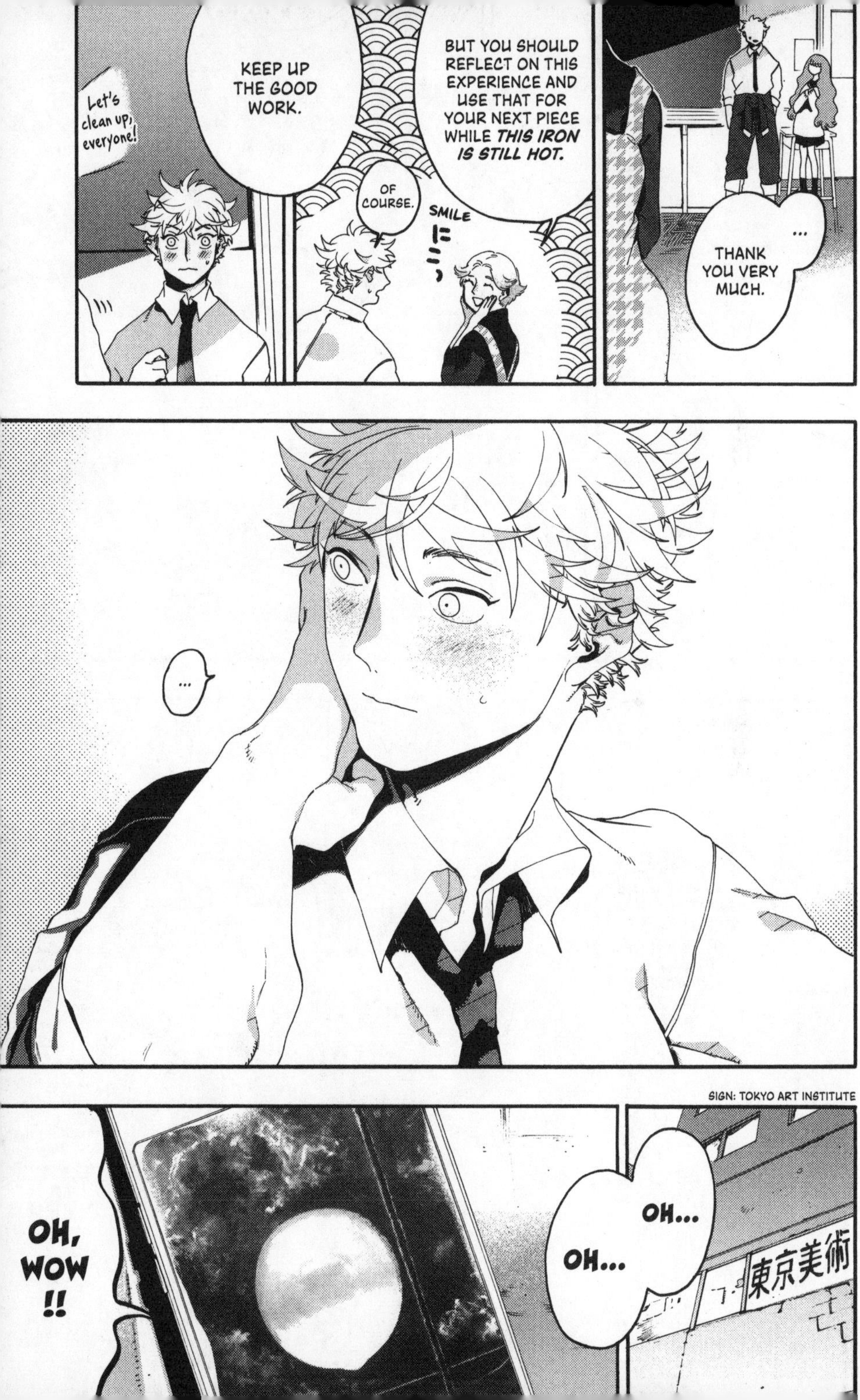
...
THANK YOU VERY MUCH.
KEEP UP THE GOOD WORK.
BUT YOU SHOULD REFLECT ON THIS EXPERIENCE AND USE THAT FOR YOUR NEXT PIECE WHILE ***THIS IRON IS STILL HOT.***
OF COURSE.
SMILE
にこっ
Let's clean up, everyone!
...
SIGN: TOKYO ART INSTITUTE
東京美術
OH...
OH...
OH, WOW!!

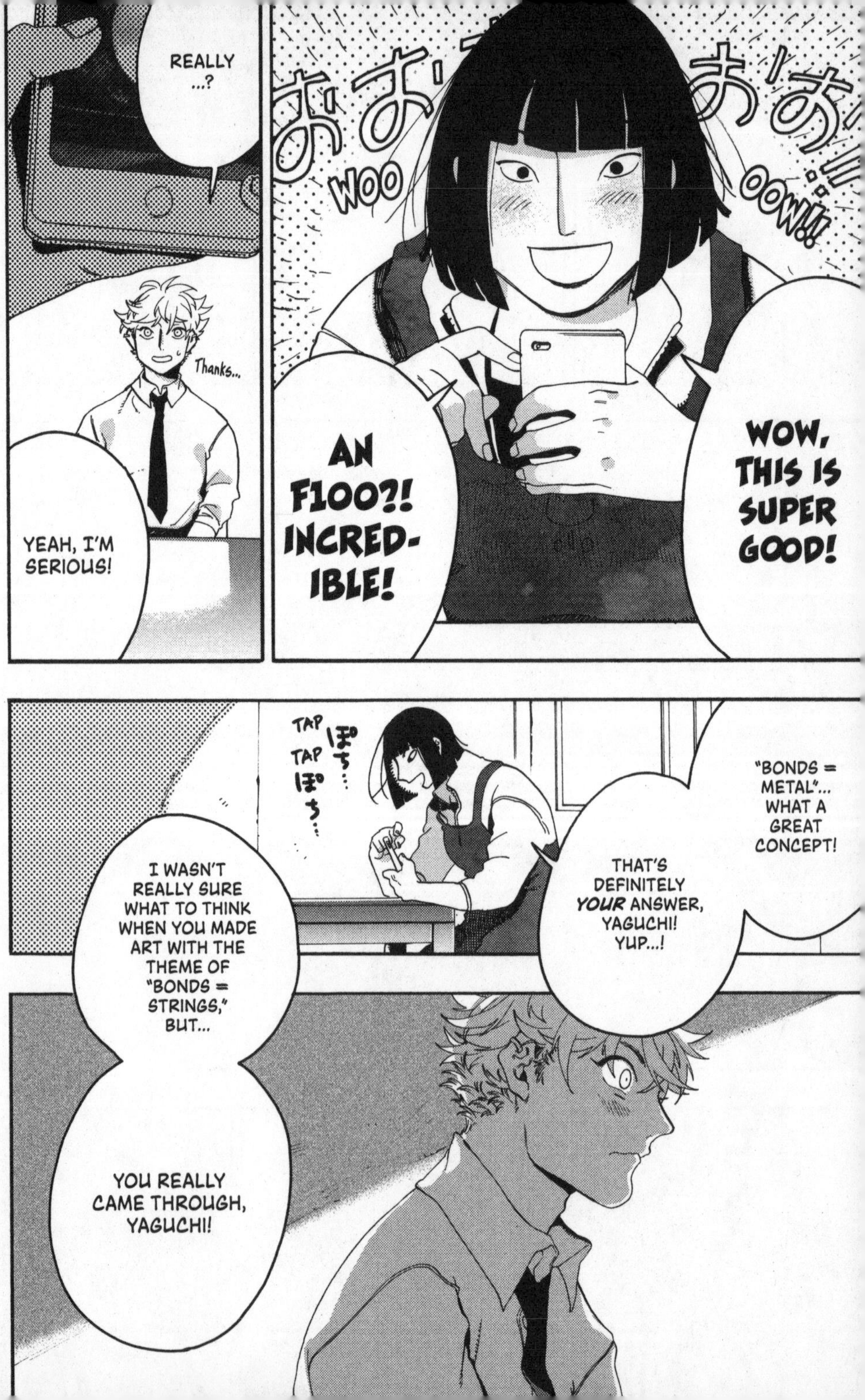
おお
おお!!
WOO
OOW!!
WOW, THIS IS SUPER GOOD!
AN F100?! INCRED-IBLE!
REALLY ...?
Thanks...
YEAH, I'M SERIOUS!
"BONDS = METAL"... WHAT A GREAT CONCEPT!
TAP ぽち...
TAP ぽち...
THAT'S DEFINITELY *YOUR* ANSWER, YAGUCHI! YUP...!
I WASN'T REALLY SURE WHAT TO THINK WHEN YOU MADE ART WITH THE THEME OF "BONDS = STRINGS," BUT...
YOU REALLY CAME THROUGH, YAGUCHI!

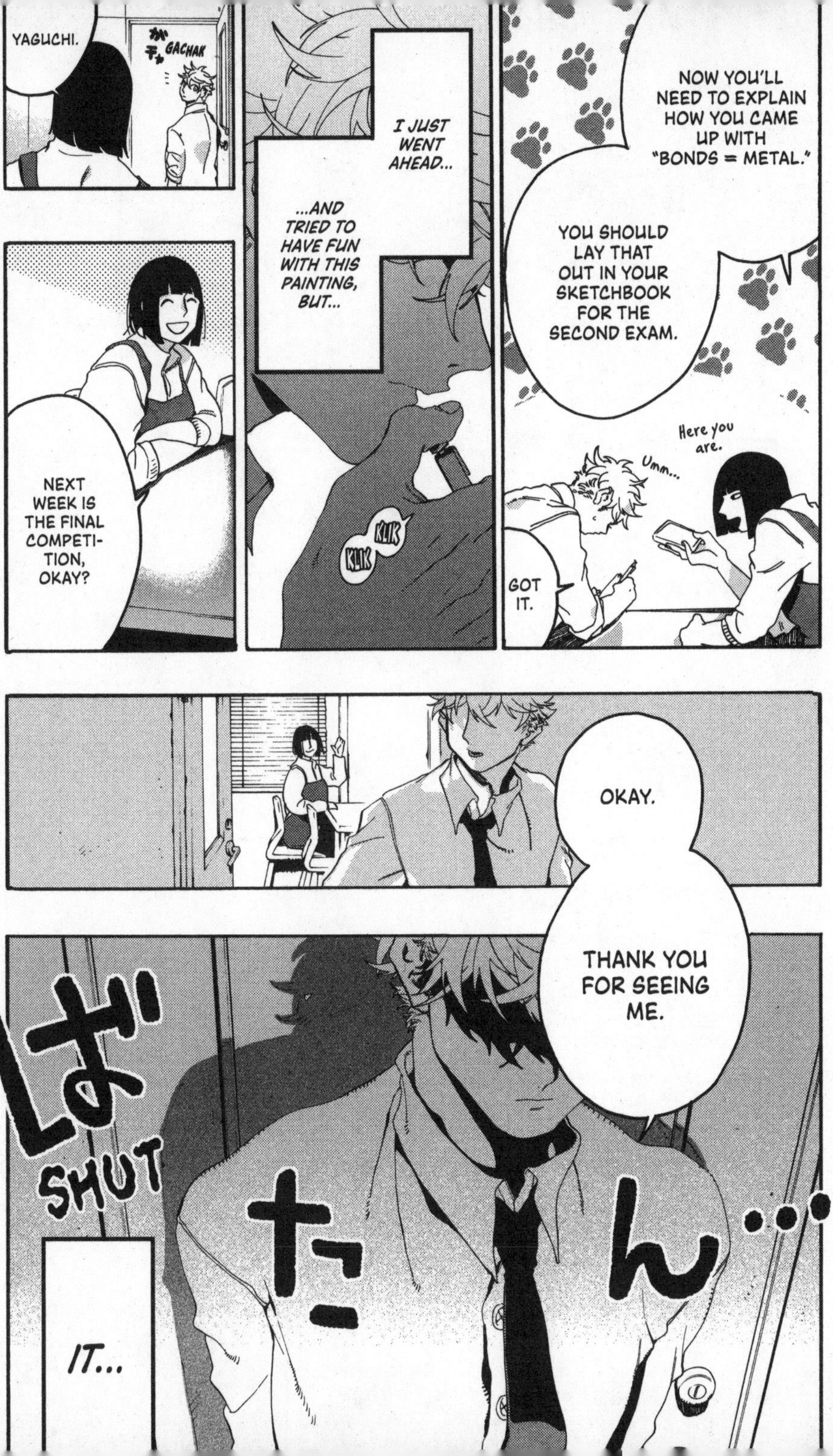
NOW YOU'LL NEED TO EXPLAIN HOW YOU CAME UP WITH "BONDS = METAL."
YOU SHOULD LAY THAT OUT IN YOUR SKETCHBOOK FOR THE SECOND EXAM.
Here you are.
Umm...
GOT IT.
I JUST WENT AHEAD...
...AND TRIED TO HAVE FUN WITH THIS PAINTING, BUT...
KLIK
KLIK
YAGUCHI.
GACHAK
NEXT WEEK IS THE FINAL COMPETITION, OKAY?
OKAY.
THANK YOU FOR SEEING ME.
ばたん…
SHUT
IT...

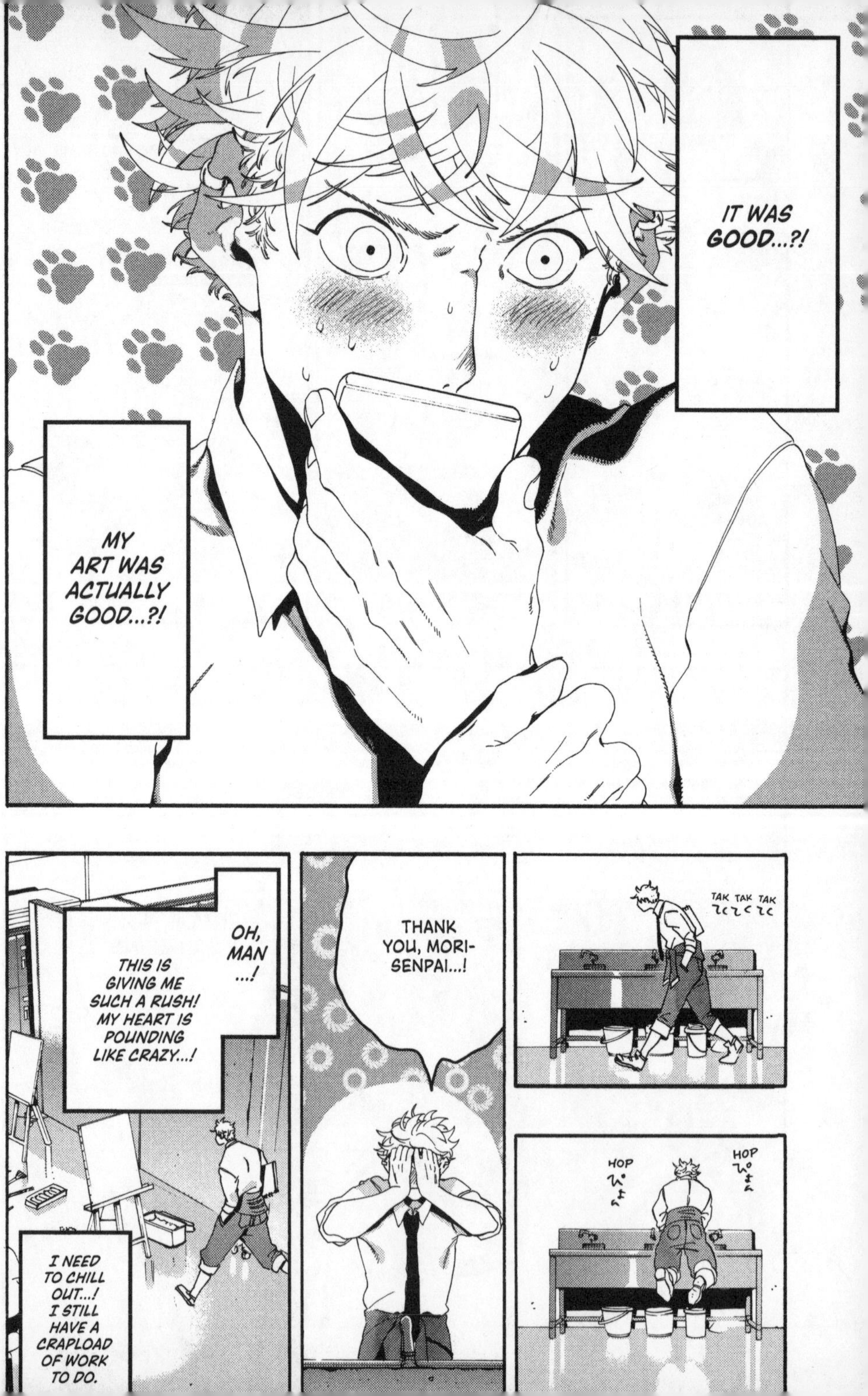
IT WAS GOOD...?!
MY ART WAS ACTUALLY GOOD...?!
TAK TAK TAK
てくてくてく
HOP
ぴょん
HOP
ぴょん
THANK YOU, MORI-SENPAI...!
OH, MAN ...!
THIS IS GIVING ME SUCH A RUSH! MY HEART IS POUNDING LIKE CRAZY...!
I NEED TO CHILL OUT...! I STILL HAVE A CRAPLOAD OF WORK TO DO.

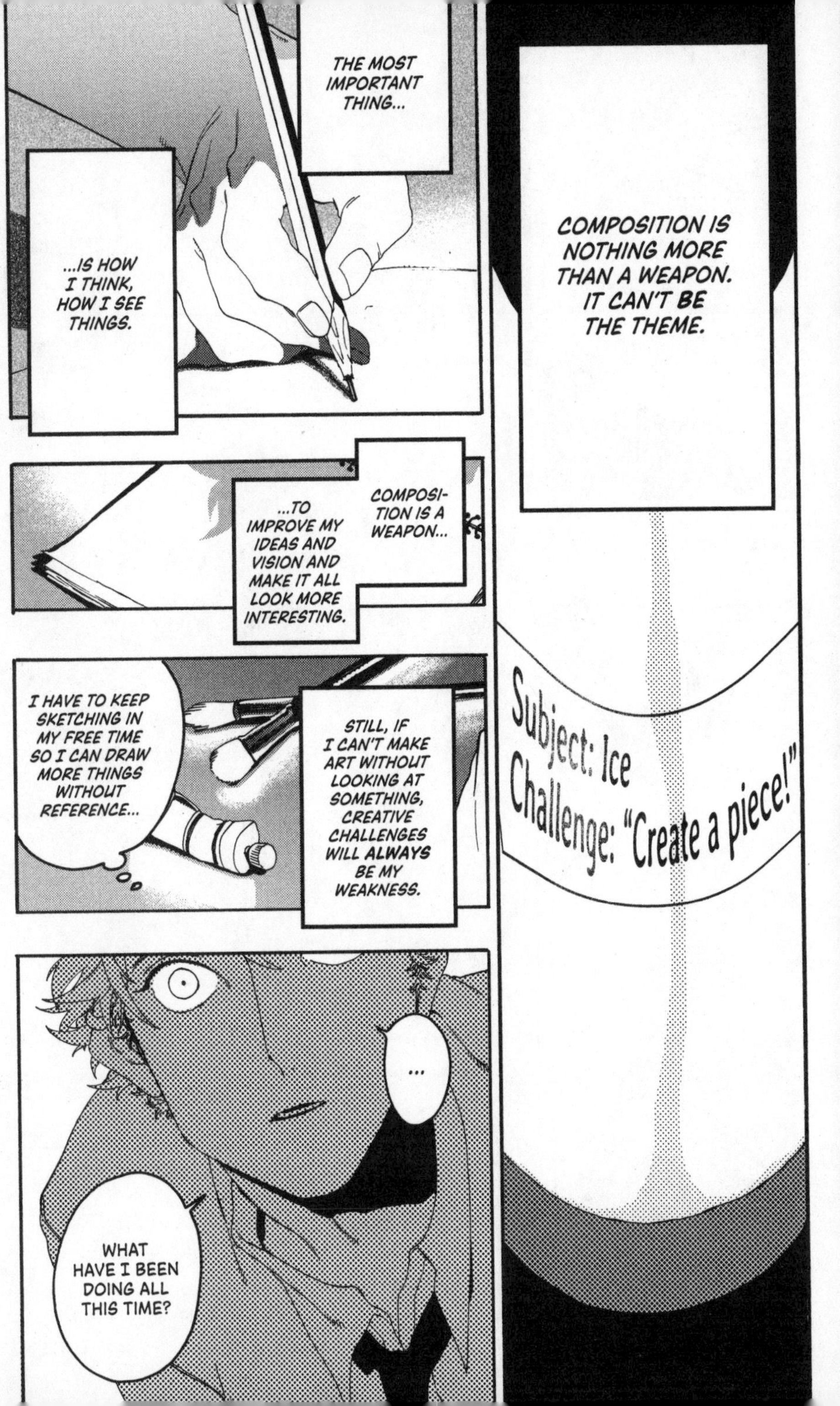
COMPOSITION IS NOTHING MORE THAN A WEAPON. IT CAN'T BE THE THEME.
Subject: Ice
Challenge: "Create a piece!"
THE MOST IMPORTANT THING...
...IS HOW I THINK, HOW I SEE THINGS.
COMPOSITION IS A WEAPON...
...TO IMPROVE MY IDEAS AND VISION AND MAKE IT ALL LOOK MORE INTERESTING.
STILL, IF I CAN'T MAKE ART WITHOUT LOOKING AT SOMETHING, CREATIVE CHALLENGES WILL ALWAYS BE MY WEAKNESS.
I HAVE TO KEEP SKETCHING IN MY FREE TIME SO I CAN DRAW MORE THINGS WITHOUT REFERENCE...
...
WHAT HAVE I BEEN DOING ALL THIS TIME?

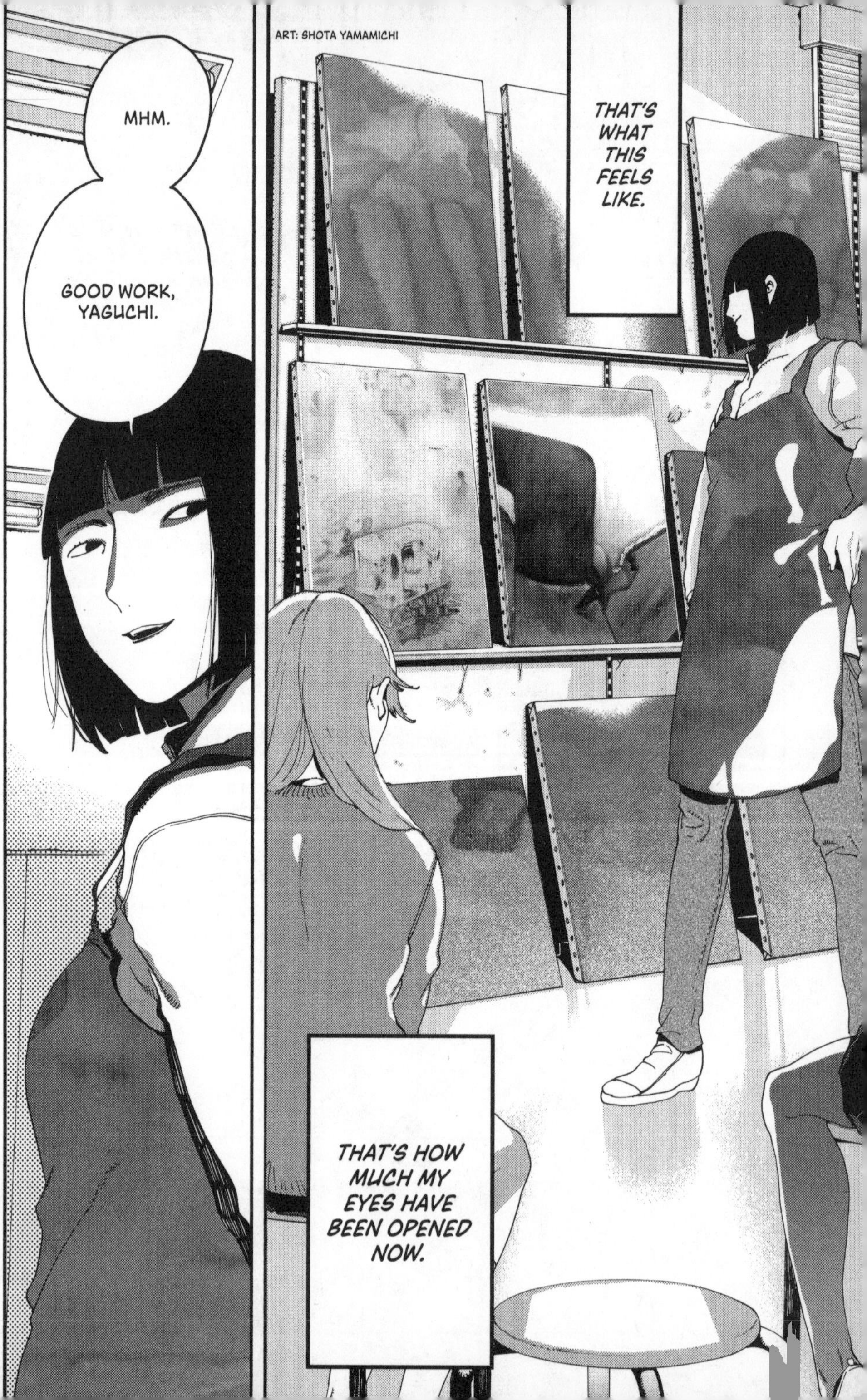
ART: SHOTA YAMAMICHI
THAT'S WHAT THIS FEELS LIKE.
THAT'S HOW MUCH MY EYES HAVE BEEN OPENED NOW.
MHM.
GOOD WORK, YAGUCHI.

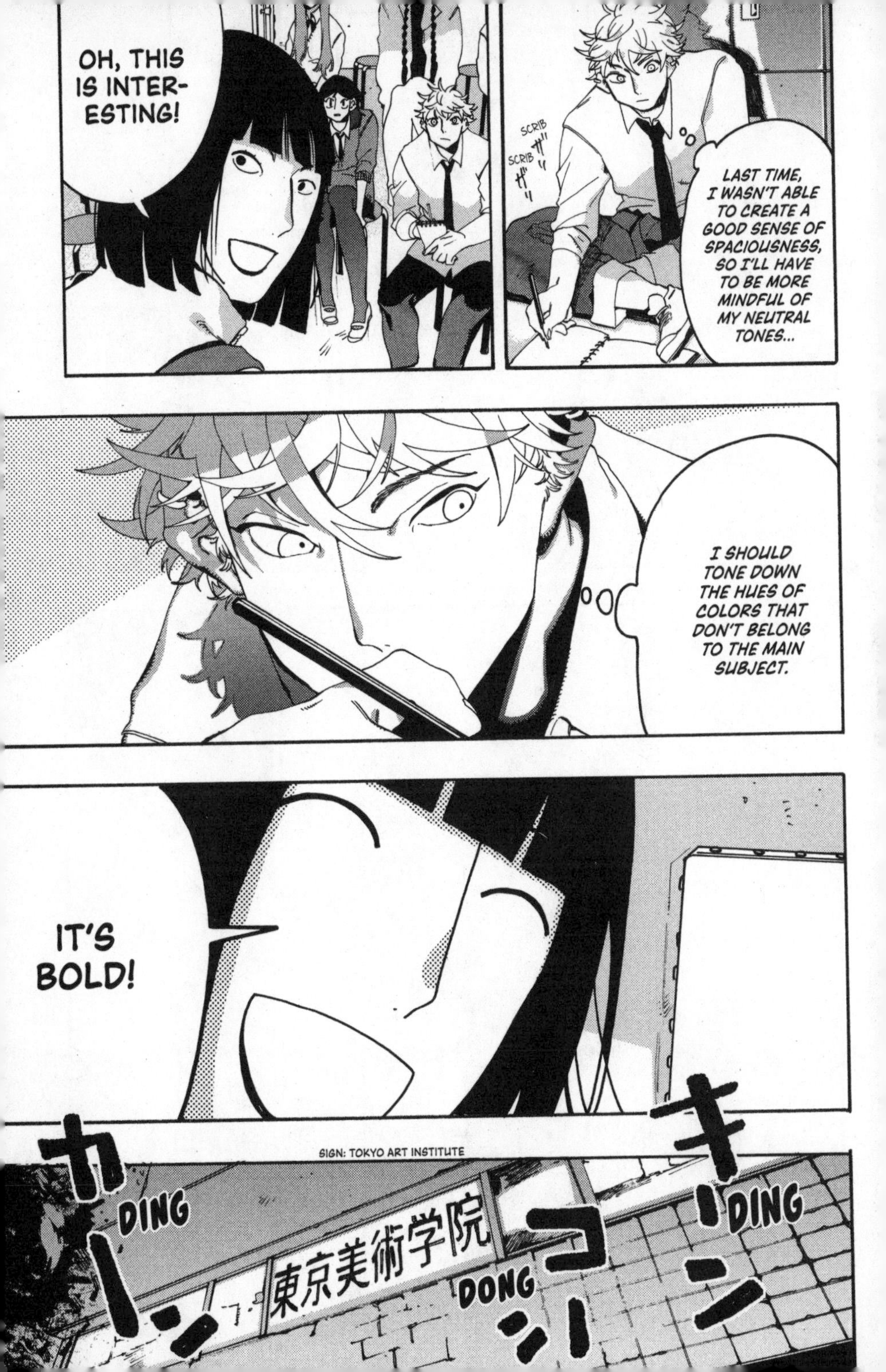
LAST TIME, I WASN'T ABLE TO CREATE A GOOD SENSE OF SPACIOUSNESS, SO I'LL HAVE TO BE MORE MINDFUL OF MY NEUTRAL TONES...
SCRIB SCRIB
OH, THIS IS INTER-ESTING!
I SHOULD TONE DOWN THE HUES OF COLORS THAT DON'T BELONG TO THE MAIN SUBJECT.
IT'S BOLD!
SIGN: TOKYO ART INSTITUTE
DING
DONG
DING
東京美術学院

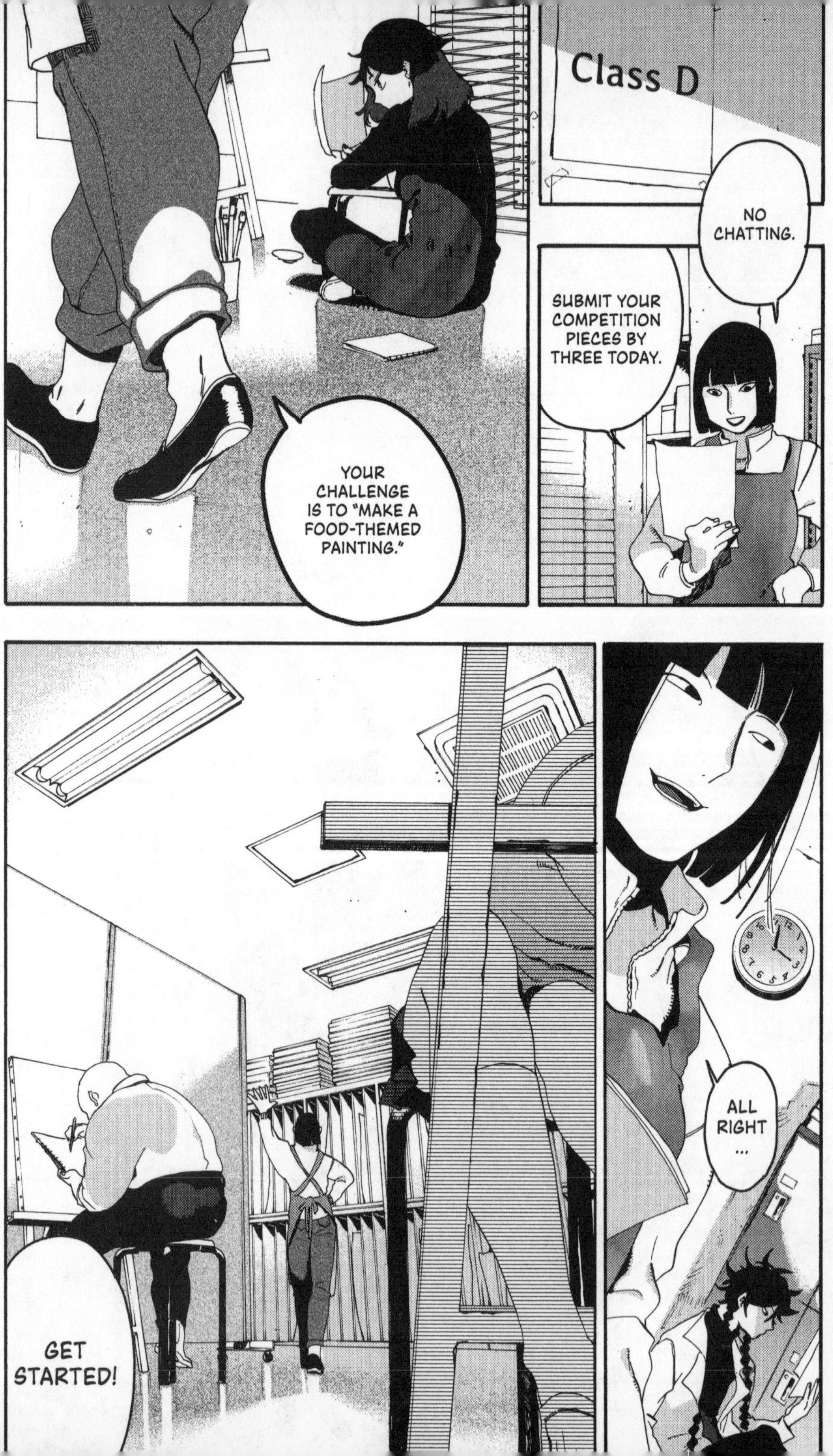
Class D
NO CHATTING.
SUBMIT YOUR COMPETITION PIECES BY THREE TODAY.
YOUR CHALLENGE IS TO "MAKE A FOOD-THEMED PAINTING."
ALL RIGHT ...
GET STARTED!

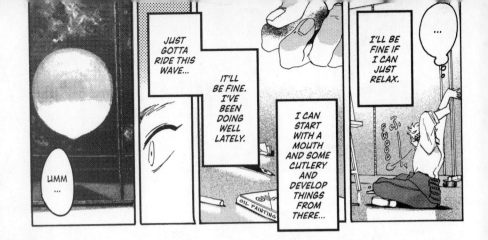

...
I'LL BE FINE IF I CAN JUST RELAX.
FWOOO
I CAN START WITH A MOUTH AND SOME CUTLERY AND DEVELOP THINGS FROM THERE...
OIL PAINTING
JUST GOTTA RIDE THIS WAVE...
IT'LL BE FINE. I'VE BEEN DOING WELL LATELY.
UMM ...
HOW EXACTLY DID I MAKE THAT LAST PAINTING?

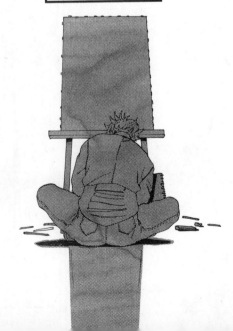

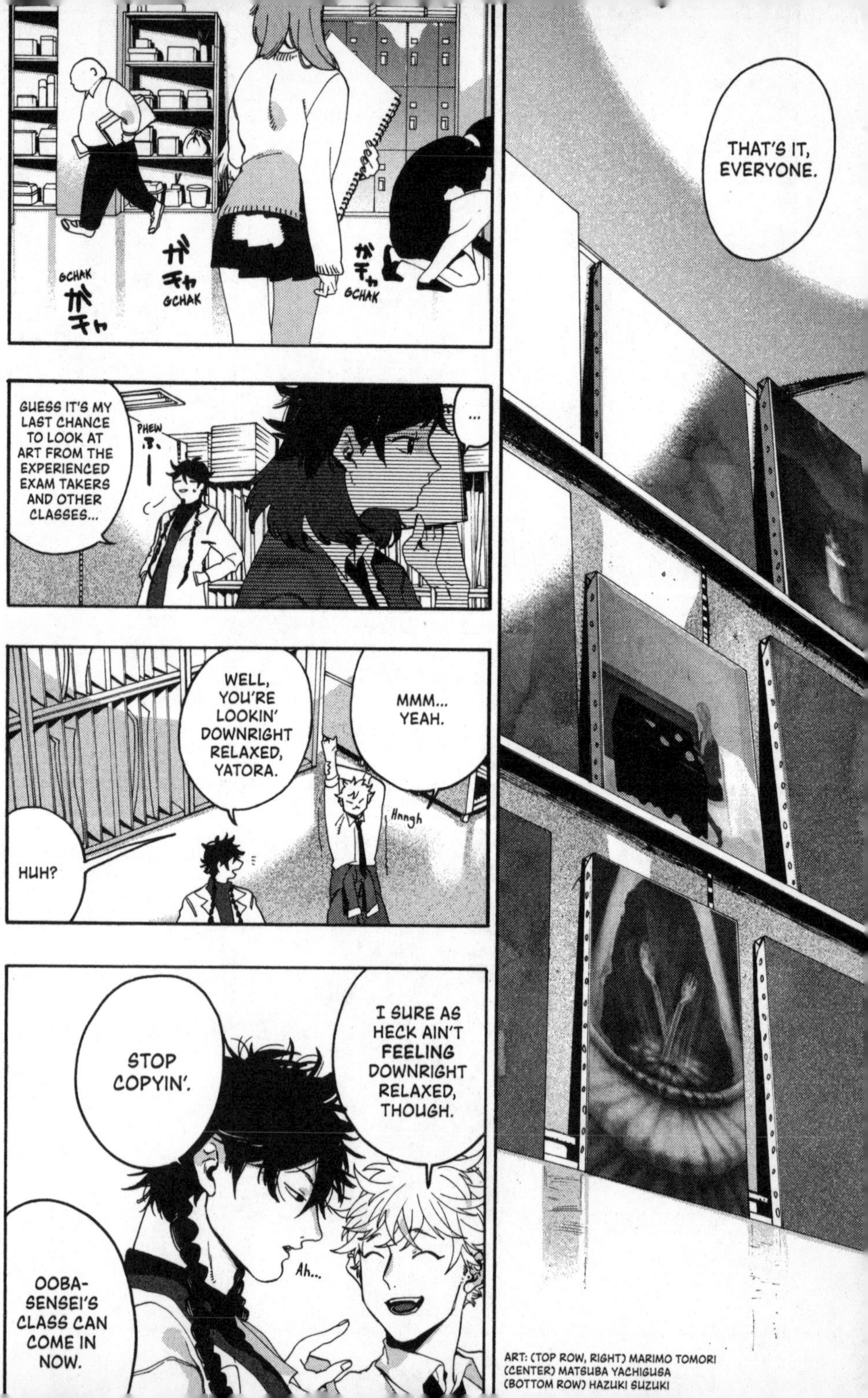
THAT'S IT, EVERYONE.
がチャ GCHAK
ガチャ GCHAK
GCHAK ガチャ
...
PHEW ふー
GUESS IT'S MY LAST CHANCE TO LOOK AT ART FROM THE EXPERIENCED EXAM TAKERS AND OTHER CLASSES...
MMM... YEAH.
WELL, YOU'RE LOOKIN' DOWNRIGHT RELAXED, YATORA.
Hnngh
HUH?
I SURE AS HECK AIN'T FEELING DOWNRIGHT RELAXED, THOUGH.
STOP COPYIN'.
Ah...
OOBA-SENSEI'S CLASS CAN COME IN NOW.
ART: (TOP ROW, RIGHT) MARIMO TOMORI
(CENTER) MATSUBA YACHIGUSA
(BOTTOM ROW) HAZUKI SUZUKI

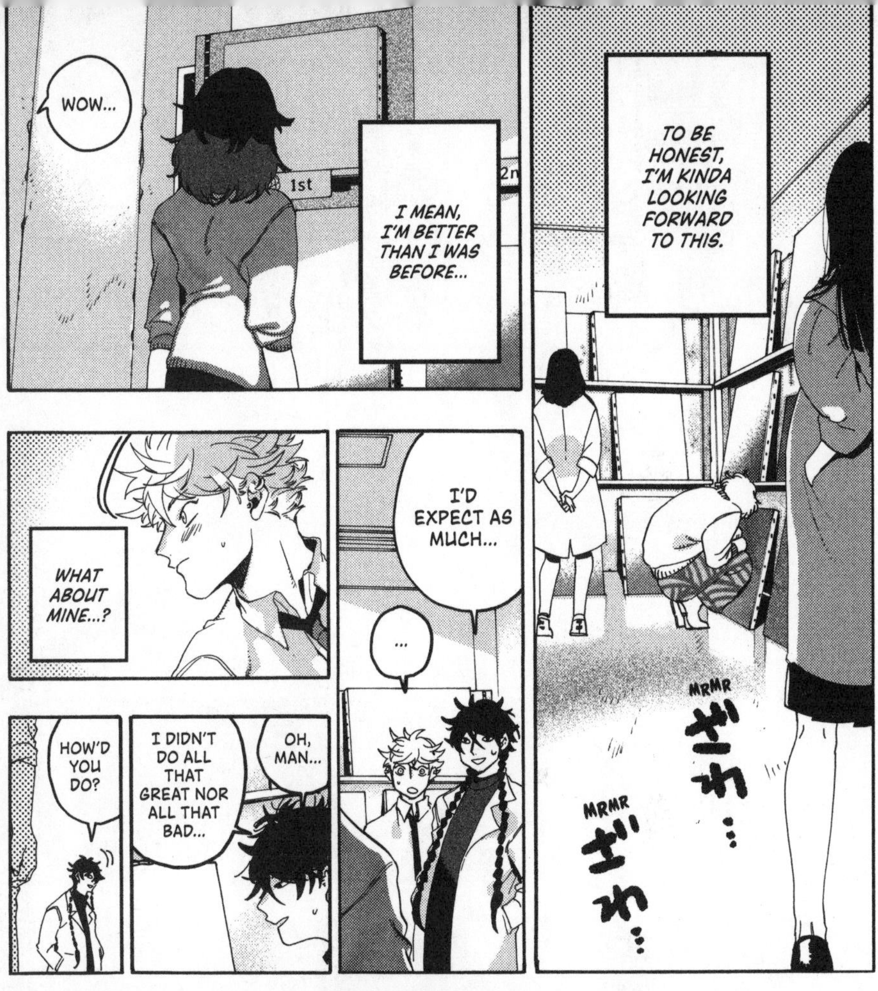
TO BE HONEST, I'M KINDA LOOKING FORWARD TO THIS.
MRMR
ざわ…
MRMR
ざわ…
WOW...
1st
I MEAN, I'M BETTER THAN I WAS BEFORE...
I'D EXPECT AS MUCH...
...
WHAT ABOUT MINE...?
OH, MAN...
I DIDN'T DO ALL THAT GREAT NOR ALL THAT BAD...
HOW'D YOU DO?

ART: SHOTA YAMAMICHI

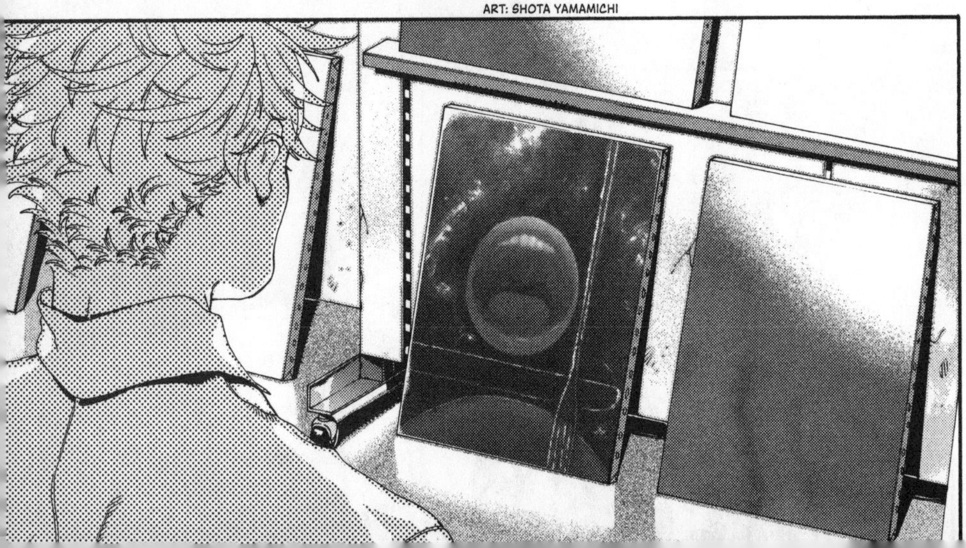

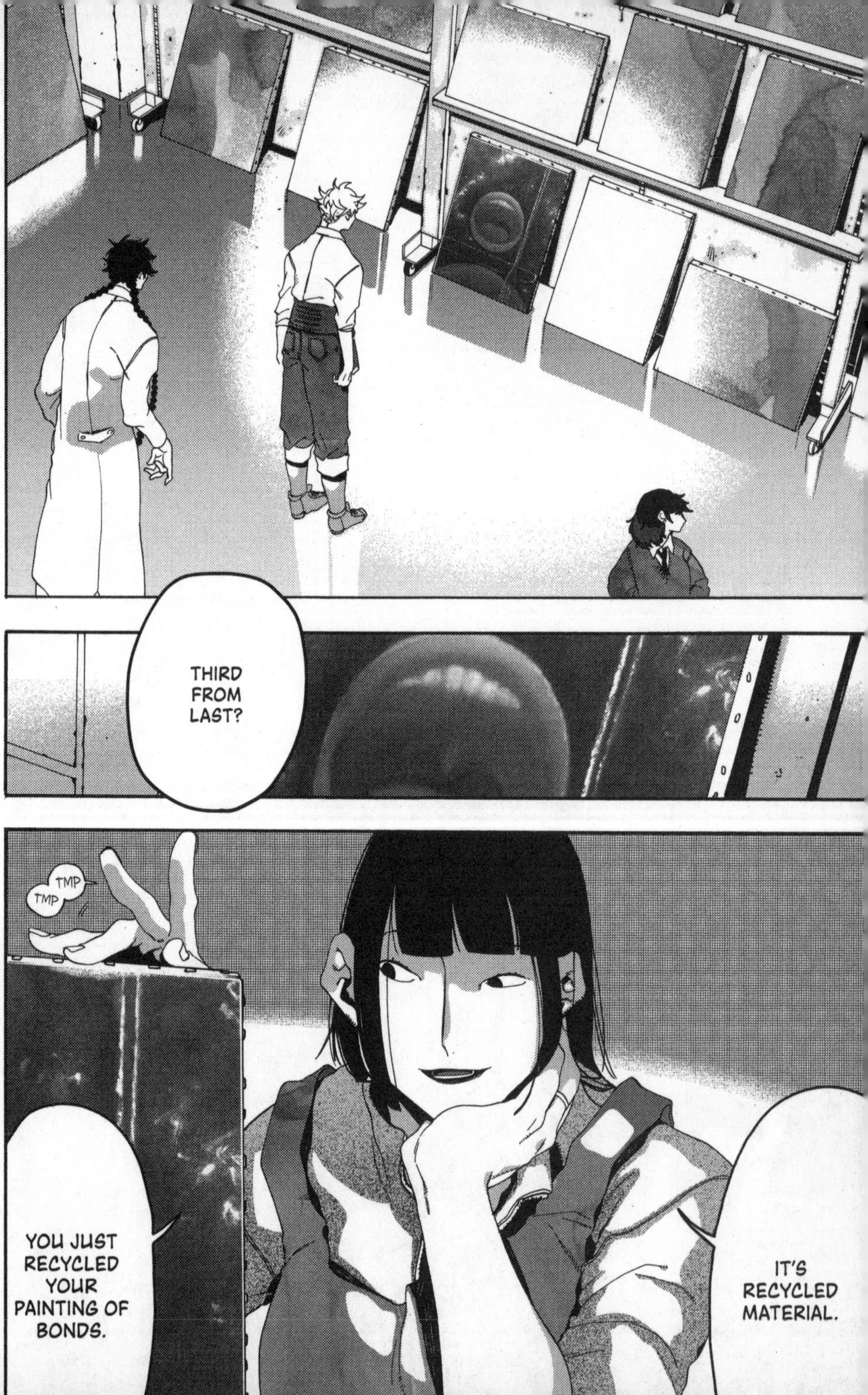
THIRD FROM LAST?
IT'S RECYCLED MATERIAL.
TMP TMP
YOU JUST RECYCLED YOUR PAINTING OF BONDS.

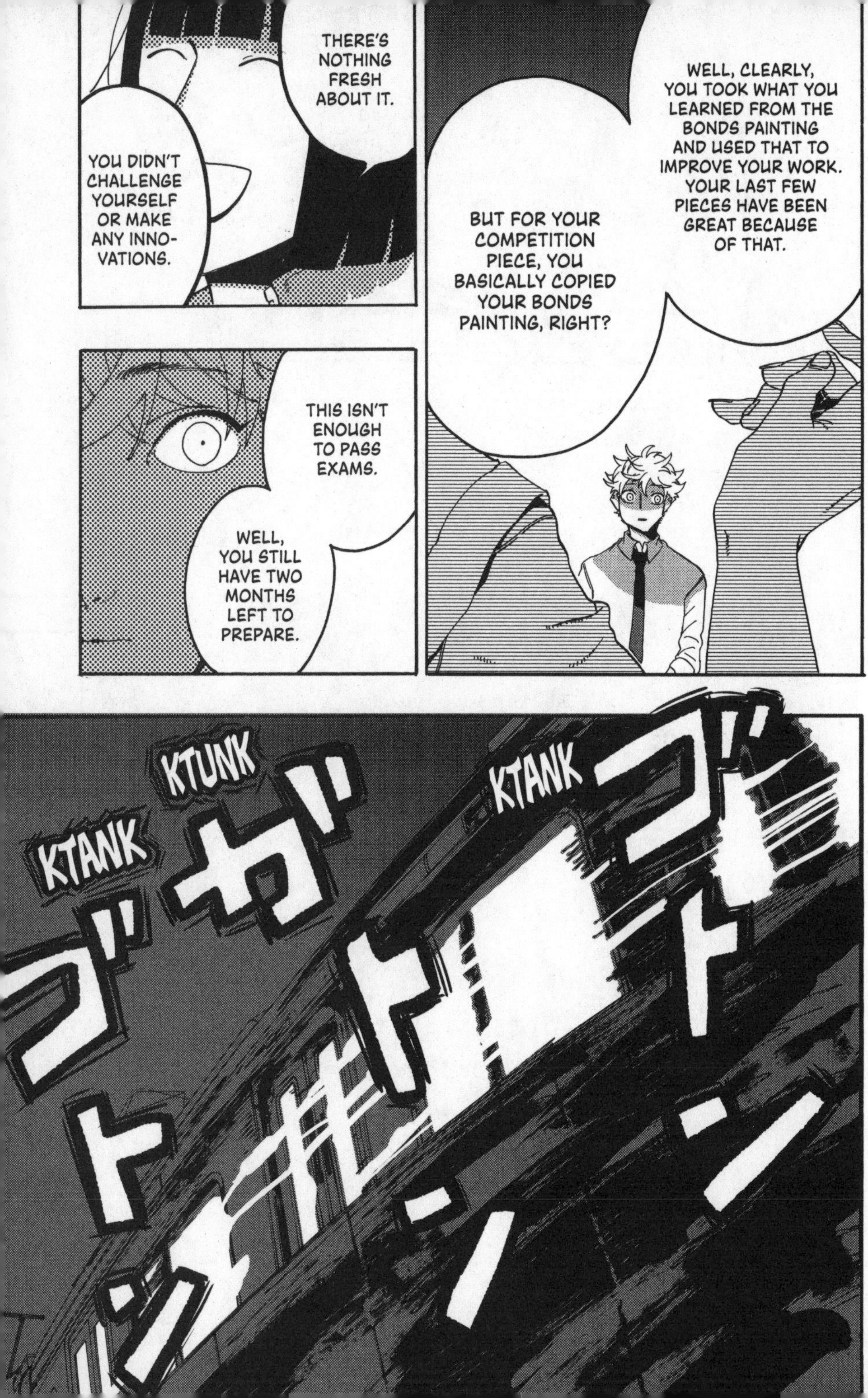
WELL, CLEARLY, YOU TOOK WHAT YOU LEARNED FROM THE BONDS PAINTING AND USED THAT TO IMPROVE YOUR WORK. YOUR LAST FEW PIECES HAVE BEEN GREAT BECAUSE OF THAT.
BUT FOR YOUR COMPETITION PIECE, YOU BASICALLY COPIED YOUR BONDS PAINTING, RIGHT?
THERE'S NOTHING FRESH ABOUT IT.
YOU DIDN'T CHALLENGE YOURSELF OR MAKE ANY INNO-VATIONS.
THIS ISN'T ENOUGH TO PASS EXAMS.
WELL, YOU STILL HAVE TWO MONTHS LEFT TO PREPARE.
KTANK
KTUNK
KTANK

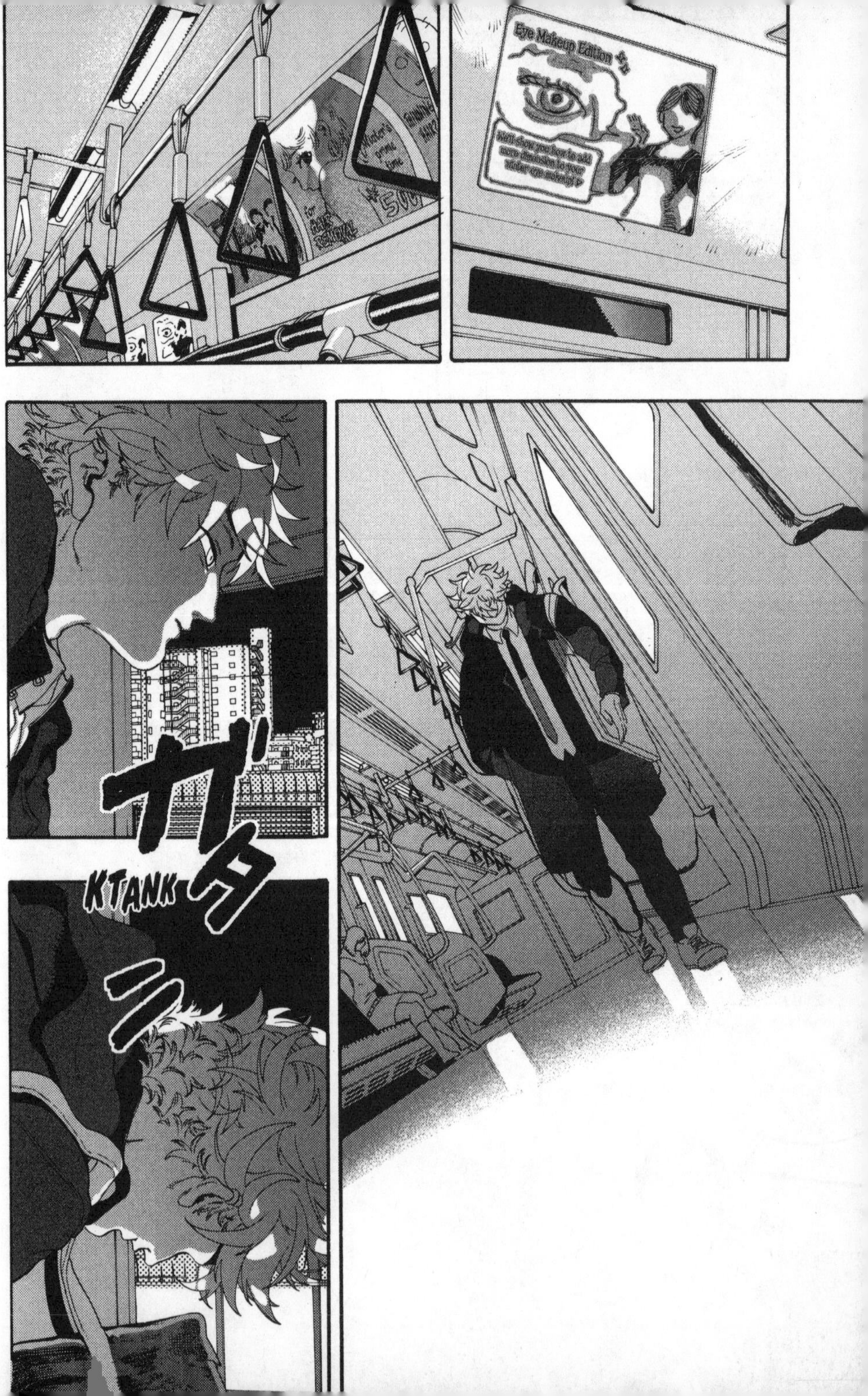
Eye Makeup Edition
We'll show you how to add more dimension to your winter eye makeup! ▸
Winter's prime time
for HAIR REMOVAL
¥500
ガタン
KTANK

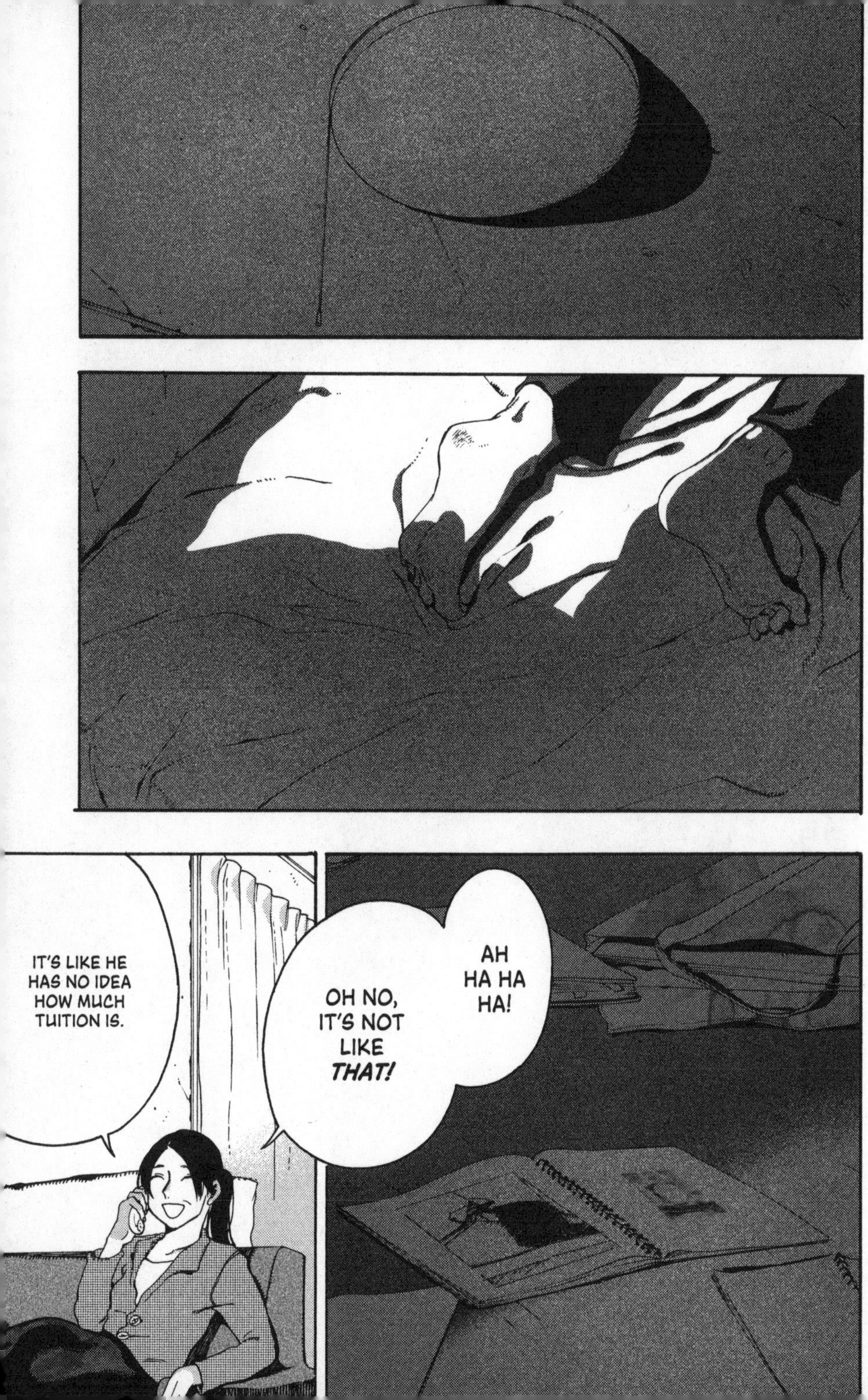
AH HA HA HA!
OH NO, IT'S NOT LIKE *THAT!*
IT'S LIKE HE HAS NO IDEA HOW MUCH TUITION IS.

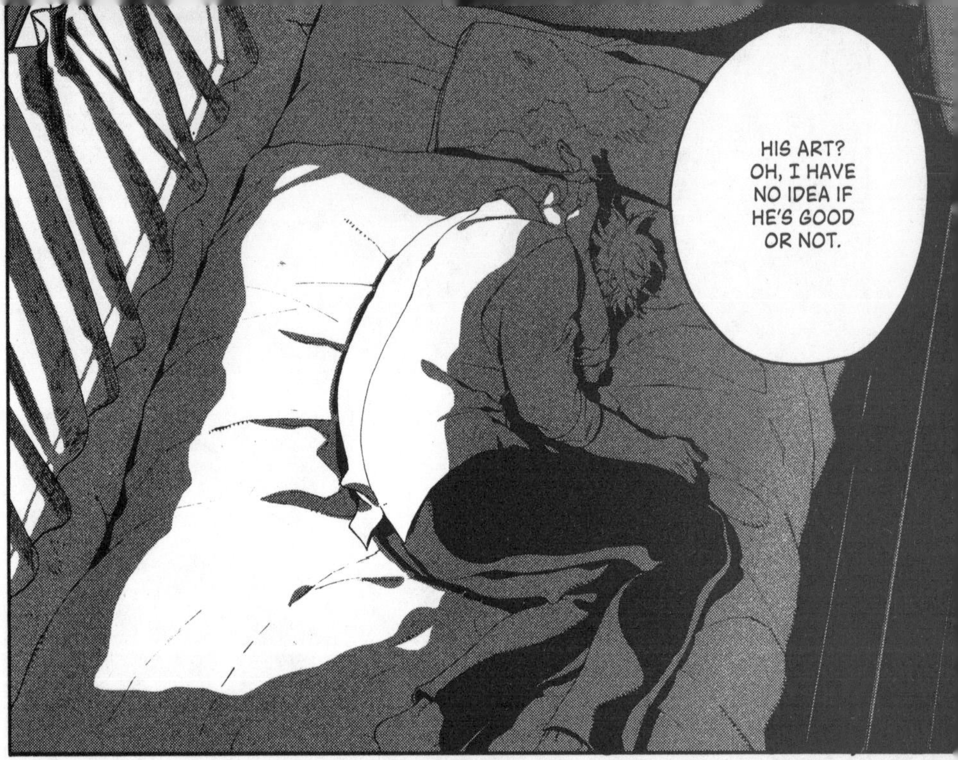
HIS ART? OH, I HAVE NO IDEA IF HE'S GOOD OR NOT.
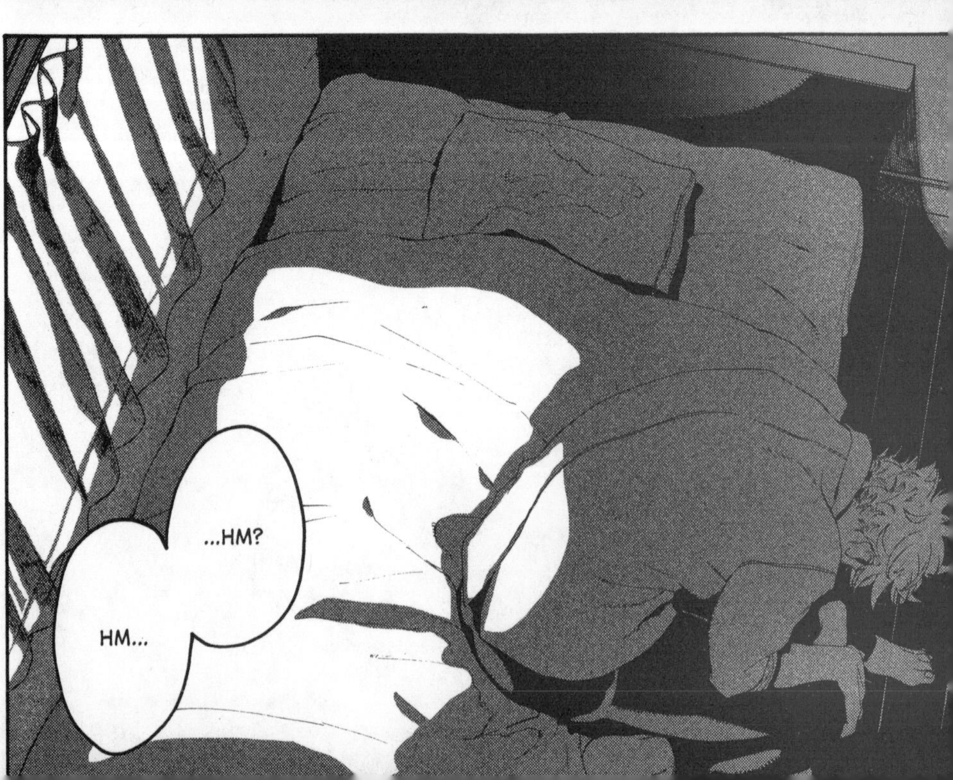
...HM?
HM...

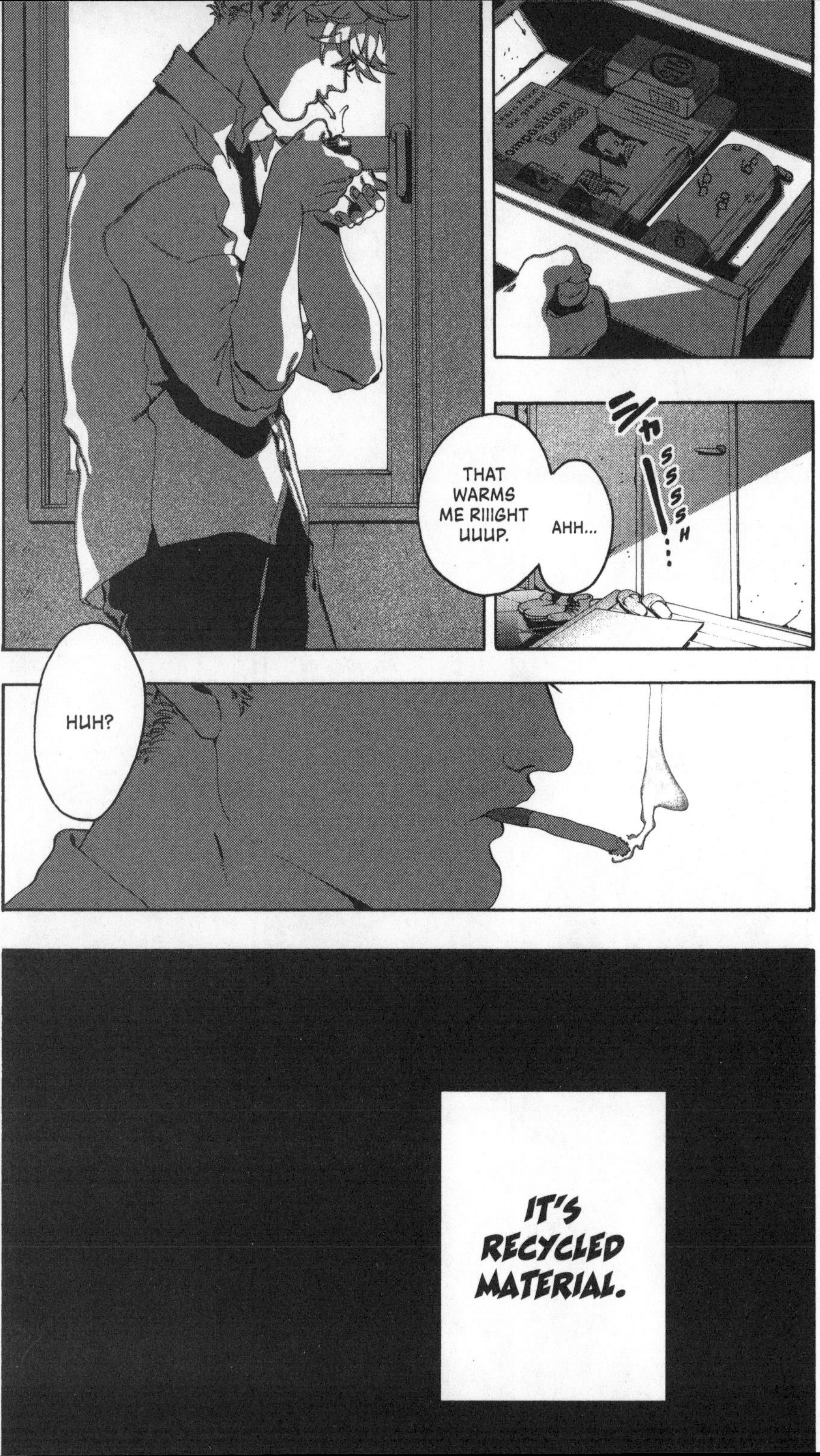
SSSSSH...
AHH...
THAT WARMS ME RIIIGHT UUUP.
HUH?
IT'S RECYCLED MATERIAL.

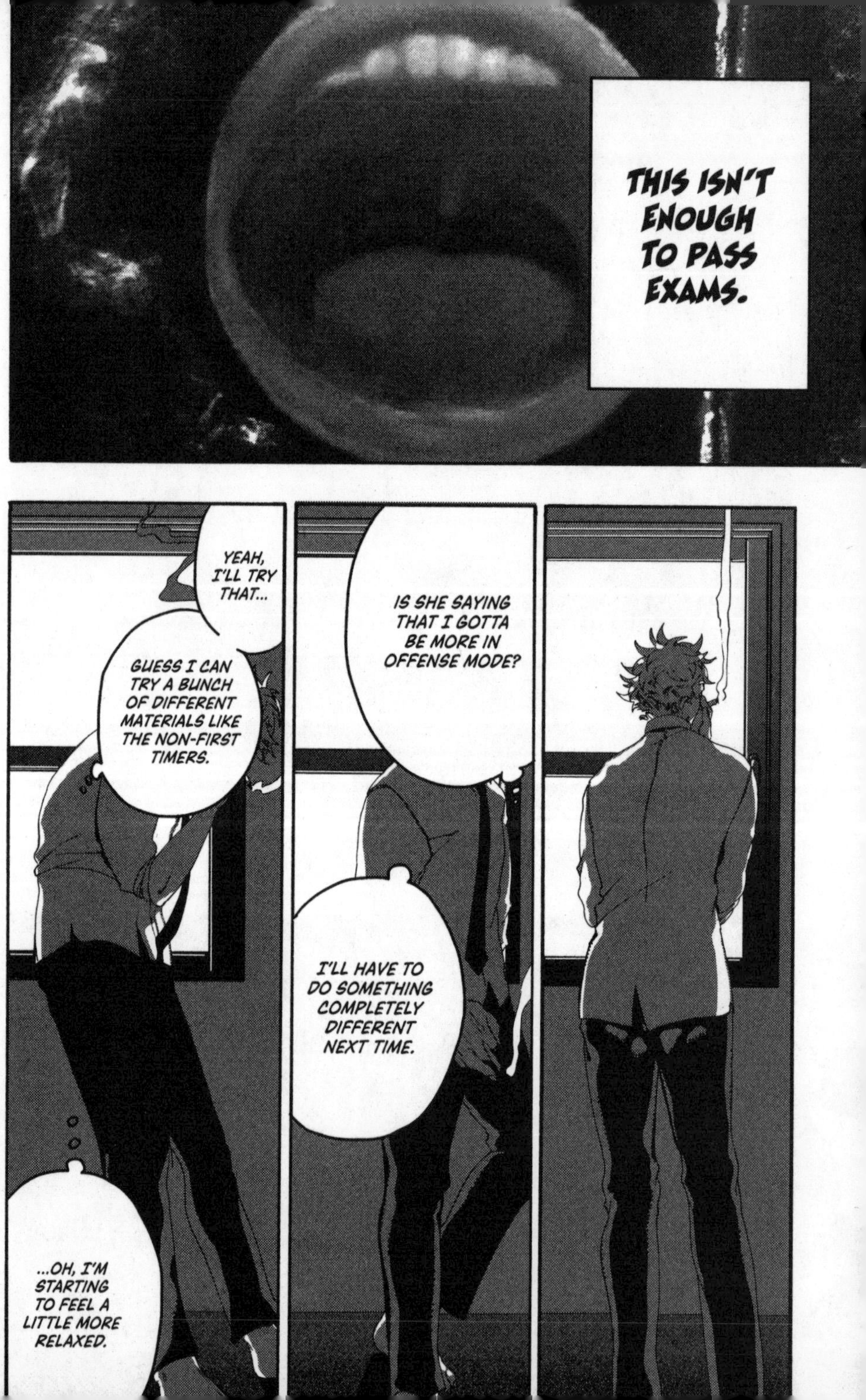
THIS ISN'T ENOUGH TO PASS EXAMS.
IS SHE SAYING THAT I GOTTA BE MORE IN OFFENSE MODE?
I'LL HAVE TO DO SOMETHING COMPLETELY DIFFERENT NEXT TIME.
YEAH, I'LL TRY THAT...
GUESS I CAN TRY A BUNCH OF DIFFERENT MATERIALS LIKE THE NON-FIRST TIMERS.
...OH, I'M STARTING TO FEEL A LITTLE MORE RELAXED.

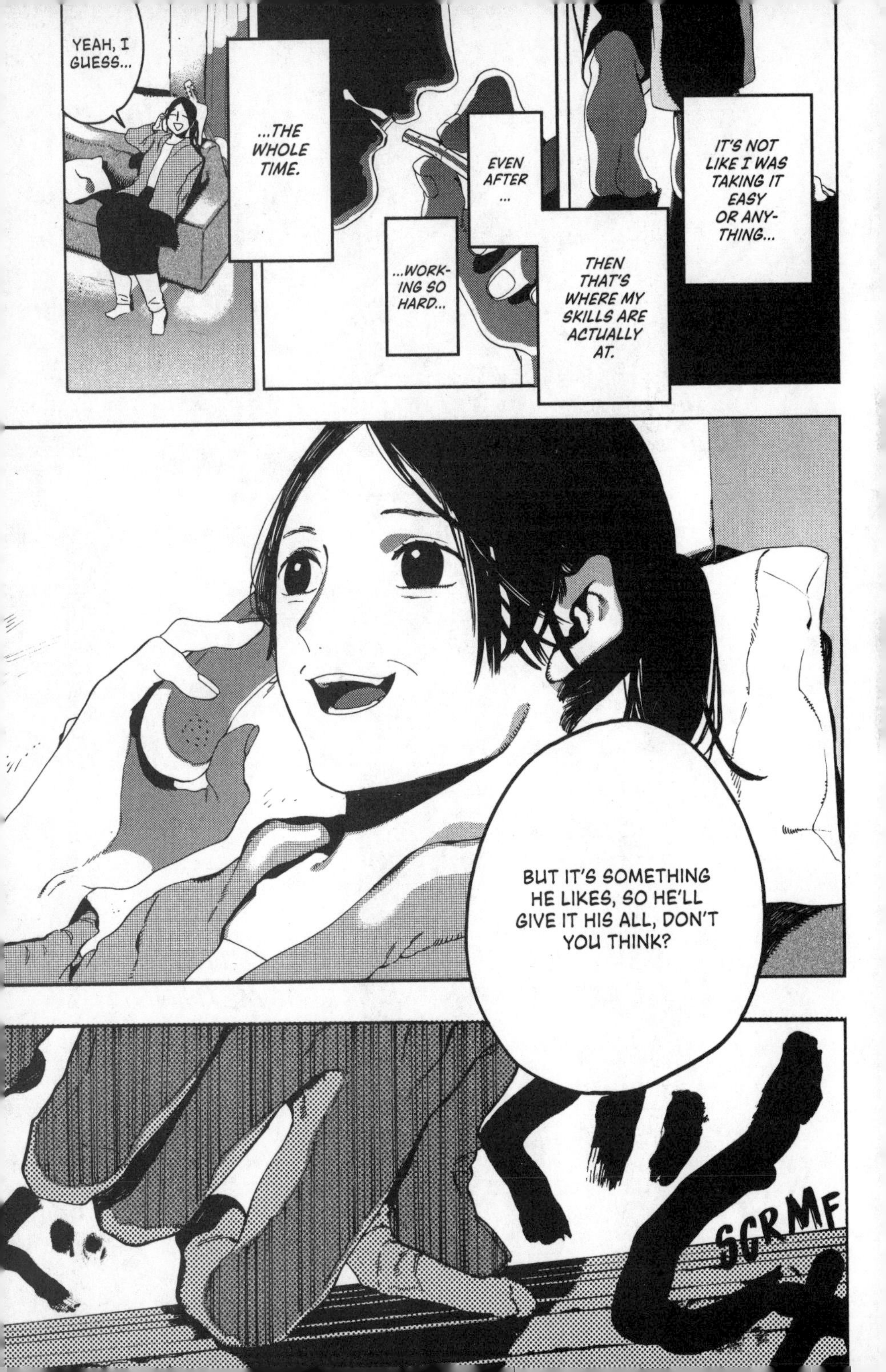
IT'S NOT LIKE I WAS TAKING IT EASY OR ANYTHING...
EVEN AFTER ...
...WORKING SO HARD...
THEN THAT'S WHERE MY SKILLS ARE ACTUALLY AT.
...THE WHOLE TIME.
YEAH, I GUESS...
BUT IT'S SOMETHING HE LIKES, SO HE'LL GIVE IT HIS ALL, DON'T YOU THINK?
SCRMF

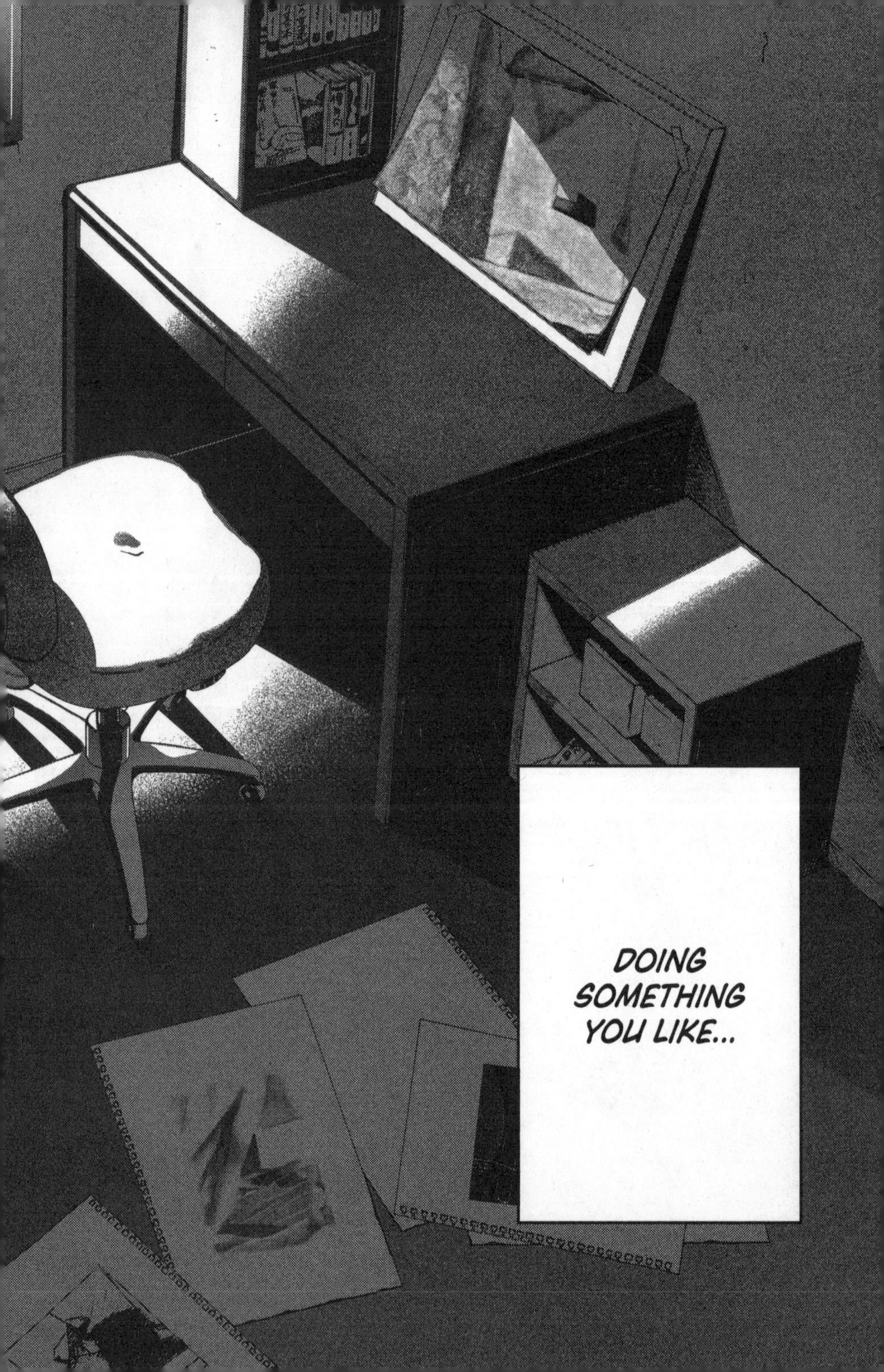
DOING SOMETHING YOU LIKE...

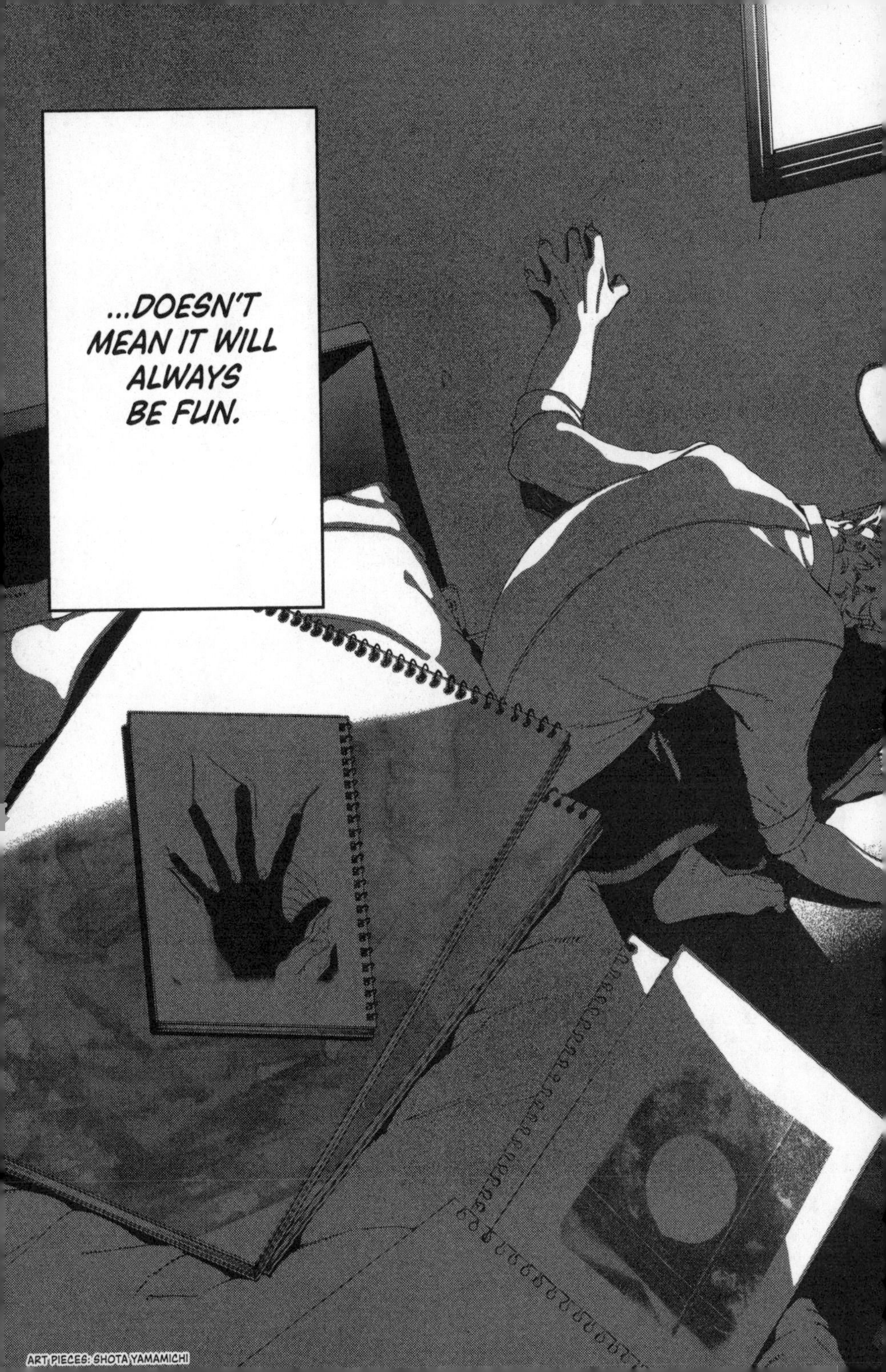
...DOESN'T MEAN IT WILL ALWAYS BE FUN.
ART PIECES: SHOTA YAMAMICHI

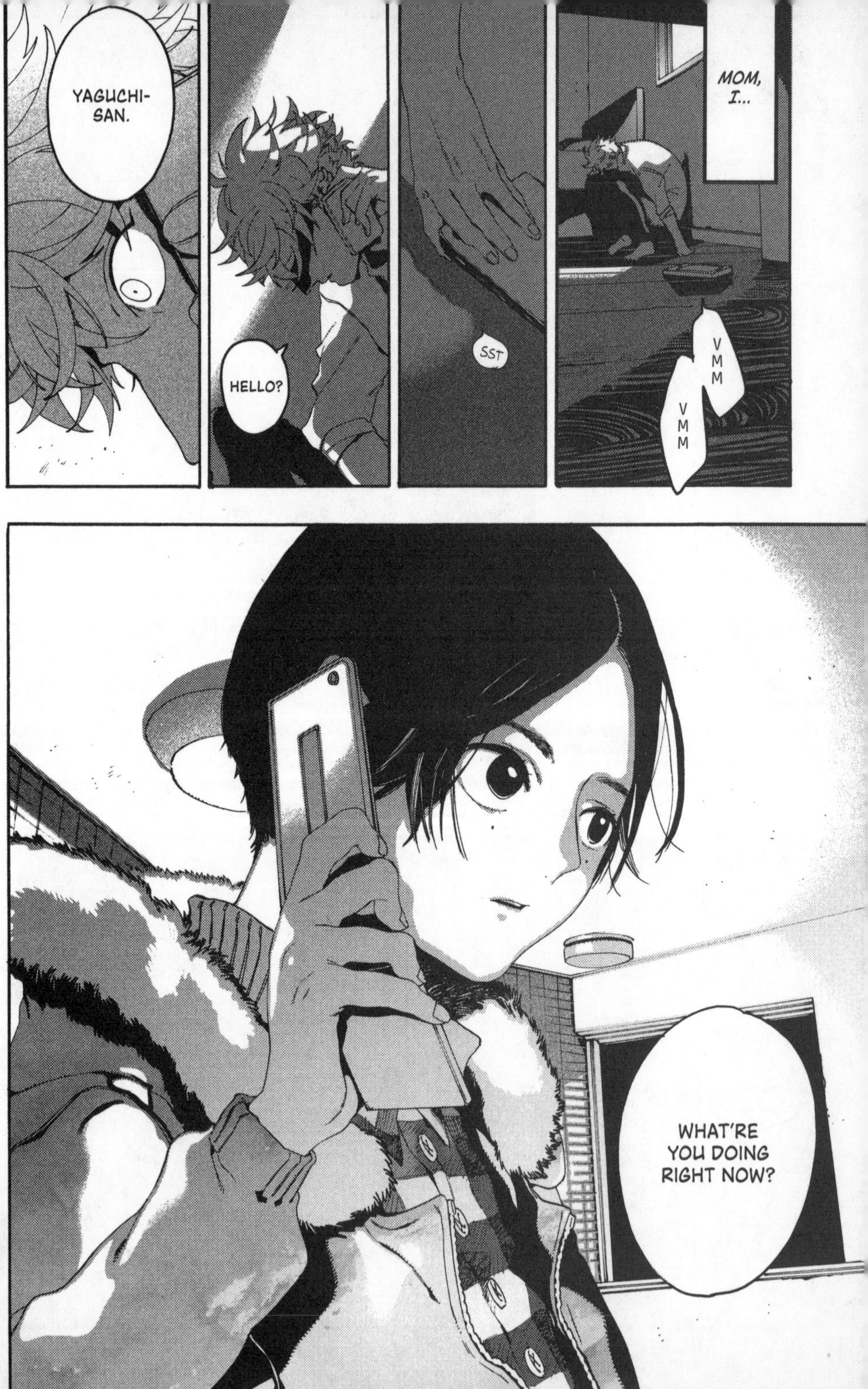
MOM, I...
VMM VMM
SST
HELLO?
YAGUCHI-SAN.
WHAT'RE YOU DOING RIGHT NOW?

STROKE 11 END

Only child

Eldest son

Only child

Eldest son

Eldest daughter

Second daughter (gyaru)

Eldest daughter

Second daughter

Eldest daught

Seco daugh (gya

Second son

Third daughter

BLUE PERIOD